Just *Lassen* to Me!
A First-generation Son's Story: Surviving a Survivor

Book Four: Survivor Surviving

Harvy Simkovits

Just *Lassen* to Me!

A First-generation Son's Story: Surviving a Survivor

Book Four: Survivor Surviving

Edition 1.2

Copyright © 1999, 2020, 2021 Harvy Simkovits

Published by Wise Press

All rights reserved. No part of this book may be reproduced, stored, or transmitted by any means—whether auditory, graphic, mechanical, or electronic—without the author's written permission, except in the case of brief excerpts used in critical articles and reviews. The unauthorized reproduction of any part of this work is illegal and is punishable by law.

This book is a work of non-fiction. Unless otherwise noted, the author and the publisher make no explicit guarantees concerning the accuracy of the information contained in this book. In many cases, the author has altered the names of people and places to protect privacy.

ISBN-13: 978-0-9773957-4-3
ISBN-10: 0-9773957-4-X
Library of Congress Control Number: 2019917664

Because of the dynamic nature of the Internet, any web addresses or links contained in this book may have changed since publication and may no longer be valid. The views expressed in this work are solely those of the author and do not necessarily reflect the views or opinions of the publisher, who hereby disclaims responsibility for them.

Memoir Series by Harvy Simkovits

Just *Lassen* to Me!
Book 1: Survivor Indoctrination
(An Amazon Bestseller)

Just *Lassen* to Me!
Book 2: Survivor Teachings

Just *Lassen* to Me!
Book 3: Survivor Learning

Just *Lassen* to Me!
Book 4: Survivor Surviving

Contents

Memoir Series by Harvy Simkovits
Welcome to the Conclusion of *Just Lassen to Me!*
Notes & Dedication

Book Four: Survivor Surviving

Part I: All the King's Money
1. New Juncture for Johnny 10
2. Next Stage for Dad and Me 27
3. A Father's Failings 37
4. A Father's Finances 57
5. A Father's Finagling 66
6. More Simkovits Travels and Travails 74
7. Late-Life Crazies 91
8. Smoking Marriage Embers 100
9. Another Frigging Family Failure 117
10. Collateral Money Damage 128
11. Always More to the Story 136

Part II: Last Days of Dad
12. Eightieth Birthday Surprise 158
13. Playing My Cards Right 172
14. Precious Things 183
15. More Card Playing 188
16. Redefining Money Moments 197
17. Reclaiming Precious Property 211
18. Hungarian-Slovak Lion in Winter 217
19. Wrenching the Pen Out of His Hand 232
20. Crimp in My Plan 246
21. Voluntary Disclosure Plan B 254
22. Reign Comes to an End 266
23. To Duma or Not Duma 286
24. Moment of Brotherly Truth 298

25. End of an Era 308
26. Ides of October 2000 319
27. Fool Me Once; Fool Me … 335

Part III: Closing the Book on Dad, Maybe

28. Cleaning Up After Johnny 340
29. End to a Father's Burden 354
30. My Abraham's Precious Legacy 369
31. Pelé Sunset 372
32. Sibling Setup 387
33. Day of Redemption – The Beginning 398
34. Day of Redemption – The Muddling 408
35. Day of Redemption – The Ending 434
36. There's Dad Again! 455
37. Day of Redemption – The Aftermath 467
38. Life after Redemption? 478
39. Montreal Funeral, May 2009 488
40. Johnny ~~Noose~~ Loose Ends 494

Acknowledgements
Author Bio

Welcome to the Conclusion of

"Just *Lassen* to Me!"

Is it possible to admire a man's accomplishments but abhor what he stands for, to crave his blessing but spurn his legacy? What if that man is your father?

Is it possible to wish for a woman's love but loathe her controlling nature, to desire a good life for her but shun being dragged into her troubles? What if that woman is your mother?

Is it possible to be forthcoming to a fellow you have grown to distrust, to want to be honest with him, but risk his turning your disclosures against you? What if that bloke is your brother?

Is it possible to seek support from your family and desperately desire to separate yourself from them, to elude their traumatic and sordid history without compromising or censoring your own developing story? What if, in longing to distance yourself, you wonder and dread that you've become a reflection of them?

Bravo for having come this far in the Johnny Simkovits and sons saga! In this final volume, the story continues to its chaotic and confounding conclusion. After leaving the family business and coming out from under the wing of his business partner and professional mentor, Harvy remains enmeshed in his father's finagling and furtive finances.

As Johnny progresses toward the end of his family and financial reign, many questions remain. What will be the disposition of the extended Simkovits clan and its patriarch's fortunes? Will the Simkovits sons get past their father's devious ways and their mutual distrust, even after their patriarch's passing?

How much will Harvy reveal to his brother, half-sister, step-mother, advisors, wife, and larger family about his father's sordid schemes and hidden money history? Will Harvy find a life separate from his father and be able to repudiate, rectify, and reconcile his dad's clandestine legacy. Will he come into his own irrespective of being the son of Johnny?

Make your judgement about all of this and all of us. Experience the rollercoaster finale of Simkovits family twists and life turns as Harvy works to survive his survivor father and make peace with his kin and, ultimately, his conscience.

HS

Notes

This memoir series continues to use Canadian spelling, terminology, and writing conventions. Also, most distance measurements are in metric.

Wise Press will donate at least 50% of the profits of this book to programs assisting victims of domestic abuse and violence.

Many individuals and organizations named in this memoir series continue to be masked to protect true identities.

Dedication

Once more, to the ones who suffered the most under the hand and from the deeds of Johnny. May they find peace in their hearts and minds, be it in this life or afterward.

Book Four:

Survivor Surviving

Part I:

All the King's Money

New Juncture for Johnny

In February 1993, my girlfriend, Gloria, and I visited Dad and Elaine at his renovated Boca Raton winter home. We were celebrating his 73rd birthday with a gang of his Montreal friends. Gloria was the only American-born person at the party. Besides her and Canadian-born Elaine, everyone else was a Canadian-immigrant snowbird who could converse in at least three languages: English, French, and at least one Eastern European dialect.

My father had hired a Polish fiddler and accordion player who were also winter vacationers from Montreal. The two men dressed in red and green vests typical for Slavic folk singers, dancers, and musicians. They serenaded guests with both lively and soothing melodies from the old country. Most everyone knew and sang the refrains in Hungarian, Slovak, Polish, Ukrainian, and Russian, all languages my father could speak.

Dad sang along, mixing words, changing syllables to spice up the lyrics. One Russian song lyric went something like, "I'm looking at your beauty with my sad eyes." Dad turned the last phrase into the Ukrainian, "…with my excited eggs." Howls of laughter emanated from the Slavic men, and blushing smiles came from their wives.

Gloria later told me, "I'm here on American soil, and I feel like a foreigner in my country." She looked at me. "By the way, what are those men howling about?"

Knowing my father's word plays, I told her.

She blushed too.

Gloria and I had met six months after I had left Margie. Unlike Margie, she had a more easygoing personality. My closest Boston friend called Gloria "an adorable person," and she was. My gal had an engaging smile and a wide-mouth laugh that could fill a room. She wore her brownish-red hair in a curly perm that dropped onto her shoulders.

Gloria and I had met at a Christmas party at our Boston racquet club. There, she and I danced, talked, and laughed with ease. She enjoyed hiking, tennis, and skiing as much as I did. I felt light around her.

After my father first met Gloria at one of his Peru house garden parties, he jested with me privately, "Margie was too thin." He gritted his teeth and closed his fist. "I like Gloria because she has a little more to grab onto."

I cringed and smiled at the same time. I told myself that I wouldn't match my father's three marriages and other women on the side. I hoped he was staying faithful to Elaine.

Dad had bought the three-bedroom ranch house in the Royal Palm gated community, situated between the intercoastal waterway and Federal Highway 1 in Boca. It was a two-mile drive to the boardwalk at Hillsboro Beach. There Dad and I went for early morning walks with Muffie, Elaine's Tibetan terrier. As it had been with Elaine's Hungarian Puli, Orphee, Dad was enamoured with Muffie and continually played fetch with her. To Elaine's chagrin, he fed the dog scraps off his plate as he had done with her former pet.

The Boca house had a mesh-screen enclosed swimming pool, complete with a rooftop solar heater to warm the water to near bathtub temperatures. Every day while I stayed *chez* Dad, he watched as I swam across that small, kidney-shaped pool, timing me for twenty minutes. I'd be across its length in five good breaststrokes, and then I'd turn around to do it again, and again, and again. He never tired of our having such moments together.

I particularly enjoyed the fruit trees at my father's Boca property: one orange and one grapefruit. They filled the small backyard adjacent to the pool. My father rose early every morning to pick the fruit right off the branches before breakfast. He squeezed fresh juice for guests who stayed over, Gloria and I included.

As he had done with his Peru, NY property, Dad went on a construction spree to spruce up his and Elaine's new southern home. He turned a small library into a big family room, and he opened and renovated the kitchen. Using his electro-technician skills, my father single-handedly rewired the whole house for stereo, both inside and out by the pool.

Elaine later complained, "Your dear father just had to pull speaker and power wires through the attic by himself, as he did in my Pointe-Claire house years ago." She pointed upward. "But it's loose fiberglass up there! He itched and scratched for days until that stuff worked its way out of his skin."

Elaine, too, kept busy by furnishing their new digs with wall mirrors and black-and-white furniture everywhere. Colour came from large paintings that filled the walls. Some of the pictures were mural-size, purchased from Slovak- and Hungarian-Canadian snowbird friends who were amateur painters.

As in Peru, NY, Dad and Elaine didn't permit any guests, including Steve and me, to come and visit until the renovations were complete. When I saw it finished, I went *ooh*, *ah*, and *wow* until my mouth was sore.

Today, at Dad's celebration, we mingled outside by the pool, complete with an open bar area that connected to the kitchen. The Slavic men chain-smoked strong cigarettes they had brought with them from Quebec. While Beth and I sipped respectively on a piña colada and a rum punch, Dad and his pals stuck to Russian vodka, straight or on the rocks.

My father approached Gloria and me. He smiled and said, "Those sweet drinks are for the ladies."

I pointed to my mouth and retorted, "I know, Dad, but I don't need that straight stuff to grow any more hair on my tongue."

He chuckled and continued to walk around and talk with every guest. He made sure that their hands were filled with drinks and canapés, and they were having a good time. Every so often, he'd grab a bosom buddy, and they sang along with the music. They laughed, clinked glasses, and downed healthy swigs.

I watched my father work his pool party. Like a sun worshiper, he soaked in the heat of his comrades' attention.

I thought of the many years our family used to come to Florida from Montreal. For almost every winter while my brother and I were growing up, Dad drove us to Miami, Hollywood, or Fort Lauderdale for the Christmas and New Year holidays. Our winter trips to Florida had surely beat the blustering Canadian blizzards.

My biggest regret was that my late mother, in her final years, never had a chance to take these long southerly sojourns that my father now took with Elaine. Though I didn't hold a grudge against Elaine for anything to do with my mother, I still felt a loss for what Mom's life could have been like with Dad during his retirement.

Dad's Boca birthday was not a time to dwell on such skeletons. I was glad that my brother bowed out of Dad's birthday party here in Boca; it offered me more of my father's attention. I think Dad, too, felt freer with Steve not present. I worked to stay focused on Gloria and give her a sense of my forebearers' cuisine, music, people, and culture.

Ensuring that Gloria had a good time at my father's party was what mattered most.

* * *

New Juncture for Johnny

Six weeks after Dad's Boca birthday, Elaine called my home office in Boston. It was a Monday morning.

My stepmother was matter-of-fact. "Harvy, I'm sorry to tell you, but your father had a serious stroke yesterday. He's in the hospital on blood thinners." She spoke as if she were taking no breaths between her sentences. "Right now, his left side is paralyzed, but the doctor says that movement could come back in time. The good thing is that he's out of danger."

I had anticipated such a phone call from Elaine one day, whether my father would have a heart attack, stroke, or another severe health emergency. But her call still came as a surprise. "How did it happen?" I quickly asked, forcing my breath out of me.

Though her voice expressed concern, she was business-like. "The stroke was progressive, happening gradually over several hours. It started yesterday morning. Your father could hardly get out of bed."

She continued to speak rapidly. "I put Johnny into a hot bath and immediately called his doctor in Montreal. When I reached the doctor, he told me to get him to the hospital right away. I called the ambulance, and they were here in ten minutes."

She stopped for a millisecond to catch her breath. "Your father couldn't get himself out of the tub, and I couldn't lift him by myself. When the EMTs got here, they had to pick him up buck naked and carry him out on a stretcher."

She paused for a long breath and then continued to speak rapid-fire. "When they got Johnny to the Emergency Room, the doctor found out he had a blockage in the artery in his neck. By then, his whole left side was frozen."

The words were pouring out of her like a fully opened faucet. "The emergency room team immediately put Johnny on anti-stroke meds and blood thinners. It's too early to say how much motion he'll recover. He'll need lots of physical therapy."

There was another pause. Elaine shifted gears, now speaking slower. "Your father's asking for you to come down here. How quickly can you be here? Can you stay for the week? You'd be a big help to him and me."

"Oh my," I said. I was two thousand kilometers away, but I felt my father's gravitational force field through Elaine's voice. I didn't hesitate.

"Okay, I'll check flights and cancel my appointments. Can I get back to you later this morning?"

"Sure, Harvy, reach me at home." She was speaking more normally. "I'm going to spend this afternoon and evening in the hospital with your father. I really can use your help to be with him."

Her voice accelerated again. "I need to get our house down here closed so we can get back to Montreal as soon as Johnny is physically able. We had planned to drive back in two weeks, but the stroke has put a hold on that." Again, the words were flowing out of her like smoke out of a drag-racing car on a high-speed track. "I'm trying to get him into rehab as soon as possible so he can start physical therapy. He can get a good start on it here and then continue in Montreal."

I interrupted. "Okay, Elaine. I'll come as soon as I can get myself organized."

"Thank you, Harvy." She took a long breath. "I know he had a choice of asking you or Steve to come down here, and he wants you. Maybe he figures your brother's too busy with his wife and two small kids."

Yah, Steve is always busy with something. If it weren't with his family, then it was with his church work. And if not with his church, then it was in helping his Mormon friends and the church's missionaries.

But now wasn't the time to get into that. "Sure, Elaine," I said. "I'll try to be there tomorrow or the next day at the latest. Let me catch my breath."

She said, "Okay, Harvy. Thank you." She then hung up.

I put down the phone and sat stunned for a moment. I knew that Dad's careless live-for-today self-neglect would catch up with him eventually. I wondered if this could be the beginning of his end.

If he survived the stroke, which Elaine said he would, how long might he last with a partially paralyzed body? Would he play golf again, be able to lift his grandchildren, stand and walk, drive a car, or even grab both of my shoulders to offer kisses on both of my cheeks?

My hand closed into a fist. *What a schmuck he is for letting this happen to him!* Through his business heydays, my father continually entertained customers and colleagues in smoke-clogged restaurants, and he filled ashtrays with umpteen cigarette butts. He ate fatty meats with the passion of a

Hungarian butcher. He drank hard liquor with everyone, clinking glasses and offering *chin-chins* as if there would be no tomorrow. Now there may be many fewer tomorrows for him, for he had played Russian roulette with his Slavic *yaytsa*.

Though Steve and I had urged him to stop smoking, he paid no mind. "Smoking relaxes me," he told us. "And I'd rather do that than put sweet cakes in my mouth and then blow up like a balloon."

I took in deep breaths as I further digested Elaine's news. My father's smoking like a Canadian chimney and drinking like a Russian fish may have now caused a grizzly bear hit to his health. I wondered how I might have to pay for his vices besides now having to drop everything in Boston to attend to him in a Boca rehab hospital.

I stared at a blank wall for a few seconds. I considered what my father's sudden illness might mean for him and me regarding his offshore money. Will changes come there too?

I rose from my chair and went to my office door. "Gloria!" I yelled down the stairs. She had spent the night at my condo and was making coffee in the kitchen.

"What's going on?" came her reply.

"My Dad's in trouble. He had a stroke yesterday and is now lying half-paralyzed in a Boca hospital. I've got to get down there right away."

* * *

The following day, Elaine picked me up at the Fort Lauderdale airport. After I had entered the car, she put her hand on my arm. "Your Dad is out of the hospital and is now in a rehab centre ten minutes from our home. I'm taking you straight there." Though her eyes looked tired, her face was fresh. She looked away and then back at me. "He's starting physical therapy in another day or two, as soon as the doctors there assess his condition and recommend a treatment plan."

I held my breath as we drove to the facility. I didn't know what I would encounter regarding my father or what he would face regarding his injured body.

When I walked into his room, Dad was lying in bed with the bed's back tilted upward. He was watching TV. Attached to one arm was an IV.

When he saw me, he raised his right arm and hand. His eyes welled. "I'm so happy to see you, son." His speech slurred, "I'm so glad you could come." He took my hand into his right hand and squeezed it hard. "Look what happened to me. I can't do anything on my left side."

He looked toward the left half of his body and then back at me. Nothing moved on that side of his frame. Also, the left half of his face sagged, the muscles and skin drooping like a clock in a Salvador Dali painting.

I pushed aside my shock and worked to be optimistic. "I heard from Elaine that you'll be okay, Dad. After some physical therapy, you'll be back on your feet." I hoped I was right. I was trying to encourage my usually optimistic father.

"How long can you stay with me?" he asked.

"I can be here for the rest of this week."

His voice quivered. "Not longer than that?"

"We'll see Dad," I said matter-of-factly. "Now tell me what they are doing for you here? When can I talk to your doctor? Has he seen you today?"

As Elaine had said, my dad was out of danger, but the stroke had done its damage. He could feel touch but couldn't move anything on his left side, except for his eyelid.

Within a day, some movement started to come back to his afflicted hand and foot. Within another day, the hospital had him performing both physical and occupational therapy every day. By the end of the week, he could lift and move both his left arm and left leg. But he couldn't stand without people assisting, one on each side of him.

The best news was that I could see the resolve in my father's eyes, the will to overcome his disability. During physical therapy sessions, he exerted his muscles with determination to pull levers, lift weights, and squeeze balls. The doctor said he could regain full motion, but it would take a year or more of hard work. Dad would have to lose twenty or thirty pounds of body mass. He'd have to exercise his muscles every day to build and sustain new motor pathways in his brain. I hoped his motivation would last.

Dad had been a hard worker all his life, but I bet he never expected this kind of project. Every day, I stayed by his side and remained optimistic for his full recovery. Unlike nine years earlier, when Dad had had an angina attack, I suspected my father wouldn't recover as quickly from this body blow.

After a few days of therapy, Dad was able to play gin rummy with me, which we did for hours. He sat unaided in a wheelchair, holding his cards between the fingers and thumb of his afflicted hand as it lay supported by the bedside table. My now "one-arm-bandit" father played with his able hand, and I let that hand win more often than it lost. Unlike his usual sly playing—pretending he had nothing and then winning in one final turn—he worked to lay down his cards as soon as he could. That way, he'd have fewer cards to hold in his weakened hand.

No matter how good my cards were, I held onto them longer than necessary, giving Dad a better chance to win. I smiled and said, "You see, Dad, you still have your good luck. You're beating the pants off me."

He smiled back as best he could with his half-paralyzed face. He muttered, "I guess you can't outsmart an old fox."

I was hoping I could.

One day later that week, during our card-playing, I asked him, "So, Dad, how did the stroke happen? Did you have any warning?"

He looked at me, his eyes down. "I was stupid, son," he offered gruffly. His voice struggled as if it were a rough motorcycle engine needing lubricant. "A couple of days before the attack, I was standing on a step stool and reaching into the grapefruit tree." He raised his able arm to demonstrate. "I was trying to get the fruit from higher in the tree."

His voice rose. "All of a sudden, I got dizzy. I slipped off the stool and fell to the ground." His good arm came down and banged the table. He shook his head. "I felt so stupid about falling that I didn't say anything to Elaine."

Oh, God! He had had a warning and ignored it. "That's too bad, Dad," I said. I let out a sigh for his having played his stroke card. "I hope you're going to stop smoking and take better care of yourself. I'd hate to see you have another attack."

"Yes, son; I have learned my lesson." He raised his right hand as if he were doing a pledge on the Bible. "I haven't put one filthy cigarette into my mouth since I got to the hospital, and I'm not going to touch another for as long as I live." He swept his unaffected arm away as if he were casting off his last smoke.

He offered a half-smile. "And I'll eat nothing but chicken and bean soups until I lose twenty-five pounds."

"Okay, Dad. That's the spirit."

Then my father offered something which I had wondered about but dared not ask. Sitting in his wheelchair, a blanket laying over his legs, he used his able hand to pull me a bit closer. He annunciated as best as he could, quietly saying, "When we get back to Montreal, I want you to come to my Lux bank the next time you're in town. You know the place, in Alexis Nihon Plaza. If I'm going to be this way, I need to make some changes."

I nodded. I had first gone to Dad's offshore Global Trade Bank a couple of years earlier, in 1991. He had put his signature on a charitable annuity agreement to siphon a chunk of his pension funds into an offshore university annuity for me after his death. The scheme would allow my father's estate to evade income taxes on a portion of his pension assets.

I had played along with Dad's financial deception—keeping that money charade hidden from the tax authorities and my brother—such that I'd obtain tax-free income from that annuity for the rest of my life. Dad had signed the clandestine agreement without a second thought. I had agreed to keep my mum about it, but I covertly considered I could change my mind after my father's passing. With his recent stroke, Dad and I were one step closer to that eventuality.

I nodded my understanding to my father. I wondered what changes he specifically envisioned for our anticipated visit to his offshore bank. I figured he could no longer drive himself there to count his offshore dollars or grab tax-free cash. He might need me to be a money mule.

I didn't know if I wanted that kind of job, but I said nothing more until I learned more about what my father had planned. I had no idea how much cash he had stashed there, but I might find out soon.

I looked down toward the floor. It seemed that Dad's thinking abilities were not too damaged by his stroke. I counted that as a good thing, though the next weeks and months would reveal more.

Over the following days and nights, I wondered if I cared for my father only because of his money. Was I as addicted to the promise of his offshore stash just as cigarettes, alcohol, gambling, and womanizing had hooked him?

How would I ever know for sure?

* * *

While being with Dad during his rehab sessions, I watched as he performed his daily physical and occupational therapy. Both he and I were encouraged by how much more he could do each time.

Later in the week, the orderlies let me help him into a wheelchair. I pushed him down the corridor to a communal room where other debilitated people hung out. After we had sat there for a few moments, Dad turned to me. "Harvy, please bring me back to my room." When I asked why, he said, "I'd rather be there." I surmised that he didn't like to be around old and sick people, though he was one too.

Gloria called every day to see how my father and I were doing. Dad told me, "You found yourself a very nice girl. I hope you'll have a good and long life with her." I felt proud that my dad liked my new choice in a partner, though it peeved me that he referred to Gloria as a "girl."

My brother called us a few times that week. Our father told him, "I'll be fine. I'm working hard in the hospital. I'll see you when I get back."

I overheard Steve reply, "Keep up the good work, Dad." Our father then passed the phone to me to fill Steve in on our dad's progress. I offered short health and doctor reports, and we left our conversations there. I felt a little irritated that my brother was getting away scot-free from tending to our father, but I figured he'd have his turn in Montreal. I was the lucky one to be living in Boston and only having to sacrifice a week of my time right now.

While I sat with my father, Elaine got the Boca house ready for its seasonal closing. Every day before supper, she came to visit for an hour or two. She brought yet another bouquet or get-well card from a friend.

One evening, after Elaine and Dad had covered a litany of house business, she asked, "How's it going with your therapy and the food here?"

He pointed to me. "Harvy will tell you how I'm getting stronger every day."

I nodded and raised my thumb in agreement.

Dad then added, "But I hate the crap they serve here. I need a good *halušky* [a hearty Slavic dish of potato dumplings and sheep's milk cheese]."

Elaine glared at him. "Now, Johnny! It's going be a long time before you have something like that again." She pointed her finger at him and spoke like a mother to a naughty child. "And I hope you're not wasting the food they're giving you here."

My father looked at her and gestured again toward me. "No, Harvy's eating most of it."

She gave me the same intense look.

I presented a grin as if I were a child caught with a hand in a cookie jar.

"It figures," she offered. "I can't trust the two of you together." She smiled as if what we did was par for the course for this father and son.

I wanted to tell her that I partook in my father's meals only because Dad wouldn't eat most of them. But he spoke first. "I don't like what they serve here. I really could use a good Weiner Schnitzel. It's not too heavy." I couldn't tell if he was serious or not.

She pointed her finger again. "From now on, Mister, it'll be bean and vegetable soups when I get you home. You'll have to lose a lot of weight if you want to walk on your own again." She huffed. "Consider your time here as the start of your diet."

My father was used to soup diets, eating such for weeks as mid-day and evening meals. Hearty soups—without the usual rye bread that he loved—helped him lose 10 to 15 pounds in a couple of months.

"So bring me some hot bean soup next time you come." Dad's tone was harsh. "It's better than the shit they serve here."

She hesitated, then smiled. "Okay, Johnny. You're the boss."

He pointed at her and smiled. "And don't you forget that!"

I was glad that there was little tension between the two of them at this needy time for my father. From the moment I arrived at the rehab hospital, Dad hadn't complained even once about Elaine, as he had done repeatedly behind her back from the moment they had married. It was one shining star breaking through an otherwise overcast week for our Simkovits family.

Before the week ended, I got up my nerve to ask my father about his marriage. I smiled. "So, Dad, tell me. Why did you really marry Elaine?"

I could see the wheels churning in his head for a moment. He looked down and then back at me. His face was straight when he offered, "Because I couldn't drink her under the table."

My father pointed my way. "One night, while she and I were getting together and having supper together at the Troika, we polished off a half-bottle of vodka."

I imagined my dad and Elaine dressed in their best, telling stories, laughing, and singing along with the roving minstrels at that lively, upscale Russian establishment.

Dad grinned as best he could and added, "Before we finished the bottle, I knew she was the woman for me."

There were parts of Elaine's and my father's personalities that were well suited for each other. Most importantly, if my father was still thinking this way about his wife, he certainly had a good distance left in him. Perhaps there would also be many more miles remaining in their marriage.

That evening at the hospital, as Elaine and I were about to leave my father's side, he looked at me, a soft expression in his eyes. "Son, can you stay longer here with me? Do you have to go back on Sunday?"

He had asked me the same question every evening that week. I responded the same way I did the last few days. "Sorry, Dad, but I have client meetings to attend in Boston next week. I also need to get back to Gloria." I took a breath. "You seem to be doing better. I'll come and see you in Montreal as soon as you get resettled there."

He nodded, and we kissed each other on both cheeks. Elaine received the same from him, with a "Goodnight sweetheart" attached.

"See you in the morning," I said. Elaine and I turned to walk out. As I approached the door, I looked over my shoulder. Dad's head was already turned toward the television as if we had never been there.

On my last hospital visit with my father, he could stand and walk short distances with a walker as long as someone was next to him. Later, we had dinner in his room. I again read the paper as he watched TV. His sad eyes looked longingly at me, and he asked the same question as if he had never asked it before. "Can you stay here a little longer, son?"

I was getting annoyed. I pointed to my hand. "Dad, when you ask for my hand, I give it to you." I gestured to my arm. "And then you ask for my arm, and I give that to you too." I then pointed to my torso. "But then you want my body." I took a breath. "I'm sorry, but I have things to do at home."

His voice elevated. "No, son; I don't do that!" He turned his eyes to the TV and said nothing more. My point made, I looked back at my newspaper.

When Elaine took me to the airport for my return flight to Boston, she assured me. "He'll be fine, Harvy. Your father's in good hands in the rehab facility here. He's working hard to get back his strength. We'll see how he is in a few weeks. I can then attempt the drive back to Montreal."

There was a caring expression in her eyes as she touched my arm. "Thank you for coming down for the week. I know Johnny appreciated your being here, and I did too. It allowed me time to get things ready at the house before we leave for Montreal."

"I'm glad I could be of help," I said.

I had an impulse. A couple of times during the week, I asked Elaine how she was doing. She gave me short "I'm fine, Harvy" answers. I now asked, "Are you going to stop smoking too?"

She looked away for a moment then turned her eyes back to me. "I've cut back considerably since your father's stroke." She took a long breath. "But with all that's going on, I'm waiting until I get Johnny back to Montreal before I work to quit completely." She sighed. "Our Canadian friends have left Florida for the season, and I'm feeling very alone down here with your father. It'll be less stressful when I have him back in Montreal."

I nodded and offered, "I'll see you in a few weeks then. I'll plan to come to Montreal right after you're back."

I said nothing of my father's and my planned Global Trade Bank outing. I hoped Dad would keep his word about that pending visit. It had taken a couple of years of hearing him say, "Harvy, I want you to come to my Lux bank," before he took me on our first visit there.

I had no idea what Elaine knew of Dad's stashed money. Hell, if I was going to say something about it. If I did, would she divulge to me what she knew, or would she pretend that she knew more than she did? Then again, how much would I tell her? I didn't want to test that boundary and have an uncomfortable conversation that could cut against me. I didn't want to put what Dad had promised me at risk, and I hoped he would keep his promise.

I kissed Elaine on the cheek and exited the car to enter the airport.

* * *

Dad spent four full weeks at the Boca Raton rehab hospital. By the end, he could stand and walk on his own with a walker. In time, he'd work up to a cane. The rehab centre had done a great job of having him perform daily activities of life. He relearned to cut his food and feed himself, get in and out of chairs, beds, and cars, dress and undress, tie his shoes, talk without mumbling, and do other activities which one with full motor abilities never gave a second thought.

Elaine closed the Boca house by herself, packed my father into the passenger seat of his large Lexus, and drove back to Montreal in two long days. They stopped overnight and several times each day to allow Dad to walk and exercise his afflicted arm and leg. At night, Elaine massaged his debilitated muscles to improve blood circulation. When they arrived in Montreal, she took my father to his doctor and arranged for physical therapy at home. She also found a masseur to give him a full-body rub every week. Elaine was trying to do her best for Dad, and I appreciated her efforts.

It would be nearly two years before my father got back what he could. By that time, he hobbled slowly with a cane—sometimes lifting and other times dragging his bad left leg. He was able to drive again for short distances, using his good right leg on the pedals. He lifted his afflicted leg in and out of the car as if it were a block of wood.

My father played golf occasionally with buddies, using a cart to carry him. He employed a half swing, using his strong leg for balance and his able arm for power. (But after a few years of ball slices and duffs, even his closest comrades stopped asking him to come out for rounds.) Dad's facial muscles came back to a degree, but his smile would never be more than three-quarters.

The good news was that my father had stopped smoking. He drank only one vodka-on-the-rocks in the evening—with doctor's permission—to make himself a little happier during supper and sleepier afterward. But Dad never danced again at Montreal's Slovak and Hungarian Balls, and he never again worked the room to greet friends and make acquaintances.

From now on, at parties, people came over to greet him while he remained seated. He'd grab their hand firmly with his able hand—his other hand holding his cane—and offer, "All I need is a little more power."

Male friends would shake my father's unaffected hand while the women would kiss him on both cheeks. They all said, "You look great, Johnny. You'll be at a hundred percent in no time." But the universe had taken a big chunk from my father's gregariousness, and "a hundred percent" became a slowly fading fantasy. He no longer became involved in any business ventures.

I never asked Dad what life was like for him as a disabled person. It must have been frustrating, if not infuriating, to drag his left leg. It must have been painful not to perform home improvement and maintenance projects that were once second nature. Though he continued his physical therapy, his recovery never surpassed a three-quarters retrieval of what he lost by having the stroke.

I felt sad seeing my father no longer being his vivacious and commanding self. I felt disappointed, perhaps even aggravated, that the survivor I had revered my whole life had irreparably damaged his body (and maybe his mind too) and now needed ongoing care.

And a part of me felt scared. I wondered what my father's disability would mean for Elaine, Steve, and me. Might we all have to be at his beck and call as he withered away in the last phase of his life? The stroke had altered my father's fortunes forever, and only time would tell what effect it would have for his and our dealings, both onshore and off.

* * * *

Next Stage for Dad and Me

On my next trip to Montreal, after my father and Elaine had returned home, Dad asked that I pick him up at his office and drive us to the Global Trade Bank. Not Elaine, my brother, or Dad's bookkeeper, Rob, knew where we were heading.

In the car, Dad didn't smoke his usual stogie. Instead, he held his walking cane. Gesturing with his unaffected arm and hand, he started to talk. His voice was gruff. "Do you remember Simon, the bank manager who you met a few years ago when we did that university annuity agreement?"

"Yes, Dad, I do."

My father's spirits perked as he raised his voice along with his able hand. "Simon was a smart fellow. He made lots of money for me with good overseas investments." He patted my arm. "I took him out on the town many times, to the Troika and other places. He was a lot of fun to be with."

Dad called Mr. Simon just "Simon" because it was his custom to call professionals by their last name. He didn't offer more about his ventures and forays with the bank manager, and I didn't ask. My father's kind of pleasures—unlimited liquid libations, a litany of Players and Pall Malls, lively Slavic tales, Eastern European folk melodies, and the occasional loose lady—wasn't my kind of fun. I regretted my indulgence in some of those sordid pleasures in my younger years as Johnny's son. I suspected that most of those vices would now no longer be Dad's kind of fun.

Dad's voice quieted. "Unfortunately, Simon is no longer with the bank's Montreal branch." He worked to enunciate his words. "Before Simon left, he told me the bank's head office doesn't like its managers to get too friendly with their clients and to show anyone preference, so they moved him back to Lux." He took a long breath. "Even though the new manager, Hoffmann, makes decent money for me, he's not as good or as lively as Simon was."

I, too, had found Mr. Simon to be very personable. When I first met him, he had shown sincere interest in me. He had asked many questions about my life in Boston and why I left Montreal. Simon was a testament to how pleasant banking professionals could be in the money-hiding, tax-evading business.

"Is Hilde, the bank's receptionist, still there?" I asked.

"Yes, and she's still a good looker for an old broad." Dad chuckled through his garbled voice. His comment told me his stroke hadn't taken away all his faculties. "But I hear she's going to retire."

Dad repeated himself as if he had forgotten what he had said. "The new manager is Hoffmann. He's okay but not as good as Simon."

Mr. Hoffmann and Hilde were tucked behind the same Global Trade Bank's double security doors in a nondescript hallway halfway up one Alexis Nihon Plaza tower. Dad hobbled while I ambled next to him into Hoffmann's office. I held onto Dad's cane in my right hand as he held onto my left arm with his good right hand.

Upon seeing Hoffmann, Dad announced, "I brought my son, Harvy, with me." He shook the manager's hand, maneuvered in front of a chair, and then plopped down into it. He gestured with his right hand to the left side of his body. "See what happened to me! I had a big stroke a couple of months ago, and I'm still having trouble moving my left side."

Mr. Hoffmann nodded, and he shook my hand firmly. He looked back at my father. "I'm very sorry to hear about your situation. I hope you will be okay soon." The man seemed formal in his ways, speaking slowly and in a banker's monotone. Unlike Simon, who used larger arm movements and a big smile when greeting someone, Hoffmann was blank-faced and business-like.

My father offered his new line. "I just need more power on my left side."

Mr. Hoffmann nodded but said nothing more about Dad's condition.

I sat still while Dad and the manager got down to business. Dad looked at him. "You can talk openly with my son. I want Harvy to be up to date with the recent activity regarding my money here at the bank."

Dad's stroke propelled him to reveal his offshore wealth to me. But a part of me wished there only was a small sum stashed here, making his illegitimate money a modest problem. But the way my father had spoken to me over the years about his stash in Luxemburg, I figured there was well over a million bucks squirreled away offshore.

I shivered as I contemplated the bigger secret I'd now have to keep. I had been anticipating this moment like a perpetual best man hoping for his wedding day. It had been twenty-one years since my father took me with him to open his first offshore bank account in Zurich, Switzerland. All this time, I had been at arm's length from his money. Now, at thirty-eight years old, I was close enough to touch the walls of its container. It both felt good and smelled bad at the same time.

Mr. Hoffmann looked at my father. "I had your current statements faxed to me this morning by our Lux office." He turned to me. "Everything is kept at our head office. Luxembourg is a tax-free state, and its laws protect everything we do at the Global Trade Bank. We keep no account paperwork here. Once we review these documents, what you don't take with you will be shredded immediately by me."

So that's how they keep the Canadian government at bay. Even if Revenue Canada and the RCMP knock down the bank's double security doors, they'll find nothing unless it was on the table in the middle of a meeting like this one. I glanced toward the door to see if anyone was trying to break in.

"Let us review these accounts one by one," the manager said.

Oh, Dad has more than one account hidden here? Might multiple accounts make him feel richer?

Hoffmann continued. "Let's look at your main account first." He passed out the first set of documents. "As you know, Mr. Simkovits, this account holds secure investments, like cash, bonds, and CDs in both Canadian and U.S. currencies."

As Hoffmann spoke about the account, I looked carefully at the paperwork. My eyebrows rose when I saw the current balance. It was for multiple millions of dollars. I wondered how my father had amassed such assets. Had Mr. Simon been a money-making maven, like a veritable Luxembourgian Michael Milken?

The manager continued to talk about the assets, income, and money transfers my father had made. He mentioned that, during the past year, Dad had removed only $30,000USD in cash from the account.

Hoffmann soon passed out the documents for a second account. It was a smaller stash—in the mid-six-figures—and held riskier investments. One position was a private venture fund that the manager said my father couldn't cash for another six years. The rest comprised of tradeable equity funds. I wondered if this was my father's mad money, assets on which he was willing to take more risk.

A third account, the smallest, held the money my father had invested, in the early 1980s, into a Supporters of Independent University annuity. His former colleague, Ben Cohen, had urged Dad to make that investment, couched as a donation. Hoffmann offered, "As per your agreement with the bank, I can give you any amounts over the original amount. Would you like a cheque, or do you want to take it as cash through the ATM downstairs?"

Dad said, "We'll take the cash out from downstairs." He turned to me. "Over the ten years I've had that annuity, and with the initial tax deduction I received from my donation, that investment has more than paid for itself." He pointed to the pocket of his pants that held his wallet. "With my Global Trade Bank identity card, I'll show you how to get money from the ATM in case you ever get cash for me."

I nodded and calmly said, "Okay, Dad." I now wondered if I would have to be a money mule for my father's hidden hoard. Would I have to come in disguise or hide my face from ATM cameras? I dreaded the thought.

Hoffmann passed out the statement of a fourth account, with sums again in the mid-six-figures. That document showed another set of secure investments, similar to Dad's multi-million dollar account.

It seemed that Dad preferred securities were CDs and bonds, which produced recurring income. My father had once told me, "Playing the stock market is like gambling your money away, and I hate to lose." I found it ironic that Dad didn't take gambles in the equities markets, considering the financial risks he had made in operating a business and the legal jeopardy he took in stashing his money offshore.

Six years earlier, during the summer of 1987, Dad had once played the equities market. A Hungarian stockbroker friend had convinced him to put $150,000 of his legit assets into stocks. The subsequent October, on what the financial industry would call Black Monday, my father lost nearly half of what he had invested. He couldn't even get hold of his broker on that precipitous day because the fellow was getting married in Budapest. When the broker returned from overseas, Dad blew his top at the guy and immediately fired him. He cashed out his equity losses and put what remained back into CDs.

I found my curiosity rising as Hoffmann went over Dad's fourth statement. I felt it was becoming okay for me to ask questions. I figured I needed to be knowledgeable if I would be more involved in my father's offshore money. I glanced at the bank manager. "Mr. Hoffmann, I understand the rationale for those other three accounts, but what's the purpose of this fourth account? Its holdings are very similar to the first one you showed us."

The manager looked puzzled, as if he had never expected that question. He turned to my father. "Your son is right, Mr. Simkovits. This account holds similar assets as your main account, yet I'm not sure why it's separate. Might you remember why you have it?"

My dad looked puzzled too. He mumbled, "Simon used that years ago for something else." I could see him wracking his brain, but no light turned on. "We don't need it. We can move the assets from there into my big account and then close this one."

I spoke up. "Dad, before you do that, I have an idea." Though I had a bad feeling in my gut about my father's money-hiding games and tax-evading ploys, a part of me liked being helpful. And here was a chance to gain offshore points with my father. "Dad, what if you use this smaller account as your main source of cash. You don't seem to be drawing much money from your accounts here, thus allowing your assets to grow over time. So why not take the cash you need from this smaller account and leave the big account alone?"

My father's eyes narrowed. "What's the difference where I take the money from?" His tone was both irritable and perplexed.

My mind was firing fast, and I wasn't quite sure what was propelling it. "Think about it, Dad. If you never touch the big account, and if you ever get caught by Revenue Canada, then you can say there's only this small account and declare just that one to the government." I pointed to Dad's statements. "Over the ensuing years, your largest portfolio will become more hidden in the background because there won't be a cash trail in or out of it."

Both my father and the bank manager stared at me. I continued to talk. "Another reason to do it is because of Steve. If he ever found out about this money—or when you pass away, and I think I have to show him something regarding your assets over here—then I can present him only these one or two small accounts. He doesn't have to know about the big one."

I pointed to the statement that showed the funds held for Independent University. I said, "That small annuity fund will disappear on its own in the donation to the university at your death—so that one isn't a problem. By having your cash come from the small account, it would protect your big one." I looked at him. "It would be safer for both of us."

I pointed again. "And when that other small account, the one that holds those venture fund investments, generates income or the assets are cashed, then you can use that money to feed your small day-to-day account. Once again, over time, it will be as if the biggest portfolio never existed." I pointed to the three of us. "Only we will know."

With those words, I was beginning to sound like my father. I hoped he and Hoffman saw my idea as a way to cut the risk not only for Dad but also for me after my father's eventual death.

The wheels turned slowly in my father's mind as his eyes shifted back and forth. After what seemed like an eternity of minutes but was perhaps a handful of seconds, he said, "That's an excellent idea, son." He turned to the manager. "Let's do it."

My dad then added something I didn't expect. "And let's give Harvy power of attorney over this smaller day-to-day account." He turned back to me. "Harvy, as of today, you'll have signing authority over this portion of my money here. If I ever need you to get any funds or move cash elsewhere, you'd be able to do it."

Oh, my! For two decades, I had been waiting for some influence over my father's offshore assets. This move was a huge step in that direction.

I thought more carefully for a few seconds. With my name on one of Dad's offshore accounts, wouldn't my hands now become as dirty as his? Would I have to file falsehoods on my annual U.S. tax returns—in my adopted country where I was a resident alien—about having access to a foreign bank account? Might the American government deport me back to Canada if they found out? Or, could I be thrown into a white-collar American jail cell reserved for tax evaders?

Why did I have to open my frigging mouth?!

I offered my usual, "Okay, Dad, whatever you think is best." But I was troubled by taking on the finger-dirtying responsibility my father had unexpectedly bestowed on me.

For years, I had yearned for my father's trust, but he now thrust me into the black money muck with him. What would happen if Revenue Canada found out I had signing authority on this offshore account? It was one thing to have my father thrown into federal jail for tax fraud, but it's quite another if I would be right there beside him. Might this power of attorney step become a stride that could catapult me into jailhouse stripes? I had many more years to lose than my father had.

Sweat formed under my collar. Could I back out of Dad's desire to grant me access to his smaller offshore account? What would he think if I declined this exclusive invite into his clandestine world?

Stay calm, Harvy. Don't overreact. As I had done times before, I sat frozen in my chair as if nothing wrong were happening. *There's nothing to worry about if I consider it his money, not mine.*

Hoffmann left the room to get the needed papers for signing. While my father and I sat waiting, Dad repeated, "That was a good idea, son. And there will be less for your brother to know if he has to know something."

I nodded and sucked in my angst. "Yes, Dad," I said meekly.

My head screamed. *What the hell am I doing?*

When Hoffmann returned, both Dad and I signed the power of attorney papers. Here and now was the first time I signed any document at a bank where my father enacted his illegitimate offshore business. I took deep breaths to keep my hand steady such that my signature looked normal.

Hoffmann gestured toward Dad across the table. "Mr. Simkovits, you can revoke this power of attorney at any time." That meant I had sway over this smaller account for as long as Dad allowed me to have it.

The banker continued looking at my father. "The power of attorney will be revoked automatically at your death. At that time, your last will becomes the governing document for all your funds with our bank."

Dad nodded. "Yes, I understand." He then offered another thought I hadn't expected. "My son here will be involved in helping me redraft my will."

I was surprised by my father's statement but didn't let on. I wasn't sure he meant what he had said or if he had said it only for Mr. Hoffmann's sake. I made a mental note to ask Dad later about his will.

My father took his copies of the documents and bank account statements and stuffed them into his inside jacket pocket. We said goodbye to Hoffmann and headed for the exit.

While we waited for the elevator in the quiet lobby, my father turned to me and spoke softly. "Harvy, I'll show you where I keep the bank's statements hidden in my private office." He pointed upward. "There's a loose false ceiling panel above my small office safe." He patted his jacket's breast pocket. "I can show you how to move that panel to hide these papers." He pointed downward. "With my bad leg, I can't stand on a chair anymore."

"Okay, Dad," I said, but a part of me didn't want to know. I had had enough clandestine money affairs for one day. I said, "I have to go to a meeting right after I get you back to the office. I'll come by tomorrow before I go to the airport to fly back to Boston."

"Okay, son. And when will I see you again in Montreal?"

There was my dad once more trying to drag me deeper into a father's hole. I said my customary, "I'll let you know."

But I wanted to spin away from the black hole of my father's hidden cash and never to return. Though I had behaved like a money-hiding, tax-evading pro that day, I wasn't sure I had the stomach for such offshore chicanery the way my father had.

* * *

When we returned to my father's office, my brother was there waiting. I hadn't expected him, but our dad acted as if he had. He kissed Steve, saying, "Good to see you, son." He hobbled to his chair, holding onto desks to steady himself as he crossed the room.

My heart started to pound. As far as I knew, my brother was in the dark about Dad's offshore money. Part of me felt guilty for what I had learned today. I hoped Steve wouldn't sense my uneasiness. I shook my brother's hands and spoke as calmly as I could. "Hi, Steve, it's been a long time." I turned to Dad. "Can I make coffee for you?" I looked back at my brother but couldn't look directly into his eyes. "What about sherbal tea for you, Steve?"

Steve shook his head. My father responded, "Okay, I'll take a coffee."

I slinked over to the kitchen area to start the brew before Steve saw my culpable face or the sweat on my brow. I wanted to run out of there, but I didn't want to leave suddenly. Something then raised my temperature as high as the false ceiling panel where Dad stashed his offshore papers. Dad turned to Steve. "Harvy and I just came from my Lux bank."

My ears were ringing as Dad continued. "There's not much remaining there—I spent most of it for the new house I bought in Florida." He spoke slowly to annunciate his words better. "What remains will be gradually spent down, or it will completely disappear when I die, going to a university in Lux." His voice was as sincere as Canadian pumpkin pie. I knew he was telling Steve only what he wanted his first son to learn.

I couldn't believe what I had heard. *Steve knows about Dad's offshore money!! And he now knows that I know.* I had never known how much Dad had told my brother, but it was now as clear as Dad's evening vodka. He had let Steve in on some things, though he had repeatedly said that Steve knew nothing.

For my brother's ears, Dad minimized his holdings and pretended they would disappear at his death. I was the only son to know the whole truth—or did I? I was beside myself. Right in front of me, my father was lying through his Hungarian-Slovak teeth to his first offspring. It seemed natural for him to be blatantly dishonest.

My heart raced; my gut ached; my head filled with angst. I was betraying my brother and dead mother, being an accomplice to my father, and false to my conscience. Was I becoming like Dad? I didn't believe I'd deliberately lie as he now did, but I wasn't placing truths on any office desk today.

Steve didn't even glance toward me; he continued to look at our father. "Okay, Dad," he offered, as I always had said to my father's finagling ways. My brother didn't ask any questions. Maybe he didn't want me to know what he knew, as I didn't want him to know what I was aware of. How would I ever know if our dad had shared secrets with Steve that they were keeping from me?

Into what kind of bind and quandary has our father put all of us? Formidable and foreboding was the pact that Dad and I had created concerning his hidden money—a covenant that became more unlivable each day. *Doesn't the guy realize what he's doing? Then again, do I know what I'm doing?*

Dad continued to talk to my brother about other things. Our father sat in his chair while Steve leaned back against a desk, his arms folded. They spoke as if I weren't there. I stood quietly by the coffee maker, hardly able to look their way. As the black brew poured into the coffee pot, my stomach felt as if it were filling with acid. What a schmuck Dad was not to warn me that he would blurt out to Steve our secret, and right here in front of me.

After serving Dad, I said I had to leave for a meeting. "I'll come back tomorrow to say goodbye before my flight back to Boston."

"Okay, son; come early, so you aren't rushed." Perhaps he was asking me to leave time to show me where he hid those Global Trade Bank papers or to share the plans for his will. I'd know only when I'd return and only if my father was ready to tell me.

I glanced at my brother. "Steve, could you take Dad home later?"

"Sure, Harvy, and see you next time." I had no idea what his face looked like, for I didn't dare look at him. I nodded quickly and turned to exit the front door into fresher air.

I looked at the darkening sky outside. My mind got away from me. I wondered which Simkovits son would rise higher on Dad's mound of offshore cash. Was my coming out on top of this pile going to be worth it?

My disdain for my brother buttressed me, but I also felt sick to my stomach. *If Dad was a schmuck, then what was I?*

I didn't have an answer.

* * * *

A Father's Failings

Months after Dad's stroke, Elaine told me, "Your father can no longer do the work he used to do at our Lake Champlain home. He can hardly lift a broom and sweep." Her spirit was down. "Other than hobbling up and down the driveway to exercise his legs, he sits and watches TV all day." She took a breath. "We don't have to be in Peru, NY, to do that."

It may have been too much for Elaine to manage that massive, old, stone house on her own, plus taking care of my father. Dad soon listed their lakeshore home for sale.

That summer of '93, Dad and Elaine held their annual Canadian Slovak Professional & Business Association barbeque *chez* Simkovits. They raised a white tent, arranged a dozen tables and a hundred chairs, and hired Polish musicians. The association's President, Joe, commanded the barbecue where he grilled hand-selected Delmonico steaks to perfection. Joe cooked calves' liver and hot dogs as appetizers, a Johnny Simkovits tradition borrowed from Montreal's Swartz's Deli.

Guests' faces sported smiles, but the party wasn't the same as in previous years. My father sat rather than mingled with guests. He abstained from his typical chain-smoking, bottomless drinking, and boisterous singing. Instead, people came forward to greet him. Women bent down to kiss him on the cheeks as if he were The Godfather himself. They offered, "You look great, Johnny." The men added, "Keep up the good work, and you'll be back to yourself in no time."

Dad took in the attention with as much of a grin as he could gather. He grabbed hands and kissed cheeks from his good right side. Elaine was full of smiles, complete with spirited hellos and sad goodbyes. She had arranged the prep, cooking, and cleanup crews, and she rushed around to ensure everything was as it should be. Doing the work without Dad's help must have been challenging.

After I had tried to help by carrying out full platers and returning empty ones, Elaine told me, "Harvy, enjoy yourself and be with your father. The people from the Slovak Association are doing most of the cuisine and serving. I hired a company to put up and take down the tents, tables, chairs, etc. I have help to pick up and clean up afterward."

With 100 people on the property, I knew she had been flat-out for days before and after the festivities. She must have been exhausted.

I became stunned when Dad told me he had put his Peru home on the market. I had impressed my share of girlfriends at that beautiful stone mini-mansion. But I also had mixed feelings about visiting that exquisite house on the shores of Lake Champlain because my mother had never had such niceties. The way my father's friends accepted Dad's new life with Elaine, acting as if my mother had never existed, made me feel blue and empty. Though I put on a good face for his guests, I never felt fully myself *chez* Dad.

I asked my father how he felt about selling the retirement home he had lived in for over a decade. Pointing to his impaired side, he offered, "I have to, son. The way I am, I can no longer keep up the place."

Hearing sadness in his voice, I sensed his feeling of loss. The Peru property had reminded him of his grandfather's nearly three decades of retirement on a hilltop farm outside of Košice. That grandfather had reached 93, retiring in the house he had lived in for most of his life and outliving three wives. The father of my father's father died while he was asleep in his bed after he had had his last nightly stiff drink of plum brandy.

I suspected Dad had wanted a similar ending to a likewise long life. But his life-changing stroke had taken away his most cherished retirement wishes.

* * *

On a September evening later that year, as the leaves turned, Dad, Elaine, and I were having supper at Luigio's. After we had finished a round of drinks, Elaine exclaimed, "It's not so easy to sell that lakeshore house!"

Dad and I looked at her as she continued. "The economy hasn't fully recovered from the recent recession. The vacation home market in Upstate New York is awful. Nothing is selling. We've received no offers." She turned to my father. "What about calling Greg Mann in Plattsburgh?"

Though I didn't know the fellow, maybe Elaine thought my father would be more amenable to her sudden suggestion if I were present. But Dad's good hand tightened around his empty vodka glass, and he banged it on the table. "I'll never sell the house to that bastard. Don't you dare call him!"

Dad's anger still sent shakes through my spine, yet it didn't faze Elaine. She looked at me as she took a sip of wine. "Harvy, Greg Mann is a local Plattsburgh businessman." Her voice was calm, and her demeanor businesslike. "Mann had vied for that house twelve years ago when your dad snatched it from under his nose."

"How so, Elaine?" I said. I suspected my father would be less edgy if I showed interest.

Dad turned his attention to his supper as Elaine continued. "Mann is about your father's age, and he still runs a building contractor business in the Plattsburgh area. He had wanted that house, but he thought he could have his way with Meyer's kids after old-man Meyer [the previous owner of the house] died." She took another sip of wine. "When we found out the house was for sale, your father placed a deposit while Mann was still dickering with Meyer's kids about the purchase price."

Elaine held onto her wine glass and swirled the liquid slightly. "I heard that after Mann had lost the house to us, he started to stockpile granite to construct his own stone house on the lake. I don't think he's built it yet. He might be open to another chance at our place."

Elaine was working to elicit my support. What she had said did make sense. I looked at Dad. "It might seem a bit odd, but what's the problem in asking Mann if he'd be interested in buying your place, especially if he hasn't yet built his house?"

Dad's eyebrows lowered as he sensed what his spouse was doing. He growled, "Mann was pissed about losing the Meyer house to me. He sued both the Meyer children and me after we had signed the Purchase and Sale Agreement." He raised his good arm to make his point. "The suit became stuck in New York State court for six months. We had to delay house renovations until I was sure I had a clear title." He then raised his voice as he glared at Elaine. "Greg Mann is the last guy I want to talk to. I'd rather give the house away than call him."

I stayed quiet. Elaine looked at me and then back at Dad. "Okay, Johnny; we'll keep on looking."

I knew that this conversation wasn't over.

As fall arrived and outdoor temperatures dropped, Dad's Peru house remained unsold. Knowing that the selling season for lakeside property dwindled in the winter months, my father and Elaine spoke to a number of their local-area friends. One was Henry, a neighbour who owned a lakeside, log-cabin-style summer restaurant just south of Dad's property.

As the 1993 summer season ended, Dad, Elaine, and I were having brunch at Henry's. Henry came by our table to chat. "It's going to be hard to see you guys leave the area," he said. "Have you found a buyer yet?"

My father blurted out, half-jokingly, "No, but how about you, Henry? I'll give you a good deal."

The restauranteur smiled and pointed outside. "You know I already have my house up on the main road." He gestured toward the floor. "And I have my hands full with this place. What do I need another house for?"

Undeterred, my father continued. "So find me a buyer; you know a lot of people in the area." His voice was gruff but understandable. "We no longer have our place listed with an agent; so, we can work out a private arrangement. I'll give you ten percent if you find somebody for me."

I noted that Dad didn't say 10% of what.

Henry quickly came back. "Okay, I'll ask around."

"Thanks, Henry," my father added. "You're a good friend. We'll certainly miss you when we're no longer here."

Elaine spoke up. "And we'll continue to come to visit. When you're open here in the summer, we'll come down from Montreal."

Some days later, Elaine got a call from Henry.

"Hi, Elaine," Henry said. "I think I've found someone who'd be interested in your home. But before I tell Johnny, I thought I'd talk to you."

"Okay, go on. And what's the big secret?"

He spoke in a soft tone. "After we had chatted at my restaurant, I called Greg Mann. I know things aren't kosher between Johnny and him, but I told Mann that you're looking for a buyer for your house. He's interested, but he doesn't know if Johnny would negotiate with him."

After a long pause, Elaine offered, "Okay, Henry, leave it with me. I'll see what I can do."

"By the way," Henry came back, "Johnny promised me ten percent if I found a buyer. I really could use the money, especially now that my restaurant is closing for the season."

"Henry, I have to find the right time and way to bring this up with Johnny. You know how he dislikes Mann. Give me a little time."

Having no other prospects and winter heating bills looming, Henry made the connection between Mann and Dad. Weeks later, my father, Elaine, and I were having another Luigio's supper. Dad huffed as he swigged his evening vodka. "That Mann is an SOB!" He gritted his teeth. "He's dickering with me about the house's price as he did with the Meyer kids."

I spoke quietly, not looking directly into my father's eyes. "I'm sorry to hear that, Dad. Do you mind my asking you what he's offering?"

Dad's voice was harsh. "The place is worth well over a million. He's offering only $500,000 U.S. to buy the property from JHS." He pointed to himself. "And he's willing to give another $185,000 U.S. in cash for the furniture, antiques, boat, equipment, and other shit we have there." He took another sip of his drink. "That way, JHS doesn't have to pay capital gains tax on a bigger sales price."

"Would you make any money on the deal?" I was always interested in my father's money-making.

Dad looked at me. "JHS originally bought the place for $250,000 U.S. I then put in another $200,000 into house renovations. That doesn't include work I did myself, including having our JHS factory workers come down over several weeks to do the den construction." Dad was counting things out with his fingers. "I put in a satellite dish, bought a motorboat and a riding mower, and who knows what other baloney. He looked at Elaine. "And Elaine spent $50,000 on new furniture." His fist hit the table. "At Mann's price, I'd make no money."

Elaine offered, "Your only alternative is to hold onto the property, but that will cost money too."

Dad's face looked flush with irritation. "I'll think about it," he said.

Elaine held her tongue.

Knowing my father, he wouldn't sell anything at a loss if he could help it. I did wonder how much his stroke had affected his ability to negotiate deals. Elaine was there to help him, though she was highly motivated to sell.

I decided to keep my nose out of their property business. I said, "Do whatever you think best, Dad."

A month later, we were back at Luigio's. Dad had taken the Mann deal, but not without more complaining. "Mann was such an SOB!" he bellowed after downing his vodka. His voice was terse. "He wouldn't budge an inch. He knew I was desperate to sell."

Elaine came in. "Johnny, you had no other prospects. At least you got your money out."

The way my father looked at her, I could sense he was growling inside, but he offered nothing more. Instead, he gnawed his lamb shank.

Elaine came back. "Johnny, will you pay Henry the commission promised him?"

Dad stared at his empty glass. "I told Mann that if I gave him his price, he'd have to take care of Henry for me."

Elaine's tone turned forceful. "Henry called me right after we had signed the P&S. I told him what you said. He said that Mann wasn't going to give him anything."

She leaned forward, her arms on the table. "Henry then told me he's in financial trouble, and he might lose his restaurant." Her voice quieted, "I heard through the grapevine that he lost lots of money gambling at Atlantic City. He might even lose his marriage over it." Her voice returned to normal. "He wants to know if you could pay something, even half of what you promised." She looked at me. "The man seems desperate."

Dad replied with greater force. "I can't give him anything! With Mann, I hardly got back the money that I had invested."

Elaine now defended Dad. "I said that to Henry when he called me a second time." She took a breath. "Because Johnny made that verbal agreement with Mann, I told Henry he should go back to Mann, even send him a lawyer's letter." Her eyes now looked at her wine glass on the table. "I don't know what happened after that, but Henry and your father haven't talked since."

I finished my drink but said nothing. Henry had been one of Dad's gracious friends, never asking him for anything until now. Though I felt terrible for the guy, it seemed he knew how to find misfortune. I held my tongue as I wondered once more about the people with whom my father surrounded himself. As the saying goes, *If you lie down with dogs, you can get up with fleas.*

Then again, who and what was the dog I was lying with?

* * *

A Father's Failings

My father's business and friendship failings were starting to add up. Looking back six months before Dad's stroke, in the fall of 1992, I had visited Dad in his Montreal office.

Even before I sat down, I could see that he was fuming. He clenched his hand in a fist, and his voice bellowed, "Remember those prefab construction panels we were going to build in Slovakia through Canexco?" He took a short breath. "Our Bratislava partners stole the design from us." He huffed as he walked back and forth across the room. "They copied our design and opened a separate company in Slovakia."

Dad had made several trips to his homeland's capital to create and build a new company with Slovak partners. He had received a grant from a Quebec export agency. On one visit to Bratislava, Canexco demonstrated its capability. With help from its partners, Canexco erected a sizable office structure on the site of that year's Bratislava Building Show. The edifice, built within a week, was fully functional office space.

Canexco showed the power and potential of those patented panels to prominent Slovak dignitaries. Knowing my father and his kind, I imagined many bottles of plum brandy downed in negotiations, perhaps even given as gifts. My father had come back from that trip with boasts about their success.

After hearing my father's new revelation about his overseas partners' duplicity, I became incensed by his brethren's betrayal. I raised an open palm. "How did that happen? Couldn't you have protected yourself?"

He banged a fist on his desk. The fluorescent ceiling light above us flickered. "We tried, son! I had our Slovak partners sign intellectual property papers, and we put an intellectual property clause into the company we formed in Slovakia, in which Canexco here in Canada owned half the shares." He pointed to his private office. "We kept the drawings of our construction panel right here in my office. We thought we had all the bases covered."

My voice nearly matched my father's volume. "So, what happened? How did they steal your design?"

Dad huffed again. "After our Slovak partners signed the deal, they sent their structural engineer here to validate that the panel design was sound from an engineering standpoint. And we allowed them to do that." He pointed to the floor. "We showed their guy the detailed drawings. We didn't let him take away any pictures or documents or personal notes."

I shrugged. "So, what happened?"

Dad's face turned glum. "We later found out that the engineer had a photographic memory. He could duplicate what he saw well enough so that our Slovak partners didn't need us anymore. They turned around and abandoned the joint venture, opened a new company, and started from scratch without us."

Dad once more banged his fist on the table. The light in the ceiling above flickered again. "Those bastards just made a couple of changes to our design so they could say their panel was different from ours."

I couldn't believe it. Dad's countrymen cheated their Canadian comrades. Maybe that was the way among Slovak men; perhaps my father had gotten his business education that way too. I didn't want to disparage Dad's compatriots, but the evidence was building.

I sat in a swivel chair. "Is there anything you can do to sue those guys for breach of contract or for stealing the intellectual property?"

My father presented his palm in capitulation. "We could have tried, son, but that would have cost lots of money to do over there in Slovakia. And because of their recent separation from the Czech Republic, their court system isn't fully functioning. Who knows if we could do anything through those courts or see any money from a lawsuit."

He raised his voice again, along with his fist. "Canexco got screwed, my Canadian partner and I got screwed, and Brian—our panel engineer from Ottawa who put a lot of his time into this project—got screwed too. There's nothing we can do except forget about the whole thing."

I elevated my hands. "What about the Slovak consulate and Quebec government people who introduced you to these shyster Bratislava businessmen? Can they do anything?"

Dad plopped himself into the high-back chair behind his desk. His voice quieted. "I tried, son. I complained to them because they had brought the building panel project to our doorstep in 1990."

He shook his head. "But there was nothing they could do. After making the connection and providing government funding for Canexco, they had no other involvement." He pointed to himself. "They expected that we were going to do the proper due diligence on those people."

I couldn't believe what I was hearing. Dad had spent over two years on the Canexco project. He developed an alliance with a Slovak building contractor in Montreal, Mr. Dubinsky. My father obtained the Quebec government's grant to support the export marketing of the panel technology. He negotiated for a manufacturing licence from Brian, the structural engineer who held a Canadian licence for the panel design. Together they flew to Czechoslovakia several times to meet with their Slovak counterparts, government officials, and the building contractors who erected the panel buildings. My father's dream of building a business while helping his country was now dead and buried in his homeland.

I was curious. "How much money did you lose, Dad? Was it bad?"

Dad quieted down. "What was wasted was mostly my time and the effort of Mr. Dubinsky. We had a Quebec export marketing grant that was paying 50% of our startup marketing and negotiation costs, up to $75,000."

He unexpectedly winked. "But you know me, son. I inflated my invoices from Slovakia so that the government here ended paying nearly 75% of the over $100,000 we spent." It seemed that judicious pen strokes by Dad on hand-written Slovak invoices offered Canexco a higher reimbursement. "JHS's net exposure was maybe $25,000 to $30,000 Canadian."

Once a businessman shyster, always a businessman shyster. I smirked at my father's never-ending money gamesmanship. JHS could easily absorb Canexco's loss. At least the project had kept Dad busy for a couple of years.

"What about Mr. Dubinsky? Did he lose any money too?"

"Dubinsky had no money to put into the project. JHS had invested the initial capital, but Dubinsky brought his construction expertise." Dad paused for a moment. His face looked hesitant, and then he added, "I'm glad I'm out of the partnership with him too. He was doing Canexco's bookkeeping. I later found out from our accountants that he was writing extra cheques to himself."

"What! Your Slovak business friend was screwing you too? Did you say or do anything?" I didn't know if Dad was right about Dubinsky, or was my father's assertion just another reason to close Canexco.

Dad shook his head like a school kid who was reticent to squeal on a chum to the teacher. "I said nothing to him. We just closed Canexco, and JHS took back the cash that remained in the company." He batted his hand. "It's over now."

I couldn't believe my ears. I had known my father to have threatened unsavoury partners in the past. "Dad, why didn't you confront Mr. Dubinsky for taking money from Canexco?"

My father's face looked like an old grizzly bear that was shying away from a fight. "Dubinsky is a longtime friend through the Slovak community." He added nothing more.

It seemed as if my father's soft heart for his people had surpassed his business tough-mindedness. Or might Dubinsky have something on Dad, considering my father had perpetrated Canexco's finagling with the Quebec government program? It's hard to raise your finger at someone when they could point one back at you.

I swiveled back and forth in my chair. "What's Steve going to do now that Canexco is dead? Is he going to find another job?"

Dad had involved my brother in his Slovak venture to offer him something productive outside of his church activities. Canexco would be Dad's way to start a business for Steve and make a businessperson out of him.

My father's face turned as stiff and glum as Canexco's sheetrock on its building panel. He tapped his finger on his desk, and his voice remained calm as he explained, "After Canexco went kaput, Steve formed another company in partnership with Brian. They call it Structural Building Panels, Inc."

He jammed his index finger down onto the desk. "SBP will build inexpensive townhouses in Ottawa, using the same panel technology on which Brian holds a user licence. Your brother felt bad that Brian got nothing from Canexco, so he started a new venture with the guy." Perhaps my brother was trying to prove to our dad that he could run a successful business.

Though we were the only ones in his office, Dad's voice quieted as if he didn't want anyone to overhear. "I don't trust Brian. He's going to screw your brother. And your brother is gladly bending over and letting it happen."

"What do you mean, Dad?"

"Brian has no money to put into SBP, and no bank is willing to lend their company any cash since Ottawa real estate is still in recession. So your brother bugged me for a month about a JHS loan against his preferred shares in the company. JHS lent him $175,000, the value of his shares, so he and

Brian could have working capital for their new business. With that money, they're going to build their first townhouse."

What?! My father had never trusted Steve with money, and now he had given him a boatload. I began to shake with anger, but my father threw more fuel on my rising fire. "They actually needed $350,000 to build their first building, so I lent SBP another $175,000 from JHS."

My voice rose to the ceiling. "You lent money to those guys!? I thought you didn't trust Brian." The ceiling lights flickered once more.

Dad raised an open hand. "I felt bad that Steve now has nothing to do since Canexco went under." His voice stayed calm. "There's nothing to worry about regarding JHS's money. Steve and Brian signed a first mortgage to JHS on the two-unit townhouse they are building." He tapped his desk again with his index finger. "They can't sell any units without first paying back JHS."

My father looked at the floor. "But unlike what I did for JHS's money, your brother put his $175,000 into SBP's Ottawa bank account without any security or collateral from Brian and with no financial controls in place. Brian manages the SBP books and writes the cheques." Dad's voice grew terse. "Brian could *foot-scoff* [Dad's polite term for *fuck off*] with your brother's money anytime, and there's nothing Steve could do about it."

It was disconcerting how Dad revealed such things to me only after he had consummated the deed. I wagered in my mind that he wanted my help with Steve. My father always looked to others to do his cleanup work.

My voice stayed elevated. "Did you tell Steve what you're now telling me about protecting his money? Because it's his money in SBP, he should be the only one to sign cheques."

My father nodded. "I did, son, many times, but Steve doesn't listen to me. He says he trusts Brian." He glared into my eyes as he pointed his finger at me. "Harvy, can you talk sense into your brother? Can you tell him that he's making a big mistake?" *There it was!* Dad wanted me to fix his first-son mess.

I needed more information. "Tell me, Dad, why don't you trust Brian?" I had met the man only once before, at JHS, near the start of the Canexco project. He wasn't a fast talker like some of Dad's shady colleagues from the Cayman Islands. The way Brian came across, with practical ideas for the Canexco venture, he seemed to be a stand-up and competent guy.

Dad glanced down and then back at me. "When Brian worked on Canexco, he expected to be paid $50,000 for his consulting services over the two years that the venture was getting started. However, when those bums from Bratislava stole the design, I told Brian that Canexco was closing and couldn't pay him anything."

Dad took a long breath. "Brian's probably upset at me about that, but there was nothing I could do. JHS lost actual money on that project; Brian only lost his time." His voice rose. "Canexco did pay his expenses here in Canada for his Canexco efforts, and we paid for his travel to Slovakia."

I glanced at my brother's old office desk. There, Dad had yelled at Steve many times for making lousy purchasing decisions or trusting suppliers who gave excuses as to why merchandise was late or costing more. My voice turned edgy as I stared at my father. "So Brian now has an incentive to steal from Steve, especially if things don't take off with those townhouses."

Dad's face looked glum. "And I expect that their business won't take off because the housing market is still soft in Ottawa. They'll have a hard time selling the two units they're building there." He made a fist. "Brian will grab what money he can and run." He pointed to the floor. "The lien I have on the townhouse they're going to build will protect JHS's money." He waved his finger in my direction. "But Steve's money is exposed." He repeated, "Harvy, can you talk to him? Your brother won't listen to me."

I stared at my father. "Couldn't you have said no to those loans, Dad?"

He raised a hand in surrender, and he shook his head. "I couldn't, son. Your brother was chasing me for his money in the company. It's his money, just like you have the same amount within your preferred shares in JHS."

Dad didn't mention how he had used most of Steve's and my money, locked into those JHS shares, to pay Mom in their divorce settlement. In retrospect, that settlement may have been a good thing; otherwise, Steve might have gotten hundreds of thousands more from JHS for SBP.

But that settled family history was long behind us. Unlike my brother, I never had the nerve to ask my father for that much cash, even if it would come from my JHS shares. My brother had had the *yaytsa* to ask.

I looked at my father. "Okay, Dad. I'll talk to Steve."

* * *

Dad arranged for Steve to be at JHS two weeks later, during my next visit to Montreal. I dressed in my navy blue consulting uniform while Steve wore everyday slacks, a shirt, and a tie. After pleasantries, I asked point-blank, "Steve, is it a good idea to give Brian full control over your money?"

My brother looked directly at me. "I trust Brian. He won't deceive me."

It crossed my mind that what Steve was doing with Brian was like what I had done when I invested in WISE, but I didn't mention that similarity. Bolstered by having gotten my money out of WISE with a profit, I saw my situation differently. I felt that I had chosen an honourable partner in Moe. But maybe Steve felt the same way about Brian.

I spoke calmly but firmly. "Steve, there would be no issue of trust if you have a system of accountability in place." I pointed his way. "Like if you alone had cheque signing authority over your money." I jammed my finger down onto the desk as my father might. "Maybe things are good between you and Brian now, but you're giving him an opening to take from you in the future. If your building project doesn't take off, or if he ever gets desperate for money, he could jump ship and take your cash. And you won't even know until he's gone." I held myself back from raising my voice in the way Dad might.

Steve smirked as if I were clueless. Maybe he saw me as Dad's surrogate—which I was. "That's not going to happen, Harvy," he said. "I have total confidence in Brian. He gives me statements every month about what and why he spends."

Talking to my brother was like speaking to a Slovak mule—a behavior he had perhaps learned from our predecessor. I was probably the last person from whom Steve wanted business guidance or opinions. We left our conversation there.

Predictably, problems emerged with my brother's investment. At the start of 1993 (now three months before Dad's stroke), I had another conversation with Steve while we were together at JHS. SBP's two-unit townhouse was nearly complete and on the market, and SBP's cash was exhausted. As Dad had foreseen, home buyers were scarce.

Steve and I again sat across from each other in Dad's private office. This time, Steve admitted, "I've allowed Brian liberties with SBP's money." His face stayed expressionless, as it habitually was with me, as he spoke matter-of-factly. "But I can't suddenly say I want solo cheque signing authority. I promised to trust him, and he returned that promise to me."

My brother looked down while he lifted his arms just above his waist. "If I ask Brian to change our banking arrangements, I might as well say that I don't trust him. He'll then have good reason to take cash from our company."

"Steve, can you ask for a weekly review of his spending?"

"That would be the same thing, Harvy. Brian sends me monthly statements, and we go over things, but I can't see everything he buys. If I double-check what he does or change his signing authority at the bank, I might as well tell him I don't want to be his partner."

My brother huffed. "There's something else, Harvy. I want to do business honestly, with integrity, unlike Dad, who takes advantage one way or another." He then offered something that surprised me. "I saw the way Dad inflated his Canexco bills in Slovakia so he could get more expenses reimbursed from the Quebec government."

So Steve knows about that! He had never before revealed what he knew about Dad's conniving ways.

He huffed again. "After the Canexco project had collapsed, Dad left Brian in the lurch. I don't want to be that way."

Steve wanted to prove to our father that he could succeed as an honest businessman. That was more important to him than taking Brian's hands away from what few cookies remained in the SBP jar.

I nodded my understanding. I suspected that my brother wanted my acceptance as much as he wished for our father's recognition. I looked at him. "I admire your trust in Brian, but trust without accountability makes no sense. It creates questions—just like what's happening between you and Brian now. It will erode your relationship over time."

Steve nodded, turned his head away, and he said nothing more. He had done what he had done. My brother wasn't going to do anything that would cause him to be seen as mistrusting, even though we all knew how naïve Steve was in overseeing his money. In trying to be unlike Dad, my brother had thrown business prudence out with his partnership bathwater.

By March of 1993 (a month before Dad's stroke), Steve and Brian sold one of SBP's two townhouses for a small profit. Over the phone, Dad told me the news. "Hallelujah!" he exclaimed facetiously.

My father added, "Instead of paying JHS back half its loan, Steve and Brian asked me to transfer JHS's mortgage solely onto the second townhouse unit. That released the first unit's sales proceeds—about $180,000—to SBP."

Dad again was telling me things after they happened. He continued. "Steve and Brian said they still needed to maintain the full JHS loan so that they could start building a second townhouse." He took a breath. "I agreed to the mortgage transfer because the second unit of their first project will secure JHS's money. But Steve's cash remains exposed."

Oh-oh! Why couldn't Dad have set new conditions when he assigned JHS's loan on the remaining townhouse—like making Steve the only SBP cheques signer? I didn't say that because, by now, it was too late. I was also tired of both Steve's SBP affair and Dad's telling me things only afterward.

I gave no further mind to Steve's townhouse project. Why should I sweat over a mess Steve was creating for only himself? With JHS's lien on SBP's second townhouse, JHS was going to come out whole. *No sweat off my JHS shares*. I hoped my brother wouldn't lose his money. But if he were reckless enough to let Brian steal it and not heed Dad's and my warnings, then it would be his loss alone to bear.

Four months later (the summer after my father's stroke), SBP sold the second townhouse. SBP returned the loan and interest it owed to JHS. Both Dad and I let out a sigh of relief that JHS was made whole.

My brother wasn't as lucky. By that fall, once again in Dad's back office, Steve spoke to me matter-of-factly. "After the first unit had sold, and the proceeds deposited into SBP's bank account, Brian started to write cheques to himself until our SBP account was empty." My brother took a long breath. "The money from the second unit's sale repaid JHS. But Brian absconded with the proceeds from the first unit's sale."

Brian had done as Dad had foreseen. But then again, both Dad and Steve had been eyes-wide-open enablers. Steve seemed disheartened about the whole affair. Soon afterward, in Dad's back office, my brother sat with me, his hands held together on his lap. There was little emotion in his voice. Perhaps he didn't want his little brother to see how dejected he was.

It was too late for an "I told you so." Instead, I said, "I'm sorry it happened, Steve." I didn't say: *What the hell were you thinking? How could you let this happen again?!* I didn't want to sound like our father.

Eight years earlier, Steve had lent $10,000 to a "trusted" Canadian friend he had met in Israel. The fellow had wanted to start a new business in Toronto, and Steve loaned him the money to help him and his wife relocate to Toronto. But Steve never saw a penny of his loan returned. He couldn't even sue the guy because the so-called friend had put all his assets into his wife's name. Steve later vowed to Dad to never repeat his error, but he now had done it again with Brian.

At our next Luigio's supper together, my father blustered, "How could Steve have been so stupid to trust Brian?!" Those words reverberated simultaneously in my head. I didn't say how Dad had eyes wide-open enabled the situation.

I offered, "Dad, I was at a family business conference recently. There I learned that wise business owners tell their adult children, 'If you want help with a new business venture, I'll help you with half the money you need to raise, but only if you can find other investors for the rest.'"

I looked intensely at my father but tried to keep my tone subdued. "By saying that to their offspring, the parent is not the bad guy, and the adult child learns how to raise money. If the son or daughter can't raise the additional funds, then the parent isn't to blame."

My father's eyes were stern. "Right now, Harvy, it's too late for that kind of advice!" He looked away and said nothing more. I consoled myself that I was preparing him for the next time Steve came calling for cash.

Though a part of me felt sad for Steve, his repeated money blunder gave me more cause to keep my father's offshore secrets hidden from him. Neither Dad nor I could afford my brother's over-trusting nature. Steve could do considerable damage to both the legitimate and the illicit holdings that Dad had amassed over half a lifetime.

In the ensuing months, lawsuits went flying back and forth among Brian, Dad, and Steve. Private investigations showed that Brian paid off personal debts with the cash he had taken from SBP. Since he owned no other assets, Steve dropped his suit against Brian, and Brian dropped his countersuit against Steve. But Brian pursued a $50,000 lawsuit against Dad until, months later, that suit became summarily dismissed in an Ottawa court.

For months afterward, Dad sounded out of his stroke-ridden mouth to me, Elaine, every friend and business colleague, and even to his Slovak priest, "How stupid Steve was in getting into business with a crook. How could he have been so irresponsible, pissing away so much money?" He said nothing about his Canexco business failure and how his countrymen had taken him on a duplicitous business ride.

* * *

Dad and his first son were now right back where they had started years earlier. After the Canexco and SBP's failures, my brother didn't seek another job or venture. Instead, his church called him—or maybe Steve offered himself—to volunteer in his local Mormon Family History Centre. He later became the manager for the regional centre that served several wards. Steve also cajoled Dad to go on trips to Slovakia to do family history research.

I figured that Steve's family research was an excuse for him not to seek employment. When I confronted Dad about it, he responded, "Your brother wants my help to dig up our dead relatives. What should I do, say no? And should I see him have no money to live on?"

Though I felt that was exactly right, I decided to stop haranguing Dad about his unwavering enabling of his first son. I was tired of banging my hand—or head—on our supper table at Luigio's to wake my father from what he was doing. The final time we talked about it, I told him, "You know, Dad, the Mormon church expects its followers to work so that they can tithe a percentage of their income to the church. Can't Steve earn and contribute his own money rather than give away a portion of what you give him?"

Dad's held his lips tightly together as his eyes looked down. His gruff, stroke-damaged voice was quieter than usual. It was as if he had run out of bravado about his first son. "I can't cut him off," he said. "I feel too responsible for the way he turned out." Like a hardened addict, Dad couldn't stop his money tap. At least he took responsibility for his habit.

Seeing that I was making my father miserable, I quit my attack. Who was I to judge either of them? *What will be, will be, with those two.* In a cosmic, biblical, or comic way, they were meant for each other. I vowed again never to be like either one of them.

Dad raised his right hand as a peacemaking gesture. "You know, Harvy, only you will have what I have over there in Lux."

I nodded. Dad still had a tight hold on me regarding his offshore legacy, though I couldn't admit it. Maybe I was as addicted to my father's offshore stash as my brother was to his onshore cash. I consoled myself by thinking Dad's statement of support recognized that I had made something of myself.

Over our supper table, my father beckoned with his hand for me to come a little closer. I leaned in as he whispered gruffly. "When I'm gone, if

Steve ever loses his half of my legitimate money, or if he gets himself into trouble and needs something, I hope you'll help him out here and there."

It wasn't the first time my father had asked that of me, just as his stepmother had asked him to look out for his half-brother, Edo. Though my eyes wandered toward the restaurant's exit door, I stayed fixed in my seat. As I had always done, I nodded to his request. I wondered if Steve and I would relive Edo and Dad's relationship, with each of them genuinely loving and profoundly resenting the other.

I considered my definition of "if Steve needs something." According to what I knew of his faith, Mormon followers sought to become good servants of God in this life so that they could rise to a stately heaven in the afterlife. They didn't work necessarily to amass material things. They offered prayers and did good deeds on earth to gain everlasting salvation in the afterlife. If my brother ever "got into trouble," he had his church and faith to lean on. To the letter of my father's wishes, I could get away with never having to give Steve a dime from Dad's offshore money.

I promised myself once more that I'd never become my brother's keeper. I vowed I'd act more intelligently with Dad's stash rather than allow it to lie dormant offshore. I had looked into socially responsible investing through associations like the *Investor Circle* and *Businesses for Social Responsibility*. I wanted to put Dad's money to work to benefit our planet in some way. Those types of business deeds would become my kind of spiritual enlightenment.

* * * *

A Father's Finances

As the summer of 1993 turned into fall, Dad told me. "Harvy, I want you to come with me to see Peternik, my notary."

I believed I knew why, but I still asked, "Okay, what's that about?"

He replied, "I want your help to rewrite my last will. I'll make an appointment with Peternik for the next time you are in Montreal. Let me know when you can be free for a few hours."

Months earlier, when Dad and I had met with the Global Trade Bank branch manager, he mentioned obtaining my help for his will. Steve's recent business debacle, on top of our father's stroke, may have compelled Dad to act on his whim. I was okay with my father not including Steve in the notary visit, but I wondered what he had in mind for his estate.

I nodded my acceptance of my father's request. Before any conversation with a banker, lawyer, accountant, or notary, I never questioned my father's motives. Though I'd find out more when we got to Peternik's, I did some thinking beforehand.

The next time I was in Montreal, I drove Dad to Mr. Peternik's office. Peternik had been Dad's notary for more than twenty years. Rather than employing a lawyer for his legal transactions, it was more cost-effective to use a notary. Canada allowed licensed notaries to draft and make legal any contract, lease, wills, or other official documents.

Mr. Peternik was perhaps my elder by a decade. He had inherited the client practice of his predecessor, who Dad employed from the time he had started Montreal Phono. In the personality of the short, slender, and soft-spoken Peternik, as in his mentor, Dad had found someone who wouldn't ask too many questions concerning motives behind transactions. The guy was honest, straight as an arrow, but he never pried. Maybe that's why Dad kept on going back to him.

Peternik worked in a small downtown office with no reception area or secretary. We said our hellos as we entered his dark, drab, dusty, and cramped office. My father hobbled to a big, cozy chair and let himself fall back into its seat. He held tightly onto his cane and raised his arms for balance.

He pointed to me and immediately got down to business. "Peternik, I want Harvy's ideas about how we should draft my last will. I'm not a spring chicken anymore, and my stroke is limiting me." He pointed upward. "A brick could fall on my head any time, and then *Boom!* I'm gone."

Over the years, Dad had mentioned the brick line many times. That was the way he wanted to go, with no prolonged illness and maybe not even knowing what hit him until he was looking down from above.

Peternik looked at my father. "What about your other son, Stephen? Shouldn't he be in this conversation too?"

Dad's voice rose. "I don't trust him as much as I trust Harvy. Steve pissed away $175,000 of the company's assets on a bullshit business venture with a crooked partner. Harvy knows my affairs better, so I want him involved."

I nodded, kept my face straight, but said nothing. Peternik looked at me and then back at Dad. "Okay, Mr. Simkovits. I'll be happy to do it any way you want. Tell me about your wishes."

Dad started. "Most of my money is in my company, JHS Holding."

That wasn't completely correct. Most of Dad's money was in his illicit offshore accounts in Luxembourg. His statement to Peternik considered only his assets in Canada, revealing only what he wanted the notary to know.

Dad continued. "Steve and Harvy hold the common shares in JHS, so they already own most of the company's assets. I hold only a million dollars in preferred shares and enough controlling shares to give me a voting majority. My shares in JHS will be fully taxable upon my death, and the boys will have to pay those taxes from my estate."

I cringed but said nothing. To our dad, Steve and I were still "the boys."

Peternik interrupted. "There is a normal clause we put into a will about your executors completing your final income taxes and paying tax liabilities."

Dad, his voice raspy and low, continued as if he hadn't heard what the notary had said. "And the same thing goes with what remains in my company pension. There are well over one-and-a-half million dollars there too."

Dad didn't say that he designated much of that pension money for me through his pending Supporters of Independent University annuity. I kept my mouth shut about that too.

Peternik and I remained quiet as my father continued his slow, gruff-voiced treatise. "Outside of those things, and some cash at my banks in Montreal and Boca, what else I own is my house in Boca and our home in Montreal's West Island, where Elaine and I now live in." (They transplanted to a new West Island house after they had sold their Peru, NY home.)

He raised his good hand. "All my other income comes from deferred life annuities. Those payments will end when I die." He pointed to me. "Or the money will go to Harvy and Steve if I die before a full fifteen years of payments are complete, in another seven years from now, in 2000."

I shifted in my seat. Though I appreciated Dad being open about his assets, a part of me was uncomfortable with this death talk and having this money conversation behind my brother's back. But Steve had proven himself not worthy of this essential assembly on the fate of our father's finances. My brother had made his first son's bed, and he would find less cash under it after our dad passed away.

Peternik interrupted again. "The disposition of your registered retirement pension and deferred life annuities doesn't have to be put into your will. I assume you have formally named beneficiaries for those assets."

Dad had heard the notary this time. He nodded. "Yes, I did that already. Both Steve and Harvy are my beneficiaries for both of those things."

"And, if you want, Mr. Simkovits, we can list your assets in a document separate to your will. Things can change between now and when you will pass away. We can update that list every so often."

Dad nodded again. "Okay."

The notary raised his hand to make a point. "What's important to know now is who you want as estate executors, to whom you want to leave your assets, and how much to each."

My father looked at me. The left side of his face drooped, and his voice was gruff. "Harvy, I don't want to slap your brother in the face by making you the only executor to my estate. With you two acting jointly, he won't be able to do anything irresponsible. And, with both of you controlling JHS after I'm gone, you'll have to get along."

I looked at my father and worked to keep my face relaxed. "Yes, Dad; I agree. It would be strange if I were your sole executor."

Steve might then blame me for his exclusion and resist my ideas and suggestions for JHS's holdings. Dad's company still owned Dad's old factory building, five other sizable properties in Quebec and Ontario, plus a bunch of cash. I nodded. "It's best that Steve and I stay co-executors."

Peternik looked at my father. "You could make your executor an independent third-party, like a close family friend, or a person like me who knows your family and your wishes." He pointed to himself.

"No," my father responded. "Steve and Harvy can do it. They'd have more control and flexibility that way." Dad didn't want to place excessive restrictions on my brother and me. A third-party executor would have to abide by the written letter of Dad's will. Steve and I would have more flexibility as co-executors, as long as we'd agree.

Peternik nodded, and his face was blank and unreadable. "So then, how would you like your assets distributed?"

Dad didn't hesitate. "Except for a couple of special bequests, I want my assets to go equally to Steve and Harvy." He looked at Peternik's dark mahogany desk. His voice remained raspy. "But I'm worried about the money. I don't want my kids to piss it away or for Steve to give it away to his church."

I had been thinking about this moment from the time my father had asked me to come here with him. "Dad," I offered, "what if you state that your assets would come to Steve and me over ten or fifteen years? You could give us a third or a quarter of those assets every five years. This way, if Steve or I lose the first portion, we'll know that more will come later."

If it helped my father feel secure, I didn't mind his legitimate money coming to my brother and me over some extended period. I had learned to be patient concerning my expected legacy. Having my consulting career, I could support myself well enough without our dad's money.

Dad looked at me, and his eyes opened wide. "That's a good idea, son."

My father's appreciation made me smile inside.

Dad looked at Peternik. "Let's give my money to the kids over fifteen years after my death. They could have a quarter of my estate when I die and a quarter every five years after that until the money is completely distributed."

Dad turned to me, a small three-quarter smile on his face. "This will give you many chances to lose the money—at least four times!"

He pointed upward as he looked at me. "But don't make too many mistakes. I'll then ask St. Peter if I can come down here so that I can punch the two of you in the nose." He made a fist with his right hand.

I chuckled. "Don't worry, Dad. I'll do my best not to lose the money." My voice dropped. "But, I can't vouch for Steve."

"I know, son," he said with resignation. "But in spreading the money over many years, he'll have less opportunity to throw it away all at once."

"What about your special bequests?" Peternik asked. "How much and to whom?"

I jumped in. "Before you speak about other specific people, Dad, I have another idea."

"What's that, son?"

I took a long breath. "There's another way to ensure that Steve and I don't throw away your assets on stupid things." Dad's eyes were on me. "You can put something into your will for our children, your grandchildren." I raised both of my hands, one representing me and the other representing my brother. I kept my fingers closed in my left hand and raised two fingers in my right hand. "I don't have any kids yet, but Steve has two." I presented a couple of fingers in my left hand. "And I'd have kids with Gloria if things continue to go well between us."

My father smiled at the notion. He'd enjoy seeing me have children with the right woman. Dad relished showering my brother's kids with gifts for birthdays, Christmas, and for no particular reason. Almost every time he saw his young grandchildren, he'd put a one- or two-dollar Canadian coin into their hands, saying, "It's for your piggy bank. Save it for something special."

Dad looked puzzled. "What do you think I should do there, Harvy? How much money should I put aside for your kids, and for what?"

I pointed his way. "I know you're big on education. You wanted Steve and me to go as far as we could in university. Why not do the same for your grandkids? You can specify in your will that you want an amount of money put aside for each grandchild. Steve and I would use the money strictly for their university education. This way, they'd have to finish high school, get into a college, and learn something."

Dad turned to Peternik. "Can we do that?"

"You can do anything, Mr. Simkovits. It's a matter of what you want. Gifts like that can be transferred into a trust by your executors for the benefit of your grandchildren."

Dad looked back at me. "How much money should we be thinking about?"

I had it figured out. "If we are talking about a U.S university over a decade from now, when Steve's children would be old enough to attend college, then you could instruct Steve and me to put a certain sum into a trust for each child." I threw out a six-digit dollar figure. "Steve and I then couldn't spend that amount on ourselves, only for *your* grandkids' college education." I pointed to my father again.

Dad pondered for a moment. "That sounds good, Harvy. And that would be a good incentive for you to get married and have kids too." He smiled as best he could. "I like that." Dad looked at his notary again. "Let's do it that way."

I hoped I wasn't short-changing myself with my suggestion, for I didn't yet have kids. This college fund move with Dad's estate seemed right and fair, and it made him happy. Let my father feel he had done something good for his grandchildren, whether I'd have any offspring or not.

Peternik nodded. "Okay, Mr. Simkovits. Do you have other bequests?"

Dad looked down at the floor. He held onto his cane as if it were a permanent appendage. "I feel somewhat responsible for my daughter, Emilia," he offered. "I want to leave something to her and her son."

Though I shunned my half-sister, I did like Igor. When he and his mother had visited Canada, or when Dad had traveled to Slovakia, I heard that Igor gave my father a helping hand without being asked twice. He even played gin rummy with his grandpa after everybody else had tired of it.

I nodded and kept my voice calm. "Whatever would make you feel good, Dad. But I suggest you spread it over some years so that they don't waste it like you're afraid that Steve and I might do."

My father looked at me. "That's good, son." He looked at the notary and offered a modest five-figure number for his daughter and her son. It was small PEI potatoes compared to the big Idaho spuds that Steve and I would obtain. Dad added, "Spread it out over five years for Emilia and ten years for Igor. I'll spell their last name for you."

My eyebrows rose. I didn't say anything, though a part of me was relieved that Dad's bequest was relatively small. I didn't ask how my father had discerned the amount. *Did he apply a low value to those relationships?*

Maybe he felt he had given Emilia enough both by having her come to North America for an extended holiday and by helping her in other ways over the years. Or maybe he felt he hadn't been as close to his daughter as he had been with his sons. Then again, it might be Old Testament scriptures or Slovak male chauvinism at play in Dad passing the bulk of his legacy only to his sons.

Regardless, his modest bequest would go further in Czechoslovakia than it would here in Canada. I wasn't going to argue for or against my father's wishes on behalf of a half-sister and nephew I hardly knew.

Peternik looked once more at my father. "Anything else?" he asked.

"Not really." Dad's face looked blank.

"What about Edo?" I asked. I wondered whether my father had forgotten his half-brother. "Don't you want to leave something for him?"

Dad's eyes narrowed and intensified; his voice rose. "I've taken care of Edo in other ways," he said gruffly. "He doesn't need to be in my will."

I hadn't expected my father's harsh response. I said nothing more about my uncle, leaving any further inquiry for another time. "Okay, Dad, is there anything else you want to put in your will?"

My father's ire quieted as quickly as it had risen. "No, son; there's nothing else. If Peternik has everything he needs, then we can go."

Peternik said matter-of-factly, "I have what I need."

Dad stood slowly, utilizing his cane for support. Peternik stood too and reached for Dad's hand. "I'll bring the papers for your signature within a week or two. Should I send a copy to Harvy beforehand?"

"Yes, that's fine." My father looked at me. "Harvy, please give Mr. Peternik your business card."

My confidence grew about the bulk of my father's legitimate estate remaining in Steve's and my hands. How much Steve would know and have of Dad's hidden, offshore legacy would be totally up to me. As long as I stayed reasonably close to my father, and he wouldn't do anything foolish with his money, then time would be on my side.

Within a month, Dad signed his will at his old factory office. Dad's bookkeeper, Rob, signed as a witness, though I suspected he didn't know the details written in the document. Peternik then signed and embossed his notarial seal. I was the only other one there to witness the event.

* * *

Right after leaving the notary, I took Dad out for supper to give Elaine free time. After my father had finished his vodka, I roused my courage. "Dad, why did you decide to keep Edo out of your will?"

My father's eyes narrowed, his face turned red, and his voice rose. "Edo doesn't deserve anything more from me. He was a loafer and boozer all his life. He never took any advice I gave him."

I was sorry for opening a sibling spigot—though a part of me felt the same way about my brother if one could call his religion a vice.

Dad continued his brazen spiel. "I helped Edo a lot in Canada. He made nothing of himself." Dad pointed to himself. "I was the one who bailed him out when he nearly killed a pedestrian while driving drunk. I hired a lawyer who kept him out of jail. He lost his licence for only a year."

My father hadn't finished his treatise. He pointed to the chair next to him and bellowed, "Five years ago, I told Edo to go back to Slovakia to take care of his sick mother—my stepmother—until she died. He inherited what she had, including her apartment condo, which was worth something. I asked nothing from her estate. Then I brought Edo back to Canada so that he could obtain his Canadian pension in Slovakia." Dad batted his other hand in the air. "I did enough for him!"

I avoided my father's eyes and stayed calm. I was glad we had arrived at the restaurant early this evening, and we were the only ones there. "Okay, Dad. I'm sorry that Edo displeased you."

Dad had never considered that he might have had a hand in what his brother had become, as he had had a part in his sons' making. Though Dad knew his half-brother couldn't hold his liquor at festive occasions, he kept on pushing drinks into Edo's hand. He expected Edo to learn to handle the alcohol or know when to stop. My uncle was lucky to have married a Slovak woman who straightened him out more than his mother or brother could.

I considered that Steve and I could offer something more to our uncle after Dad's passing. Not having been a big saver, Edo could benefit from additional income for the rest of his life. I expected Steve to be amenable, for he too cared about our uncle.

I looked at Dad. "So, how's your physiotherapy going?"

* * * *

A Father's Finagling

Nearly a decade earlier, at the end of '84, Dad had closed JHS's manufacturing operations. He then turned JHS Electronex into an asset holding company and renamed it JHS Holding. Some years later, Dad told Steve and me that the company no longer needed Roger Delliard's big accounting firm to do JHS annual audit and tax returns. Roger was soon to retire, so Dad was considering a change of accountant.

By 1990, I heard ardently from Dad that he was looking for a new accounting firm. So I suggested my friend, Geoff Levi, a partner in a smaller firm that dealt with small businesses. Geoff and I had met years earlier in the Young Entrepreneurs Organization. His manner was calm, his voice a confident monotone, and his words thought out.

Geoff said he had worked with many small business clients like my father, and he kept them out of trouble with Revenue Canada. If Dad ever tried to pull a fast one with his holding company's books, Geoff had the strength to say, "Johnny, stop playing around with the government." I had had my eye on Geoff for years as a potential replacement for Roger. The fall of 1990 seemed the right time to broach the subject with Dad.

After meeting Geoff, Dad agreed to try his firm for the year-end review of JHS's books. My father became especially keen when Geoff quoted half the cost to perform JHS's annual financial report and tax returns compared to what Dad had paid Roger Delliard's big firm. After Geoff had completed the review in the spring of '91, Dad agreed to make Geoff JHS's regular accountant.

I felt particularly pleased with Dad's decision. His move was a sign of his starting to share control over JHS's finances by engaging a professional who was my friend and peer. Geoff would also keep my brother and me informed of Dad's financial moves with JHS, especially if our father proposed wrong-headed ones.

* * *

Three years later, on a windy afternoon in May 1994, Geoff came for the fourth time to present JHS's annual statements and tax returns to my father, Steve, and me. Rob, now a fourteen-year bookkeeping veteran of JHS, was also present. From the time Geoff had started doing JHS's annual review, Dad invited Steve and me to participate in discussions about the company's income and assets. I was pleased to be included and be informed of JHS's overall financial situation.

Early in the meeting, Dad again got in his critical remark about my brother's failed SBP. "Steve lost $175,000 on his Ottawa building project this past year," he blustered with disdain in his rasping voice.

I could see a wince on my brother's face. Not Rob, nor Geoff, nor I responded to Dad's cutting comment. We had caught his chronic complaint many times before.

Geoff made his presentation of JHS's 1993 revenues, expenses, and tax liabilities. Along the way, he offered, "JHS made about $198,000 this year and will have to pay $99,000 in federal and provincial income taxes."

"How is that?" my father yelled. He looked sternly at Geoff. "We distributed most of our JHS earnings to the kids so we could take advantage of their lower tax brackets. The company's income should have been very little, maybe even nothing."

Though I cringed once more at Dad's "the kids" reference, I allowed Geoff to do the talking. I, too, wondered what might have enlarged JHS's revenues and tax liability this past year.

Geoff looked directly at my father and spoke without a waiver. "That's true, Johnny; JHS made the normal distributions to Steve and Harvy. But there was the Peru house. JHS made over $175,000 Canadian in taxable income on that sale."

My father raised his voice louder as if the damage from his stroke had superseded his civility. "How is that so? JHS sold that house for what we bought it for, plus the improvements I put into it over the years. There should have been no gain."

Geoff eyed his notes and responded calmly. "We looked closely at the books, Johnny. JHS bought the property from CANEX Company in 1988 for $315,000 Canadian."

Uh, oh! Unlike Roger, Geoff knew nothing about CANEX, Dad's clandestine offshore corporation. I understood from Dad that he had closed CANEX after JHS bought the Peru property from that Cayman entity. I wondered how much my father was going to tell Geoff about it. I also didn't know how much my brother knew about Dad's finagling with his Peru house.

I sat quietly across the room as I tried to wrack my brain for the unexpected taxable gain on the Peru home sale. As the company's bookkeeper all these years, Rob surely knew about JHS's purchase of the home from CANEX. But did he also know that Dad had owned CANEX?

My stomach turned queasy. I felt as if I were in a *Perry Mason* courtroom scene. *What might be revealed by whom?* I wondered if Dad would drag Geoff onto sordid offshore sands, or would he leave the CANEX skeleton buried on a Grand Cayman beach?

If Geoff got a whiff of CANEX not having been an arm's length enterprise, he may feel compromised and recuse himself from JHS. I decided to say nothing and see how Dad wanted this conversation to play out. I was glad I wasn't in either his or Rob's shoes to try to explain the situation.

Geoff continued. "JHS sold the house for $500,000 U.S. last year, which converted to over $665,000 Canadian. It led to a total capital gain of over $350,000." He looked at my father. "As you know, half of that gross gain is taxable at your corporate rate; the rest goes into your JHS Corporate Dividend Account, which you can legally remove tax-free to JHS shareholders." Though Geoff motioned toward the three of us, I knew that the tax-free half of that capital gain would probably go into Dad's pocket. There was no incentive for him to share such a large sum with Steve and me.

Dad came back a little loudly. "But we made a lot of improvements to that house over the years. The house's cost basis should reflect that."

Geoff looked puzzled. "There were no improvements booked against that house in your ledgers." He looked at Rob. "Did my auditor miss something?"

The room became deadly silent. Alarm bells now rang in my head. Dad had made hundreds of thousands of dollars of improvements to that home. Why wasn't it reflected in the cost of the property?

After what had seemed like an eerie eternity of silence, Geoff repeated, "Is something wrong? Did we miss anything?" His face looked confused while he gazed with sincere puzzlement at my father. Geoff's hand was open and beckoning.

After a few more long seconds, Dad turned to Rob and spoke calmly. "Rob, where were those house improvements reflected in our ledgers?"

Okay. Dad's speaking in code, being coy. I looked across the room to my brother. His face was as expressionless as I was trying to keep mine. I was glad that Geoff's and everyone else's eyes were now on our bookkeeper.

Rob was standing to my right. He was leaning back against his desk. Though his hands grabbed firmly onto the back of his swivel chair in front of him, his backside fidgeted. I could see his eyes moving about as if he were searching his mind for an answer.

After a moment, Rob responded, his voice meagre but calm. "Johnny, I think we made those expenditures before JHS bought the property from CANEX." He showed an open hand. "I guess there were no further improvements made after 1988, the year the house transferred to JHS." He spoke timidly, perhaps not knowing what reaction would come from his boss.

An explosion went off in my head. *Oh, my God!* Dad had transferred the Peru house from CANEX to JHS in '88 at the same price his Cayman Corporation had bought the home from the Meyer family six years earlier. *How could Dad and Rob have been so stupid?!* JHS thus didn't pay CANEX for the over $200,000USD of improvements that Dad had made while CANEX owned the property. Some of those improvements came from JHS-purchased materials and JHS's in-house labour. But there had been money that Dad had spent in New York State, like for the new kitchen and garage.

Oh, my God!! I became enraged at Rob as I was infuriated at my father, but I tried not to expose my feelings. Whatever Rob did or didn't know about CANEX, he let my father make the Peru house transfer to JHS without accounting for the property's higher cost basis. He should have known better. *What a schmuck he is too!*

I kept myself as collected as I could. I took a stab at trying to find a way out of my father's lake-house quagmire. "Geoff, if I may?" My friend turned to me while I continued. "It seems that some improvements were made to the house before CANEX officially transferred the property to JHS in '88." I didn't say who had paid for those improvements. "Is there any way we could still include those costs in the house's cost basis?"

Geoff looked at me curiously, as if he knew he wasn't obtaining the whole picture. He took what I gave him and responded unequivocally. "That would have to be reflected as a capital gain or a loss for CANEX. It has nothing to do with JHS's cost basis." He gazed at my father. "What was CANEX anyway?"

Uh, oh, again! How much truth was Dad now going to spill on the floor in front of Geoff? Is he going to divulge that CANEX had been a shell corporation, used to shield a bunch of JHS's earnings from Revenue Canada?

Dad had an answer. He spoke calmly. "It was an international trading company we had worked with when JHS Electronex had been in business." He took a breath. "But CANEX no longer exists." He left it there.

Geoff continued. "At this point, if you want to make a change in the Peru house's cost basis, you'd have to go back to your company statements for 1988 to reflect a higher purchase price for the house." He took a long breath and shook his head. "But I don't think you'd want to do that."

"Why not?" I asked. Everyone was letting me ask the questions. Perhaps I was asking the right ones.

Geoff responded. "That's five fiscal years ago. Going back five years could raise eyebrows at Revenue Canada. They could force an audit and want to take a look at the intervening years. They also might want to know more about this CANEX Company."

Uh, oh, once more! That's not good.

Geoff probably knew enough of my father's ways to suggest Dad steer away from a government audit. My friend looked at Dad and continued calmly. "Also, my firm wasn't your accountant back then and couldn't represent you. You'd have to go to your previous accountants if you want to pursue that course."

Is Geoff trying to protect himself and his firm?

I spoke again. "Geoff, is it too late to distribute those excess gains this year to my brother and me? We might be in a lower tax bracket than JHS."

My friend looked directly at me, his face a little tight. "You and Steve each took your regular bonus this past year. It would look odd to the government if you took more. They frown on siphoning excess profits to directors to avoid a higher corporate tax." He spoke calmly yet firmly. "They could reverse your bonus decision and put that revenue back into JHS's returns and then force you to pay the corporate tax. Or they might turn those excess bonuses into corporate dividends, and then you and Steve would have to pay a higher personal tax rate, and possibly a penalty."

Gosh! I suspected upping our bonus wouldn't have been a problem with JHS's previous accountants. Perhaps our engaging Geoff as JHS auditor cut back on us in other ways.

I nodded my understanding and offered nothing more. I was now sure that Dad was paddling up a Revenue Canada creek concerning the corporate taxes JHS needed to pay on the Peru house's gain. All eyes turned to him.

Dad looked down at his desk and then back at Geoff. I could hear my quick and short breaths as the seconds ticked away. Dad's voice remained calm. "Okay, let's leave it as it is." He offered nothing more, acting as if he were paying a simple supplier's invoice.

I couldn't believe my ears! My father shrugged off his and Rob's blatant error as if nothing terrible had happened. The room was quiet for another moment. No one spoke while everyone looked at Geoff. I had no idea what my friend was thinking regarding this awkward conversation, but I hoped he would end it here. He offered, "Okay, we'll go with that," and he moved on to something else. He'd never ask more about CANEX.

Across the room, my brother had said nothing throughout the conversation. It seemed as if he had listened carefully, but I wasn't sure whether he understood. I suspected that both of us were glad that Dad's CANEX days were history, and he wasn't going to reopen that can of offshore sandworms. In his stroke weakened condition, I suspected my father, at 74, didn't want to grapple with Revenue Canada tax auditors.

Dad asked Rob to prepare company cheques totaling $99,000 to the Quebec and Canadian governments to pay the taxes due. Perhaps my father now figured the tax payment was a hidden cost of doing his asset concealing and tax-evading business.

I'd never ask him or Rob more about their oversight. That money misdeed was long behind us in JHS's review mirror. Also, Geoff never again brought up the subject of CANEX nor asked me privately about the firm.

* * *

Some good things came from Dad's miscalculation regarding the Peru house sale. From that day forward, my father never uttered another word about how my brother had lost money in his Ottawa property business. Dad's combined Canexco botch and Peru house transfer bungle now nearly matched my brother's SBP business blunder. The pissed-away-money ledger between them seemed to have balanced.

I wondered if I could have caught Dad's house transaction error. Though I hadn't been privy to JHS's statements back in '88, I wished I had been a little smarter to pick up on the issue. And how could Rob, along with Roger Delliard's accounting firm, and my master tax-avoiding father, have missed it? Their error now caused the government to make off with lots of JHS's cash.

At that precipitous moment during our annual meeting with Geoff, another good thing happened. My anger and disappointment toward my brother ceased. I stopped chastising him in my mind for his SBP money mishandling. What Steve had lost—the value of his preferred shares in JHS—was technically his. Only he should begrudge himself for that loss.

Considering Dad's Canexco disaster, my brother's Ottawa building project fiasco, the Peru house capital gains miscalculation, 1993 was not a prosperous year for JHS and our Simkovits clan. As I drove away from our year-end meeting, I thought, *We won't survive many more money mistakes like these.*

I wondered if Dad's missteps had been a sign that he was losing his mental edge. To be proficient at playing tax-evading games, he had better not lose track of what goes with what, onshore and off. Any slip in bringing an offshore asset (the Peru house) into the onshore world (via JHS's purchase) could take a toll on the wallet. *Was moving money offshore even worth it?*

And what about Rob? He didn't seem to be on top of Dad's financial affairs as much as I had hoped. As I drove away, I wondered if I should later confront him about his transaction transgression. But I decided to let that go, for that calculus had been more my father's failing than Rob's.

I felt a sudden surge of fright as I headed for the highway. I recalled that it had been Al Capone's bookkeeper who, in the end, made the U.S. Fed's case that finally put Capone behind bars.

* * * *

More Simkovits Travels and Travails

As 1993 headed into autumn, Dad called me in Boston. Though I regularly called him Sunday evenings to see how he was doing, he rang me mid-week. He was surprisingly upbeat. "Harvy, I'd like you to come with Elaine, Steve, and me to Czechoslovakia in November."

Though his country had split into the Czech and Slovak Republics two years earlier, Dad still referred to them by their former name. He had been disappointed by his homeland's separation.

He had once told me, "That goddamned Prime Minister Mečiar of Slovakia thinks he knows everything. I met him when he was the leader of the Slovak province; it was before the two countries separated." He sounded frustrated. "Mečiar came to the Bratislava building show where Canexco participated, and I talked to him." His voice elevated. "I told him that he and the Czech prime minister shouldn't split up Czechoslovakia, that the country is stronger together than apart."

Dad had jammed his index finger onto his desk as his voice rose in disgust. "But he and that Prime Minister Václav Klaus of the Czech Republic decided to separate the two states without even consulting the people. There was no referendum." His voice remained bitter. "Even Czechoslovakia's President, Václav Havel, was against the split. He resigned his presidency, as he had previously threatened to do, so he wouldn't have to oversee the separation."

As we continued to speak on the phone, my father kept on his family vacation track. Though he no longer conducted business in his homeland, he enjoyed visiting every year. He offered, "We'll fly into Munich and drive from there to Prague, then to Košice and Budapest. We'll spend time in Karlovy Vary outside of Prague and a night or two in the Tatra Mountains in Slovakia—all places we've been together when you and Steve were kids."

Though we had never been to Karlovy Vary, a spa resort town that went back to Roman times, I said, "Yes, Dad; I remember."

He went on in his raspy voice. "I want to make this trip with you before I can't travel any longer. I want to show you where I was born and where I lived in Košice." He took a quick breath. "Can you please come with us? We can fly there together from Montreal."

I had made a similar vacation trip seventeen years earlier, in 1976, with Dad and Mom. That trip nearly turned disastrous when my mother tried to smuggle digital calculators past Czechoslovak border guards. The prospect of this time being in a packed car with my disabled Dad and obstinate brother was not appealing.

Even though I could tolerate Elaine for the length of a homeland trip, would I feel comfortable with her filling in for my mother through the same roads and countryside I had previously traveled with Mom and Dad? Could I stomach being with my brother for a stretch? If Steve didn't want to do something, all the horses in the Czech and Slovak Republics couldn't drag him into doing it.

I spoke timidly. "How long would the trip be, Dad?"

"Just two weeks, son, in the middle of November when the airfares are cheaper. I'll pay for everything. I'll get you guys a separate hotel room from Elaine and me. Please say you'll come."

I was grateful that Dad wouldn't place us into one big room as we had done on family vacations during my younger years. "Is Steve's spouse going to come?" I asked. My brother's wife was a kind soul, a kindergarten teacher by training. On the other hand, she could go on and on about her food allergies, body ailments, and the myriad alternative cures she was undertaking.

"No," Dad responded. "She has to stay home with their young kids."

In that case, my father wouldn't invite Gloria, now my fiancée.

I needed time to think. I continued to speak softly. "Dad, I'll have to check my client schedule. Can I get back to you tomorrow?"

"Sure, son, but please come. It would make me very happy to have you be with us. With my stroke, this may be the last time we could make such a trip together." He took a deep breath and went on with his pitch. "There are members of my family in Košice that I want you to meet. You have third cousins there who also have the last name of Simkovits. Their mother, my second cousin's wife, is still alive. Steve and I located them when we did family history investigations there a couple of years ago."

Gee! More extended family with whom to get entangled. I wondered if they'd have their hands out for my dad's money the way my half-sister did. I recalled how my father had given cash handouts to his kin whenever our family had visited Czechoslovakia. When our family had been there in '68, '72, and '76, Dad filled a restaurant with dozens of high-spirited Slovak family members.

Those Košice parties had been festive events, with lots of smiles and laughs and rich Slovak food. But I had been repulsed by the yellowed- and missing-toothed Slovak men of my father's era. They could put down potent plum brandy as if it were sweet sherry. They smoked Russian cigarettes as if they were black licorice—just as my father did with his Canadian brands. Unable to speak my parents' Slovak, but only their Hungarian, which Slovak schools no longer taught once Soviet Communists took over the country, I could hardly connect with anyone. My only consolation in those days had been to eat the rich and tasty food that reminded me of my mother's cooking.

I cringed at my pettiness. Perhaps I was falsely seeing my father's Slovak family as greedy people who expected to be looked after, just as my Simkovits siblings expected.

I thought about Steve. I didn't want to scour the Slovakia countryside to find deceased relatives so that my brother could seal them for eternity in his church. "Does Steve want to conduct more family history while we are there?" I asked. That was his pastime, not mine.

"No, we've completed that," Dad responded. "But I'd like to show you the little hill villages outside of Košice, where my grandfather and great grandfather lived. Steve and I were able to track the Simkovits family back for 200 years, to the late 1700s."

My voice sank. I was running out of excuses. "Okay, Dad; I'll see what I can do."

Overnight, I mulled over Dad's offer. If he was going to parade his wife and first son across his homeland, I felt I had to be there. We were speaking about my relatives too, and I shouldn't dishonour them by not coming. As Dad said, this may be the last occasion we could travel together; I didn't want to disappoint him. He and Steve had taken many Eastern Europe trips these last few years, interviewing family and digging up history. I needed to take my rightful place on my father's other side. But I wondered how much of my sensibilities would remain after spending two weeks with them.

I called Dad the next day. "I thought about it; I can come for one week. I'll buy my ticket to fly to Prague from Boston, and then I'll fly back here from Košice. You can pick me up and drop me off at those airports." My voice was firm, but it wasn't sharp. "That's what I can do."

He came back. "You won't be able to drive our car because we are renting it in Munich."

"That's okay with me. You'll have Steve and Elaine for that." I suspected that my father, being just six months past his stroke, wouldn't drive. "I'll be happy to sit in the back."

After a long pause, he offered, "Okay, son. You arrange for your tickets from Boston, but I'll reimburse their cost. We'll pick you up at the Prague airport. Here are the dates we are traveling..." My efficient father had everything already arranged.

I told myself that I was making this trip only for Dad, though Elaine and I did get along. Who knows, I might even have a good time with my brother if he didn't go on about his religion. If my participation would make Dad happy, it was only one week out of my life. No big sacrifice.

There's something good about expecting the worst. It makes everything that happens afterward seem better. It's like the sheer rock faces and jagged, bare peaks of the High Tatra Mountains of northern Slovakia transitioning into the rolling farm hills leading into Košice.

When I was less jet-lagged, my second night in Prague, Steve arranged that he and I see my mother's eldest brother, Geza, now 83 years old. Not being well-to-do, my uncle, along with his son and daughter-in-law, plus his grandchild, lived together in a one-bedroom apartment on the far side of the Vltava River from downtown Prague. I wondered how any family of four could live in such tight quarters.

Over our supper, I found out. "By living with my father," my older cousin explained, "I not only can take care of him but also have the right to inherit his apartment after he dies." I understood that this was a common practice in a former communist country.

Dad and Elaine stayed away from this supper. My father didn't feel Elaine would be welcome in his former brother-in-law's home, and he was right. My uncle was relieved not to see the woman that had replaced his sister, though he did mention, "I always liked your father."

Over a traditional Czech meal, cooked by my cousin's wife, my cousin mildly boasted about how they lived only ten minutes via streetcar to the heart of Prague, a 1000-year-old city that had stayed untouched by war. He added, "New life has come to the city now the communists are gone."

Earlier that day, my father had pointed to many old town buildings, saying, "The bloody Soviets allowed the city to rot. Plaster and concrete are falling from everywhere." He huffed, "Thank goodness that those bums left, and a new democratic government is restoring these beautiful old buildings."

After saying goodbye to our uncle and cousin, Steve and I made the 45-minute walk back to our hotel. We strolled along and across the Vltava River, following the streetcar route into the city. As we walked, my brother filled me in on some of his family history research.

"No official records remain of Mom's family here in Slovakia and Hungary," he started. "The Nazis destroyed the Jewish archives housed in the synagogues." He shook his head. "I could only go back as far as Mom's grandparents, basically what Uncle Geza remembered and told me the last time I was here."

He was matter-of-fact. "Geza also mentioned that their Friedmann family had had two other siblings, but they died young. One, a boy, died soon after birth. The other, a girl, got sick and died at six years old." His voice dropped. "But nothing he said can be officially confirmed."

"I didn't know about the other two siblings," I replied. "That's too bad about the lost records. It would have been nice to know more about where Mom's family originated."

"The most we know is that her ancestors lived in Košice from the time Jews were allowed to live in the city, some time in the 1800s. According to Geza, it sounds as if their predecessors were fairly poor folks. Only Mom's generation was able to get ahead in their lives by becoming tradespeople."

He counted out Mom's siblings on his fingers. "Mom became a seamstress; Geza was a Hungarian bookstore clerk here in Prague; Uncle Victor became a music teacher; Uncle Lali was a hat maker." It gnawed at me that my brother was talking as if he were a school teacher, telling me things I had known for practically my whole life.

While Steve continued to speak of our mother's family, I became aware that I felt much less angst than usual in being with him. Maybe he was trying to reach out to me, putting on his best self for the sake of our surviving family. I continued to let him take on the knowledgeable big-brother role that he seemed to want to play. Our mother would have wanted us to get along in her native land.

The uneasiness I held toward Steve was nothing compared to the torment my mother had gone through with her brother Lali in Canada. Outside of that mishigas, Mom cherished her siblings. She was happiest when she was with them. At this moment with Steve, it was appropriate to be considerate. I allowed him to guide our conversation about Mom's family.

On our third day in the Czech Republic, we drove ninety minutes to the spa resort town of Karlovy Vary. Dad, Elaine, and I had dinner in the grand dining room of the Grandhotel Pup with its high ceilings, ornate candelabras, and luxurious golden draperies. The neo-Baroque style building, built around 1900, resembled a grand chateau.

Steve said he wasn't hungry. Instead of having dinner with us, he went for a walk through the town. The main street wound downhill through a wide gorge that cut through the mountain by natural hot springs over the millenniums. Up against each other, boutique hotels, shops, restaurants, and mineral spas—constructed right into the mountainside—hugged both sides of the steep-walled valley. Steve liked to explore new places, and he may have wanted a break from being with Dad and Elaine. He had already spent many days with them before I arrived in Prague.

Our father couldn't walk much, and the outside temperature was near freezing. He, Elaine, and I decided to stay inside. The hotel's dining room looked like the grand ballroom in Montreal's Ritz Carleton. Yet, this late in the tourist season, there were more servers than guests.

We ordered my father's favourite—goulash soup. While we waited for the course, Dad looked at Elaine and me and raised his voice. "Why can't Steve stay with us? Why does he always have to do something else?"

Elaine jumped in. "Johnny, you know that Steve marches to his own drummer."

Dad pointed to himself and then to Elaine and me. "It seems as if being with me and us isn't important to him."

I didn't say a word. I figured Steve's going off on his own was because he had worked with our father for too long. He also didn't warm to Elaine as I did. I, too, felt peeved (or was it envy?) to see my brother doing his own thing. Though I chose to stay closer to Dad, Steve's approach had its benefits.

After the waiters had served the food, my father slurped the delicious goulash soup, utilizing the bread to slop up the broth. To prop up his body while eating, he kept his weakened left arm on the edge of the table in front of him. His head hung low, almost into his bowl. It was the way he had eaten soup all his life, and no one ever remarked on it.

The next day, we drove ten hours to reach another chateau-like hotel, The Grandhotel in Stary Smokovec, Slovakia. The town was a winter skiing and summer hiking village in the High Tatras Mountains. Dad crowed in the car. "The High Tatras are nicknamed The Slovak Alps, with over 25 peaks that are at least 3000 meters high." He pointed. "Another village down the road, Štrbské Pleso, was the location of many ski jumping and Junior World Cup championships through the 1980s and into the 90s."

Steve and I said, "Yes, Dad." We had heard those tidbits before.

While Dad rested in his hotel room after we had arrived, Steve went for another walk. Elaine and I shopped for Bohemian lead crystal in the hotel and the village. I didn't say it to her, but I wanted to add to my mother's crystal collection that I inherited after she had died.

Mom had amassed Bohemian glass vases, serving trays and bowls, decanters, and matching wine, liquor, and champagne glasses. She had accumulated them through thirty years of overseas trade with her Košice sister, Irén, who had sent Mom crystal care packages twice a year.

My mother had displayed her myriad crystal pieces all over our house. She carefully dusted and wiped each piece every few months. Her eyes lit up as she opened packages of new arrivals from her sister as if they had been babies delivered by the stork. She washed each new piece carefully in the kitchen sink. Anytime a vase got chipped or broken in shipment, tears filled her eyes, a Hungarian "God forbid!" spilled out of her mouth, and her hand covered her heart.

After Mom had died, I filled two large curio cabinets with her collection. I stored a couple of boxes in my basement packed with extra sets of wine, champagne, and liquor glasses. Steve never wanted more than a few of her vases.

I enjoyed the beauty and sturdiness of Bohemian crystal, something one could also say about my mother. She'd have been happy to know that I kept her crystal collection going, as she would have been to be a part of this homeland trip with her three loves—but certainly not with Dad's third wife.

At the Grandhotel's gift shop, I found a set of cut wine glasses and a big fruit bowl with a set of smaller side bowls. I knew that Gloria and I would use them regularly—she appreciated both the crystal and what such things meant to me. As my mother had done during our family trips to her home country, I'd find a way to lug my twenty-five pounds of booty back to Boston.

Over our next few days in Košice, we saw many of Dad's relatives, including Uncle Edo and his wife, Eboya. By now, all of Mom's Košice clan had either passed away or departed Slovakia. Except for my late Aunt Irén and Uncle Geza, the rest of Mom's siblings and their families had escaped to North America. Though none of them had been religious, perhaps my mother's kin had seen no future for themselves as Jews in Slovakia.

I later learned that fewer than 3000 Jews currently lived in Slovakia while 90,000 had resided there before the Second Great War. During WWII, over 70,000 Jews were deported by the Slovak fascists or killed by the Nazis.

Many survivors of those atrocities then immigrated to Israel and North America in the late 1940s, as my mother did with my father.

Aunt Irén had lived out her life in Košice until both her husband and then she passed away. After my Uncle Victor had lived in Canada for 20 years, he retired back to Košice, and he too was now underground. In this unexpected and disturbing way, the Nazis had come close to accomplishing their "final solution" by killing or driving out nearly every Jew from Eastern Europe. The Soviets then supported that cause via their anti-religion policies.

My heart hurt for having no more relatives from my mother's family in the city of their birth and heritage. I had spent much time with them in my youth—by having taken many summer vacation trips here with my parents or by having them, one at a time, live with us in Montreal for six-month stints. Though I felt disheartened about Slovakia's fascist and communist history, I couldn't discuss that with Elaine present. With her Canadian upbringing and heritage, she wouldn't have understood.

The day after we had arrived in Košice, Steve drove us through the hills north of the city to locate graves of dead Simkovitses. In small farming villages like Velka Lodina and Kavečany, my brother and father showed us cemeteries where we found Dad's great-grand relatives with the name Šimkovič (the Slavic form of Simkovits). Though I wasn't fascinated with dead predecessors and old gravesites, I paid attention while Dad and Steve shared what they knew about each buried kin. They went back and forth about one male predecessor who had been a church organist and witnessed many local marriages.

Steve pointed out that most of the rural Šimkovičes were simple farmers. Dad's father had left his father's farm to become a successful cabinet maker in Košice. While my brother spoke, I suddenly realized that our entrepreneurial father was very much an aberration in our Simkovits lineage. Like the rest of Dad's ancestors, Steve and I didn't have much of a "build a business" bent—though I did run an independent consulting practice.

I wondered why I felt uncomfortable by Steve and Dad's banter. Did I fear Steve unilaterally baptizing all Šimkovičes into his church, sealing us forever into Mormon heaven? Maybe I was envious because Steve had spent so much time with Dad in his native land these last few years.

Even worse, was Dad unconsciously manipulating Steve and me to keep us closer to him? I wondered how I was so entwined with these two, drawn toward my father and repulsed by my brother. I forced smiles for camera shots. *Are we having fun yet?* The cold November temperatures didn't help my mood.

While in Košice, we had supper with the widow of Dad's second cousin at her single-family home on the outskirts of town. Her two sons and their wives joined us. Though the elderly matriarch, Maria, spoke Hungarian, her children only spoke Slovak plus a little English.

After one lengthy interaction in Slovak with Maria, in which she pointed to her two sons, Dad turned to the rest of us and provided a short translation. "Alec is a medical doctor, and Tomas is an electrical engineer." He smiled. "Here in Slovakia, engineering is a more highly regarded profession than medicine, so Tomas makes a better salary than his older brother."

That was perhaps another reason why Dad had wanted Steve and me to become electrical engineers. I nodded back at my father, trying to show my interest and not discomfort. Part of me still hoped I hadn't disappointed him by not following in his technical and business footsteps.

During the meal, I couldn't stop glancing at Alec. His face reminded me of someone, and I wondered if and where I might have seen him before. I recognized the straight face, narrow nose, and long jawline that neither Dad nor I sported, but I couldn't place who he looked like. His broad and slightly-forced smile looked familiar, but I was at a loss.

Then it came to me. I looked at my brother and then back at Alec. *Oh, my God! These two could be brothers!*

I grabbed my glass of wine, took a swig, and said nothing about my sudden awareness. Was this a coincidence, or my imagination, or a recessive gene at work? Their facial resemblance and expressions were unnervingly similar. All these years, I had thought my brother had gotten his looks from my mother's side of our family. I had Dad's rounder face and prominent nose, with everyone at home telling me how much I looked like him.

Now, the first son of my father's second cousin seemed to have an uncanny resemblance to Steve. All this time, I had considered myself the truer and purer Simkovits offspring, my father's preferred son. My brother now seemed to be in the same Simkovits gene pool as I was.

Like Steve, my elder third cousin may have gone counter to his father's wishes, becoming a doctor instead of the more prized engineer. It was eerie that his younger sibling held an engineering degree, as I did. I looked once more at my younger third cousin's face. *Thank God he looks nothing like me!* I was relieved that no one else noticed or said anything about the similarities between Alec and Steve. I said nothing about it, for I didn't want the conversation to focus on my brother.

For years, I wondered if I had imagined things in my distant cousin's face. A year after my father's death, I met Alec again on a visit to Slovakia. I was once more amazed at the resemblance between my brother and him. I told him about the likeness, but he waved off my statement as if he hadn't wanted to consider it. Was that a typical first-son reaction?

From the moment we started our Czechoslovakia trip, I couldn't sleep more than four hours each night. Usually able to nod off in a car or plane, I had no success sleeping in our Mercedes while travelling cross-country. After a few days, my eyes burned with such fatigue that it was painful to keep them open.

While we drove the eight hours from Prague to the Tatra Mountains of Slovakia, I tried to drift off in the back seat, my arms folded across my chest to keep warm. While Steve drove without a word, Dad hummed to Slavic tunes on the radio, and Elaine, sitting next to me, read a Slovakia guidebook.

Drifting in and out, I found myself annoyed for our playing "one happy family." I became mired in thoughts: my father casting my mother aside for Elaine, his disappointment in my brother's religion and business blunders, and his body-ravaging stroke. I couldn't get rest.

Dad and Steve seemed to have no trouble stuffing our family's past into a glove compartment as we drove across our father's native land. Did my brother's daily prayers and Dad's war survival give them desensitizing powers?

I turned in my seat and worked to find a comfortable position. I used my jacket as a pillow. Maybe I couldn't accept my brother behind the steering wheel of our homeland tour. I wondered why I disliked him so. Did it have to do with his ethically pure, religious superiority? Was I the only one to see through his being-closer-to-God-and-heaven veil that masked his counter-dependency dance with our father? Perhaps I was projecting onto my brother my self-disdain about my sinister dependency on our father.

I kept my tired eyes shut so they'd burn less. In my view, our father had never acknowledged my brother as a man. Dad had more than once told me, "Harvy, I'm glad you found a career you like, and I'm happy you are supporting yourself." At times, he also offered, "I like the way you think." I never heard him provide such praise to Steve. Then again, Steve was never in earshot when Dad had praised me.

I worked to slow my breathing and listen to the hum of our car's tires on the road. Through the years, Steve and I had worked together at Dad's company, and we had cooperated when we handled our mother's estate after her death. But I couldn't recall a single time my brother had said, "Harvy, you're right. Let's do it your way," or "Yes, little brother, I agree with or defer to your better judgment." He always, always, always had to have things his way. It ticked me off! Then again, maybe Steve was equally annoyed with me because I worked to please Dad, striving to be our father's favourite.

There was nothing I had seen in my brother's face these last few days that divulged his true feelings toward me. He was a blank screen on which I could project my angst. Was he that way to irk me, or was he doing it for his self-preservation?

Please, can I get some sleep?! Yet, I could not pack my thoughts, along with our luggage, into the car's trunk.

When we arrived at the Tatras, Elaine saw my tired eyes. She suggested I take Valium that she had brought with her. To my relief, half a pill helped me get six hours straight that night. I was far from rested, but it was much better than the three to four hours of sleep I had gotten in each of the previous three nights.

By the time I flew back to Boston, I was exhausted. For the next twenty-four hours at home, I hardly got out of bed. Though our Czechoslovakia voyage was more enjoyable than expected, I was relieved my dutiful participation in our family travels was over. I had had enough Simkovits contact and contemplations for one journey. It was good to be back in my saner life with Gloria, where we could focus on our future.

* * *

Something else had happened during our family trip. On our last night in Prague, the phone unexpectedly rang while we all had tea in Dad and Elaine's hotel room. Elaine picked it up. "Hi Tom," she said to someone I didn't know. "Do you need to speak to Johnny?" She held onto the receiver. "Oh, my!" she said. She turned to us, her face white. "Ralph Lieb died suddenly on Saturday."

Ten years younger than my father, Ralph had been the President of Gusdorf Canada, the lessee of Dad's factory building. Ralph was not only a good tenant but also a good friend to his landlord. He dropped in on my father at the end of many workdays to see how he was faring. They chatted about business and family before Ralph departed home. Whether it was an act of kindness or need, Ralph had leaned on my father as a sounding board for his business and personal challenges. There was chemistry between those two.

I had first met Ralph about a year earlier, in the same week when Dad first took me to the Global Trade Bank, where he housed his offshore money. Ralph and I had talked about my coming to his office to interview him for my client newsletter. My father then said that Ralph had ongoing health problems. He added, "He could use your consulting help to get his key people better organized."

It took me a while to get back to Ralph. It took months more for us to coordinate a time to meet. We finally met in Montreal the month before Dad's Czechoslovakia trip.

I asked Ralph many questions about his business operations and company leadership, and I took copious notes. As a consultant to small businesses, I was impressed by Ralph, a rare breed of general-manager entrepreneurs. Most small business owners are typically adept in one or two business areas: marketing, product development, operations, or finance. Ralph had a good handle on all those disciplines. His growing company and versatile management approach would make a good cover story for my client newsletter. I hoped he would remain a tenant in my father's building for many years to come.

"Wow! Wow! Wow!" came out of my father's mouth when he heard Elaine say that Ralph had passed away. "What happened?" he almost shouted.

Elaine raised a finger to have us wait a minute until she got the whole story from Tom. During those seconds, my stroke-challenged father squirmed in his chair as if he carried carpenter ants in his underpants. Elaine asked Tom, "When is the funeral?" and she got an answer. She finally hung up.

"It's terrible what happened," she offered matter-of-factly. Elaine then sat down; her face was blank but almost white. She looked at Steve and me. "That was Tom, Ralph's Toronto sales manager."

Dad was bursting. "I can't believe it! Ralph was in his early sixties. Please tell me what happened!" Steve and I were nodding too.

"Okay, Johnny," she said coolly, keeping her emotions in check. She looked at Dad. "You know that Ralph and Nancy were at Tom's wedding this weekend. Because Ralph has a good singing voice, he went on stage to sing something to the bride and groom." As she spoke, she motioned her hand up and then down. "When he finished his delivery, he walked back to his seat." Her hand dropped toward the floor. "Instead of sitting down, he collapsed on the ground and died right on the spot." She took a long breath. "Tom found out from Rob where we're staying in Prague. Tom says that Nancy is beside herself. She doesn't want to talk to anyone right now."

"When's the funeral?" my brother asked.

"In three days, on Thursday."

"I can't believe it," my father repeated. He was shaking in his chair. "Ralph was such a good friend." Tears were rolling down his cheeks.

Elaine stayed cool, like a collected mother to an overreacting child. "But you know he had heart trouble, Johnny. He's been telling you that for a couple of years. He was perhaps going to need a transplant. And he probably didn't tell Nancy too much because he didn't want to worry her." She shook her head. "It got the better of him before he had the chance to have surgery."

Not wanting my father to get overwrought, I offered, "I can't believe it either. I feel bad too. I met with Ralph last month, and he seemed fine."

My father reached over and put his hand on my arm. He looked at me through his half-sagging face. "After your meeting, Ralph told me he wanted to hire you to help him in his business." His reddened eyes welled once more. "Ralph visited me every day he was in the office. I'm going to miss him terribly. He was such a good friend." He took a breath and looked at Elaine. "I feel like I want to go home tomorrow to be at his funeral."

Elaine retorted, her voice slightly terse. "Johnny, Ralph is dead! There's nothing we can do about it. Nancy also doesn't want to see anyone right now.

She has a lot on her plate, including Ralph's business. Going home tomorrow won't accomplish anything. Stephen and Harvy are here with us, and we should finish the trip. We can go see Nancy after we get back."

Dad looked at her, his eyes intense and wet. With his able hand, he banged his cane on the floor. "I want to go home! I want to go to his funeral."

Steve stayed quiet. Had this been our mother and father arguing, he might have jumped in to discuss the situation. Around Elaine, he hung back.

I had never gotten in the middle of my parents' fighting, and I felt it wasn't my place to intervene between my father and Elaine. But I didn't want this conversation to get out of hand and see my father burst a blood vessel via a screaming match with his wife. For the remainder of our trip, Steve and I would have to live with any fallout.

I had recently completed post-graduate training in my organization development field. My newly tuned senses were compelling me to act, not to let this argument escalate. I turned to Elaine. "I can see that Dad is very upset by Ralph's death. We need to talk about it more."

I looked at her as if she were the only person in the room, though I did want my brother to hear. I wasn't sure whether my father would understand what I was about to say, but that was less important right now. I asserted, "Dark clouds are forming around us concerning Ralph's death, and you are trying to keep those clouds from coming into this room." I raised my hands as if I were trying to stop the wind. "It's hard to hold back a storm. But if we let that storm form and then pass, there might be clearer skies behind it."

Elaine was quick on the uptake. Her face relaxed. "Okay, Harvy. How should we do that?"

I didn't look at Steve but turned to my father, "Dad, can you say more about why you are so upset about Ralph's death. How and why did he mean so much to you?"

For the next hour, my father talked almost nonstop. He told us how he met Ralph years ago when the man had been the sales manager at Gusdorf, and he later became promoted to General Manager there. He offered, "JHS and Gusdorf did business together a few times during those years. Ralph was a straight shooter and fair negotiator. When Ralph said something, he did it."

Dad pointed to the ceiling. "His word was as good as God's." I wondered if our father had said that for my brother's sake.

Dad shared how he thought about Gusdorf's company as the perfect tenant when JHS needed a new one in '87. He tapped his cane on the floor. "I helped Ralph buy out the Canadian division of Gusdorf when the U.S. parent company wanted to jettison it. I loaned Ralph $150,000 so that he could put together enough money to buy the business from its parent."

Elaine offered how she and Dad had many times gone to supper with Ralph and Nancy. "Ralph was such a gentleman," she offered. "He always pulled out the chair for Nancy." (I wondered if she said that as a criticism of Dad, but my father's stroke now made it a moot point.)

She took a long breath. "They were such a good couple; Ralph loved that woman, and Nancy loved him back." Her face looked pensive. "I wondered what Nancy is now going to do with Ralph's business, considering she has never once stepped into that plant. It was always Ralph's baby."

Steve offered what he knew of Ralph—all good things. I mentioned how knowledgeable and professional Ralph seemed about his business when I interviewed him. "It's too bad that I won't get a chance to work with him as a client."

Elaine touched my arm. "Maybe you can still be of help to Nancy."

After sixty minutes of sitting Shiva for Ralph in our hotel room, Elaine turned to Dad. "How are you feeling now, Johnny?"

"I'm tired," he replied. "Let's go to bed. Tomorrow we can continue our trip to Slovakia." He turned to me, "Goodnight, son." He turned to my brother. "Goodnight to you too, Steve."

Elaine nodded at me. Dad's distraught mood had formed, passed, and dissipated into the ether. Nothing more needed to be said by anyone. I wiped my forehead in relief.

Steve and I departed. While we walked to our room next door, Steve said nothing about how I had saved the moment regarding the drama that had played out with Dad and Elaine. He only mentioned what he thought we should do in the Tatras when we'd arrive the next day.

What was it about my brother that he couldn't even say, "Nice work, Harvy!"? Then again, where did I obtain my need for his acknowledgement?

My recent professional training helped me respond to situations rising before me (like my father's reaction to Ralph's sudden death). However, I still wasn't good at initiating conversations that needed to be raised (like airing family issues with my brother).

It was as if our father had placed a dead moose under my brother's and my Grandhotel beds. Neither Steve nor I were willing to deal with the stink coming from our suppressed distaste for each other. Perhaps I didn't want my brother accosting me with his righteous scripture, and maybe he didn't want my righteousness about being our father's favourite.

Going to bed that evening, I tried to ignore the moose stench in our room. It seemed that my brother and I would prefer to live with the smell of our troubled Simkovits family rather than deal with it. Maybe neither one of us thought we could successfully address the lingering odor by airing out our issues.

It turned out that Nancy did continue Ralph's business, and she brought her son on board as a potential successor. Though Nancy and I had one conversation, she chose not to use my services. I was okay with that because I would have felt awkward working for my father's tenant. Maybe Dad (and Moe Gross) could handle such complex connections, but, at the time, I liked to keep my business and personal relationships clean and single-purposed.

Nancy became successful in building her husband's business, to the point that she moved out of Dad's factory building five years later, and she constructed a larger plant. But five years after that, she, too, died unexpectedly, and I heard that her son took over. But a few years after that, the company went bankrupt, probably due to the unexpected rise of the value of the Canadian dollar and thus drying up the company's USA market. Or might it have been due to a still unseasoned successor?

I wondered what Steve's and my life would be like after our father's passing. Would we get past our family history and rise to guide JHS toward a productive future? Or would we fall because of our discordant history with each other?

* * * *

Late Life Crazies

Even before Dad had his stroke, he had more than once confided, "I used to be a free man, but Elaine has now got me hooked!" His voice was terse. "She's trying to control me. I can't do what I want anymore." His eyes were intense as he glared at me. "And she costs me money, always buying baloney for our homes."

From the day when Dad and Elaine had tied the knot in Plattsburgh, NY, in 1988, Dad's private complaints about his third wife had not subsided. Things did look better between them during Dad's rehab in Boca. But some months after they had returned to Montreal from Florida in the spring of '93, life turned rotten in Dad's Denmark. He chimed out to me, "Elaine doesn't care about me but only about herself and her mother. She always goes to Jean's house and leaves me alone at home." He fumed, "And Jean doesn't care about me either."

Though I knew those notions were not correct, my solace was that Elaine wasn't around to hear the crap I was hearing.

Perhaps I was misguided, but I said little to Dad's outbursts, thinking that it wasn't my place to put myself between him and Elaine. Once, I did offer, "Dad, don't you think Elaine needs space for herself? You can't expect her to be by your side the whole time."

He became adamant, and his voice elevated. "Elaine can do what she wants during the day when I'm in the office. At night, she's supposed to be with me!" Dad expected Elaine, as he had expected of my mother, to sit by her Hungarian-Slovak man's side as he watched (or snored through) evening television shows and not even question what station he wanted to view. Dad expected the "to love, cherish, honour, and obey" marriage line to be meant only for wives.

Maybe Dad wanted a woman's undivided attention and affection, something he may have lacked as a child because of his mother's premature death. My mother always worked to give that to him. But I gathered that Elaine, as I did, found it hard to breathe freely around this man who was of his place and time.

I hoped my father's flare-ups would burn or sputter out, but they didn't. His vitriol got worse in the months and years after his stroke.

After selling their Peru house, Dad and Elaine moved into a modern three-bedroom home in Montreal's West Island. It was a new home in a new development, complete with a cathedral ceiling entryway, a sweeping staircase to a second-floor landing, and a large open kitchen. Dad invited me to stay with Elaine and him whenever I came to Montreal to see clients, which now was about once a month for several days at a time.

One evening, after supper, I hung around with my father while Elaine stepped out to do errands. Dad and I watched TV. Ten minutes after Elaine had left, he raised his voice. "Elaine's mother is a two-faced bitch! She only cares about herself!" He made a fist with his good hand. "And she talks all the time, *yackety-yak*." It seemed as if Dad couldn't stop his spewing. "Elaine always goes to see her when I'm home and spends no time with me. When her mother is with us, she takes over the conversation; I don't get to talk."

The petit Jean was a talker like Elaine could be, but I hardly found her overbearing. I backed or turned away from her when I had had enough of her chit-chat, and she got the message. Dad's complaints reminded me of something he had said concerning my mother: "She cares more about her family than she does about me." It had been his wretched tune during their thirty-year marriage.

I figured that Dad's stroke had precipitated his incessant whining. Because of his harshness this time, I couldn't let it pass. Perhaps I should have raised my voice, but I spoke calmly, hoping my father would match my tone.

Just *Lassen* to Me!   93

"Dad, Jean is very nice to you. She comes around and spends time with you. She asks nothing of you, unlike other people who take advantage of your generosity." I pointed to him. "She's certainly not like Mack."

I never liked Dad's lawyer. He was a *schnorrer*—the kind of guy that would call my father, ask him to go out for supper at the Troika, then expect my father to pay the bill, which Dad did without being asked or without complaint. Elaine had mentioned Mack's methods, and it irked me.

To my statement, Dad repeated, "Jean's a two-faced bitch! She only cares about herself." It was as if he hadn't heard a word I had said. Like a repeating song on a scratched vinyl record, he continued his gruff refrain every few minutes. After defending Jean and Elaine once more, I focused on the TV and sank deeper into the couch.

Dad maintained his intermittent rant. I hoped he'd get it out of his system before Elaine returned. I didn't want him to screw up another marriage, especially to a woman who seemed to be doing her utmost for him. Of course, Elaine wasn't the slave my mother had been, but she was the best thing Dad had going.

Elaine suddenly walked in through the garage entrance next to the den. In her hands were shopping bags and dry cleaning. Her voice was sharp. "Who's the two-faced bitch you're talking about, Johnny?"

Dad stopped dead in his rant. I could see his eyes shifting back and forth. I sank even deeper into the couch, hoping to make myself disappear. My father turned slightly toward Elaine and spoke calmly. "Hi, sweetheart. I was talking about that Mrs. Dubin at the Slovak Church. She doesn't care about anybody but herself."

Astonishment struck me. My heart raced, but I sat frozen. It was a good thing Elaine was standing behind the couch and didn't see my troubled face. I said nothing, not wanting to get in the middle. Elaine spoke sternly at my father and said something to defend Mrs. Dubin. My father said nothing more, his eyes turning back to the TV. When Elaine walked into the bedroom, I shook my head. *Dad, what the hell are you doing?*

I soon retired for the evening. I sat on my bed in an upstairs guest room and thought about what had happened. *Where's Dad going to wind up?* Where the heck would he go if his marriage fails?

My father was dead wrong about Elaine and Jean. Elaine took him to doctor and physical therapy appointments, making him breakfast and supper, managing their home. But my father was insatiable. What he wanted was to have a doting mother fused with a worldly mistress. A woman like my mother would have continued to serve Dad without question or fatigue. She would have washed and ironed his clothes, down to his sweaty undershirts and stinky socks. In Dad's Eastern European world, a man was the king of the castle, even if its walls were crumbling to the ground. For him, a wife served the king with her hand, foot, and every other body part.

A North-American-raised woman, Elaine was not a traditional housewife. She cooked, but she also ordered takeout and liked to go out to restaurants. Though Elaine cleaned, she hired cleaners to do hard scrubbing and heavy lifting. This wife sat by her man as he watched television programs, but she'd read a fashion or home décor magazine or a good mystery novel. There was nothing wrong with that in my marriage manual, but it wasn't enough for my father.

The irony was palpable. When Dad was with my mother, he had sought out a sophisticated woman like Elaine to show off to his friends. Now that he had Elaine, he wanted a caretaker as my homemaker mother had been. I wondered if he could ever accept the choices he had made.

Sitting on my bed in Dad's home, I felt as if I were sitting alone on a station platform, waiting for two oncoming trains to wreck in front of me. As when my father had, thirteen years earlier, left my mother for good, I sensed there was little I could do to stop the pending crash.

I prayed I would be wrong.

* * *

Weeks later, while I was again spending the night at Dad's home, Elaine confided, "Since your father had his stroke, there's less he can do for himself. He's getting more irritable and harder to please."

I looked at her. "How's my father's physical therapy going? Maybe if he stepped it up, he could do more for himself."

Her eyes looked down. She offered, "I'm sorry I brought Johnny back from Florida so soon. The Boca rehab hospital had been doing a great job with him." Her tone was downcast. "But after a month there, your father and I wanted to get back to Montreal." Her voice rose. "And he didn't want to spend the extra money to be in full-time rehab."

"So what's happening here? How much physio is he getting?"

She looked glum. "Quebec health insurance only pays for ninety minutes of therapy, three times a week." She shook her head. "It's not enough, but your father doesn't want to pay out of his pocket for more. In Florida, they had Johnny busy every morning and afternoon, three hours a day. He was progressing more quickly."

I nodded. I understood Elaine's lament. As he had done in business for thirty years, Dad was Simkovits penny-wise and investment dollar foolish regarding his health. When I later asked him about his therapy in Quebec, he responded emphatically, "What I'm getting here is good enough."

Once a Simkovits mule, always a Simkovits mule. Maybe all our male forbears had been that way, and perhaps my brother and I were the same.

I shook my head to Elaine's response. "That's too bad."

Though Dad could drive his car, he was no longer the gregarious garden-party host. Outside of his regular therapy and short daily hobbles down the block near his office—with Rob, Steve, or me whenever I was in town—Dad spent most of his time sitting. I don't know how Elaine held herself together with a disabled older man who now could barely hold a fork in his left hand or smile with his whole face. I was glad I lived a distance away, but I still felt tightly coupled with my father in other ways.

I looked across the kitchen table at Elaine. "Can I do something that I learned in one of my training programs?" I was hoping to ease her tension.

"Sure, Harvy," she responded. "What's that?"

I put my two fists in front of her as if I were holding something in each. "Okay, please pretend I have an ice cream cone in each hand. One is vanilla, the other chocolate." I put my hands in front of her. "Please choose one."

Her eyes stared at my hands. "Okay, Harvy. I'll play along." She pointed. "I'll choose chocolate."

I moved that hand away and left the one that held the imaginary vanilla ice cream cone. "Okay, Elaine. Here's the vanilla cone. Now choose again!"

She looked at my hand for a moment and then at me. "Well, if that's what I got, I guess I'll take the vanilla."

I left my hand there. "Now pretend I'm holding Johnny Simkovits in my hand. Now choose again!"

She stared again at my hand for a few long seconds. She then burst out laughing. "Okay, I get it, Harvy." She looked at me, a smile on her face. "I'll see what I can do with your father."

I wasn't sure if I did that little exercise for Elaine's benefit, Dad's benefit, or my own. I certainly wanted her to stay invested in my father; otherwise, he'd become Steve's and my charge. If it were up to my brother and me, we'd probably ship him into assisted living, which he would have hated. He'd see such a move as putting him out to pasture, and he might be right.

I felt my father shouldn't squander his best retirement benefit.

* * *

Six months later, in early 1994, and a few months after returning from our family trip to Slovakia, I visited Dad and Elaine in Florida. Elaine once more confided, "In January, I drove your father down here from Montreal. We regularly stopped, staying over in hotels for two nights so he could walk and do his exercises. For the rest of our trip, all he had to do was sit there." She looked away. "But I guess he didn't like the way I drove."

I wasn't familiar with Elaine's driving, for I was the one behind the wheel whenever we drove somewhere in Montreal or Florida. I did remember the way Elaine had piloted Dad's boat on Lake Champlain. She gunned that craft across the lake, enjoying the wind on her face and the scenery rushing past.

Across their Boca house's kitchen table, Elaine's face tightened. Her voice turned terse. She looked to one side. "When we arrived at our Boca house, I came around to his side of the car to help him get out. When he stood and steadied himself with his cane, he took his good hand and swung at me, hitting me flat on the cheek." She looked right at me. "I stood stunned for a moment, not knowing what to say or do." She swung her hand. "Then, he took another shot and hit me again."

I put my hand to my forehead and looked down. "Oh, no!" I said.

I wanted to ask, *What did you do?* I had known Dad to have hit my mother, more than once, during their thirty-year marriage. When he did, Mom worked to get away from him. She ran into another room and shut the door behind her. When Dad had hit her on the day he left her for good, she ran out of the house to get away.

I wondered if Elaine had the nerve to hit back at my now weakened father. Could she give him a taste of his bullying MO? Had she carried that out, she would have also done it for my mother and me.

Elaine answered my question before I asked it. She raised her tone. "I looked at your father and said, 'It's a good thing that you're a sick man; otherwise, you'd be on the ground right now!'" She steadied her voice. "I then left him by the car and went into the house alone."

She took a long breath. "That was the first and only time in sixteen years that Johnny hit me. I was simply stunned." She looked away and then back at me. "He neither said anything afterward nor showed remorse. Harvy, he's now an angry man, as if the rest of the world should have had that stroke and not him."

"Wow!" I said. I guessed she wouldn't hit an invalid. I didn't say anything about the abuse that Dad had rendered on my mother. I didn't offer anything about the guilt I felt for pretending Mom's abuse never happened. I sat frozen in disbelief, not knowing what to say or do. As it had been with my mother, I hoped this revived Johnny Simkovits nightmare would disappear.

Perhaps Elaine saw my discomfort, for she moved on in our conversation. She surprised me once more when she declared, "I think I'm going to ask Edo to come back from Slovakia and be here for Johnny. I can't take care of your father by myself." She looked straight at me. "Edo could be a big help, assisting him with his exercises, spending time with him, and such."

"Wow!" I said again. *Poor Edo!* I thought. A little over a year ago, the man had left Canada for the second time. What's Eboya going to say when Edo tells her he's returning to Canada to be a buffer between his brother and sister-in-law?

I pondered Elaine's idea for a few seconds. I spoke slowly. "If Edo is willing to do it, I think it makes sense." Dad might complain vehemently about Edo, but I didn't think he'd ever take a swipe at his brother. I felt sad for Edo having to come back to be an invalid-sitter. But his re-entry into Dad and Elaine's life could be worthwhile if it would keep their marriage intact.

Elaine continued. "Edo can go to church with your father every Sunday." She looked slightly to one side as if she were talking to herself as much as she was talking to me. "Your father has become a religious man since his stroke. From the day we got back from Florida last spring, he has wanted to go to church every Sunday. All these years, he maybe went for Christmas and Easter. Suddenly, he's re-found his religion. It's as if he's afraid of dying and wants God on his side."

She talked fast; her conversation gas pedal approached the floorboard. "And your father never wants to be left alone. I can't leave his side for ten minutes without him asking me to come and sit with him. Every time I leave the house, he asks me, over and over, where I've been."

I was dumbfounded by what she was saying, but none of it seemed ridiculous. Dad had lost something in his stroke, and Elaine needed her sanity if their marriage was going to stay intact. I looked down and then up at her.

"Whatever you think best, Elaine." I hoped that her strategy with Edo was going to work out for everyone.

I don't know how my father and Elaine got Edo to return—and to abandon Eboya—for another stretch, but he did come. In the spring of '94, soon after Dad and Elaine had come back from wintering in Florida, Edo flew back to Canada for a second recall.

I hoped that Edo's presence would be suitable for Dad, even though it might be a torment for my uncle here and his wife back home. As far as I knew, my father never hit Elaine again. Maybe he couldn't surprise her once more.

As for me, I was glad I wasn't the one who'd have to watch over my increasingly volatile and irrational father. I thanked my stars again for my move to Boston five years earlier. I was pleased that I had my own separate life at a distance from the rest of my family, and I was grateful I didn't have to live day-to-day with Dad's growing late-life craziness.

Or was I once again fooling myself?

* * *

Smoking Marriage Embers

In the summer of 1993, three years after my separation and divorce from Margie, Gloria and I were making wedding plans. We arranged to get married in Geneva, Switzerland, in June of 1994. Our friends asked, "Why Geneva?" I answered, "Because Paris won't have us, and Geneva embraced us with open arms." Gloria smiled and added, "We're planning a three-week honeymoon in Switzerland, Provence, and Paris, so why not get married over there too?"

None of our family or friends showed for our Swiss wedding; then again, we never asked them to come. Instead, Gloria and I invited everyone to a wedding reception in Boston a month after we returned.

A few days before Gloria and I were to leave for Europe, I was in Montreal both on business and to see Dad and Elaine. My father had an important reason for my being there. He wanted to talk to my brother and me about his financial arrangement with Elaine.

A year earlier, some months after Dad's stroke, Elaine asked my father to ensure her financial security. By then, she had bent to my father's repeated requests to quit her real estate job. Elaine no longer worked to support herself.

Because she was now full-time with Dad, and he needed more care, she wanted him to put assets into her name. Until then, he had given her only a monthly stipend to cover household expenses. At several suppers back then, she told Steve and me, "If something happens to your father, I'd be a widow on the street, with no job and no place to live."

Elaine was exaggerating, but she had a point. As far as I knew, their Florida and Montreal homes were in Dad's name. Dad had told Steve and me that he and Elaine had a separate-to-property prenuptial agreement when they got married. That agreement stated he would give her $500,000 if he abandoned their marriage. If she left him, she'd get nothing. He had also said, "I'm devoted to you two boys. Elaine is still working and has her own money. She accepts that I'd leave her nothing at my death."

I thought Dad's prenup was odd, but it wasn't my business. But with Elaine now no longer working, it seemed she no longer accepted previous arrangements.

Dad planned to put money into an investment for Elaine, Steve, and me. Starting in the summer of 1993, he placed $50,000 per year into a universal life insurance policy on her life. After three years of paying premiums—assuming Dad kept them going—there would be $150,000 cash accumulated in that $1,000,000 policy. The earnings on the cash value would pay for the policy's annual premium, making the insurance self-sustaining.

Dad told us, "When Elaine dies, this policy's death benefit will go to you two as the beneficiaries. That benefit will then cover the cash I will have given her during our marriage." He pointed at us. "Elaine has agreed for me to obtain the policy for your benefit."

But Steve and I would find out much later that Dad made a somewhat different promise to Elaine regarding that policy. He told her she could borrow against the policy's cash value if she needed any money during or after his death.

The insurance policy seemed like a good investment for Steve's and my benefit. But, at that time, I wasn't sure what Elaine was getting from it. Dad never told us that the policy's cash infusions would be a growing fund for her. I never asked Elaine about her side of this matter; I didn't want to get in the middle between her and Dad.

The life insurance policy seemed to work out until Dad had an unexpected change of mood. When the second premium payment of $50,000 was due a year later, in June of 1994, my father called for a meeting at his office. My brother, my father's lawyer Mack, and I were in attendance that day. It was two days before my wedding and honeymoon trip to Switzerland.

After we had sat down, Dad said, "I'm pissed off with Elaine. I want to cancel the insurance policy on her life and get my money back. She doesn't take good care of me, so I don't want to do anything for her."

Mack added, "I don't blame you, Johnny. You're giving her a good life, and you don't owe her anything." Mack never seemed to like Elaine or to take her side. Maybe he was that way with any client's wife, including his own. He aligned with my father's want-everything-but-give-nothing ways.

I didn't intervene on Elaine's behalf because I wasn't clear about Dad's promise to her via that insurance policy. Or perhaps I didn't want to go against both Dad and Mack. But I did want to slow down the conversation and find a middle ground. I turned to my father. "Dad, before you cancel, can we phone your agent and see if there are other options? Now that a year has passed, you may not be able to get back your initial $50,000 investment."

Dad reiterated loudly, "I don't want to spend a penny more on this policy. I give Elaine enough, and she doesn't deserve more."

I wanted to know more about what was behind my father's statements, but he seemed in no mood for questions. "Okay, Dad," I said. "Let's call Leslie [the agent] and see how much money you can get back, or see what else he might suggest. I would hate to see you lose your entire investment."

My father called Leslie's office, and the agent came on the line. Dad put him on the speakerphone and said, "I have Harvy, Steve, and Mack here with me. We want to cancel the policy on Elaine's life; I no longer have the money for this investment." Dad knew that Elaine and Leslie were friends. He needed a crowd behind him to show that he had a lot of support for his decision. He didn't reveal to Leslie his real reasons to curtail the policy.

There was a long pause on the other end of the line. Leslie then offered, "You know, Johnny, you'll get very little money back. Now that you are in, I would advise you not to cancel. If you want to cut back your investment, you can skip the payment for a year or two and make it up later."

"I don't want to invest anything more!" Dad huffed. "How much would I get back if I cancel today?" His voice was loud and impatient.

Leslie talked slowly and calmly. "I'd have to check with the insurance company, but my guess would be, with the upfront sales charges and cancellation fees, maybe twenty to twenty-two thousand dollars. It would be a big loss for you."

Dad had initially made the policy sound like a good investment for Steve and me rather than a promise for Elaine's financial security. Trying to be helpful, I employed my knowledge of life insurance. I offered, "Dad, I don't think you want to lose $30,000 on this investment." I turned to the phone. "Leslie, could we get away with lowering the face-value death benefit of the policy to perhaps a third of a million rather than the full $1,000,000? This way, the policy would be pretty much fully paid, and my father wouldn't have to put any new cash into it."

After many seconds of silence on the other end of the phone, Leslie responded, "That could be possible. I would need to check the policy contract and ask the insurance company for their legal opinion. I can get back to you later today."

I looked at my father. "If the insurance company says that's okay, Dad, would you consider that option? Then the $50,000 you have put in won't go to waste, and it would give Steve and me perhaps a $350,000 death benefit when Elaine passes away instead of the original million dollars."

Dad's face softened. "Okay, son; that's a good idea." He spoke into the phone. "Leslie, if we can do that, then send me the paperwork right away, and I'll sign it. Steve, Mack, any problems with that?"

They said, "No," and "That sounds okay."

"Okay, Johnny," Leslie said. "I'll look into it right away and get back to you. By the way, do you mind my asking why you no longer want to maintain the policy the way we arranged it for your kids and Elaine?"

Dad's tone stayed terse. "I don't want to spend the money."

Later that day, my father told me that Leslie had called to say that lowering the insurance policy's face value would be possible. Dad's initial investment would then be enough to keep the lesser policy funded for many years to come. Dad said he was going to sign the papers when he got them from Leslie.

Proud of myself for my idea, I thought everything was now right with Dad's world. I drove him back to his Montreal West Island home that evening after he, Steve, and I had supper out. It was a quick meal; I never liked to linger when my brother came along.

When we arrived at Dad's home, Elaine wasn't there. Dad suspected she was at her mother's and would be back "who knows the fuck when." As the minutes and hours ticked away on Dad's grandfather clock, there was no sign of Elaine. I had a flight back to Boston early the following morning. Gloria and I were to pack for Switzerland and catch an evening flight overseas. Dad and I decided to go to bed early, anticipating that Elaine would arrive soon.

Several hours later, screams echoed in the house and woke me. Elaine was yelling at Dad vehemently. "You didn't keep your promise!"

I was stunned. I didn't understand why Elaine was screaming. I then heard her talk about the insurance policy. "You promised you weren't going to change that policy! You promised that you were going to have it arranged for me. You goddamn bastard!"

Even though my bedroom door was closed, I could hear her as if she were standing right outside it. Elaine's rage had me frozen under my covers, the way I had been as a kid when my parents fought in the middle of the night.

Dad started to plead. "Darling, please; that's not true."

I knew he was lying. I now had a fuller picture of that insurance policy and the financial promise Dad had made to Elaine.

She kept on screaming. "You are such a liar! Leslie told me about your meeting earlier today with Mack and the boys."

Dad kept on pleading innocence. He said, "You heard it wrong from Leslie." He inserted "sweetheart" and "darling" at the beginning and end of every sentence.

She kept yelling. "You lying bastard!"

Screaming matches had been a regular pastime between my parents. They would go at each other as if they had trained for years. If angry yelling were an Olympic sport, Slovaks and Hungarians would medal. My parents' screaming had churned my stomach, hurt my ears, given me headaches, and made me shiver. Though I had a thicker skin for it with my consulting clients—sometimes having to come between raging business partners—I got wet under my collar when I heard the same from family.

Since they had tied the knot, I heard Elaine raise her voice more than once to my dad. I knew it was her way to get his attention or to put him in his place. This time it was different. She was in a full-throated fury against my father. Perhaps it had built over many months or years of tolerating his "sweetheart" and "darling" bullshit.

I sat up in bed. *I can't frigging believe it!* I didn't know what I should do. *Should I put myself between those two?* I wondered what this moment would mean for their marriage; would it be over in this clash? I thought about how I was just hours away from flying to Boston then Europe to get married and have a honeymoon. *Couldn't Elaine have allowed me to leave Tombstone in the morning before she started shooting up this O.K. Corral tonight?*

After what had seemed like an eternity, yet it may have been only a few minutes, I decided to get up from my bed. I walked to the bedroom door, grabbed the doorknob, and then stood still for a few seconds. *Should I get involved in my father's bullshit?*

Elaine continued to scream. Something compelled me to open the door and walk onto the second-floor landing overlooking the living room. I didn't dare go downstairs, worried that she would surmise that I had come to defend my father. *Hell, if I wanted to be in her line of fire!* I hoped she'd see me standing on the landing and then calm down.

Elaine was still at it with Dad. "I'm getting my things and sleeping over at my mother's tonight," she shouted. "I don't know if I want to see you tomorrow." She walked into their bedroom and came out a few moments later carrying a handbag.

Dad implored, "Please, sweetheart; it's a misunderstanding. Please don't go." My two-faced father could be as sweet as Austrian apple strudel coated with powdered sugar.

Her tone turned a bit subdued as she repeated, "Johnny, you're such a liar." At least she didn't swear like a Hungarian-Slovak.

On her way to the front door, Elaine saw me on the upstairs landing. She looked up and stopped in her tracks. Her voice calmed, but her hand was still in a fist. "I'm sorry, Harvy, to put you through this." She turned her head forward, walked out the front door, and slammed it behind her.

After a few long seconds of deafening quiet, Dad looked at me and batted his hand. "Go to bed, son. She'll calm down. It'll be better tomorrow."

After her display, I wasn't sure. I said, "Goodnight, Dad. I'll see you when I get back from Europe." He knew I'd be gone before he woke in the morning. He'd then be on his own.

I went back to bed and got what sleep I could. I rose before sunrise and called a cab for the airport. My heart pumped fast and hard until I walked out of the house's front door. I didn't want to get further embroiled in my father's marriage mess. As far as I was concerned, he had created this chaos with his wife, so he'd need to fix it—if he could.

I was livid regarding that stupid life insurance policy. *What a schmuck I was for getting involved!* I no longer wanted to be included in his and Elaine's financial matters, even if it was to my detriment.

When I got home to Boston, I didn't say a word to Gloria about what had happened between Dad and Elaine. Hell, if I'd let my father's financial fiascos ruin our wedding and honeymoon. But I had no idea what I'd be up against on my next trip to Montreal.

* * *

Three weeks later, in mid-July, Gloria and I returned from Europe with wedding bands on our fingers. We had hiked in Grindelwald, Switzerland, in the days before our wedding. Before tying the knot in Geneva, we rode the gondola up the Aiguille de Midi at Chamonix, France.

After our wedding ceremony, we went on an evening supper cruise on Lac d'Annecy in France. We spent our wedding night at a former monk abbey turned village inn. Over the following two weeks, we stayed a few nights in a guesthouse carved into the mountainside at Les Baux-de-Provence, and we lounged on French Riviera beaches at Sainte-Maxime and Cannes. We then rode the high-speed train to Paris, staying in an *auberge* above a French bakery café. Our only whiffs of trouble came from deciding what kind of coffee and croissants we wanted for breakfast each day.

As soon as Gloria and I returned to Boston, Elaine called a "meeting of the Simkovitses" for when I would next be in Montreal. From what I could gather from Dad, the air seemed to have calmed between him and her. However, I figured there was stuff she wanted to get off her chest to the rest of us. I was apprehensive but agreed to be at the meeting, more for her sake than for Dad.

Elaine had always provided value to my father, be it in her taking care of him or giving advice regarding his business affairs. Though she could have been my adversary, as my brother was, I saw her more as an ally. Dad owed her for sticking with him, as he had owed my mother.

By now, Edo had returned from Slovakia to live with Dad and Elaine in their West Island home. After hugging my uncle, I kidded him. "Hey, Edo! How does it feel to be back in Canada?"

He looked perturbed and shrugged his shoulders. "What can I do? Eboya's not happy, but Johnny needs me."

I nodded but added nothing more. I didn't want to add more fuel to a smoldering sibling fire.

Before we sat down to supper, Dad showed me his new walking cane. It was a smooth, tapered, black stick with a long, smooth, solid sterling silver handle. He smiled. "Edo brought me the handle from Slovakia. He inherited it from his mother after she died." He pointed to himself. "It belonged to my father's father. I had the handle put onto this new stick." His grin widened. "Both my father and grandfather had used it for mushroom picking."

He turned the cane upside down and moved it back and forth near the floor. "It's used like this to move the underbrush away to find mushrooms."

Like his predecessors, Dad had enjoyed looking for fresh mushrooms around his Peru, NY home and previously at his country digs in the Laurentian Mountains, north of Montreal. After an overnight summer rain, he'd arise at sunrise to scour the shady areas for edible mushrooms—he could tell which ones were fit for consumption. My father gathered the fungi into a clean dishcloth like a peasant farmer, with one end of the cloth tucked into his pants.

In the kitchen, Dad cut the mushrooms into thin slices, laying them on sheets of newspaper. Over the ensuing hours, as the mushrooms dried, tiny insects crawled out of the fungi and died on the newsprint. Dad was then ready to gather his uninfested booty and make a milky soup for his dinner. The hot concoction brought a smile to his face.

Seeing the bugs come out of those toadstools and being unsure about the toxicity of the newsprint ink, I never took a chance with Dad's recipe. Maybe that's why, from then on, I regularly removed the mushrooms from my soups, salads, and pizzas.

Dad was happy to have his father's sterling silver stick handle. It would become a permanent accouterment to his wardrobe and walking routine, though his gait would never again be steady enough for mushroom picking. I hoped my father's good mood—from having a treasured item from his father—would last through this evening, maybe even the rest of his marriage.

During our supper, neither Elaine nor Dad mentioned the altercation they had had a month earlier. We spoke about my recent marriage event and honeymoon trip. We went over the plans for Gloria's and my Boston wedding reception to come at the end of the month.

When supper was over, Elaine excused Edo. The rest of us remained at the dining room table. After clearing, she sat down and looked at Steve and me. She spoke firmly and frankly. "As you boys know, I'm not working anymore to support myself. Johnny wants me to be by his side more and travel with him whenever he gets the urge. I can't do that freely until there's a financial arrangement between us." She repeated what she had said before. "If something happened to him tomorrow, I'd be out on the street."

I knew she had owned her first home in Montreal and then sold it for a profit. I didn't think she was impoverished, but I didn't know how much money she had. It was true that after six years of marriage, she hadn't gotten much from Dad other than some expensive jewelry and a monthly allowance.

Dad spoke, sounding frustrated. "Sweetheart, I said I'd take care of you."

She looked at him, her voice unwavering. "Johnny, I want Steve and Harvy to know too. You can promise things but then drag your feet. I'd like to know what you have planned and when you'll have it done."

Steve and I stayed silent as we looked back and forth between Elaine and Dad. Our father's voice was even rougher than a month earlier. "I told you that I've already met with my insurance agent, Maury Reemer," he said. "We're working to arrange a lifetime annuity for you with my pension funds. If something happens to me, then you'll have a steady income for the rest of your life. As long as I'm alive, I'm still supporting you, giving you money every month."

"Okay, Johnny. Let me know when and where you'll consummate that annuity deal, and I'll be there."

Elaine looked at Steve and me. "Do you guys have any thoughts on this?"

I tried not to squirm in my chair. I didn't like to feel squeezed between Dad and Elaine. I looked at them. "You should do what you think best."

Steve nodded his agreement, but he didn't quite look at anyone.

I knew my future was secure with Dad's accumulating offshore wealth. Steve and I would be taken care of by what monies and properties remained in JHS Holding Company. It seemed fitting and proper to sacrifice a part of my father's pension funds to take care of Elaine.

None of us, Dad included, should have any complaints. Elaine would be there for him until his final days, so she deserved something substantial. The money he'd put into that annuity would come from his taxable pension money, saving him or his estate a hefty 53% marginal tax rate on those assets. Elaine would get more mileage from Dad's retirement money, considering she'd be in a lower tax bracket. It would be a win-win, and then peace would rain on our Simkovits family.

As for me, I'd share my assets differently with my new wife. Both Gloria and I worked and contributed to our household costs, though I provided more due to my higher earnings. In time, all I owned would be hers and vice versa—though she had told me she expected little from me if our marriage didn't work out.

But unlike with my first wife, there were no signs of our marriage being rocky. Sharing our assets was a part of sharing our lives, benefiting us and our children's future. Not only was it the right thing to do, but there would be financial benefits to our combined estate when one or both of us would die. As a Canadian citizen married to an American, and with the proper trusts configured, I'd receive the same estate tax exemptions in the U.S. as Gloria would obtain.

Like my father, I kept my interests in mind. But, unlike my father, I kept Gloria's and my combined interests in mind too.

As Elaine had done when she stymied Dad's plans for Bahamian residency, she had orchestrated this evening well. Steve and I rarely had any influence with Dad, but Elaine had our father voice his intentions, with Steve and I acting as witnesses. She also received my brother's and my tacit agreement for our father to set aside a chunk of his legitimate pension funds for her.

A few days later, I saw Dad privately at his office. Once again, he yammered on regarding Elaine trying to control him and wanting his money. This time, I spoke to him more firmly yet without raising my voice. "Dad, what's it worth to have Elaine stay with you? You have to give her something. You promised her, and now you have to deliver."

He shut his mouth and didn't say another harsh word for the moment.

I became curious. "By the way, Dad, how much of your pension funds are you going to set aside for her?"

Dad responded calmly. "It needs to be enough to give her a decent and steady income after I'm gone, perhaps $100,000 per year. We're arranging to transfer a million dollars from my pension into a deferred annuity in her name. That money would grow tax-free until she is required to receive income either after I die or when she turns 69." He tapped his knuckles on the table. "She'll have a good income for the rest of her life, and the government wouldn't tax it until she receives it."

Though that sum was more money than he had given my mother eight years earlier in their divorce, the amount seemed reasonable. Elaine could be taking care of Dad for another ten or twenty years. The better she did that, and the longer he lived, the larger that retirement fund would be for her. It made good financial sense.

Dad didn't say anything about it then, and I didn't remember it myself. He had also promised me a million dollars of his pension funds, earmarked via his tax-free annuity agreement with the Supporters of Independent University.

When Dad's promise crossed my mind later, my heart skipped a beat or two. But I consoled myself; *It'll be okay*. By the time he dies, Dad would have enough pension assets to fund not only Elaine's annuity but also that Independent University annuity. Instead of sharing Dad's pension fund with my brother, I'd be splitting it with my stepmother. And my half might come tax-free if I kept to Dad's plan of not declaring the ensuing income.

Though that clandestine option unnerved me, I felt I had little to worry about. I could wait until after Dad's death before I decided what to do with that university annuity. In my case, the only losers would be my brother and the Canadian government.

What they don't know won't hurt them.

* * *

Later that month, Gloria and I held our wedding reception at the Audubon's Habitat Center & Sanctuary in a Boston suburb. Their facility could seat ninety guests and a six-piece band for our celebration—small but lively.

Gloria had asked to have the Habitat Center's banquet people arrange the reception outdoors so people could dance under the stars. By midafternoon on our wedding day, dark, ominous thunderheads sent servers to set up inside, just before the heavens burst open in a late afternoon thunderstorm. After twenty minutes of drenching downpour, the clouds parted. The setting sun refracted and reflected off water droplets, giving everything a radiant glow. Gloria and I were glowing too.

Though Dad and Elaine had driven down the previous day, Steve and his family hadn't. They didn't show for the pre-reception photography and cocktail party. I said to Gloria, "My brother punches in and out on his own time clock. Let's not delay supper for him." I wasn't going to be like my father with my brother, holding up the meal until Steve got there. Gloria agreed.

As the waiters served supper, I perused my note cards before making my welcome speech. I used a knife to ring my wine glass to get everyone's attention. I stood and said, "Thank you all for coming to what I consider to be the best day of my life, being here with my wonderful Gloria."

I looked at my bride. She wore a beautiful cream-beige dress that flowed down to the floor, complete with a wide-brimmed matching hat. I sported in a new, tan, light wool suit. Because both of us were previously married, we decided to forgo the traditional wedding of whites and blacks. There were no best men or bridesmaids either.

I turned to the crowd. A serious look came over my face. "But I want to know where you all were when we got married a month ago in Geneva? None of you showed!" There were chuckles in the room. "What! Didn't you get the invitation? Gloria and I waited and waited at the Geneva marriage hall for you."

More laughter came from the audience. Everyone knew that we had had a private ceremony overseas for the heck of it. We had spoken our oaths in front of an administrator in an ornate Swiss hall. Our witnesses were two secretaries who had sported t-shirts and shorts.

I batted my hand in the air. "I know! I know! You just wanted to crash the party."

The room filled with laughter.

I smirked. "Joking aside, Gloria and I are glad you all are here to share this special day with us." I paused to absorb the moment and look around at the faces in the room. I raised my glass to everyone. "Enjoy your time at our special celebration . . . and we'll pass around a hat later."

The crowd chuckled again. I smiled as I felt the love of family and friends in this beautiful setting.

I barely got into my seat when Steve and his wife walked in unexpectedly. In front of everyone, they came through a sliding door next to our table. *I guess it was too hard for them to find the front door.*

With perhaps peeved faces, Gloria and I quickly motioned them to sit at the place we had saved. Grinning ear to ear, Steve offered. "Sorry, Harvy, but there was a lot of construction traffic on the highway from Montreal."

I knew that traffic alone couldn't account for their more than three-hour delay. I didn't say *Yah, right, Steve.*

Gloria and I looked at each other, the momentary annoyance in our faces subsiding, and we said nothing. Neither of us wanted any negative sibling or in-law feelings to darken our mood, as the dark rain clouds an hour earlier could have done. I offered a feeble, "You missed the photography." Steve shrugged, said nothing in return, and they sat down.

After the main course, Gloria and then I stood again to give our prepared speeches. We toasted our family and friends from near and far. We talked about our friendship, love, and devotion to each other.

Afterward, one by one, as in a Quaker meeting, friends and family stood at random to give their respects and blessings. Guests reiterated how wonderful this day was and how Gloria and I were right for each other. In my head and heart, I agreed. She and I were people who liked to please, especially each other. *I'm going to get it right this time!* I wasn't going to stand a third time in front of any judge, justice, or minister the way my father had done.

After a few friends had spoken, Dad rose at our head table. He held himself steady by employing his able right hand to grab the table's edge. My father then leaned his body against the tabletop and held himself steady with his weak left hand. He lifted his wine glass with his right hand and tilted it toward Gloria and me. "I congratulate the two of you for a wonderful reception in this beautiful place. I wish you a happy and prosperous life—including children." He winked at me the best he could with his good eyelid.

"Here! Here!" came from another voice in the room. Everyone chuckled.

Continuing to steady his body against the table, Dad lifted his glass again. "I toast you for a good, long-lasting marriage."

I half-smiled. *Yah! My father never had anything like that with any of his wives.*

Dad ended his speech there and sat down slowly. I was grateful that his tune was short and sweet, even though it seemed a little off-key.

After other relatives and friends had risen to offer warm words, Elaine wanted to do her part. She stood, shook off the cocktail that she had finished, then looked around the room. "What a beautiful evening," she motioned with her glass, "for all of us to celebrate Harvy and Gloria's future together." She looked at us, her eyes glaring. "Congratulations, you two!"

Her voice turned slightly edgy. "As I look around our head table, I see that there are many past marriages represented here."

Uh, oh! I hope she's going to speak only for herself. Elaine knew that both Gloria and I had been around the marriage block before. She and Dad had been at my first wedding and reception in Montreal. I didn't want her to revisit that past.

My stepmother took a long breath and continued. "Both Johnny and I know from experience that marriages are difficult to keep going. It requires hard work and a continual commitment from both partners."

She looked at my brother as he sat on the other side of Gloria. "You know a lot about that, don't you, Stephen? Over the years, your marriage has had its ups and downs. You've had your religious beliefs to hold onto, to keep you going." She took a breath. "Maybe you can tell us about how that has helped make your marriage work." She then sat down, her eyes remaining on my brother.

Gloria suddenly turned toward me, her back to Steve. There was a look of shock, even horror, on her face. She sensed what would happen next, but I didn't have to read her eyes to know.

It was as if Steve's bishop had asked him to talk at a prayer recital. My brother stood and started to cite passages from his religious books and beliefs. The heavenly floodgates opened from his Mormon mouth. He rambled on for two, then three, then four minutes. Though he spoke of faith in God and devotion to the church, he was unprepared. His sentence strands were jumbled together like a bowl of spaghetti that had spilled onto the table.

Gloria turned to me again, dread on her face. She quietly whispered in my ear. "Harvy, you have to stop him. He's going on and on about nothing having to do with us, but only about his religion."

I whispered back. "What do you want me to do? I can't just shut him up." I prayed that my religious brother would soon end his biblical chatter.

Another minute passed. Gloria and I were squirming in our seats, trying to look composed for our guests. The room was deadly silent except for my brother's ramblings. I glanced at Elaine. She was staring into the crowd, no discernable look on her face. I don't know what inspired my wife, but she reached toward my brother and tugged at his pant leg.

Steve got Gloria's message. After speaking another disjointed sentence or two, he ended his piece and sat down. Though I felt cold sweat rolling down my back from wondering what our friends were thinking, I was relieved my brother had stopped his spiel. Thank goodness that someone stood from an adjacent table and proposed a toast as if nothing had been amiss.

After supper, our friends came to Gloria and me. "It's been a very nice wedding. You two know how to set the mood." One comrade looked my way. "By the way, Harvy, what was your brother talking about?"

I waved my hand away. "It's not important; it's just Mormon stuff. Glad you're having a good time."

Gloria and I later surmised that Elaine couldn't deal with the warm comments people had expressed in public that evening. In her marriage to Dad, we figured she never received the wedding reception and speeches that were as heartfelt. What marriage strains lay inside her had oozed out in urging my brother to speak.

But Elaine's urgings and Steve's ramblings couldn't compete with the rest of our other guests who held affection in their hearts and maybe a drink or two in their bellies. Or perhaps it was the lively dance music that subsequently captured their attention. Other than the two of us, it seemed no one else had paid much attention to what Elaine had enacted, what Steve had expressed, and what Gloria had ended.

Near the end of the reception, as Gloria and I were saying goodbye to family and friends, my brother came to us. His face was long. "I'm sorry if my speech went on a bit too long."

Gloria smiled. "Don't worry about it, Steve. Elaine reeled you into it."

I put my hand on his shoulder. "You took Elaine's bait, brother, and you swam a long way with it." I smiled too. "But, no one noticed."

I turned toward another guest who had come forward, not giving Steve a chance to say more. My brother nodded and walked away to join his wife. Gloria and I were not going to give in to any hard feelings that evening, for that would have been giving into Elaine's thoughtlessness, whether or not she had intended it.

Elaine never said anything about her goading Steve into speaking, and hardly did anyone else. Both Gloria and I did surmise that there could be more trouble brewing on Dad's home front. I wondered what would come next from those two, but now wasn't the time for that contemplation.

* * * *

Another Frigging Family Failure

Three weeks later, my father called me in Boston. He was fuming. "Edo and I left the house. We moved into the Quality Suites here in the West Island." He was talking as fast as his stroke-ridden face would let him. "I've had enough with that bitch. I'm fucking fed up with her."

For a millisecond, I thought my dad was talking about Elaine's dog, Muffie. His voice shook like an erupting volcano; I had to pull the phone away from my ear. "She only cares about herself, her mother, and getting my money." I imagined him banging his fist on his office desk. "I'm not going back to her, ever!"

Uh, oh! The bad cards had been piling up between those two, but I never thought my father, now 74 years old, would be the one to pull the up-and-leave card with his wife.

And what must my uncle be thinking about his big brother's craziness? Edo had come back to Canada to help Dad with his physiotherapy, go to church with him, and keep him company. Now he was sitting in a hotel suite just minutes from Dad and Elaine's home, with his big brother screaming profanities.

I stammered, "Wow, Dad! When and how did this happen?"

"We *foot-scoffed* out of there a couple of days ago. I can't stand that woman anymore."

"Are you sure you want to do this? You've been living with her for, my gosh, fourteen years."

"I'm not going back to that bitch!" he shouted. He took a breath and then asked matter-of-factly, "When are you coming to Montreal?"

My voice hesitated. "My next planned business trip there is next week."

"Okay, I'll see you then. We are staying in room 203 here at the Quality Suites. Make a note of it. I'll make sure there's a key for you at the reception desk. There's enough room for you to stay here with Edo and me." He hung up the phone.

Gloria was at work, so I had no one to talk to about my father's sudden madness. I spoke to myself for a few minutes. "What the hell is going on? What the heck happened?" Dad was angry beyond belief, not a good thing. *Maybe Steve knows something.*

I sat for a few more minutes, swiveling and rocking in my chair. *Should I call my brother?*

I looked out the window then back at my phone. I dialed Dad's home number.

I was shaking with fright when Elaine answered. "Hi, Elaine, It's Harvy. I just talked to my father. He sounded distraught. What's going on?"

She was matter-of-fact. "Your father has wanted to pick a fight ever since we came back from your wedding."

She took a long breath. "You know how Steve picks up your father and Edo every Tuesday morning?"

"Yes."

"Well, Steve takes them to your father's office and then carts them to the hospital for your father's physical therapy. They go out for dinner, return to the office, and are home by five o'clock. It's nice of Steve to do that because I'd otherwise have to be with Johnny 24/7."

"Okay," I said, thinking again that I was glad that I lived in Boston.

Elaine's voice stayed steady. "Well, this Tuesday, I dressed your father, gave him and Edo breakfast, and had them ready for Steve by nine o'clock. Your father kissed me goodbye, told me that he loved me, and then Edo and I helped him down the stairs and into Steve's minivan."

Elaine's voice elevated a touch. "Then, around two o'clock, the doorbell rang. It was a messenger with a lawyer's letter from Mack's office!"

Her pace picked up. "In disbelief, I called your father at his office and said, 'Johnny, what is this? Mack's office served me papers.'" She took a breath but kept up her pace. "Johnny then started screaming, 'You bitch, all you want is my money, and he hung up!" She took another long breath. "Harvy, I was beside myself with disbelief!"

I was speechless too. A couple of months earlier, Elaine had screamed bloody murder and slammed the front door on Dad only hours before I left for my overseas wedding and honeymoon. Maybe Dad needed to show his wife that he could also slam a door, throwing a king of spades on her queen of hearts.

Elaine kept on talking. "A couple of hours later, Steve called to say he was taking Johnny and Edo to a hotel. He asked if I would pack a bag for them. When Steve came to retrieve the bag around five o'clock, he said, 'I don't know what he's doing, but I'll try to talk some sense into him.'"

Elaine paused. My mind raced. *What the hell is going on?! How the hell is Dad going to take care of himself? What does Edo think about his brother's blustering baloney?* I didn't know what to say to Elaine.

She spoke again, "Harvy, I'd have your father back if he wants to come home."

I took a long breath. "Dad sounded pretty mad when he talked to me." I didn't think I could talk much sense into him in his current state. "I'll try to talk to him over the weekend and when I'm in Montreal next week." I hoped he'd come to his senses on his own or after Steve would speak to him.

"Okay, Harvy," Elaine added. "He should know that my door is open."

I talked to my father both that weekend and the following week in Montreal. He continued to stew and grumble. "She's a bitch! I never want to see her again! I've had it with her and her mother!"

I spoke to Steve, but he knew nothing more than I did. He added, "Dad said that if I tried to intervene in what's going on between him and Elaine, he'd disinherit me." He quoted a Bible passage: "Beware of wolves in sheep's clothing." I wasn't sure whether he was referring to Dad or Elaine.

I didn't think Steve wanted to get involved in Dad's marriage. He never became as close to Elaine as I had become. It seemed it didn't matter to him whether Dad went back to her or not.

I wanted my father to return to his wife. Who else did he have? Edo? Would his baby brother take care of him for the rest of his life, walk with him around the block, give him physical therapy, and massage his legs every night before bed? Indeed, I wouldn't, and neither did I think Steve would.

At every ensuing conversation, Dad continued to gripe about his wife. His vitriol lasted not just for one week or two weeks but three long weeks. He seemed determined not to step back into his home as long as Elaine was there. I felt my mother had been right. *What an old fool he was!*

I didn't call Elaine again because I had nothing encouraging to report. Over one supper at his Montreal hotel, I asked my father, "What are you going to do without Elaine for the rest of your life?"

He didn't hesitate. "Edo and I will find an apartment, and he'll take care of me."

I looked at Edo. His face was blank; he said nothing. I turned back to my father. "But what about Eboya?"

Dad answered with a straight face. "She can come here to visit anytime she wants."

Edo shrugged and looked away.

By mid-September, in the fourth week after having left his third wife, Dad's attitude shifted. I supposed that even a madman could hold insane anger only for so long. I was in Montreal once more to see clients. I stayed again with Dad and Edo for a couple of nights in their hotel suite.

Dad and Edo slept in a king bed, sharing the space as they had sometimes done as kids. I slept on the living room's sofa bed. I don't know why I didn't insist on getting a hotel room away from my father's craziness. Though I never got a good night's sleep on that pull-out, maybe I was surveilling what was going on between Dad and Elaine. Or was I as attached to my father as Edo was?

Every hour or two that evening, Dad called Elaine. She never answered, but he left her messages. His voice was gentle. "Sweetheart, please pick up the phone. Please call me back. I'm sorry; I miss you. I want to come home."

I couldn't believe my ears on my father's sudden change of heart. I prayed in my mind from under my covers. *Elaine, please call him back and allow him to go home.*

I wondered if I truly wanted them to get back together. Dad had been a complete ass to her, and he deserved a cold shoulder in return. I became fed up with his 180-degree reversal madness. I never called Elaine to see what was going on for her. *Let Dad lie alone in the crappy marriage bed he had made.* To my chagrin, I was lying not far from that bed.

Weeks later, my father called me in Boston. He sounded happy. "Elaine is going to have me back. She just wants her financial situation settled."

It was now two months since Dad had left Elaine. I was surprised she agreed to reopen her arms to an ailing, volatile man who talked out of both sides of his stroke-ridden face. I figured she would consider that option if her financial future were secure.

My father shared more. "Elaine doesn't want you or Steve involved in our arrangement. I'm going to engage Mack and Maury Reemer. They'll work out a deal with her lawyer."

Elaine has a lawyer! Dad had screamed profanities when my mother hired a lawyer after my father had left her for the final time. This time, Dad seemed to accept Elaine's attorney in stride.

He continued. "I will give Elaine perpetual income for the rest of her life from an annuity I'll purchase with my pension money." Dad's move meant that she'd obtain income immediately, not having to wait until Dad's death.

I later mentioned my conversation with Dad to Gloria, offering, "It's hard to believe. After all that my father had done and said to her, Elaine is willing to have him back."

Gloria was as dumbfounded as I was. We agreed the best thing was to stay out of their matter. Dad and Elaine would have to work this out on their own if they could.

After another few weeks, I was again visiting my father in Montreal. From the moment I walked into his offices, he was up in arms. "Even my fucking lawyer won't agree to what I want to give Elaine."

"What!?" I said.

Dad threw his reading glasses onto the desk. "Mack said something stupid to Elaine's lawyer, and now Elaine wants to have our house as a part of our settlement." He threw his hands in the air. "I fired that *Schmack!*"

I put my hands up to try to deflect my father's ire. "Dad, please calm down." I didn't want him to have another health event. "Tell me what happened."

Dad quieted, and he slowed his speech a tad. "Mack disagreed with my giving Elaine 1.1 million dollars of my pension so she could have $100,000 of annual income for her lifetime. He said something stupid to her lawyer. Elaine then got mad, and now she wants our West Island house in her name."

He banged the table with his flat hand. "I got pissed at Mack; I fired the guy. He's no longer making the financial arrangement with Elaine's lawyer."

Dad picked up and waved a paper in his right hand and then banged the document down on the desk. "Mack now wants me to sign a fucking legal 'love letter.' It says I can't hold him responsible for what I want to give Elaine. He wants to be off the hook if I later change my mind."

I was glad that Mack was out of the picture; I never liked that guy. "So, what are you going to do now?"

Dad quieted. "Reemer is now handling the situation for me. He has an idea of how I could transfer $1.1 million from my pension funds tax-free into a pension in Elaine's name and to have her obtain a steady income from it right away."

"That's interesting." I looked intently at him. "But why is it now 1.1 million? I thought it was going to be only a million."

"It's because bloody interest rates have gone down. I need to put more capital into it." He raised his voice a notch. "But I don't care; I want to go back home. And I'm going to transfer the house over to her as well." He took a big breath. "I want it to be over."

Maybe Dad was getting tired of living in a small hotel suite with his brother, eating the same bland hotel food every morning and evening. That kind of living would drive me batty, and it seemed as if my father were heading in that direction. He had once said that he and Elaine had a prenuptial agreement that entitled her to half a million dollars if he upped and left her. I guessed that the agreement didn't apply to his now wanting to return to her.

Though I was skeptical about why Elaine would have my father back, I figured whatever she got would be worth it. Though I'd feel a loss for the money going her way, I wasn't the one who would have to take care of him for the rest of his life. No one could handle my father the way she could. He had no acceptable alternative.

I hoped that my angst and my father's *agita* would soon be over.

After more weeks of back and forth, Dad and Elaine struck and signed a deal. He told me about it on my next trip to Montreal. "The notary is transferring the house into her name. And to give her an annual income of $100,000, I had to put 1.2 million dollars of my pension into an annuity."

I tried not to raise my tone. "Gee, Dad, last time you said it was going to be 1.1 million."

"Yes, it was going to be that when I talked about it weeks ago with Reemer. But goddamned interest rates have come down again. I had to invest more capital from my pension so that she'd get a steady income each year. Reemer and the insurance company calculated the investment." Dad seemed desperate to get back a woman who didn't have the same open arms my mother had had for him.

My father added another nuance. "Elaine also wanted a cost-of-living adjustment each year, so I had to put another $250,000 into a separate annuity vehicle for her. She could draw from that as the cost-of-living increases." He pointed my way. "But don't worry, son. If she doesn't need that extra money, it will stay and grow within the annuity. That money will then go to Steve and you when Elaine dies."

"What! How does that work?"

"You can ask Reemer yourself. He's going to be here soon." He gestured toward the coffee maker. "Grab a coffee, use the phone if you need to, and wait for him."

When the agent arrived, a smile was bursting from his face about what he had done for Dad. Maury said, "I'm going to manage that extra cash that will stay with the insurance company." He pointed to himself. "Elaine needs my permission to release any funds from that separate account. I'll only do that as inflation goes up each year, giving Elaine a few more dollars. More than likely, that asset will grow faster than what she takes out of it. It should stay intact for you and Steve to have when she passes away."

Maury's chest puffed out. "Elaine's attorney was impressed as to how I was able to legally transfer a client's pension into an annuity in their spouse's name. Now that the Canadian tax laws have changed regarding pensions, I showed her how I could create a whole new vehicle for spousal separation settlements." His smile went from ear to ear. "Elaine's attorney even asked for my card so that she could do the same for other clients of hers."

These insurance guys are always selling! Luckily, Maury was better than most.

Maury was more than a decade younger than Dad, so I didn't ask who would manage the money in that second insurance vehicle when Maury retires or passes away. I assumed his firm would still control those funds and then give what remained to Steve and me upon Elaine's passing.

Once the papers were signed on the spousal annuities and the house transfer to Elaine, Dad called me. He chirped jubilantly, "Elaine is getting the house ready for my return."

But days turned into weeks. Every time we talked, my father said, "I don't know why, but she doesn't answer my calls."

Neither Steve nor I contacted Elaine to find out what was going on at her end. Our sideline approach to Dad's marriage scrum was still in play.

After more days had passed, Dad called around to his friends. He then called me, his voice roaring again. "Elaine sold our West Island house!" His tone was harsh and whiny, like a wolfhound that had its supper bone taken away. "She took my money and moved to Vancouver without telling me! She took all the house furniture and my grandfather clock too!"

And her annuity payments too. I couldn't believe it, but a part of me maybe did. She left Dad the way he had dumped her and other women in his life.

For the following weeks, Dad shouted a new mantra on our calls. "I CAN'T FUCKING BELIEVE SHE WOULD DO THAT TO ME!" The next time I saw him in Montreal, he flung his good fist into the air. "She took my goddamned grandfather clock. It was a present from my friends." His face contorted as if he had drunk hot and bitter coffee.

I later heard from Steve, who now visited Dad's office more often, that Dad had obtained Elaine's number in Vancouver. My brother told me that

Dad called her every day and yelled into her answering machine, "I want my grandfather clock back! You shouldn't have taken it!" He said nothing about how she had *foot-scoffed* with his money and his hopes.

Elaine eventually sent the seven-foot-tall clock back to Dad. He later told me, "She shipped it back to me at my expense, along with divorce papers." He added, "I signed the papers, and I never, ever want to see that bitch again."

All I could say was, "I'm sorry it happened." I felt terrible for him. I had no idea what I could have done to have prevented their marriage train wreck.

But was I sorry for my old man? He had made his turbulent marriage bed and now had to lie in his divorce mess. And Steve and I had to pay for it too, with that much less of an inheritance. I didn't know at whom to be pissed off more, Elaine or my father. I didn't know if I should curse or admire her for having walked away with more money than any other woman in Dad's life.

I found it ironic that my father married Elaine some months before my wedding to Margie, and then he divorced her some months after my second nuptials to Gloria. It hurt my head to try to make any sense of that.

Worst of all, I felt as if my *yaytsa* had been rendered impotent in Dad's third separation and divorce. I was in a daze for days, saying nothing about my bitterness to either my wife or my brother. There was not a thing that I or anybody could do. Nothing could bring back what we had lost.

Dad's grandfather clock sat in his office in the corner of his old factory building for the rest of his days. That 7-foot tall timepiece was a testament to his failed third marriage. Its symbolism mimicked the fountain he had installed outside the kitchen window of his Peru, NY house—to remind Elaine of their failed attempt at finding potable well water.

Once a week, Dad cranked the gears of that Emperor clock to keep it ticking and chiming. He performed that ritual until the day he could crank those gears no longer.

* * *

As the years passed, I heard tidbits about Elaine's life post-Johnny. Dad or Maury mentioned what they knew. Over supper one day, I relayed my understandings to Gloria. "After a time in Vancouver, Elaine met and married a retired army colonel. But within another year, she divorced him too. It seems he was abusive, but I don't know in what way."

My astute wife looked at me with amazement. "That's too bad. It seems there's a pattern in her life about being attracted to such men. Didn't you once say her first husband was that way?"

"Yes, from what little I know." I grinned a bit. "I guess she's trying to catch up to my father in the marriage and divorce department." I took a breath. "And there's more. After she had divorced that Vancouver guy, she upped and moved again, this time to Boca Raton, FL."

She stared at me. "Isn't that where your father had his winter home?"

"Yup," I said.

Her face looked puzzled. "So, what's Elaine doing in Boca?"

I told her what I knew. "She's has friends there. One helped her get her Florida real estate licence. She started a real estate agency in the high-end home market and now has dozens of agents working for her."

"Wow," Gloria added. "That woman always has something going on."

What I didn't tell Gloria was another tidbit Dad had shared. After some time had passed, he tried to get back in touch with Elaine during the months he wintered in Florida. My father told me he repeated a trick that had won over Elaine nearly twenty years earlier.

He showed a slight smile as he said, "I ask my good friends to invite both Elaine and me for supper to their home. Elaine comes once in a while." He looked at me with a straight face, no misgivings in his tone. "During our evening together, I slip her a gift, like a piece of jewellery or cash. I place it into her jacket pocket or handbag without anyone else noticing." His eyes looked sad. "I still want her back."

"So, what happened with that?" I asked him.

He looked down. "Elaine took my gifts, but she hasn't decided to come back to me."

I guessed she saw past Dad's repeated suppertime ploy and had had enough of the conniving and run-down man he had become. In his reduced mental state, Dad couldn't take a hint. I asked or said nothing more about it.

For the rest of my father's life, I never shared with anyone my resentment toward Elaine. I was angry at my ex-stepmother. She had upped and abandoned my father, absconding with a bunch of his money.

A few years later, Maury Reemer had a medical emergency and retired from the insurance business. Elaine took the opportunity to engage her insurance friend, Leslie, to transfer Dad's $250,000 supplemental annuity into Leslie's control. I became distraught when the original insurance company told me about the transfer, and there was nothing I could do about it. Neither Steve nor I would now see a dime from those dollars. I was then as sure as a Canadian $1000 bill that Elaine, in the end, had taken what advantage she could of my father.

Perhaps Elaine had been driven by my father's conniving and craziness. Maybe she did what she had to do to save herself. I handed it to her for being the only woman to get away with giving Johnny Simkovits a dose of his own money medicine. I guessed that a North American goose could take advantage of a Hungarian-Slovak gander as much as the other way around.

* * * *

Collateral Money Damage

One early morning—a week or two after Dad's divorce had been finalized—I was sleeping in my bed in Boston. Gloria lay next to me. I suddenly awoke and bolted upright. *Oh, my God!*

I had suddenly realized what Dad had done by giving away most of his pension fund to Elaine. There might be only four or five hundred thousand left in that fund. With the turbulence that had transpired between him and Elaine, I forgot about his promise to fund the one-million-dollar Independent University annuity for me. *How would his estate now pay for that?*

My heart raced; sweat started to form on my face; I put my hand on my chest. "Oh, my God!" came tumbling out of my mouth. *How did I forget?*

My moaning awakened Gloria. "What's going on, honey?"

I had never told her about the university annuity that my father had arranged for me, let alone anything else about Dad's hidden stash. I didn't want to burden her or to have her think less of her husband by telling her what I knew about my father's offshore finances. I needed time to think through this revelation. Might Dad have other taxable assets he could put toward that university annuity?

I blinked to get the tiredness out of my eyes. *Maybe Dad's pension move was a Godsend.* Part of me wanted to forget and forgo that nonkosher annuity. Maybe Elaine had done me a favour by taking away most of Dad's pension assets. Though it would mean less money for me, I was never comfortable with that clandestine contract. Hell, if I wanted to steal away every year—after Dad's death—to branches of the Global Trade Bank scattered around the world to collect cash from that tax-evading scheme. I loathed the idea of one day having to explain to the IRS, or even Gloria, how I was obtaining untaxed cash.

I was now an established independent consultant, doing well in my field. I was a married man with an honest wife. She would frown on anything that wasn't above board. She and I prided ourselves on our integrity in our client work and personal lives. Would I risk fooling around with undeclared assets, dragging my new wife and any future kids into an offshore gutter?

My father's having more cash in his pockets certainly didn't make his life any happier. His offshore finagling had become a slow-working poison in my gut. Maybe my life would be much better, certainly simpler, without that Independent University annuity.

On the other hand, would the university chase my brother and me regarding that not-totally-aboveboard annuity agreement (in the guise of a legitimate charitable donation) that Dad had destined for my benefit?

I needed to think through my dilemma. Was Dad's signature on that agreement legally binding? Should I tell my father what I now understood about his dwindling pension funds? Perhaps I had to find an estate lawyer to help me think through my dilemma. Did I know anyone who could help me? Whom could I trust?

Gloria placed her hand on my arm. She asked, "Harvy, are you okay?"

I turned to her and gave a partial answer. "I just realized that when my father gave most of his pension money to Elaine, it now complicates other things in his estate."

She sighed. "Harvy! Don't think about that now. Go back to sleep."

"You're right, honey." I reached over and kissed her. I lay back down beside her and closed my eyes. But I wasn't able to return to slumber.

* * *

In April '95, Dad returned from wintering at his Boca Raton home. Edo and a Hungarian couple—friends of Dad's—had stayed there too. The wife, Edna, cooked for them. The husband, Billy, a sports therapist, helped Dad every day with his physical therapy. Billy also chauffeured the group around town when needed. Because of Dad's crowded Florida house, I visited him only once that winter. While I was there, he told me, "I'm going to put the house up for sale."

I was shocked and saddened about Dad letting go of that large three-bedroom Royal Palms ranch with its orange and grapefruit trees. Dad had had many birthday parties there, with rich Hungarian food and lively Eastern European musicians. I asked him, "After all the work you've done here, why do you want to leave?"

His voice was firm but subdued. "I found a smaller three-bedroom condo in Deerfield; it's on Hillsboro Mile, right on the beach. And it will cost me only half of what I can get for the Boca property. It'll be easier and cheaper for me to maintain." His eyes turned down. "And it won't remind me of Elaine."

I nodded my understanding.

Dad changed the subject. "For now, Billy is giving me therapy every day while we are still here in Boca. We work together in the pool, in the house, and while walking on the street. He said I'd be as good as new by the end of the winter."

With Billy's help, Dad walked a little more assuredly with his cane. He now lifted instead of dragged his afflicted leg, and he could employ his left arm and hand a bit more fluently. My father's Montreal friends would later notice how much he had improved, yet he still seemed far from 100%.

A couple of weeks after Dad had returned from Florida, I visited him in his Montreal office. He was dismayed. He handed me a document and exclaimed. "I housed and fed Billy and Edna the whole winter. Now the guy sends me a big bill for his daily therapy services."

I glanced at the invoice. It showed an amount due of $5000 for the over three months they had worked together. "What was your arrangement with Billy?"

"I was going to give them a place to stay during the winter, and he was going to give me physical therapy."

"Did you put that in writing?"

Dad shook his head.

"Can you tell him that you are surprised by his bill, that you understood that this was a quid pro quo?"

Dad took the invoice from my hand and placed it onto a tray on his desk. "It's okay, son. I'll handle it."

I wasn't sure what he had in mind. "Would you like me to call Billy?"

He shook his head. "No, it's okay. He's a friend; I don't want to upset him."

"What if you send his bill back with a note saying you're charging him and his wife the same amount, or even half of it, for their room and board?"

Dad shook his head again. He didn't say anything more.

From what I later learned from Rob, Dad paid Billy the total amount. But Dad never again received physiotherapy from the guy nor allowed him and his wife to stay the winter *chez* Dad.

I wondered if such vague money arrangements were becoming a sign of things to come with my declining businessman father.

* * *

A couple of months later, Geoff Levi returned to JHS for another end-of-year financial review of JHS. After the sale of the Peru house, the company had accumulated $175,000 of tax-free cash in its Corporate Dividend Account. (That account represented half of the house's capital gain that was not subject to income tax.) Dad wanted to take that cash out of the company for himself, something he could legitimately do as the controlling shareholder.

As I had hoped in such situations, Geoff talked to me beforehand. "Harvy, there are two ways your father can remove that cash from JHS." My friend was his monotone self. "The first way is for him to take a dividend against his one million preferred shares. Doing it that way would leave his preferred share-value intact—he'd still own a million shares."

I was a bit confused. "So what's the problem with my father doing that? He's allowed to take dividends on his preferred shares."

"There's no problem, Harvy. But there's another way to do it that would be more advantageous to you and your brother."

"Okay..." I didn't know where he was going.

"Your father can instead redeem $175,000 against his preferred shares and be left with 825,000 shares instead of his original million."

"So, what's the difference?"

Geoff spoke softly. "Think about it in the long run. If he does it the first way, he'll remain with more shares in the company. When the day comes that he passes away, the whole $1,000,000 will be taxable in his estate. But if he does it the second way, then he'll have only $825,000 that is taxable."

"Okay, I get it. The second way will keep more assets in JHS when he dies, which then increases the value of Steve's and my shares in JHS."

Geoff nodded. "That's exactly right. His estate, too, would save taxes when he dies, about $90,000. That money will remain in JHS rather than go to Revenue Canada via your father's estate." He looked at me. "So, how do you think we should approach your father about this?"

I thought for a moment. "Let's be open and straight with him. Explain it both ways, and then tell him you'd recommend the second way because it keeps more money in the company for the future."

Geoff came back as if he had already had that answer in his head. "I can accept that, Harvy. Your father structured the company years ago so that its accumulating profits would go to you and your brother. If he went the route of declaring a dividend, he'd be defeating his original purpose. The second way will defer the tax into the future until you and Steve sell or redeem your shares." His lips formed a smile. "And it's always good to defer taxes."

"Right, Geoff. That makes sense."

A week later, Dad, Steve, Geoff, Rob, and I were in the office. Geoff explained the situation to Dad precisely the way he and I had discussed it. Even Steve nodded his understanding and approval.

I don't know if my father misunderstood or thought something was happening behind his back, for he was skeptical. "I don't want to reduce my shareholdings," he gruffly stammered. "Make the withdrawal a dividend."

Geoff explained it again, but my father's eyes turned glassy as if the explanation had gone over his head. Geoff pivoted to other subjects on his agenda, and Dad didn't mention the dividend issue again.

Toward the end of the meeting, Dad and Rob got busy preparing cheques to the government, signing JHS's income tax returns, and giving Dad a cheque for $175,000. In that lull, Geoff gravitated toward my brother and me. His face showed concern. "What do you two think about this dividend to your father? I don't think he fully understands the implications."

Steve and I glanced at each other and then looked back at Geoff. I spoke softly. "If Steve agrees, we can do it the way you recommended."

Steve asked, "Does our father have to put his signature on the share redemption?"

Geoff looked at both of us. "No, we don't need a signature. But he'll eventually see the reduction in his shares in next year's JHS statements and this year's corporate minutes. We'd also have to direct your company's lawyer to make those adjustments in the corporate books."

From the time Dad and Mack had a falling out regarding Dad's divorce settlement, Mack no longer worked for JHS. At the recommendation of a close business friend, our father allowed Steve and me to interview and hire a new corporate lawyer, Sam. He, like Geoff, was about our age.

I turned to Geoff and continued talking in a low tone. "Steve and I can tell Sam to accept your instructions on the shares. And I don't know if Dad looks carefully at those tax statements and corporate minutes anymore." I repeated, "Let's then do it the way you recommended."

Steve nodded and said, "Okay."

"Then it's agreed," Geoff said.

This situation marked the first time that these sons of Johnny worked to overturn a financial decision that our father had made. Then again, did our father make his choice with complete understanding? He didn't seem to grasp the reality of what he was doing. Dad's decision would undercut his purpose in passing JHS's assets to Steve and me in the most tax-efficient way.

I was grateful that my accounting friend was here to guide us through the transaction. I felt the three of us had done the right thing, but I remained uneasy about Dad finding out.

Dad did find out what Geoff and we had done. He called another accountant—an older guy named Pierre—for an opposing opinion. For many years, Pierre had pursued Dad for JHS's accounting business.

Months after our gathering with Geoff, I was again visiting Dad at JHS. He showed me a letter that Pierre had written. The letter rambled about how my father had had another choice in taking his $175,000 tax-free dividend from the company. It said that Dad didn't have to reduce his share ownership. Pierre didn't say that what Geoff had done was incorrect or wrong. He only said that Dad had had another option.

After I had finished reading Pierre's letter, I looked at my father. "Dad, the way we did it was the best way in the long run. There'll be less tax to pay on your estate when you pass away."

Dad wasn't listening. "Geoff didn't do his job!" he bellowed. "I fired him, and Pierre is now JHS's accountant."

I couldn't believe it. Our father's move seemed irrational. The very first time that Steve and I flexed our biceps with the company's finances, Dad put a pin into them to show that kid balloons were all we had. *Son-of-a-bitch!*

I repeated my rationale, but Dad stopped listening. He said nothing about Steve or me working in cahoots with Geoff. Dad had consummated the deed of firing Geoff and hiring Pierre; I couldn't sway him otherwise.

I called Geoff later. "I'm sorry, I had no idea my father would pull something like that. He's not been thinking straight since his stroke and divorce from Elaine." I took a breath. "But I promise that when Steve and I have full control of the company, you'll be back at JHS."

Geoff's attitude was philosophical. "I've seen stuff like this before in family businesses. I'm sorry he did what he did, but that doesn't change anything. While he's alive, your father has control."

Dad continued to squeeze his sons' *yaytsa* concerning JHS. From then on, Steve and I were no longer privy to the company's annual financial review. He and Pierre conducted everything in private, and Pierre never suggested that Steve and I should attend. Our father, in effect, had banished us from what he had always called "our company." Perhaps he was now doing to us what he had perceived our having done to him with Geoff.

Dad's message was clear: JHS was his and only his until the day he died. He did offer, "JHS's annual statements are in the cabinet in my office. You two can look at them anytime you want." But Steve and I knew that the statements were only a summary of the company's financial condition, with little detail about how Dad was spending or placing the company's assets.

Steve and I later conferred. "Son-of-a-bee," I said, trying not to swear in front of my devout brother. "Dad has, in effect, marginalized us from his holding company."

"Yes," my brother said, his tone subdued. "There's nothing we can do."

Steve and I figured our father was trying to bring a sense of control back into his life after losing Elaine. Our only consolation was that Dad couldn't reverse his preferred share reduction that we enacted the previous year. Steve and I would have a bit more to our name when our day came, as long as Dad didn't squander the company's assets.

To Steve's and my benefit, Dad no longer took income from JHS—he didn't need to because of his many deferred annuities. He also continued to bestow year-end bonuses to Steve and me, thus not cutting us off completely.

My brother and I were unanimous once more. Whether Pierre had been doing Dad's bidding or leveraging himself into our father's favour, his days as JHS's accountant would end the moment our father no longer had control. My brother and I agreed unequivocally that we now had a common enemy.

* * * *

Always More to the Story

I didn't see or talk to Elaine again until years after my father's passing. I figured it was time to let go of my resentment toward her—she had always been good to me. My beef had been squarely on Dad for his foolishness.

One of Elaine's friends gave me her email address. I contacted her, and she and I started trading messages for holidays and birthdays. I told her about my young kids, and she asked questions about them. I asked her about her life and her real estate business in Boca. After a couple of years of back and forth, I asked to interview her for my memoir. I told her, "I want to get the story straight from you rather than guess at what I don't know."

After a few days, I got a message back. "Okay, Harvy. But are you sure you want to go there? Those were senseless and hurtful times."

I wrote back. "You can tell me as much or as little as you want. There's probably nothing you'd say about my father that would surprise me."

She emailed back, "Okay, Harvy. I'm game if you are."

When I next visited Florida, she and I spent a few hours together in her new Boca Raton abode. She hugged and kissed me as if the nearly fifteen-year gap in our lives had never existed. She looked as young as I had remembered her, and I could still see what attracted my father to her. Her handsome face, round cheeks, sculpted hair, and well-proportioned body would turn the head of any high roller.

Elaine's Boca home was even more modern and stylish than the one she and Dad had had in Florida. The house sported high ceilings, black and white furniture, and lacquered cabinets, making it look like a model home. I exclaimed, "Wow!" around every corner.

As she showed another room, she offered, "As a part of my real estate business, I buy a new house every few years in order to renovate and redecorate it." She swept her arm around like a Vanna White. "This place will be ready to be put back onto the market within another year. I'll sell it for a profit and then start over again with a new place. It's my way of building my nest egg."

Elaine had always been an intelligent business lady, and she never hung onto anything past its time. I did wonder why she felt she had to work so hard. As far as I knew, she had no dependents. After three unsuccessful marriages, perhaps life fiercely drove her to stay independent of any man.

Elaine poured two glasses of wine. She smiled. "We'll probably need this for our chat."

I smiled back. "You're probably right; let's keep the bottle close."

We sat on two high-back leather chairs separated by a small round table. The chairs stood askew, so Elaine and I didn't have to face each other directly. She asked about Gloria, having last seen her at our wedding reception. My ex-stepmother had myriad questions about our kids (we now had a daughter along with our son), my consulting work, and even my brother and his family who still lived in Montreal.

I turned the conversation to the old Peru house, a place she had enjoyed with my father. I told her I had driven by it recently during one of my trips to Montreal from Boston. I said, "It looks the same as when you and Dad lived there." I added that the new owner, Greg Mann, had built a new two-floor bungalow adjacent to the main house. That bungalow matched the exterior of the original home.

She grinned. "So, I guess we now know what Mr. Mann did with the granite he stockpiled for years after your father and I had stolen that house from under his nose."

She turned to me, her face serious. "You know, Harvy, your father shouldn't have sold his Boca ranch house. That gated community is prime property. It would have been worth a lot more today."

"Yes, I miss that place too." I didn't tell her that Dad sold that house because he didn't want it reminding him of her. He might have gone mad if he had had to see those decorated walls and black-and-white furniture every winter for the rest of his life. Then again, perhaps he had gone crazy, his stroke having precipitated that madness.

I asked her, "How did you and my father originally get together?" Though I had known much of the story, I was seeking additional nuances. I was also looking for a comfortable place to start before I got to more challenging parts of our conversation.

Elaine recounted how Dad's companion, Albert Vidor, had introduced her to Dad when she worked as a real estate agent in Champlain, NY. "That Vidor tried to pull a fast one on your father," she said, her voice a bit curt. "He told Johnny that a large NY State property I had shown them was subdividable when it wasn't."

She took a long breath. "After I called your father to warn him about not making a big mistake with that place, he asked me out for supper in Montreal." She looked away and then back toward me. "I didn't know he was still married to your mother. He hid that fact and his wedding ring from me."

A twinkle came to her eye. "I make it a rule not to date my clients, but this time I made an exception." She looked right at me. "Did you know that I was thirty-four years old when I met your father, and he was twenty-four years older than me?"

I nodded. Though Elaine was attractive, she was way too intense for my taste. I enjoyed her company and zeal, but her perpetual propensity to fill a conversational void could wear down an introverted guy like me.

I surmised my father had been worn down by her, especially after his stroke, possibly as much as she had felt worn down by him. I remembered many a family supper gathering where Dad stayed silent as Elaine talked about everything and nothing. I admired that quality in her, to make something interesting out of the mundane, but it also felt overwhelming. Maybe, in the end, my Slavic father felt overpowered by her and tried to reclaim his alpha dog status by leaving her. But his need to dominate worked to his detriment.

Elaine added, "Well, Harvy, you probably know the rest of the story. When I found out he was married—nearly a year after we had met!—I was livid and cut off contact with him." Her voice was hard and matter-of-fact.

"Many months later, he asked his long-time friends, Aras and Celia, to call me to have supper with them. When I arrived, your father was there."

Her voice softened. "After supper, Johnny said that he wanted us to get back together and that he was going to leave your mother." She took a breath. "I told him he could contact me when all that was behind him."

She looked away. "Then, in August of 1980, without any warning, he was at my doorstep telling me he was out of your mother's home and wanting to move in. He got his lawyer, Mack, on his car phone to convince me to take him in." She took a long breath. "Your father certainly had his ways to get what he wanted."

He certainly did! Dad's manipulative methods could make one put aside common sense.

I nodded. I then summoned my courage and asked my most pressing question, the one that had changed everything for my father. "Why did you, in the end, not get back with him after the lawyers completed your financial settlement?"

She didn't hesitate. "Harvy, I could no longer deal with your father's lies and abusiveness." She turned to look directly at me. "It came to the point that if he said that it was raining outside, I'd have to go to the window, pull the curtain, and check for myself." She lifted her wine glass. "My mother had an expression for it. 'You can watch a thief, even a drunk, but you can't watch a liar.' Boy, did that prove right!"

Elaine took a long sip of her wine and leaned back in her chair. "To be honest, I had intended to let him return after we had completed our financial arrangement. However, after we signed our deal, I woke the next morning and asked myself, 'After seventeen years of mistreatment, could I continue to live with that man?'"

I nodded again. Elaine didn't need to explain further. Whether she dumped my father at the last minute or not, I understood what she had said and done. (I also wished my mother could have done the same, but her love and dependency had blinded her senses.) I, too, had felt my father's money manipulations, though I had kept his offshore shenanigans a secret and had gone along willingly.

Elaine's eyes intensified. "Did you know that through our financial negotiations with Reemer and Mack, your father had the gall to foreclose on the house I was living in?"

"What do you mean, Elaine? Didn't he own that house?"

She pointed to herself. "No, both your father and I legally owned it, though he had paid for it."

That was the first I had heard of that. Dad had told me that he had bought and owned their West Island Montreal house outright.

Elaine's voice elevated as she continued. "But then he took a mortgage from JHS on nearly the full value of the house so that JHS could have a lien on the property. At one point, when your father wasn't getting his way in our financial negotiations, I received a 'love letter' from Mack. It was a foreclosure notice from JHS. It demanded that I vacate the premises."

Her voice rose. "I couldn't believe your father was throwing me out of my house. I was livid. I called Johnny and screamed bloody murder at him. I told him that if he wants to negotiate in good faith, he'll have to keep his *schmack* lawyer out of it."

Her voice calmed. "I had to put my foot down with that man, or he'd walk all over me. I wasn't going to be an 'ova.'"

I became confused. I offered, "I understand that 'ova' is Slavic for 'Mrs.' In Eastern Europe, people called my mother 'Anna Simkovitsova' when she was married to my father. So I'm not sure I fully get your reference."

"Harvy, to Slavic men *'ova'* really means 'owned by' or 'property of.'" She kept up her pace. "Unfortunately, your mother had been raised during such times in Eastern Europe. She had lived that way with your father, but I wasn't raised that way." She pointed to herself. "I was no one's property that could just be used up or thrown out."

I looked away, allowing the kicked-up dust of our interchange to settle. Elaine was right about my mother. And the woman across from me wasn't a serve-your-master *ova*.

I certainly had no desire for my wife to be my 'ova.' Gloria and I both worked and contributed to our household, sharing in the chores and child-rearing. Not everything had to be perfectly equal. She liked to do more of the cooking while I preferred to clean up and put things away. She did the laundry while I did the regular repair work in and around our home. We each changed diapers and fed our young kids, and we each read them bedtime stories on alternate nights. I didn't want my parents' relationship where the dad slogged away at work all day and entertained customers by night, and the mom cooked, cleaned, and took care of the kids by day and then served her man when he came home.

Elaine continued as if she could talk forever. "There was one time when your father and I were vacationing in Dubrovnik, Croatia, on the Adriatic Sea. It was when we travelled a lot, before he had his stroke. We were sitting by the hotel pool, your father reading a Slavic newspaper." She raised her arms. "A big tour bus came rolling into the resort." She held those arms forward as if she were mimicking my father's head buried in a newspaper. She then raised her head and pointed upward. "Your father looked up and saw these older ladies walk off the bus. He then turned to me and said, 'Look at those rich bitches.'"

Elaine's head jerked back as if Dad had struck her in the face with his remark. "I was surprised by what he had said. I asked him, 'What do you mean by that, Johnny?'"

She turned my way. "He looked at me and said, 'Those old bitches outlive their husbands and then spend the rest of their lives feeding off their money.'"

Elaine's eyes opened wide and were intense. "I couldn't believe what he was saying." Her head cocked forward as she pointed a finger. "I gave him a piece of my mind, saying, 'Now, Johnny, how could you say that. If those husbands had taken better care of themselves, then they'd be here too. Don't you think those older women would have loved having their spouses with them?'"

She threw her hand in the air. "Your father grunted and went back to reading his paper." She pointed to me again. "He was a man of his Eastern European heritage. There was little anyone, even I, could do to change what his culture had embedded deeply inside him. I loved him dearly, but I felt I was fighting a losing battle."

I nodded again. What Elaine had seen as "helping Johnny change for the better," my dad saw as "she's trying to control me."

Elaine shifted conversation gears like the professional car racer she had once been. "You know I was there at the hospital when your dad was dying."

"Yes, I heard something about that." Dad's last partner, Suzie, had told me that she had walked into Dad's hospital room one morning to find Elaine there with my father.

After his divorce from Elaine, Dad had found Suzie, a kind and caring woman. They lived together for nearly five years until Dad became hospitalized with a fatal illness. I didn't know many details about how Dad and Suzie had gotten together, except they knew each other from the Montreal Slovak Church. I also knew that Suzie was a French Canadian, widowed after a long marriage to her Slovak husband. Being very attached to their church, she volunteered at and cooked for church events.

Elaine continued. "One morning, I tried to sneak in-and-out of Johnny's hospital room. Remember when you emailed me to say that your father was usually alone in his room at that time of day. I wanted to say goodbye before he passed away."

"Okay," I said. I hardly remembered that request and was glad I had avoided being there during a potentially awkward moment between two of Dad's women.

"You know, Harvy, Suzie would be welcome in my home. I have no grudges against her. She had nothing to do with the demise of my marriage to your father."

Elaine took one of her rare breaths. "Suzie and I met only that one time, and our interaction wasn't confrontational. Anyway, she would have known I had visited Johnny, for I had left many photographs with him. I had albums of your family (you, Steve, the grandchildren—happier times) that I had stored in my mother's basement. I put some of the pictures in frames and placed them in his room and on his bedside tray." She raised a hand. "Your father also loved red roses. I picked up a vase of them at the hospital florist and put them on a side table in his room."

"I remembered seeing those flowers by Dad's bedside," I said.

She didn't lose a beat. "I was glad I visited. I showed Johnny the photos and talked about old times. He was still coherent; it gave him good thoughts!"

Elaine looked away and then back at me. "Then Suzie walked in as I was getting ready to leave. I don't know if she knew who I was because we had never met. She came up to me and said quietly, 'Do you know who I am?'"

Elaine pointed to herself, opened her eyes wide, raised her voice a tad, leaned forward, and pointed to herself. "I looked right back at her and said, 'Do *you* know who *I* am?'" She then chuckled.

Elaine leaned back once more. "That was all we said to each other before I retrieved my things and walked out of that room. I never saw your father or Suzie again."

Once again, Elaine proved she was no shrinking "ova." I felt overwhelmed by her force. She seldom was the first to wear down in a conversation.

I chose not to say anything about Suzie unless Elaine asked me, which she didn't. I didn't ask her about her third marriage and divorce in Vancouver before she departed Canada for Florida. I didn't want to stir our whole messy family pot in one sitting.

My ex-stepmother looked my way and shifted gears once more. "After your father had retired in '84, he started to let himself go. He slowly lost control of his waistline. I tried to help him, preparing the right foods, watching what he ordered at restaurants, but he resisted my suggestions." She smirked as she pointed to herself. "He called my salads 'food for rabbits.'"

I didn't say that my father's chronic complaints about her had increased with his waistline, especially after their marriage in '88. There was no sense wading through the dirt that should remain in his grave.

She continued. "Johnny tried to get back into shape, but it was a constant battle. There was one time when we went to the Snowdon Deli, near where we lived. He was working to be good—he ordered only the chicken soup. When the waiter came with a big stack of rye bread, I told the guy to take it away. But your father batted his hand and said, 'It's okay; let him leave it there; I won't touch it.' Your father didn't, and I was impressed.

"However, when I went to pay the bill at the register with your father's credit card, I looked back at our table. Johnny was stuffing that bread into his jacket pockets." She mimicked my father by grabbing pretend bread in front of her and pocketing it into an imaginary jacket.

Her eyes appeared incredulous when she added, "I couldn't believe what he was doing. I went back to the table and told him, 'Johnny, you're only fooling yourself.' He looked like a kid with his hand in his mother's baking pantry." She shook her head. "He never heeded my words."

I nodded again. Many times, Dad had said one thing but done another.

She took another breath. "But everything changed when Johnny had his stroke in '93. After that, he always asked me at restaurants, 'Sweetheart, can I eat this? Darling, can I eat that?' He had never gotten to know what was healthy for him, and now he was desperately trying to make up for his failings. Even though he tried to watch himself, it was too late; the damage was done."

"Yes, I know. Dad was a stubborn man and set in his ways."

I turned toward her and summoned my courage. "You know, Elaine. No woman, not even my mother, ever got as much money from my father as you got from him."

She stopped in her tracks for a long second. Then she looked at me. "But what I received was small compared to what your father had owned."

Her statement shook me. "What do you mean, Elaine?"

She raised her hand but not her voice. "Once in a while, your father bragged to his friends that he had thirty to thirty-five million stashed here and there, and he was looking for good investments." Her voice was straight and true. "He could easily afford what I had asked and gotten from him."

I knew better. "No way, Elaine! What you are saying of his wealth is many times more than what he had had. He was a bragger. He once told me that your Peru house was worth two million when what he later got was only a third of that, the furniture included."

She paused, her eyes focused on me. "Oh, I didn't know."

My curiosity kept me going. "Dad had told Steve and me that you and he had had a prenuptial agreement that stated what you would have gotten if he left you."

Her eyes stayed fixed on me as her voice rose a few decibels. "That's the first I've heard of that! We had no prenup when we married." Her voice was steady. "I was still working back then, making a good living. There was nothing I wanted from your father until he asked me to curtail my career and be full-time with him."

I took a breath. "That would explain a lot," I said, holding back my surprise. "Dad had said that you and he had had a prenup, but we never found such an agreement among his personal papers." I spoke softly, trying to be gracious. "I guess you weren't the only one who needed to look behind the curtain to see if it was raining outside when my father said so."

Dad's bragging about his bigger-than-real wealth cut back on him with Elaine. No wonder she had pushed for a settlement that amounted to perhaps one year's interest on his self-aggrandized assets. Though I had been displeased that Elaine had received so much money from my father, maybe she deserved the pounds of cash she had carved out of him. I admired this lady for giving Johnny Simkovits a taste of his stinking Hungarian salami. It was something that Mom, Steve, or I couldn't have done.

Elaine looked at me and changed the topic once more. "What happened to your father's brother, Edo?" Did he go back to Slovakia to be with Eboya?"

I pointed upward. "Edo was a saint during the fifteen months after Dad had left you. He went with Dad to live in a retirement residence near JHS's old factory office. Those two were joined at the hip until Edo went back to Slovakia at the end of '95, about six months after you and Dad had officially divorced."

I didn't say that Suzie moved in with my father on the same day Edo had returned to Slovakia. Dad couldn't fend for himself without being attached to a woman. The Montreal Slovak Church offered widow possibilities, which might say something about longevity of Slavic men.

I knew little about Dad and Suzie's courtship other than his mentioning her to me while we talked during one of our regular Sunday evening calls. I met her only after she had moved into his assisted living residence. What I did know was that, once Suzie accepted Dad's offer to live together, Edo was happy to be dismissed from his duties of attending to his brother.

"So Edo and Eboya are doing okay?" she asked.

"Yes, as far as I know. The summer after Dad had died, Gloria, our son, and I visited him, among seeing my other family in Košice." I grinned. "Eboya made us a scrumptious chicken paprikash."

Elaine smiled. "That Eboya was always a good cook." She stood, walked over to another table, and brought back a book. "When I came down here to Boca, I joined a women's group. We created this recipe book. I contributed a few of your father and Eboya's Slovak and Hungarian dishes."

"Yes, Dad had been an excellent cook."

His cooking could rival any high-end establishment. Every friend who devoured a Johnny Simkovits meal said he should open a restaurant in

Montreal. My father always retorted, "I'd go bust if I did that. I buy the best, most expensive meats and ingredients for my cooking, and I spend a long time preparing. That's no way to do business, only pleasure."

Elaine continued. "The proceeds from the sale of these cookbooks go to a women's shelter down here in South Florida." She put the book into my hand. "Here, take this copy."

"Thanks, Elaine," I said, taking the book. I paged through it and spotted one of my father's recipes. "It's good you wrote this down. Dad only cooked via memory."

"Yes, I stood beside him in the kitchen many times, trying to gather how much of this ingredient and that spice he put into his dishes." She smiled. "He got annoyed at my asking him, again and again, what he exactly meant by a 'pinch' or 'dash.'"

"I'll take it home and show Gloria," I said. "We'll do a Hungarian night for our friends." My wife and I occasionally made Hungarian *lecso* meals. Our kids also enjoyed those dishes, soaking up the sauces with deli rye bread.

I took a big breath. "There's one other thing about Edo." My eyes looked down at the floor. "I felt my father never appreciated the sacrifices his brother had made for him." I tapped my hands on the arms of the chair. "Dad didn't leave anything in his will for Edo. Both Steve and I were bothered by that." I took a breath. "To make it up to Edo, we told him Dad left him money, to be paid annually for the rest of his life."

Elaine's eyes glanced away and then came back. "It seems your father hurt those who loved and cared about him the most."

I nodded. "Yes, that's right." *And you hardly know the half of it!*

I raised my empty wine glass and pointed it toward Elaine. "I guess it's time for a little more of this. Where's that bottle?"

Though a part of me had been curious, I never did and never would ask Elaine about her knowledge of my father's offshore affairs. I assumed she had been in the dark about Dad's personal Cayman corporation and his money "over there" in Luxembourg. I preferred not to know what she knew, how, or when. I'd never want to implicate her in any way.

* * *

A few years later, after more visits to Elaine's home, more glasses of chardonnay, and emails back and forth about my father, Elaine emailed me unexpectedly. "Harvy, I've been thinking about it. I'll soon be in the process of rewriting my will. I've decided to put you and Steve into it."

I was well enough off financially that I didn't expect anything from her.

I wrote her back. "That's very nice of you, Elaine, but you don't have to feel obliged."

I was speaking for myself. Let my brother talk for himself, though Elaine hadn't copied him in her email.

Tongue in cheek, I added, "Before you make that gift, you might want to read my memoir about my father. ☺"

Over the ensuing years, I sent Elaine sections of my manuscript. I wanted her input regarding what I might have missed, and I figured she wanted to know what I went through with my father. In the middle of her reading, she emailed again. "Okay, I'm working on my will now. I want to put your kids into it. Can you give me their full names?"

I emailed her back: "So kind of you, Elaine. But before you do, can we meet for dinner and talk about it when I'm next in Florida? I'll be down there soon for quiet time to write and to get out of our chilly Boston weather."

Boston had a more temperate climate than Montreal. But as I got older, my adopted hometown started to feel less warm. Annual winter trips to Florida became one of my pastimes, as it had been when Dad had his house in Boca and subsequent condo in Deerfield.

Elaine and I met for dinner at the Sea Watch restaurant by the ocean in Pompano, a place my father had enjoyed. I told her. "If something would happen to you sooner than later, I don't think my kids are yet old enough to be responsible with any large sum of money."

I asked her to make her bequest to my irrevocable trust, where Gloria and the kids were my beneficiaries. I smiled. "And I do hope you are around a long time to come. Who else can tell me so many stories about my father?"

She responded right away. "Okay, Harvy, email me the particulars. I'll make the bequest to your kids via your trust. It would make me feel good to give them something."

"So kind of you, Elaine," I said. And it was.

More years later, after reading more of my book chapters, Elaine wrote me a series of emails.

> I'm sleeplessly walking the floors tonight after reading what you wrote about those last months of your father and me, and how it all transpired. You don't have it straight, and I feel like I'm reliving the audacity of that man."

I was taken aback by Elaine's forcefulness, the first time that I felt the brunt of her indignation. I read on quickly.

> That day your father left me, the papers I got from his lawyer stated I had to hire an attorney and have them enter a Notice of Appearance on my behalf within 72 hours. I didn't have an attorney, nor had I spoken to one, but I now had to get one. I started calling friends to see who they could recommend. I hired someone within two days.
>
> On that day your father left, one of the legal papers I received had Mack's imprint. Mack had orchestrated the whole thing, an opportunity for that man to take megabuck fees once more from your father. If Mack had been a good friend, he would have counselled your dad to stay in the marriage. He wouldn't have put Johnny in the position (as sick and lame as he was) of spending months in that hotel suite and then living in an assisted-living place with Edo.

Mack seemed to have been the facilitator of both the beginning and end of Dad and Elaine's not-quite-made-in-heaven union. My mother had held similar opinions about the lawyer. Perhaps she and Elaine didn't realize how much Mack was just a reflection of Johnny.

Elaine's note continued.

> While the lawyers worked out our divorce settlement, I continued to take your father to doctor appointments (when he called me) and out to supper. When he said he had rented the assisted-living apartment near JHS, I offered to give him the furniture in our den, including the lazy boy chairs, TV, entertainment centre, and even his grandfather clock. But he had already bought furniture for his apartment through a business friend. He had me come to his new place after the furniture was delivered. I brought him dishes, pots, pans, etc.

The mess went on for months.........then, suddenly, Johnny was flying with Edo to our house in Florida. His Hungarian masseur, Billy, would stay with him down there and already had left Montreal, driving down with his wife. They were to pick up Johnny and Edo at the Fort Lauderdale airport. I had to go to Johnny's apartment to pack his clothes. And I made sure his and Edo's passports were in order, along with their travel papers. For months that man screamed "bitch" at me in one conversation then called me "sweetheart" in the next........

Johnny called from Florida regularly, and he wanted me to go down there. My Montreal lawyer advised me not to. Anyway, Johnny already had three people there taking care of him. When he came back in April, I was once again his chauffeur to doctors, out to supper, etc.

I held my breath, and my heart beat hard for the nuttiness that had transpired. I kept on reading.

I was slowly becoming a basket case!! Whenever the lawyers thought they had a financial deal between us, Johnny changed his mind and wouldn't sign. One day my attorney called to say we would be signing at Maury Reemer's office. Off we went to meet Johnny, his attorney, and Maury. When the lawyers placed the settlement papers in front of him for his signature, he stood and started screaming again. 'You bitch...all you want is my money!!'

I immediately got up to leave. Johnny then said, 'Where are you going?' I replied, 'I'm not paying an attorney $350 per hour to sit here and listen to this.' We walked out, much to his amazement. After that, we got nothing signed for months.

When the day came when we finally signed the divorce papers, I decided to sell the Montreal house and move to Vancouver for a year. I had a girlfriend there, and I felt I needed to get the peace I wouldn't get in Montreal. Also, I had 19 years in Quebec but needed a full 20 years working in Canada to collect my Canadian pension in the U.S.

> I didn't tell your father I was moving, but I did call him to ask if I could send him his grandfather clock. He said, "No, keep it at the house." So I moved it to Vancouver, along with my other things. When he found out, he called and screamed at me for taking his clock. I said, 'Johnny, I've offered that clock to you on two different occasions. If you want it, I'll ship it to you at your expense,'.....which is what I did.

I hadn't known that Dad and Elaine had still seen each other throughout their separation and divorce proceedings. I did know that those times had been senseless, but they had been even crazier than I had imagined. I emailed her back:

> Thank you, Elaine, for enlightening me. I certainly want to capture those events as accurately, completely, and honestly as possible. I'm sorry that my writings have kept you up at night.

After reading about what Dad had told me concerning their Florida rendezvous, Elaine sent me another email. I was glad her tone was a bit more subdued.

> I had met your father only once in Florida while he was living in his Deerfield condo.
>
> Our friend, Jane, called me one day to say your father wanted to meet me for lunch and whether I'd agree to meet. Her husband, Walter, would pick Johnny up and bring him to their house where I could rendezvous with him. After numerous invites, I finally agreed.
>
> Your father must have told Suzie that Walter was taking him to his bank in Miami. He certainly didn't tell her he was stealing away to have lunch with me............
>
> When I went to their house, I asked Jane to join us. She asked, 'Are you sure?' I responded, 'Yes, Jane, I have nothing to hide, and there isn't anything you don't know about this relationship!' So I drove us to the Radisson Bridge Hotel, next to the Intracoastal. He didn't bring any gifts, nor did he stash any money in my pocket!

> At one point, I told Johnny, 'You'd better be careful. Suzie could claim support from you down the road now that you're living common-law.'
>
> He had that figured out. He replied, 'Oh no; I give Suzie a cheque every week, and I write 'housekeeping' on it!'

My father worked every legal angle with his women, anting a devoted partner but no strings attached. My mother would have turned in her grave in knowing his callousness, but I supposed she already had.

Elaine went on.

> Going back to Maury Reemer, after the divorce papers had been signed and filed, Johnny called him one day from the office. He told Maury that he wanted me back, and he asked what would be the financial consequences if we got back together.
>
> Reemer was a little surprised (needless to say, since I had been 'the bitch' to him for many months). He told your father that the government would probably look at our divorce as a means of transferring his pension assets to his wife without paying any income tax. Johnny would probably have to pay the taxes due at the time of distribution, plus any penalties. Your father asked him how much that would be. Reemer said he'd figure it out and call back. I was there with your father, listening to the entire conversation.
>
> Reemer called back shortly afterward. This time, I didn't hear what Maury said, but your father's loud reply was, 'I don't care how much it is. I'll pay for it. I want her back!' Needless to say, that didn't happen after what he had put me through; .... there was no more trust in our relationship.

I felt the loss of what could have been between those two had Dad given Elaine what little she had wanted from the beginning. Instead, Dad dug a deeper financial grave for himself regarding his onshore money.

Later that same day, after having read more of my manuscript, Elaine wrote once more.

> I want you to be clear, Harvy. It was your father who had served me with divorce papers. He pursued that action for many months until he found himself defeated. He realized he could not walk away from our marriage without settling with me financially in some fashion. It was only at that point that he wanted me back.
>
> And I almost went back to him. I felt sorry for him, and I had married him until death do us part. I think I regained some direction in a conversation with one of his Slovak friends who said, 'Elaine, now that Johnny has to settle with you, he'll try indirectly to get his money back. It's like buying a pair of shoes that are uncomfortable but aren't returnable, so what do you do? You put them on your feet and wear them anyway.' He was right! Your father would scheme again!
>
> I don't know if I ever told you. Near the beginning of the divorce action, Johnny said I'd never get a dime from him. He said he'd go back to Slovakia, where I could never pursue any legal action against him. I was so convinced he would (since he had Emilia and Igor over there) that my attorney utilized her connections to check the passenger manifest each week on the one direct weekly flight from Montreal Mirabel Airport to Prague!

I was dumbfounded. Elaine's story reminded me of something my brother had once said, "Beware the wolf in sheep's clothing." Perhaps Steve had been referring to Dad, but Elaine was no lamb the way my mother had been.

The next day brought more recollections from my ex-stepmother. The subject line was: "How I Closed the Deal."

> Harvy:
> You have me walking the floors again tonight after reading another bunch of pages of your manuscript..........
>
> Your father had vacillated signing any agreement for months...... It was 'Yes,' 'No,' 'Yes,' 'No'......'You bitch!!' then 'Sweetheart!' I even hired an attorney in Florida to protect

my rights in that Florida house. My lawyer there filed a *lis pendens* (litigation pending) on the Boca property so that Johnny couldn't sell the house in the interim. Your father had already orchestrated his time in Florida—hiring that Hungarian masseur and his wife to spend the winter with him and Edo. Deep down, I was happy to know Johnny would be out of the snow, but I was so frustrated that he wouldn't settle with me. I had no job at that time (your father had asked me to quit), and I was struggling to pay bills, etc.

I called my Florida attorney and asked if I could be in the Boca house. He said, 'Absolutely—you have every right to be there.' So I called our close friends, Jane and Walter, and told them I was flying in, but I knew that Johnny had changed the locks. Walter told me, 'Don't bother to get a locksmith; I'll pick you up and give you a key.' After I arrived, I retrieved the mail, mostly junk, but the property's tax bill was sitting in the pile. The following day, I faxed the bill to your father's office. Within five minutes, the phone rang. He screamed at me, saying that I had no business being in his house.

I said I had every right to be there and that he should cancel his planned trip for the winter. I planned to stay put until we settled our matters. I also reminded him that I was an American citizen, that I had the right to the quiet and peaceful enjoyment of my home, and that I would have him tied up at the border if he attempted to come to Florida. He went ballistic and hung up.

Five minutes later, he called back. He was now calm and said, 'Sweetheart, please come home, and I'll sign the papers.

I wondered what my father had meant by "come home." Did he want her to come back to Montreal so he could go to Florida, or did he mean for her to go home to him?" Maybe it had been both.

Elaine's email continued.

I said, 'No, Johnny; you've said that on several occasions. I will not get on a plane and come back until I have an agreement signed by you.'

'Okay,' he said. 'Tell me what you want, and I'll sign it.'

It was nothing more than what we had discussed for several months. I sat down and wrote out the agreement in longhand, then faxed it to Johnny for his signature. He promptly signed the document and faxed it back. Within two days, I was on a plane home with the understanding that if he did not sign the official settlement this time, I would immediately fly back to Florida and leave him stranded for the winter in Montreal.

We then met once more at Reemer's office for the official signing. Johnny was calm and pleasant to everyone. Near the end of our meeting, he turned to me and said, 'Sweetheart, I have one more thing to ask you..... Will you be buried with me?'

I looked at him and said, 'Johnny, that's a ridiculous question........... You're not dying, so I'm not going to answer.'

As we stood to leave, he took my attorney's hand, kissed it, and said, 'You're a great lawyer. If I ever need one in the future, I'll hire you!'

Such memories..............as if it were yesterday!"

Once again, that finale to their divorce was news to me. I felt overwhelmed, taken to the edge of credulity. But I had no cause to doubt Elaine's words. I didn't have a curtain I could pull back to see what had actually happened between those two.

I wrote her back.

> So bizarre! Thanks for sharing your crazy memories, and I do hope you get some rest. What an unforgettable guy my dad had been! Both vivacious charmer and contemptuous bully wrapped into one.

What else could I say?

A photo of Elaine, taken about fifteen years after divorcing Johnny. She looked as good as the day they had separated in 1994.

* * * *

Part II:

Last Days of Dad

Eightieth Birthday Surprise

It was Feb 3, 2000, my father's 80th birthday. My wife, young son, and I flew into Fort Lauderdale and arrived at Dad's Deerfield Beach condo to celebrate with him. We were there with twenty-five of my father's closest Eastern European snowbird friends and former business colleagues from Montreal.

The before-party was underway when we arrived. The guests came for drinks and hors d'oeuvres before everyone headed out for a birthday supper at the upscale Gibby's of Fort Lauderdale. Gibby's was a famous Montreal restaurant with a local branch—giving the owners a business reason to head south in the winter. Everyone *chez* Dad wore their finest attire: two- and three-piece light suits for the men and either a frilly or a flowery cocktail dress for the women. Though there were many extra pounds present from years of robust appetites, everyone carried them well.

Initially, my family and I avoided those who were chatting in the living room. We strolled into the kitchen, where my father sat quietly in his regular spot at the table. He wore his old, black-and-white speckled sports jacket. It had gotten bigger on his leaner frame since the last time I saw him. *He must have lost another ten pounds this past year.*

Dad's now thinner wrist sported a multi-function Citizens digital watch that I had bought for him a year earlier. He no longer sported his gold Rolex, saying that it was too heavy to wear day-to-day. He needed a watch with multiple alarms, and I had set those alarms for him. They beeped five times a day so he could remember to take a designated rainbow assortment of medications: blood pressure, blood-thinner, anxiety-reliever, stomach-acid-preventer, stool softener, and who-knows-what-else. It was annoying to hear that Citizens beep five times a day—though its alarms did help to keep my father alive.

In an ashtray next to Dad was a smoldering, half-finished cigarette. *I can't stand that he's still smoking!* For the last number of years, Steve and I had asked him to quit, but it was no avail. He had started again after he and Elaine had split five years ago. My father couldn't stop, still puffing over a pack a day. Irrespective of all his meds, I was amazed he was still with us.

When Dad saw me, he reached for his cigarette and stubbed it out. He yelled, "Hello, sweetheart!" When I came close, he grabbed my arm firmly with his able hand and pulled me down to place a big kiss on each cheek. "Welcome to *Flor-I-da*. I'm happy to see you. Thanks so much for coming," he said. He smiled mainly from the good side of his thinner, half-sagging face.

"Hi, Dad; you're looking great!" I lied.

My father had not looked great since he had suffered his stroke seven years earlier. Two years of physical therapy and losing over thirty pounds helped him recover three-quarters of the movement he had lost in a day. He then could walk with a cane, use a fork and knife without too much trouble, and put a smile on most of his face—that is, until his marriage to Elaine ended. After that, he went on a steady decline. Year after year, Dad's muscles slumped more as he stood, and his body leaned further to one side as he walked. He dragged his bad leg behind his good one. For meals, he employed only a fork once Suzie had cut his food.

Dad grabbed my wife with his able arm. "Hello, darling," he said. He pulled her down toward his face and gave her big smooches on each cheek.

He looked at our son, pulled out a shiny U.S. dollar coin from his jacket pocket, found our four-year-old's hand, and said, "Hi there, big guy! I've been saving this for you." He put the coin in his grandson's palm, closed the boy's fingers over it, and patted his cheek. Dad grinned. "Put it into your piggy bank at home."

"Gee, thanks, Papa," our son responded with a big smile, his eyes sparkling. He gave his grandpa a peck on the cheek. Dad swung his good arm around his grandson, smothering the boy as he squirmed with delight.

Suzie stood behind Dad, her back to us, as she talked with a woman guest. When she heard Dad's big greeting, she turned around. We exchanged warm hugs and hellos. She bent down toward our son, "I have a good book for you." From the kitchen counter, she handed him a kid's picture book. Mathew took it with a big "Thank you, Suzie!" He then sat down adjacent to my father to examine his new treasures.

Suzie was a shorter, heavier-set woman than Elaine had been, though she sported a pretty face. She had short, curly blond hair that reminded me of my mother. Like my mother, Suzie was a caretaker type. She prepared supper for Dad and massaged his legs before bedtime. She wasn't a worldly, outgoing woman as Elaine was. Suzie was happy to sit at home and watch television shows with Dad until he retired for the evening.

Suzie did enjoy having me and my brother visit Florida. She had told me, "Your father goes out and does more things when you boys are around."

We all enjoyed going to our favorite waterside restaurants for the early bird specials. We also liked to ride up and down the Intracoastal Waterway on afternoon tourist boat cruises. Dad enjoyed looking at the multi-million dollar homes and expensive boats of rich people, perhaps reminding him of the Lake Champlain property he once owned. I, too, lamented what Dad lost when he sold his unusual and exquisite stone home.

After my son had sat down next to Dad, Suzie returned her attention to the other women guests. My father tugged at my sleeve and whispered in my ear as he pointed Suzie's way. "They're always *yackety-yacking*," he said with his gruff voice, "as if they hadn't seen each other's snowbird feathers in years."

Most of Dad's *allophone* guests (Quebecers who had a mother tongue other than English or French) owned or rented condos along the strip from Fort Lauderdale to Palm Beach. Later on, my wife drew me aside in the hallway and said, "It feels strange to be the only American at your father's Florida parties." She smiled. "I'm again surrounded by these Eastern European Canadians who speak at least three languages!" She was referring to their English, French, and native Eastern European tongues.

Here in Florida, my father's ethnic friends loved comparing vacation notes. They spoke about the recent weather (South Florida versus Montreal and Toronto), when they had flown in or driven south, how long they were staying in the area, and where their favorite shops and restaurants were this season. They complimented each other for their suntans and traded the latest tricks on keeping them going—few cared about SPF numbers. Some of the men patted their bellies and hips to show they were shamefully putting on weight. They mentioned how they were trying to take better care of themselves in their later years. Some kidded, "You look so much younger than when I last saw you down here."

After a few moments of snowbird chat with Dad and my wife, I excused myself, grabbed a glass of wine, and strolled into the living room. Every man grabbed and firmly shook my hand, saying, "Good to see you here, Harvy." As my father would, they asked, "How are things in *'Bawston'*?"

Many of the wives had known me since I had been a kid. They kissed my cheeks, saying, "Don't be such a stranger. Come to see us when you are in Montreal."

I returned their smiles and said, *"Bawston's* great!" I then gave the standard American pretense. "I'm pretty busy, but I'll try to call the next time I'm in Montreal."

The one person I was glad not to see here was my father's lawyer, Mack—a former fixture at my father's environs both during Dad's business heyday and way too far into his retirement. *I'm glad Dad fired that bum years ago!*

The last time I saw Mack, sometime after Dad and Elaine's separation, it had started with a call from the attorney while I was visiting my father at his office.

"The Troika? Tonight? Yes, sure, sure," my father said in a subdued tone over the phone to his long-time lawyer. It didn't sound as if Dad were excited to hear from his old colleague.

Dad put down the receiver and turned to me. "Mack wants to entertain his nephew, Martin, tonight at the Troika. You know the fellow. Can you come with us?"

I was acquainted with Martin. Years earlier, I conducted management training work in his firm when I had worked at WISE. Martin, a shrewd businessman, liked to talk about money: making it here, spending it there, and storing it wherever. I remembered his rule for his Accounts Payable Manager: "Wait as long as you can to pay a supplier without pissing them off so much that they no longer want to do business with you."

My dad might have enjoyed Martin's line, but I knew my father had paid his key suppliers quickly, provided he got a customary one or two percent discount off the invoice. Though I enjoyed money conversations too, I preferred to keep my money axioms to myself.

Seeing a pained look on my dad's face regarding Mack's call, I agreed to go with him to the Troika. Elaine had once said how Mack could be a parasite, expecting others to pay for him. I wanted to see if that was true. With my being there, the lawyer might think twice about how far he'd go.

Over supper, Mack and Martin went on about the great Troika food and the good-looking women that came there. They nodded and pointed. "Oh, look at that foxy broad with the nice suit." They ordered Beluga caviar and rack of lamb. They drank pepper, lemon, and who-knows-what kinds of vodkas.

Martin spoke about the new fur he had bought his wife. "I can't keep that woman happy unless I get her something expensive every other month. Last time it was a diamond tennis bracelet. I spend money on her faster than I can make it in my business." It sounded as if Martin's wife liked to bathe in newly minted cash.

Poking fun at his nephew, Mack said, "I hope you get something in return."

"Yah," he smiled, "but her habits are costing big bagels."

I was glad my Gloria was not like Martin's high-maintenance spouse. Gloria was modest, not materialistic. She was happy with colourful and unusual jewellery, though I more than once surprised her with gold earrings, pendants, bracelets, or bangles for her birthdays. She was happiest when spending time with close family and friends, rather than going to expensive restaurants or being the first to go to the latest theatre performances. Gloria and I were the dress-down types away from work, and those ways suited me fine.

The whole evening with Mack and Martin turned out to be a bore. I couldn't wait to get out of there. When the waiter placed the tab on the table, I noticed that it totaled nearly $400. Mack completely ignored it. After twenty minutes, Dad put his credit card on it.

I was aghast, but I didn't want to make a scene at the table. In the car, I asked my father, "Why did you pay for that *Schmack* and his nephew?"

My father put his hand on my arm. He calmly said, "It's okay, son. It's no big deal."

I figured my father let things go with Mack. Decades earlier, Dad had shared how Mack helped him to separate his various businesses. That way, Montreal Phono and its related companies could take advantage of low small-business tax rates, saving hundreds of thousands of dollars for my father's various companies.

Conversely, Mack once got my father into a stock investment based on rumours of a company merger. But it never happened, and Dad was down over $100,000 on the stock. He became outraged at Mack, yelling profanities at him over the phone, but he never fired the guy. I didn't know why my father felt he still owed his attorney.

From the moment when my father unexpectedly brought Mack along to see Steve and me at our boarding school—to tell us that our dad was leaving our mother—my neck hairs stood out regarding the attorney. Mack continued to be a talking head for my father through the years whenever Dad felt he needed reinforcement with friends and family. It peeved me that Dad sometimes needed his lawyer to speak on his behalf with my brother and me.

Dad was willing to let the restaurant bill pass, but I couldn't let it go. The next day I called Mack. I was shaking inside. I took a big breath and told him, "I don't know the extent of your relationship with my father, but I don't think it's right that you ask him out, bring along a guest, and then expect my father to pay."

After a momentary pause, Mack replied calmly. "Harvy, we should get together when you are back in Montreal. I'll explain it then."

Though I had no idea what Mack was talking about, I said, "Okay," and we ended the conversation there. Years passed before I reached out to Mack again, but he never responded to my advances. I guessed he fired me from his life. That was fine, for I had fired him from mine.

Some years later, Suzie mentioned, "Your father occasionally takes me and some of our Slovak friends out to the Troika. We have such a good time in that place, enjoying lively music and great food." Talking as if it were nothing, she added, "Your father could spend $750 in one night there. Good thing he can afford it."

My curiosity rose about Suzie's declaration. "Oh, that's nice, Suzie. I haven't been to the Troika in years. How often do you get to go?"

"Oh, once or twice a year."

"Does Dad's old lawyer friend, Mack, ever go with you?"

She looked at me with a straight face. "No, I never met the man."

I looked back at her. "That's okay. You haven't missed anything."

Though my father still had his habit of picking up the tab, I'd never stop him from having fun with the friends that he invited. As far as I could tell, Mack never again called my father to go out, and my father never lamented the loss of that so-called friendship. Though I never asked my dad what made him feel indebted to Mack, I had gotten the satisfaction of ousting that *Schmack* from preying on my father's generosity.

Decades later, a friend pointed out what could have been going on between Mack and my father. He told it through a joke. "One day," he said, "a Jewish guy walks into a church and goes into the confessional. He says to the priest, 'Father, I'm Jewish, but I had to come and see you.' He proceeds to tell the pastor about how he cheated on his wife, how he stole money from his business partners, and how he screwed his customers. The priest then turns to him and asks, 'I'm happy to hear your confession and give you penance, my son, but why did you come here and not see your rabbi?' The Jew responds, 'Father, I can't do that. I had to tell somebody, but my rabbi knows every person I'm talking about.'" To my father, Mack had been his priest.

Though the thought of Mack irked me, it wasn't the time to focus on such *schnorrer* types at Dad's 80th birthday celebration.

Across Dad's Deerfield condo living room, I saw my brother standing away from the crowd. Steve had made the trip from Montreal, *sans famille*, putting in one of his rare Florida appearances. Three decades had passed since he and I had been in South Florida together, when our father had driven our family to Fort Lauderdale for the winter holidays. Though I now came south regularly in the winter to visit Dad for long weekends, my brother at most made a once-a-winter appearance from Montreal. Outside of this day, Steve and I had never been together at Dad's former Boca home or his Deerfield condo.

Just *Lassen* to Me!

Steve had his usual soft drink in hand. He was talking to a colleague from JHS's business past. I could see my brother was wearing his best smile, and I heard him employ his finest laugh that seemed slightly forced. My confrere within sight, I felt my typical stomach queasiness. I worked to ignore it.

Mon frère hadn't worked for a living since Dad's Canexco venture failure eight years earlier, followed by Steve's SBP business demise. Throughout and afterward, Dad and JHS kept on supporting his first son.

For the last fifteen years, since I started my professional career, both with WISE and on my own afterward, I supported myself separate from my father and his company. I guessed I still held deep-seated feelings about that difference in my brother's and my divergent lives.

Steve now volunteered full time at his church and had no qualms about Dad paying his way to a better afterlife. As with Dad's lawyer Mack, it peeved me to see my brother get away with our father's charity. My father had grumbled for years, "Steve does little in his life than work for his church." I had encouraged Dad to reduce or cut off the money tap to his first son so that my brother would learn to stand on his own feet. I had gotten nods from my father, but he never stopped the cash flow.

I resigned myself that Steve and our father lived a biblical scripture. No one, except maybe God, could conclude their never-ending story. I couldn't confront my brother the way I had faced Mack. That would be overly self-serving, for Steve obtaining less cash sooner would mean I'd have more money later. I was as much a part of our maddening Simkovits drama as he was.

I couldn't fully grasp why our father had crafted such a soap opera in our family. Did he not understand what he had done to his sons, creating our competition for his attention, affection, and affluence? Perhaps Steve and I saw each of ourselves as saints and the other as a sinner. Was our family die so deeply cast that nothing could break our troublesome and intractable narrative?

Today, Steve seemed content to talk with a former JHS business associate. Over the years, my brother had confided, "I never really enjoyed Dad's colleagues. I don't like putting on a good face at his parties."

Though I got along with most of my father's peers—getting into snowbird-like banter as any Canadian would on American turf—I still felt awkward being in the same room with my brother. My gut turned acidic whenever he and I had to share our father's aura.

Some years earlier, an unexpected revelation had bolstered Steve's life mission. When my brother was in his early 40s, he called me unexpectedly. He cleared his throat and offered, "Harvy, a doctor recently diagnosed me with severe dyslexia. It explains why I had problems in high school and college."

I paused to take in his words. "Wow, Steve," I said. "That clarifies a lot." After two years of struggling in undergraduate engineering school, Steve decided to leave college and work in our father's company.

I wished something as simple as dyslexia would explain my brother's difficult disposition with Dad and me. I added, "It's amazing that our private high school hadn't discovered your condition during our years there."

There was relief in his voice. "They didn't have the tests back then." He added something I didn't expect. "I think Dad might have dyslexia too."

"What makes you say that?"

"Have you ever seen Dad read anything more than a newspaper or a *Time* magazine? Dyslexia runs in families; I might have gotten it through him."

There he goes, blaming Dad for his offspring lot. "I never considered that," I said.

I thought about my time in school. "You know, Steve. I was a slow reader myself, and I still don't do much reading for fun. But I don't see words garbled the way dyslexic people do."

Steve came back. "Maybe get yourself checked out."

Thinking my brother was grabbing at gene pool straws, I focused the conversation back on him. "So, what are you going to do now that you know this about yourself?"

He said he was going to Queens University to do an executive MBA. "And because I'm now diagnosed, I get a free laptop to do my assignments, plus more time for exams. I should have my degree in two years."

"I wish you the best of luck with that, Steve." And I sincerely did. If Steve obtained professional credentials, he could gain marketable skills and feel more self-confident.

Just *Lassen* to Me!

During our call, I pushed my brother a little further. "What do you plan to do after you obtain your MBA?"

After a pause: "I'm not yet sure. Maybe I'll start another business."

Uh, oh! I felt my blood pressure rise. The last time my brother did that, he lost a partner and his entire investment. But I kept my mouth shut, hoping that business school would teach him to become more astute and prudent.

As our father had done for me regarding my AU/NTL program, he paid for Steve's advanced degree studies. Before the '90s ended, Steve received an executive MBA with high grades—quite the accomplishment for an adult without an undergraduate degree. But he had yet to start a business or find a work position outside of volunteering at his church.

At Dad's Deerfield condo, I couldn't ignore Steve all evening. I decided to approach him first. I meandered around guests to get closer. My brother sported a two-piece suit and Windsor-knotted tie—as Dad expected from his sons on formal occasions. If we didn't wear such attire, our father might ask, "Why did you dress like a beggar for my party?"

Coming up to Steve, I suddenly saw something unusual on his left wrist. It was a shiny black, white, and gold object. It looked like a watch, but I rarely saw my brother wear a timepiece.

After having taken another step, I realized what the item was. I had to stop to catch my breath. *My God!* On my brother's wrist was my gold Patek Philippe. It was the one I had stowed away in JHS's office safe, the watch Dad had given me as a present in '76 after I had graduated from MIT.

How could Steve be wearing MY Patek?!

I was dazed, but my brother had spotted me. "Hi, Harv," he shouted. I cringed at his calling me by a nickname that made me feel like a kid, but I said nothing. Maybe he felt the same way about me calling him Steve, though our parents had called him Stevie. Everyone else called him Stephen.

"Hi Steve,' I responded, half hugging my brother. I forced a smile, keeping my breath steady and my voice calm. I then fibbed for another time that evening. "Good to see you in Florida," I said.

He offered a broad smile, though it looked a little forced. "Ah, good to see you too, little brother," he said. His "little brother" remark reached under my skin and into my gut. I tried not to show my discomfort.

We exchanged a few snowbird remarks. I then asked, "What are you doing now that you completed your MBA? Have any work prospects?"

He responded without hesitation. "I've been putting out the word through my church friends that I'm looking for a business opportunity."

No, not that again! My brother wasn't the entrepreneurial type our father had been—others could easily hoodwink him. But I held my tongue, hoping his Mormon friends were of a better ilk. "How's that going?" I asked.

"It's funny, Harvy. People have been crawling out of the woodwork with investment ideas, but none of them have any money."

Of course! I gnawed on my tongue again. I felt off-balance by my Patek being on Steve's wrist. I offered no business advice or money warnings, for Steve never took counsel from his little brother, no matter how many college degrees and how much consulting experience I had amassed.

My mouth was dry. I looked across the room. "I'll see you a bit later. I need another drink and to say hello to other folks."

He nodded and turned away. I walked in the opposite direction.

My smile departed as my mind filled: *How did Steve get my watch, and how long has he had it?* Had he taken it from our father's office safe? Or had Dad given up on my having it and offered it to my brother? *What the hell is going on?*

I had felt uncomfortable wearing that expensive timepiece—worth $5000 as Dad said when he had given it to me twenty-four years earlier. I wore it a few times on special occasions, like the Slovak and Hungarian Balls when my father had invited me, and to Dad's big birthday parties in Montreal. After each affair, I asked him to return the watch to his safe.

I never felt right about wearing that precious Patek in my professional world. Its opulence made me feel as if I were showing off, as my father did with his fancy suits, silk ties, gold cufflinks, and his gold chains and watches. I preferred being admired for my smarts and deeds, not for what was around my neck and wrist. Though the last time I had worn the watch was at Dad's birthday celebration a decade earlier, I still considered it rightfully mine.

I walked into the bathroom for a moment and stared into the mirror. My mind got carried away. When Dad had bestowed the Patek on me, I believed that I was a revered second son, like the biblical Isaac had been to his Abraham father. I thought I had reached a higher position with my patriarch. Seeing the Patek now on Steve's wrist, I wondered if our dad had unseated me from my princely status. Was the older but less-esteemed Ishmael suddenly at our Abraham's side, becoming the primary heir to the nation of Dad?

For the last twenty-seven years, I had kept my father's furtive finances secret. I knew of his hidden bank accounts that went from Switzerland to the Cayman Islands to The Bahamas and now resided in Luxembourg. I knew of his tax-evading annuity deals with the Independent University and his property purchases in NY State and Florida utilizing his offshore assets.

Dad never trusted my brother with his sordid secrets because of Steve's morality. He was afraid that my over ethical brother would reveal such confidences to his church bishop, his wife, or the taxman. Seeing Steve now have my gold watch on his wrist, I wondered if I were no longer first in line to my father's legacy. I felt clammy sweat ooze out from under my shirt.

I shook my head, loosened my tie, and left the bathroom. I worked to keep a good face as I spoke to other guests. I ignored the growing acidity in my gut. I looked for an opportune moment to confront my brother without drawing too much attention to the conversation he and I needed to have.

Soon I saw him standing on the living room balcony. He had wandered away from the crowd as he often did when he had enough chitchat. I excused myself from one of my father's friends and strolled toward Steve.

We exchanged, "How's the family?" and "Fine, thanks." I then looked at him with curiosity. I pointed to the Patek as if I had seen it for the first time this evening. "Hey, Steve, how did you come by that watch?"

Steve hesitated for a moment. He glanced down at the Patek and offered calmly, "Dad gave it to me a while ago when I was visiting him at his office. I'm wearing it for his birthday to make him happy." He said his words in a quiet monotone, like a priest to a flock member. I couldn't read his mood.

My heart was beating hard for having to act pleasantly with Steve. I held myself back from coming across too strong or critical. If he went into his trademark stubbornness, I would lose any chance to reclaim my watch. I found a calm voice and mixed it with a tinge of concern. "I'm sorry to tell you, Steve, but the Patek is mine. I'm surprised that Dad gave it to you."

Steve looked straight at me. His eyes seemed stunned, but his face remained blank. He didn't recoil from my statement. I could tell he was waiting to hear more. I figured that what I had said made sense. Then it dawned on me as to the real reason why Dad had given Steve my Patek.

My brother and I knew our father was becoming forgetful. Sometimes, Dad got lost when he drove the three kilometers home from his office. He'd then used his car phone to call Suzie, asking her to come and find him. Seeing my watch in his office safe for years, never worn or claimed by me, Dad might have forgotten that he had given it to me, thus offering it to Steve.

As coolly as I could, I pleaded my case. I told Steve about my history with the timepiece. "Dad gave me the watch as a graduation present when I completed my bachelor's at MIT. I last wore it at his 70th birthday party when he was still with Elaine." I shared, "I, too, had mixed feelings about wearing it, so it stayed in Dad's safe all these years. Elaine even said that Dad had worn it a few times himself since I wasn't keen about putting it on."

Steve looked at the watch again. "Dad gave it to me a few months ago." He placed his opposite hand on the Patek as if he were petting it. "I don't enjoy wearing the thing. I only put it on to honor Dad for his 80th." After he had taken another breath, he looked at me. "Okay, Harvy, I'll put it back in the safe when I get to Montreal. You can get it when you're there."

Part of me wanted to yank my watch off my brother's wrist, but he was right. It might look odd or confusing to Dad if he didn't see the Patek with Steve. Irrespective of his signature stubbornness, I knew my brother took pride in his religious honesty. I trusted him to keep his word.

He continued. "When you come to JHS, we can talk about the other things Dad has in his office safe and in his safety deposit box at the bank."

In those safes were many gold coins Dad had collected from over the world, other gold watches he had bought during his prime, and gold jewellery that he had worn at different times of his life. Steve pointed to me and then himself. "We'll eventually need to figure out how to divide those things."

It crossed my mind that my brother rarely offered anything for nothing. But his condition was acceptable, considering our father had made my brother and me the co-executors and chief benefactors of his estate. I offered, "Thanks for your understanding, Steve." We shook hands on our sibling agreement. He and I had completed a covenant to share in our patriarch's promised legacy—at least a part of it that my brother knew about. But there were other things I wasn't ready to divulge.

Steve didn't know that I had met months earlier with two attorneys, first André Lefebvre and then his colleague Bernard, at one of Montreal's high-end legal firms. André determined that an annuity agreement Dad had signed with the Independent University was not binding on his estate. A month later, Bernard took me through Revenue Canada's rules for performing a voluntary disclosure on Dad's offshore assets.

I had shivered and sweated through both of those conversations. My father had expected me to keep his offshore money a secret, away from Steve and the taxman. I still feared my father might cut me off if he ever found out I was going against his wishes of keeping those assets concealed in perpetuity.

After I had met with André and Bernard, I breathed a small sigh of relief. I then knew my legal options for handling Dad's hidden legacy, though I still wasn't sure how far I'd go to unwind my father's entire offshore web. But those legal options would allow me to put our father's financial finagling into my brother's and my rearview mirror if I chose to go that route.

I now had a growing urge not to continue my father's money games. That urge no longer wished to replicate Dad's manipulating of assets away from the taxman. His vices were not my vices, nor were they my brother's. Though I admired my father's success, and I longed for Dad's legacy and his blessing as his favored son, he had had three failed marriages and three offspring who were worlds apart.

Though I knew Dad loved all of us, his kind of love came at a cost to our family. He not only had caused my mother's broken heart and my brother's contrarian nature, but he also had contributed to the estranged relationship between my brother and me and between our long-hidden Slovak half-sister and us. And that was only the tip of this patriarch's iceberg.

None of that came out of my mouth while I stood with my brother on Dad's condo balcony. Revealing what I knew about Dad's illegitimate assets would have to wait until our father was closer to death. I didn't know how much I could trust Steve with those secrets. I wondered if he and I would be able to move beyond our father's nearly three decades of money hiding.

Today, on Dad's 80th, Steve's action concerning my Patek was a small sign that he was willing to be fair with me. Regardless of our strained history, perhaps I too should be equitable with him concerning Dad's illicit legacy. My dear dead mother certainly would have wanted that for both of her sons.

* * * *

Playing My Cards Right

Dad was in better spirits whenever I came to visit him in Florida. During the previous winter of '99, I suggested going on a four-hour supper and gambling cruise out of Ft. Lauderdale. Dad immediately said, "You make the reservations, Harvy, and I'll pay for the excursion."

After an onboard seafood supper buffet, he and I headed to the blackjack tables while Suzie gravitated to the slot machines. At a $5 table, Dad pulled out $200 from his wallet and exchanged it for chips.

From the time I could remember, Dad enjoyed playing cards and gambling. In any given evening, he could win or lose five to ten thousand U.S. dollars. Dad would brag about his big winning nights, but I had to hear it from others, like Elaine, about his losing nights.

Wanting to get a sense of his current ability to think, I watched him playing from a short distance away. His youthful exuberance, along with his customary stiff scotch and smoldering stogie, were no longer there. He had a blank expression on his face as he pulled out and lit a cigarette.

To my chagrin, as Dad played, he pulled cards and doubled down when he had little chance of winning. In ten to fifteen minutes, his chips dwindled. He then took another $200 from his wallet. After he had repeated this pattern a few times, I went up to him and said, "Want to take a break, Dad?"

He said, "No, son." He moved a bunch of his chips to an open seat next to him. "Come and play with me," he added.

I played alongside him for a while but had a growing sense of shame as I saw my father lose most of his hands. After he had pulled out and thrown away more rounds of $200, and after having the $100 he had given me whittle down to near nothing, I said, "Dad, I've had enough for one night. Let's use the chips we have left to buy drinks at the bar."

"Okay, son."

On the way to the bar, we bumped into Suzie. She said, "I can't believe I lost $75 on those stupid slot machines. How did you do, Johnny?"

He waved his right hand to one side and answered her with a straight face, "I lost only $200." He pointed to me, "And Harvy lost $100."

I looked away and said nothing.

Most other nights during my long weekends visiting Dad in Deerfield, we ate at local outdoor restaurants. Once in a while, we drove to Fort Lauderdale to eat supper at the only Hungarian restaurant in the area. There, Dad ordered one of his favourites: goulash soup or Weiner Schnitzel. A Hungarian violinist played, and Dad chimed in to give voice to a familiar refrain.

But Dad's voice had lost his clean, clear baritone. He no longer initiated a tune or taught the musician a new song as he had done for decades at his beloved Troika with the roving minstrels, Sasha and Vladjec.

At an open-air restaurant that overlooked the intercostal at the Bridge Hotel in Boca, Suzie once said, "That guitar player is so good. He plays the songs we know." She looked at me. "We only come to these nice places when you are in town, Harvy. Otherwise, your father doesn't like to go out unless it's to a friend's home."

I imagined my mother might have said the same in her day. Dad had taken her out to fancy places only a couple of times a year, and it was never merely the two of them. I forced a smile. "Then it's good that I visit every month when you are here."

Dad said nothing. Over supper, neither he nor I talked much. Part of me felt irritated at him for the loss of the gregarious life he had had and the energetic person he had been.

Suzie carried the conversation for all of us. She spoke about her daughter, son-in-law, and her two grandkids in Montreal. I half-listened, half-smiled, and joined in here and there. There was perhaps too much dirty water under Dad's and my bridge for me to be fully present around him.

At the end of supper, Dad turned to me. "Give the bill to me, son. It's my pleasure to have you here with us in Florida." I nodded my acceptance but again wondered if my father was paying me off for coming to visit him. When I was a kid, he had put quarters into my hand for having solved math questions. Maybe his money was his only remaining source of manliness.

I also wondered where my father might be today if it weren't for his millions. Might he be sitting alone and miserable in an old folks' home, discarded by his family for the pain and suffering he had caused them? For Dad, his money was his source of attention and vehicle for affection. I certainly didn't want to be that way in my life and with my family.

Perhaps I held resentment for what my father had lost not only with his stroke but also in his divorces. He had discarded my mother to be with Elaine, and then he threw even more away when he left Elaine. Now he went back to find a caretaker in Suzie, as my mother had been, someone who would spend most of their time by his side. Yet I wondered if he might throw her away too.

My old man was lucky to have found a kind and gentle person in Suzie. She said she liked my father, and it looked as if she were taking good care of him. While they lived in Montreal, she was at their apartment each weekday evening when he came home from his office. She prepared hot suppers unless they went to the restaurant in their residence.

Suzie sent her partner off to his office every morning with a kiss and a sandwich packed in a paper bag. Every night, she massaged his legs before bed. She also came looking for him when he called her from his car, saying, "I took a bad turn. Please come and find me. I'm on *such-and-such* street." Without complaint, Suzie drove out to where he was and had him follow her home.

Maybe Suzie was what my father needed, but I sensed Dad saw her as a consolation prize rather than the first prize Elaine had been. Though Suzie was devoted to Dad, she wasn't as attention-grabbing or thought-provoking as Elaine had been.

Both Steve and I thought Suzie was a good companion for our father. But after a few years of living with her, Dad started to complain about her too. It was behind her back, as he had done with every woman with whom he had lived. It was his typical litany. "We spend too much time with her family," he said, his raspy voice almost shouting.

I responded calmly yet firmly, "Suzie has only one daughter, a son-in-law, and two grandchildren that she adores. You visit them only on Sunday afternoons and only when you're in Montreal. It's not a lot to ask."

He continued his rant. "Suzie's *yackety-yacking* on the phone all the time!"

"What do you expect, Dad? She does have a life besides you."

He banged his good hand on the table. "She's supposed to be with me when I'm home." He had said the same damn thing about Elaine.

I pushed back. "Doesn't Suzie take good care of you? She cooks, cleans, and rubs your legs every night too. And you're not even married to her."

Dad's voice rose. "She's with me only like a nurse. I pay her a salary every week [a stipend for food shopping and household things]. She does nothing else for me."

I couldn't understand how my father saw only the water and not the vodka in his drink glass with every woman in his life.

* * *

After Gloria had given birth to our son in '96, my father started to put wads of hundred-dollar bills into my hand whenever I came to visit him in Montreal or Deerfield. He said, "Here, son, please take this." He didn't say where he got the cash. He smiled. "I love you. Spend it as you want."

I responded, "I appreciate it, Dad, but you don't have to give me money every time I see you."

He looked at me with kind eyes, and he placed his hand gently on mine. "I want to give it to you. You have a young family; you need it. Please take it; it would make me very happy." If I refused Dad's cash, he might feel disappointed. I accepted it with a nod and a thank you. I again wondered if these perks were my reward for spending time with him.

Gloria and I were self-sufficient in our careers and life together. But in the back of my mind lay: *What would I do if Dad went crazy and gave all his money away?* Could I support my family in the long run and have a good retirement down the road? Considering Gloria and I were planning for a second child, I wasn't entirely certain about our financial future.

I wondered whether my self-doubts were real or imagined. Were they an impression that my father had implanted, a notion that I could never be successful on my own without his "Just *lassen* to me" advice and his assets housed both here and over there?

I again considered that my loyalty to my father had been a dependency, perhaps no better than my brother's dependence wrapped in his perpetual counter-dependence. Was it Dad's respect, appreciation, love, or money I was most afraid of losing? What made me intensely wish to be his preferred son? I wondered how my life might have been different had it not revolved around Dad and Steve, I being attracted to one and repulsed by the other.

My desperate desire for my father's approval, even anointment, was like an addiction, perhaps worse than Dad's smoking or gambling. It afflicted me down to my *raison d'etre*.

In the summer of '91, after Dad had met Gloria on our first visit to his Peru home, he called me a few days later. He offered, "She's a nice girl, but I think you could do better."

My mind knew that he was full of crap for judging Gloria just on a first impression. But his statement felt like a hard fist to my gut. For days, I was angry and depressed about his lack of approval for someone I cared for. I tried to close my ears to his unkind words, but those words resonated in my bones.

Months later, as Dad got to know Gloria, he changed his tune. "She is a good woman for you, son," he offered without being asked. Though my mind still fumed at him for his previous offhand comment, my gut felt relief.

As for Dad's money, I wanted to do more with it than stash it in a bank account half the way around the planet. I wished to find ways to use it to do some good in the world. A couple of years after my brother had squandered his JHS preferred shares on his SBP venture, I asked my father if I could cash in my JHS shares. It was the first time I asked him for an outlay outside of my post-graduate education. After reminding him that he needed to treat me fairly, he had Rob mail me a cheque.

I placed portions of those funds into various private-placement investments. One was a company that farmed hard-to-raise, restaurant-destined fish in an ecologically sound manner. Another was a startup venture that worked to reuse ash from coal-fired power plants to build construction materials. Yet another business created innovative grain storage technology for underdeveloped countries. If any of those took off, I'd feel good about contributing to the world in a valuable way, and I'd build my nest egg independent of my father.

I continued to take my father's handfuls of hundred-dollar bills whenever we were together, surmising he was giving cash to his every offspring.

Once, my brother confided to me, "Dad paid down some of my house mortgage. I feel a little guilty that he didn't do the same for you."

Though Dad had already told me what he had done for Steve, I was impressed with Steve's honesty and concern. I responded, "Dad probably has a ledger in his head. He gives to you in some ways, and he gives to me in others." I looked away and then back at him. "I wouldn't worry about it, Steve; it'll probably even out in the end." I didn't tell my brother that Dad had also paid down a portion of my mortgage. I didn't want to compare who had gotten more from our father.

I continued to reveal nothing to Steve about the offshore bucks that our dad had destined for me. There was still a part of me that was resolute that my brother would have no part of that hidden stash. Dad had balanced the scale with my brother by placing him in purchasing positions at other businesses, paying down his house debt, giving him a continuing salary to live on, getting him involved in Canexco, and helping him with SBP. If my brother squandered his best onshore opportunities, the greedy part of me felt there shouldn't be any skin off my offshore allowance.

But my brother had shown genuine concern about Dad being fair to both of us. I didn't know if I could legitimize Dad's hidden money without Steve's involvement. I was softening my position on my brother; I might share our dad's offshore empire with him. But it would be my decision as to how, when, and how much that would be.

For now, I was waiting to see how my hand in my father's offshore game would play out as Dad approached his last days. I looked for a defining moment that would turn his daunting game in my favour.

* * *

Before Dad's annual trip south with Suzie for the winter of 2000, his complaints about his partner escalated. "Suzie doesn't give a shit about me anymore! I don't want to go to Florida with her." His simmering pot was boiling over about yet another woman.

I remembered his chronic complaining about Elaine and what had happened to that marriage. The last thing he needed was another change of mate. After he had repeated his grievance, I thought for a moment.

I then placed a suggestion in front of him. "What if Emilia and Igor stay with you for a couple of months this winter? They could keep you company while Suzie goes out shopping or goes to visit friends." I was thinking about Suzie's sanity as much as my father's. More importantly, I no longer felt competition from my half-sister regarding my father's favours.

Dad looked intently at me, "Okay, son; I'll think about it."

A month after his 80th birthday celebration, I visited Dad in Deerfield again. By then, Emilia and Igor had already arrived. My father had picked up the gin rummy card I had put down for him.

After I had settled into my room in his condo, Dad pulled me aside. He pressed a wad of folded bills into my palm. "Here, take this. It's three thousand dollars."

I was taken aback by the higher-than-usual sum. I made a feeble protest. "I don't need your money, Dad."

He put his hand on mine. "Please, son; take it."

I nodded, took the cash from his hand, and pocketed it without counting it. It might be better to accept Dad's donations rather than have him spend the money at a South Florida restaurant akin to the Troika.

Later, in my room, I counted the wad of cash. It was not the $3000 Dad had said, but only $700. *Wow*, I thought, *Is Dad faking it or losing it?*

I didn't go back to ask him. If I didn't want or expect his outlays, what would be my point in identifying the discrepancy? I wouldn't want him to get upset about his growing forgetfulness or my questioning his intelligence. And I wasn't interested in his making up the difference.

I looked again at the money in my hands. I thought about Emilia and Igor. I wanted to be kind to them since they were here for Dad at my recommendation. I knew they had little cash coming to them from our father's will. Why not make a kind gesture to Emilia as a down payment to our future relationship after Dad's passing? If she showed appreciation and was discrete about this money, I could be generous to her again. *Nothing to lose!*

I waited until I saw Emilia having a cigarette while she stood on the condo's balcony. I put my hand on the wad in my pocket and joined her. We exchanged greetings, and I asked her how she was doing.

"Fine, fine," she said curtly. "Me and Igor not too happy to be here, but Daddy wanted it."

I nodded my understanding and then showed her what I had. I articulated my words slowly so that she could understand. I pointed to the money, then to me, and then to her. "Here, *I* want *you* to take this." I put the money in her palm. "Dad gave it to me, but I want you to have it. You are spending much time with him." I gestured toward the beach and buildings beyond. I smiled. "Go out and maybe have fun somewhere with Igor while you are here."

She looked at the money from my hand and then presented a blank face. She continued to speak in her broken English. "When Igor and I come here," she started, "Daddy give me money too. He tell me, 'Here's five thousand dollars.'" She batted her hand in the air as she said with dissatisfaction, "I counted, and it only five or six hundred."

Though it sounded like what I had given her had been nothing, she didn't return the bills. She offered me a nod but no smile or thank you.

What is it with this half-sister of mine? I nodded back but wondered why she should be disappointed. She was here for the winter on my father's dime. Wasn't that better than being in a snowy Slovakia or a cold Canada? Maybe she felt as if she were in a patriarch's pristine prison.

It seemed that Dad was pleased to have Emilia and Igor with him. Might he have promised them something for their presence and not yet delivered? Maybe Emilia was playing the slighted victim, believing she deserved more.

Since I didn't speak Slovak, and my Hungarian was insufficient, I didn't discuss the subject further. But my little experiment had conveyed a lot. I wasn't going to offer further handouts to my half-sister, as my father did.

I excused myself, went inside, and found Suzie in the kitchen. "How is it going with having Emilia and Igor here?"

Her typically sweet voice turned a touch sour. "It's okay, but Emilia acts like a princess, rarely raising a finger to cook or a hand to clean." She turned toward me. "All that woman wants to do is go shop, buying things for herself, Igor, or her two daughters in Slovakia, and have your father pay."

Suzie's tone softened as if she had caught her annoyance and put it into a kitchen drawer. "It's a good thing Igor helps out. He drives your father here and there, helps him in and out of his car, and pushes his wheelchair. Igor loves your father very much."

"Why do you think Igor cares so much?" I wondered if he might be playing to his grandfather as much as his mother was.

Suzie responded matter-of-factly. "I think he's close to Johnny because he lost his father when he was young. He sees your father as his own."

"Okay," I said. *My nephew seems to have good intentions.*

I kept on digging. "Do you know what Emilia and Igor do for work in Slovakia? And what schooling has Igor completed? Isn't he over 20 years old now?" Though I had known my half-sister and her son for over a decade, I knew little about their lives. Maybe our language barrier had been in the way, or perhaps I had constructed a fence between us.

Suzie was forthright. "Your father said that Emilia's retired from an administrative job she had in Košice. She gets a government pension plus a second pension from her deceased husband."

She took a long breath and continued. "As for Igor, he's almost 23, and he finished high school only a few years ago. He now spends most of his time helping his mother, driving her around and doing things for her." She shook her head and lowered her voice. "What he exactly does, I don't know, but it doesn't seem to be much. When your father and I visited them in Czechoslovakia last fall, Igor was inseparable from Emilia."

Over the next few days in Deerfield, I did notice Igor acting like a puppy dog around his mother. He fetched her eyeglasses and carried shopping bags for her without hesitation. Though I pondered what kind of people my half-relations were, contributors or freeloaders, I chose not to question my father about his Košice clan. I didn't want to upset him or give him the wrong message about my intentions.

I had tried for years to make responsible people of Dad's brood, but my efforts had gone for naught. *There's no sense in blowing my second-son wind against a patriarch's tide.* What Dad dished out to his kin was small potatoes compared to what lay in his estate.

As one would discard a lousy card out of a gin rummy hand, perhaps I should discard Emilia from my family constellation after Dad's death. But it might be kind to hold onto my more considerate half-nephew. Maybe Steve and I could help Igor with a college or trade school education—like Dad would do for our kids through his will. That could be fair to Igor. There's no sense in his living a life tied continually to his mother.

I nodded to Suzie, took a deep breath, and walked out of the kitchen. I still had time to see how best to play some of my cards in this confounding family game.

* * * *

Precious Things

I dropped into the JHS office after business hours in late March of 2000, a week or two before Dad would replant his wobbly feet in Canada. I went there to retrieve my Patek from his private office safe.

I collected my timepiece plus a pocket watch with a gold chain. I had bought the latter items when I wore three-piece suits to formal occasions with my first wife. I also retrieved the gold identity bracelet that Margie had given me as an engagement gift. After she and I had divorced, I placed the bracelet here so it wouldn't remind me of her. My precious things no longer seemed safe among the other valuable items stashed here.

Before I closed the safe's door, I noticed something unusual. Dad had put his Rolex in the safe over a year ago. He now wore the lightweight Citizens digital watch that I had given him.

I rummaged through the safe. I looked on every shelf and opened every compartment, but I couldn't locate the Rolex. Fifteen years earlier, when he had retired, I knew Dad had paid $10,000 for the watch. A new one like it was now double that price.

I called my brother at home. I thought he might have taken the Rolex—for safekeeping or in exchange for the Patek—after he had returned my watch to the safe. I told him the Rolex was missing.

He assured me, "Harvy, I touched nothing else when I put back your watch." I had no reason to doubt him. He added, "Maybe ask Suzie if she knows anything about it."

I called Suzie in Deerfield. Dad never answered their phone anymore, so I had no fear of reaching him by accident. "Suzie, I was checking my father's office safe for insurance papers I keep there." Though that was true, I didn't tell her my real reason. "I noticed my father's Rolex is missing. Do you know what might have happened to it?"

She answered matter-of-factly. "Yes, your father gave it as a present to Igor before he and Emilia returned to Slovakia last week. Igor was pleased about it. He wears it all the time."

Son of a bitch! My eyes looked down at the floor. "Okay, Suzie. Thanks for telling me," I said. I hoped my voice didn't reflect my shock. I said goodbye and hung up.

My heart sped. I had hoped that Steve and I might have had that watch one day. Okay, maybe I wanted it for myself. Steve rarely wore a watch, and he'd never wear Dad's showy Rolex. The Rolex had typified Dad's manhood of bygone years. I had hoped it would eventually become mine.

I took deep breaths. Maybe Igor deserved that watch for what he had provided his grandfather. Though Igor seemed tied to his mother, he did push Dad's wheelchair here, there, and everywhere, and he helped his grandfather in and out of the seat innumerable times. He also was the only one to play gin rummy with Dad when everybody else tired of it.

Though my gut felt a painful loss for the Rolex, I hoped Igor would enjoy it for the rest of his life. At least Steve and I wouldn't have to vie for it.

I called my brother again and related the discouraging news. He said, "I'm sorry to hear that, Harvy, but I would rather Igor get the Rolex than a stranger." Though I felt disappointed, perhaps Steve was right; I shouldn't feel attached or entitled to that watch.

Might Igor take $5,000 for it? Then again, why was I so petty?

Was I the only offspring who deserved anything substantial from Dad? Maybe my brother's self-righteousness had rubbed off on me. I was just one progeny in Dad's litany of family. My father was free to give what he wanted to any of us. He had made no promise to Steve or me about that Rolex, though I wished he would have said something about giving it to Igor. But

Dad rarely, if ever, informed me beforehand or asked my permission regarding anything he gave away.

I shook off my disappointment and once more looked through my father's safe. I took a mental inventory of the treasure that was there. I found Mom's gold rings and jewellery. Those items had been sitting on a shelf ever since her death a dozen years earlier. I saw several of Dad's old gold rings: one with a flat black onyx stone and one that once had held a 2 ½ carat diamond. That diamond was now long gone, and I recalled its story.

That large stone had come from a diamond and ruby brooch—the only possession Dad had from his birth mother. Dozens of tiny rubies marked the outline of three flowers. In the center of each bloom was a large diamond. Dad had replaced the three diamonds with zirconium, and he employed two of the jewels for items for himself.

Dad had the largest diamond placed into the weighty 18kt gold ring that I now held in my hand. The raised silver-gold letters "JS" were on one side. It weighed over an ounce. Dad had worn that ring since my childhood.

One winter evening during my youth, after our father had gotten home from work, he said he had seen a black cat on the plowed sidewalk in front of our house. Because Dad was superstitious, he made a snowball with his bare hands and threw it at the cat to chase it away. To his chagrin, the cold snow had shrunk his fingers, causing the diamond ring to fly into a snowbank. He spent the next thirty minutes digging through the snow, the only light coming from a street lamp. He luckily found the ring, the diamond intact.

Fifteen years later, Dad told me, "I did the same bloody thing again! I threw a snowball at a black cat walking in front of the JHS factory door." He sighed. "My ring got thrown from my finger and into the snow." He frowned. "I had to dig once more."

His face frowned. "I managed to find my ring, but the diamond setting had broken, and the diamond fell out." He huffed. "I searched and searched. I even sent my factory foreman out to dig for it, offering a reward if he found it. After forty-five minutes of digging, he came back empty-handed."

Dad took a long breath. "I had to file a claim with the insurance company." He broke a smile. "Luckily, it cost only the $500 deductible to get the diamond replaced; the insurance company paid the rest." He lifted his hand to show me his repaired ring. "My good friend, Jacoby, who has a jewellery store in the city, got me the replacement diamond."

I looked at his ring but couldn't tell if the new diamond was in any way different from the one he had had before. "You dodged a bullet there, Dad," I offered. "You better not throw any more snowballs at cats."

He chuckled. "Yes, I learned my lesson." He pointed a finger upward. "God was with me." He smiled. "That black cat didn't get the better of me."

A decade later, Dad received discouraging news about his ring. "Son of a bitch," he recounted in his office one day. "When I was in Florida, the setting on my ring got loose again, and I had it repaired once more. The jeweller there said my diamond wasn't real, just zirconium. Jacoby screwed both the insurance company and me by replacing the real diamond with an industrial one."

"Incredible, Dad! Can you sue the guy or report him to the police?"

"That's the problem, son. Jacoby's dead. A couple of years ago, a gunman got into his downtown shop, took all the jewellery from his store and safe, and then shot Jacoby to his death."

I had heard about that robbery through a story in the Montreal newspapers. "Oh, wow!" I exclaimed. "Who's running his store now? Is there anything to go after?"

Dad shook his head. "Jacoby was a one-person operation. His wife closed the store after he got killed."

I raised my hand. "I remember being at Jacoby's shop a long time ago. I was there once to pick up your ring after it had been cleaned or repaired. His place had bullet-proof glass and an incredible amount of security. How could anyone have broken in?"

Dad shook his head. "He must have known the guy who shot him. Maybe the shooter was someone who got screwed by Jacoby and was taking revenge." He growled. "I could shoot Jacoby myself for being the crook he was." He pointed in my direction. "And because the security system didn't fail, and Jacoby let the robber in, the insurance company paid nothing to his widow for the loss. She had to declare bankruptcy."

"That's amazing!" I calmed my voice. "Will you replace the diamond?"

My father shook his head. "No, it's over $10,000 for a new stone like the one I had. I don't want to spend that kind of money."

Dad didn't say it, but that black cat had gotten the better of him.

He pointed to his tie. "At least I still have my diamond tie pin."

The diamond in that pin had also come from his mother's brooch. Dad wore that pin to work every day during his business years, every night he went out on the town, and every Sunday when he went to church. I could only imagine the confessions that pin and stone might share if they could talk.

Alone in my father's private office, after calling Steve and Suzie, I looked once more at the ruby brooch that Dad's late mother had worn. I retrieved it from its box and put it in my palm, feeling its weight.

Dad had given me the second largest stone from that brooch. It was a 1 ½ carat diamond, which I had mounted onto an engagement ring for my ex. She held onto the ring after she and I had divorced. I sighed for its loss along with the Rolex. My father's precious items were dwindling like his health.

I took a long breath and shook some sense into my head. At least Dad still had his diamond tie pin plus the gold jewellery stashed here.

I wanted the brooch after Dad's passing; it held sentimental value. It went back at least two generations on the Hungarian side of our family. Dad's mother was a descendant of a wealthy Hungarian nobleman, a landowner. In return for this piece, I'd let Steve take Mom's jewellery. He could have those items for his daughter; I didn't have a daughter at the time. Steve had been closer to our mother, so he deserved her jewellery.

I put the brooch back into its box and hid it among a stack of papers in the lower part of the safe. I promised myself to make my claim for it to my brother when our dad was gone.

I left everything else as I had found it. I closed and locked the safe. I made a mental note to talk to my father about what he had in his safety deposit box at his bank. He had been storing several precious things of mine—primarily gold coins that he had bought for me over the years when our family had taken trips to Europe and the Caribbean. I needed to go to the bank with him to retrieve my items before he passed away. I didn't want any arguments with my brother as to which items belonged to whom.

* * * *

More Card Playing

After Dad had returned from Florida, the April after his 80th birthday celebration, his ability to walk degenerated in weeks. He continually repeated to Suzie, "I need a wheelchair."

Dad's long-time GP had resisted our father's earlier requests for such a device. During regular office visits, the doctor had said, "Once you put Johnny into a chair, you'll never get him out. He'll become dependent on it."

By the spring of 2000, it became apparent that Dad was hardly able—or perhaps not willing—to lift his afflicted leg and pull it forward. It took longer and longer for him to walk fifteen yards from his car to his JHS office door. He also fell to the ground a couple of times when he exited his vehicle or locked his office door. He didn't break a hip but bruised one badly.

Suzie gave in to her partner's repeated requests. She, Rob, Steve, or I now pushed his foldable wheelchair. Dad sat in it comfortably, holding onto his cane in his hand as we maneuvered him here and there.

Dad's driving had become a concern too. Up to the end of the previous year, he had driven himself to and from his office. He followed my car if we had to go somewhere in more than one car. Once, in my rearview mirror, I noticed him weaving across the road and coming close to other vehicles. I saw pedestrians and bicyclists turn their heads to see who the "crazy driver" was.

Whenever Steve or I tried to talk to Dad about his increasing disability, he made a fist and repeated, "I just need more power!" So Steve and I phoned

Dad's GP and told him of Dad's near misses and how he became lost when driving home from his office.

Dad's doctor conceded, "Okay, I'll be the bad one. When he comes to see me in April after he returns from Florida, I'll tell him that he should stop driving. I won't sign his annual licence renewal that I've been endorsing every year." The physician spoke matter-of-factly, as though he had performed such a stop-driving maneuver many times before. "This way, Johnny will just stop driving, and you'll have nothing to worry about."

Since Dad left the driving in Florida to Suzie, and he only expected to get behind the wheel upon his return to Montreal, my brother and I gratefully accepted the doctor's tactic. When Dad next saw his GP, our father accepted his doctor's verdict. He never said anything to Steve or me about the doctor's new orders; he just let others do the driving for him from that point forward.

Along with his reduced walking mobility and driving ability, Dad's spirit continued on a steady decline. It was hard to watch him, once so vital and virile, get quieter, perhaps depressed, as the months and years passed after his divorce from Elaine. Suzie had reported, "Yesterday, I counted twenty-five cigarette stubs in Johnny's ashtrays both in his office and at home."

Though my brother and I complained about his habit, Dad told us to crack open a window, turn on an air filter, or open a door or window to let in some fresh air. After his annual checkup and chest x-ray, he emphatically proclaimed, "The doctor says that my lungs are clear!"

No one could stop him from his cigarette fix or the umpteen cups of coffee he imbibed throughout the day. At least it wasn't the 100 fuming cigarettes and seemingly unending nighttime glasses of scotch or vodka that he had consumed during his business heyday. Despite his heavy nicotine, caffeine, and alcohol consumption over the years, I was amazed that my father had not contracted lung, stomach, or liver disease so far.

For sure, Dad was no longer the life of the party as he had always been. He no longer came up to people confidently and shook hands firmly. He no longer told jokes, laughed with a bursting voice, sang with great bravado, or smiled with a full face. It was sad to see his decline.

* * *

Over the years, Dad told me that a few of his former business colleagues visited him at his office. He said, "We talk about old times when JHS was still in business."

One day, an old colleague from Montreal Phono's RCA days came to visit while I was there. Dad smiled and nodded as the guy spoke about members of Dad's old RCA gang. He mentioned who had died and who was "still kicking." After the colleague had left, my father turned to me. "Harvy, do you remember who that fellow was?" I offered the man's name, and Dad nodded, "Oh, okay."

After the man left, I asked my father, "What happened to Aras?" Aras had been his long-time Troika drinking buddy. For decades, almost every Thursday night, they had gone out to their favourite Montreal haunts. They stepped out as if they had owned the city, staying past closing time as long as both the ethnic musicians played and the Stoli flowed.

Dad's eyes looked sad as he responded gruffly, "Celia is still mad at me for having left Elaine." My father blinked a few times. "Aras is ten years older than I am, and he no longer can go anywhere without Celia driving him." He looked down a bit. "He and I talk here and there on the phone."

Celia was in charge of that marriage. Though I admired her smarts as a cultured and well-educated woman, that Lithuanian was as big and tough as a linebacker. If she didn't want Aras to see my father, then it wouldn't happen.

I suspected Aras's companionship was an immense loss to Dad. From the time I was a teen, I enjoyed that man's company. He told stories about his escapades as a young buck in Vilnius, Lithuania. He once said, "My city had stunning women." He winked and raised a finger. "But you had to be careful. Not every girl who looked like a princess was for free."

Though Aras's humour was chauvinistic, he brought smiles to our faces. I was sad about his being no longer in our lives. Other longtime friends who had been closer to Elaine now no longer went out with my father or came to see him at his office. I understood my father's plight; I, too, had lost many friends after I had left my first wife.

* * *

The next time I visited my father, he was playing gin rummy with his bookkeeper, Rob. In Dad's heyday, he played that game for money—a penny a point—with his Slovak and Hungarian friends. He could rack in $5 to $10 in a given night, enough for a sandwich or two from the canteen truck that came daily to his factory door. Now he played to keep his mind occupied. He held his cards in his weaker left hand, his left arm propped on the desk. He used his right hand to pick up and put down cards.

Completing their play soon after I had walked in, Rob smiled at me. "Your father can play this card game for hours." He winked, twirled the edge of his moustache, and lowered his voice as he leaned my way. "On most days, I let the boss cheat and win." I figured if Dad could knowingly double-deal, then his mind was still working. Maybe that was his mental measure too.

Rob came into the office four days a week to be with my father. He was more a boss-keeper than a bookkeeper. He drove my father to weekly physical therapy and regular doctor's appointments, and he took him around to visit friends. Occasionally, Rob and Dad went to see the land properties JHS owned in Ottawa and on the Montreal South Shore. Rob paid Dad's personal and company bills—Dad signing the cheques, of course—and Rob kept track of JHS's and Dad's bank accounts.

My father and Rob became so attached that it felt as if Rob were his third son. Dad regularly invited Rob and his girlfriend to the Slovak Business Association meetings and Slovak Church parties. While attending one of those events, I saw Dad kissing Rob on both of his cheeks when they said their hellos and goodbyes, just as he did with Steve and me.

Rob's closeness with our dad didn't threaten Steve or me. Rob was a good guy who wanted to make a decent living. He never asked for more salary than a regular bookkeeper earned, though I didn't think he worked hard for his pay. I never said anything about it because I could see the fondness in my father's eyes for his adopted third son.

Dad had told my brother and me, "Rob's here just to help me in the office." He added, "I'm helping out the guy by giving him a job. And I let him take Fridays and some afternoons off so he could do bookkeeping work for other companies besides JHS." I surmised that Rob, rightfully so, didn't want to keep his career eggs solely in a Johnny Simkovits basket.

I wondered which one needed the other more. Neither Steve nor I would be at Dad's beck and call as much as Rob was. I spoke calmly and respectfully to the man, for he probably knew more about Dad's onshore money and business dealings than I did. But I didn't know how much he knew about Dad's offshore accounts. As with my real brother, I kept my hidden-money cards close and didn't dare utter a word about the cards I held.

Once or twice a year, Dad asked me to drive him to the Global Tarde Bank. He wanted to obtain an accounting of his offshore assets and income.

After our visit, and while we were waiting for the elevators, Dad handed me his statement copy and said quietly, "You know where to put this, son." He pointed upward, giving me an indication of the loose false ceiling panel above the safe in his private office. "Take the old statements that are there and shred them somewhere." Dad's request seemed like an everyday business transaction to him.

"Okay," I said. I kept my hand from shaking as I took the thick wad of papers from my father and stuffed them into my inside jacket pocket.

While driving back to his office, I asked, "Dad, do you get cash from over there through the bank's branch here in Montreal?"

He turned my way. "Yes, from time to time. Why do you ask?"

"I was wondering how you get down to the bank to get your money. Does Rob take you?"

He placed his hand on my arm. "*Lassen* to me, son! Don't worry about Rob. Since you are not in Montreal as much, I have a good Hungarian friend who takes me there every so often." He patted my arm. "That guy has money there too." He palmed his other hand at me. "We go to the bank's ATM in the building's lobby to get some cash."

Dad pronounced his words slowly. "As long as we take less than $10,000 at a time, there's no bank reporting to the government."

I was glad Dad had another chauffeur who could drive him to his hidden money. I was grateful he didn't mention the fellow's name. Though I was curious, the less I'd know about another person who was screwing the Canadian government out of tax money, the better I'd feel.

I wondered how Dad could retrieve up to $10,000 from an ATM in one shot. Maybe he employed the special bank card that he had once shown me—

when he first took me to the Global Trade Bank to sign the Independent University annuity deal—and perhaps the card had a high limit. I chose not to delve deeper into those money mechanics.

Dad was making cash withdrawals one way or another. If I asked too many questions, he might get me a card for the one account I held a power of attorney. I didn't want that kind of access. Knowing about Dad's hidden treasure was very different from having my hands in the chest.

I pressed on with my questions. "What about in Florida, Dad? How do you get to your money at the bank's branch there?"

"I have my Polish friend, Alec, take me."

Alec was an ex-Canadian who moved to Boca Raton and became a property manager. Dad and Alec had met through a real estate agent. Dad got friendly with the guy because he was of Eastern European descent. He was also a handyman who came over to my father's Florida home to fix a sink, hang a painting, or disconnect the car battery while Dad wasn't in Florida. The two of them occasionally played the minimal golf my father could play, with Dad hacking at the ball with half-strokes.

I was concerned about Alec. "How does that work, Dad? What does he know about your offshore bank?"

Dad's gruff voice expressed confidence as he batted his hand at me. "Alec knows nothing, son. Once a month or so, when I'm in Deerfield for the winter, he does me a favour and drives me to the Miami branch of the Global Trade Bank. I tell him I have money invested offshore and this is my way to take out my earnings. While Alec sits in the car in the parking lot, I go to one of the special bank tellers for customers like me."

He motioned forward with his able hand. "I present my Global Trade Bank card, punch my passcode into the card reader, and then indicate how much cash I want." He patted my arm. "As long as it's less than ten thousand dollars at a time, there's no problem. The government won't know anything."

I felt some relief. It sounded as if neither Rob nor Alec were privy to Dad's offshore world. I hoped a chosen son's blood would remain thicker than any hired help's water.

When Dad and I returned to JHS's office after our banking excursion, Rob had already gone for the day. I went alone to my father's private office. I closed the door behind me in case somebody walked into the front office unannounced, especially my brother.

I took off my shoes and checked to see if my hands were clean so that I wouldn't leave any prints on a ceiling tile. I pulled up a chair near Dad's grey-metal office safe. I stepped up in my stocking feet—not wanting anyone to wonder later why shoe marks were on the chair—and lifted and moved the right false ceiling panel, as I had done a few times before.

I pulled out the old papers I had hidden there the last time, replacing them with the new statements. I mumbled to myself, "I can't believe I'm still doing this." I didn't poke around to determine if anything more was up there. I didn't want to know about any other sordid secrets, financial or otherwise.

I barely glanced at the old documents in my hand, thinking that bad luck would fall upon me if I were too much of a voyeur of the details of my father's hidden hoard. I put the papers into my inside jacket pocket for later shredding at the office of one of my clients.

I wondered why my father never bought a shredder. Either he didn't want to spend the money, or he didn't want to draw attention to documents that he needed to destroy. I never asked.

For the time being, I did my chosen son's duty. I reckoned I'd repeat this secret ritual until the day when Dad would be closer to his demise.

* * *

A year earlier, in the summer of '99, on the advice of my U.S. attorney, Jay Henry, I had asked Dad if he could switch his estate executors from Steve and me to his notary, Peternik. Jay had advised that I distance myself from Dad's suspect accounts, and I tried to do that. I told my father, "I don't want Steve and me to fight over your will." Initially, he agreed to my request, but I later found out from Peternik that Dad never made the change.

Some months later, I tried another angle. I told my father, "From now on, Dad, can you ask your Hungarian friend to take you to your bank when you need to get money or go to a meeting there. It's becoming inconvenient for me to do so." It was a feeble reason, but it was the best I could devise. To my surprise, my stroke-weakened father nodded and quietly said, "Okay, son, if that's what you want."

I went further. "Dad, because I'm a U.S. resident filing taxes in the States, it might be good if you took away, at least for now, the power of attorney I have on your smaller account over there." I said my words slowly so that Dad could understand. "Every year, I have to declare in my U.S. tax returns whether I have an interest in any foreign accounts. I hate having to lie about that every time."

I didn't tell him that I hadn't lied to the IRS in all the years I had resided in the U.S. I had checked the correct box on my tax returns, declaring my interest in several legitimate Canadian accounts I still held. I correctly reported all my Canadian income and assets, and the IRS never asked for more details. I told myself that Dad's foreign accounts were his, not mine. He was the one with the tax problem, not me. I hoped I wasn't fooling myself.

I had wondered if my father might think of me as a tax-evading turncoat, but a part of me no longer cared. After twenty-seven years of confiding in me concerning his clandestine accounts, who else did Dad have to carry on his hidden legacy?

Since I had never taken a penny from any of his offshore accounts, not even from the smaller one over which I held power of attorney, I hoped he would comply with my request to remove my signing authority. I hoped he wouldn't see me like a rabbit running scared, just that I was prudent about my U.S. tax situation. "Can you do that for now, Dad," I repeated.

I wondered what might happen if my father became incapacitated or died suddenly. If he gradually lost his faculties, would Dad give me control over his accounts before he lost his senses completely? If he lost his mind overnight, then Steve and I would have to step in and declare him incompetent. That could tie my hands with his money over there, forcing me to share everything with Steve when he and I took joint control as Dad's court-appointed guardians. Though I knew I was wishful, I prayed to God and my dead mother to bring forth what they thought was best. My choices might be simpler if the universe would decide for me.

To my request about rescinding my POA on his one offshore account, Dad eyed my face and said, "Okay, son, I can do that for you."

I was not only surprised—perhaps nervous too—about the potential consequences but also glad Dad didn't press or resist. Whether he complied with my request or not, at least my conscience would be clearer regarding not having signing authority over any of his Global Trade Bank accounts. I was trying to keep my distance without totally losing my connection.

I wondered how much longer I'd have to play Dad's offshore card game. Only time would tell if I were playing my cards right.

* * * *

Redefining Money Moments

In mid-April 2000, I once again completed my U.S. tax return, checking off the right boxes that declared my legitimate foreign holdings. I wondered how much longer I would have to keep my father's offshore assets a secret. I had sleepless nights about how I would pull off the voluntary disclosure that my latest lawyer, Bernard, had described.

How was my drawn-out, offshore nightmare going to end? Would I have to wait until my dad would be in his grave? Given how he was holding on to life despite his weakened condition, there was no way to tell when that might be.

I still wasn't sure what I would tell my brother about Dad's hush-hush money or if I would include him in sharing those assets. I could share just one of Dad's offshore accounts with Steve but keep the others for myself. Living in the States, I could perform a U.S. voluntary disclosure regarding the remainder of Dad's hidden assets after we completed a smaller Canadian declaration. I was vacillating between my options.

If I told Steve about the millions our dad had hidden in Luxembourg, my life would be less complicated and my conscience a little cleaner. Steve and I could then declare Dad's hidden stash to Revenue Canada, allowing me to avoid tangling with the IRS. My mother in heaven would be pleased if I included her other son in what she had never known about nor had.

As I turned in bed, my eyes burned from lack of slumber. My jaw was sore from clenching it—perhaps from my lack of integrity. Sleeping soundly next to me was my wife. I hadn't revealed my father's money mishigas to her. I wondered what she would say when I'd tell her. Would she think less of me if I were to divulge what I knew?

I didn't have all of Dad's hidden accounts within my grasp. I had to wait for the right time to disclose my secret to my brother. I had to avoid his potentially confessing our father's hidden stash to the likes of Revenue Canada (or his church bishop) before the time was right. I had to stay patient and not let slip what I had known but never spoken about for nearly three decades. The secrecy weighed on my conscience as if someone had strapped Dad's office safe onto my back.

A couple of weeks after he had returned at the end of April from Florida, Dad called me in Boston. His voice was gruff but assertive. "Son, the next time you come to Montreal, I want you to come to my bank with me." He was speaking in code; he meant the Global Trade Bank in Montreal. I again found it ironic that an offshore bank here on Canadian soil held many of his millions.

Though I had been sidestepping such banking trips for the past year or so, I told myself not to avoid this one. Dad's failing health—his need for a wheelchair, his inability to drive, his growing intolerance of his common-law spouse, his forgetfulness about who he was talking to—was telling me I had to do something regarding his hidden assets. I had no idea what that would be, but maybe a situation would present itself on this bank visit.

"Dad, I'll be there for three or four days next month, at the end of May," I offered. "Can we do it then?"

"Okay, son; save an afternoon for me."

"Sure, Dad. Whatever you need."

* * *

By now, Gloria and I had been married for six years. I hadn't wanted to burden her with what I couldn't change. I had accepted that Dad's offshore money was my load to carry and that I had to bear it alone. I didn't want to make Gloria a co-conspirator or to have her throw me back into the sea for the secrets I held and had done little about.

My son was now four—old enough to know the difference between right and wrong. Would I haul him to an offshore bank the way my dad had done with me when I was seventeen? Would my son hold onto our secret as I had done for decades for my father, hiding it from his mother and any future siblings?

My gut wrenched at the thought of IRS tax inspectors pursuing my offspring. Would they drag my kid into a courtroom and then a jail cell because of my father and me? I didn't want my son to speculate, salivate, or suffer for the promise of an offshore treasure that would be beyond his reach until I was practically in my grave. If I perpetuated those insidious bank accounts, how would I ever explain myself to him or any other child of mine?

A few days before I headed to Montreal, Gloria and I visited friends on Cape Cod for the Memorial Day weekend. I decided to confide in my wife, to liberate what had been yearning to emerge from me. I wanted her support for what I imagined I'd be up against with my father—to bring his hidden stash into the light of the taxman. On a sunny but crisp Memorial Day morning, Gloria and I went for a long walk on Sandy Neck Beach.

I looked down at the sand as we walked along the water's edge. Gloria ambled by my side, dipping her bare feet into the chilly ocean water. I stayed on the land side of her to keep my feet on the warmer and firmer sand. She sensed I was troubled. "What's going on, honey? You seem to be elsewhere."

I hesitated. "I have to tell you something about my father and me."

I continued to walk, keeping my eyes forward. I didn't dare look in Gloria's direction or glance at her face for fear that her eyes would look right through me. As we walked, I shared with her my decades of playing along with my dad's money-hiding and tax-evading ways. I opened up about the attorneys I had recently engaged—the type of big-firm lawyers that my father loathed—to help clean up his offshore assets and my conscience. It was the first time I had ever given anyone the whole picture of my complicity. I had no one else I could trust with my soul.

Gloria listened. She held onto my arm to keep her balance as we walked in the soft sand. She said little except to ask a few questions to understand what I was telling her. Then she asked, "Does your brother know about this?"

I looked down as I walked. "Steve knows very little about Dad's hidden money." I stayed slightly ahead of her to avoid turning my face to her. "I promised Dad that I'd never tell anyone, even Steve, about the money he has over there." I took a deep breath as I pointed east, across the ocean to Europe. "I'm now scared that my father's losing control of his mind and his money."

"Will you tell your brother?" she asked.

My forehead cringed at the thought. I said, "I'll have to eventually, but I can't do it while Dad still has control over his offshore accounts." I bent over to grab a clamshell and threw it into the ocean. "I can't take a chance that Steve will go off the deep end, not keeping quiet what I know until we're ready to declare it to the Canadian authorities." I took a deep breath. "There's nothing we can do to fix the situation until I get more say over those assets or until Dad is gone."

Ideally, I didn't want my brother to know about Dad's hidden assets until I had complete control over our father's offshore fortune. And I still wasn't sure how much I'd include him in sharing those hidden assets.

I glanced at Gloria. She looked pensive. I wondered if she might leave me stranded on the Cape Cod sand. She put her hand on my shoulder and stopped me in my tracks. She looked into my eyes. "Honey, I think you have to follow your heart. As far as I can tell, you are working to do the right thing." She looked right at me with her compassionate eyes. "You are not and have never been your father."

I looked back at her, my eyes welling with relief from my feeling boxed-in for over half my life. I nodded at her and gave her a big hug. I pressed her against me as if I had needed her strength and support more than ever. She understood my pain and predicament.

I now knew my time had come. Wherever it would lead me concerning my father and my brother, I was confident I could put myself on a righteous path regarding the money my father had stashed over there for me.

* * *

It was a chilly spring afternoon at the end of May when I retrieved my father and drove to the Montreal branch of the Global Trade Bank. New buds were struggling to work their way out of maple trees and cedar hedges as another Canadian winter came to its close.

My father had traded his walking stick for a wheelchair. He could still stand and walk some steps if prodded, utilizing the cane or a person for support, but there was no point for him to risk a broken hip.

During our car ride to the bank, Dad and I said very little to each other. Unlike the first time he had taken me to his offshore Lux bank, nine years earlier, my father showed no excitement, no giddiness, and frankly, little life at all about what he had hidden from the rest of his family and the government.

When we arrived at the bank, still on the seventh floor of one of the Alexis Nihon towers, we were once more buzzed in through its double security doors. I wheeled Dad into the reception area and wondered how much longer I'd have to come here to visit his money.

The previous receptionist, Hilde, was no longer behind the front desk. A new face was there, and my father didn't greet her with the same exuberance that he had had for Hilde. After the middle-aged woman had guided us to an empty conference room, I turned to my father, "What happened to Hilde?"

He responded in a gruff voice. "Hilde retired over a year ago."

"Has it been that long since I've been here?"

He looked at me with tired eyes. "I guess so."

Nothing else had changed about the place. It was still a dull-looking, cubical-type office space with framed Luxembourg travel posters on most walls. The bank branch was now on its third manager since I had first set foot here with Dad to participate in the university annuity scheme. A couple of years later, in '93, I met the second manager, Mr. Hoffmann, soon after my father's stroke. Dad had brought me here so that I could put a new Global Trade Bank face to his hidden assets. He then authorized Hoffman to give me power of attorney over one of his smaller accounts.

The latest manager was Mr. Weber, who I had met a couple of times. Unlike the first manager, Mr. Simon, an unusually gregarious fellow for a bank manager, Mr. Weber was soft-spoken and reserved. He was one to say little more than what was needed to conduct our banking business.

While Dad and I waited in a conference room, my father looked at me. "Weber's a good man; he watches my money well." He raised his arm. "He's made six to eight percent for me each year, tax-free." He lowered his arm. "But he, and Hoffmann before him, never made as much money as Simon did during the three years he looked after me." He stopped there.

I nodded my understanding but asked no questions. I was nervous about how this day's banking conversation would go. I didn't want my anxiety to show.

When Weber walked in, he put a stack of papers on the desk. He looked at my father and reached out to shake his hand. "Good to see you, Mr. Simkovits. I hope you are doing well."

Dad gestured with his right hand to his left side, and he raised his voice. "You see what happened to me?! I now have to live in a wheelchair."

The manager nodded, "I see, Mr. Simkovits." He turned to me and reached out for my hand. "And it's good to have you here with your father, Harvy. We have not seen you in a while."

"It's good to see you too," I lied. Though I thought Mr. Weber was a nice enough fellow, I wasn't sure how good I felt about seeing a foreigner make illegitimate banking business in my native land. He and I shook hands firmly, but my gut felt as if it were full of rocks, the kind of stones that need to be pulverized by prisoners in a forced labour camp. I put on the best smile I could. "These days, I don't come to Montreal as much."

"He's too busy in *Bawston* to come and see me as often as he used to," Dad blurted, his voice as rough as ever. I couldn't tell if his words were supportive or berating.

Weber sat at the head of the table. Dad and I sat on either side of him. "How was your winter in Florida?" the manager asked, looking at my father.

"It was like every winter, but maybe a bit nicer this year. It was sunny; we had very few rainy days."

Every time I had visited Dad in Deerfield these last few years, he studied the *Sun Sentinel*'s weather report every morning. It went with his breakfast of black coffee and dry English muffin, which he dunked into the coffee like a donut. Reading the paper, he liked to compare the conditions in Southern Florida to Montreal and Boston. Every Sunday, over the phone, he'd boast exuberantly, "It's forty degrees warmer here than in Boston, and fifty-five degrees higher than in Montreal." I'd smile through the phone and respond, "That's good to know, Dad. I guess I have to come down and see you soon." My father was happy when he heard me say that.

"It's nice you had a good winter south," Weber said. "I've never had the pleasure of being in Florida. For my vacations, I return to Luxembourg to see my extended family."

Dad nodded at the manager but offered nothing more.

Weber turned to the stack of papers he had brought with him, apparently the printouts of my father's accounts. He kept a set of documents in front of him. He gave a second set to my father and a third to me. "I received these from Luxembourg this morning via fax."

It was good that the Canadian government didn't monitor electronic communications between countries, but they might one day.

As always, there were no names written on the printouts. A set of numbers indicated the account's identity. Report by report, the bank manager reviewed the investments. He summarized the respective gains and occasional losses that occurred since my father had last been there, perhaps six months earlier. Dad put on his reading glasses but took only cursory glances at the papers. Maybe he expected I would take a closer look.

The manager led the conversation. "Most everything looks excellent, Mr. Simkovits. Your investments in all currencies (in U.S. and Canadian dollars and in Euros) are making the return they are supposed to be making. Other than the one account that holds various mutual funds, the rest of your money is placed conservatively, as it has been for years, in an array of bonds and CDs."

Weber took a long banker's breath as he eyed a few pages carefully. "The only negative I see is the Euro. It has lost value to the Canadian and U.S. dollars since its introduction a couple of years ago. Your Euro-denominated bonds have experienced some unrealized foreign exchange losses at this time."

He looked at my father. "But rest assured, Mr. Simkovits, that you made solid investments in the Eurozone. Many of your bonds are linked to the Libor index, giving you a guaranteed return above that base rate. And when the Euro recovers, your investments will do very nicely."

Dad said nothing and only nodded. I wasn't sure how much he was absorbing.

I stayed with Weber's program. I asked questions to understand the asset mix of a handful of mutual funds my father had invested in regarding one of his smaller accounts.

Weber answered. "Most of these mutual funds are broad-based equity investments in the Eurozone. One, the Heritage Fund, is a private-placement fund that still has a seven-year time horizon from the time your father entered into that fund some years ago." Weber nodded in my dad's direction. "That fund is invested in a select number of growth companies, with the plan of retiring from those investments in a few more years." His eyes rose from the account statement to look at me. "I see that your father has already received some dividends and repayments from that fund, but what remains there is not a guaranteed investment as he has in the other accounts."

I nodded. "Yes, I remember that now." That Heritage fund, and other mutual funds in that one account, represented about 10% of Dad's total assets in this bank. It comprised my father's offshore "mad money"—the extent to which he felt comfortable gambling in the equities market. It was ironic, considering the risk he was taking in hiding his money from the government.

I nodded again and then mustered my courage. "Mr. Weber, can you tell me how much money my father has been taking out of his accounts this past year?" I wanted to know how much of his offshore cash he had spent.

My father didn't bat an eyelid at my question. He continued to look at Weber as if he, too, were interested in the answer.

Weber looked at the spreadsheets and did quick mental calculations. He said, "He's taken out around $250,000 U.S., which is also about how much interest and dividends his assets have generated this past year. So your father's accounts currently have about the same amount of assets as they had a year ago, except for those unrealized losses due to the falling Euro." He lifted his hand off the table and reiterated, "Those foreign exchange losses will recover in time."

I tried not to show my angst. *Where is Dad spending that kind of cash?* He gets over $200,000 Canadian from his legitimate insurance company annuities, Canadian and Quebec pensions, and his registered pension plan. That didn't include the bank interest he was getting on the gains he realized from his Peru and Boca Raton house sales and the JHS share redemption he made years ago. He wasn't living a lavish lifestyle with Suzie, so where was all that cash going?

I knew that my father had been giving some money away to me, my brother, our half-sister, and the Slovak Church. The previous year, he had transferred $30,000USD from his offshore funds to help a sick Košice relative, who had cancer, receive hospital treatment in the U.S. That had been a good use of my father's offshore cash. But how had 250,000 American bucks disappeared in only a year?

I made a mental note to ask Dad's bookkeeper about my father's spending. Rob must know what's going on regarding his legitimate bank accounts. For now, I didn't bat an eye to my father's colossal cash outlays from his offshore accounts. There was no point upending an apple cart I had no control over. And I had a more significant issue to deal with today. But how would I broach the topic of gaining a greater say over my father's money here?

The room suddenly turned quiet. The bank manager looked at me and then back at my father. I kept my eyes on the statements in front of me. Then Dad spoke unexpectedly. He pointed my way and said to Weber, "I want to give Harvy signing authority over all my accounts here. Can you do that for us?"

Wow! I hadn't expected that. For a moment, I was stunned. I tried not to show my surprise, acting as if Dad had told me such beforehand.

Weber looked again at me and then at my father. "We can easily do that, Mr. Simkovits. It would have to be in the form of a power of attorney unless you want to open new accounts in your names." It felt as if Weber had anticipated Dad's request. The banker said nothing to discourage it.

Dad responded quickly. "The power of attorney is sufficient for now." He pointed upward. "Harvy can later do whatever he wants to when I'm with Saint Peter." He showed no expression on his half-sagging face.

Weber explained further. "Mr. Simkovits, a power of attorney would give Harvy open access to your accounts while you are still alive. When you pass away, then the POA expires, and your last will shall determine the disposition of the money."

My mind was working fast. Dad's move would mean that if I wanted this money to stay hidden from my brother, who was my co-executor regarding our father's estate, then I'd have to transfer the funds into new accounts in my name before Dad passed away. That may have to happen while our father was on his deathbed or if he became fully incapacitated.

But suppose I wanted to bring this money into the light of legitimacy, revealing it to my brother and declaring it to the Canadian government. In that case, I might not have to do anything more than what Dad had requested. I could let the POA run out at Dad's death, allowing his co-executors to take control. Then not even my brother would know that I had had a direct say over these hidden funds.

I said nothing for now. I'd later worry about what I would do before or after Dad's death. Given my current intention of revealing some, most, or all of Dad's offshore money to my brother and declaring the amounts to the Canadian tax authorities, Dad's way of arranging it was okay for now. The risks were small that Dad would die unexpectedly, thus causing my loss of influence over his hidden millions. I hoped I was playing my dealt cards right.

Dad's eyes were square on the manager. "The POA is okay; let's do it."

"As you wish, Mr. Simkovits," Weber replied. He stood and left the room to get the necessary paperwork.

For a few minutes, Dad and I sat in silence. I glanced his way. He kept his head down, staring at the conference table between us. I wanted to ask, *Are you sure you're ready to do this, Dad?* But I didn't want to dissuade him from redefining the arrangement between us regarding his offshore assets.

I took long, deep breaths. For twenty-eight years, this was the moment for which I had patiently waited. While the seconds ticked off on the wall clock, this moment projected my father's trust regarding his promised legacy. My steadfast loyalty had paid off. Of his own volition, Dad was putting the keys to his offshore accounts into my hands, to have and to hold until death do us part.

I hadn't had to ask or say one single word about it. Inside Dad's failing mind, he may have figured that now was the right time. I was grateful that I wouldn't have to wrestle the cash out of his one good fist. I'd have no leverage in that match, for Dad had complete legal control over his offshore treasure.

Weber returned and placed the power of attorney papers on the desk. He asked for my identification. I gave him my driver's licence, and Weber completed the forms. I didn't ask Dad whether he had ever removed my POA on his small account, as I had asked him to do a year earlier. I didn't need or want to know. That fact was now superseded by my gaining a say over his every hidden Canadian, American, and Euro cent. I'd later work out, with my lawyer, what I'd need to do to make peace with the taxman about now having my fingers deep into my father's offshore pockets.

Weber turned the filled-in documents around, and he placed them in front of me. "I need a copy of your signature for the file." The banker leaned forward and pointed to where I needed to sign.

I complied as I worked to keep my breathing steady. I was now up to my elbows in Dad's hidden treasure chest sitting in illegal offshore sand. I didn't want to show my overexuberance, which could lead to my demise.

Weber pushed the documents across the desk to Dad. The bank manager leaned over the table even further to show my father where he needed to sign. My dad stared at the papers for a moment, perhaps pretending to read them. Though he had on his reading glasses, I was pretty sure he wouldn't understand the legalese. Dad raised his head. "Weber, are you sure I'm doing the right thing? Should I be giving this authority to Harvy?"

I held my breath and said nothing. For years, the manager had known of my father's deteriorating condition. I had come here several times to talk candidly about my father's investments. I hoped Weber would support my father's move, but I had no idea what was on the banker's mind.

Weber responded as if his lines had been rehearsed for today or said before in similar situations. "Yes, Mr. Simkovits, it's the right thing. Your son, as long as you trust him, can manage this better for you."

He gestured my way. "And it appears you do trust him by having brought him here many times to participate in these discussions." He glanced my way. "And I understand that Harvy has never done anything counter to your wishes." He looked at my father. "You need to make such plans to preserve the longevity of your assets with this bank."

Dad did trust me. I had proven my loyalty, time and time again. As far as he knew, I had held his financial secrets in total confidence. Only once had I ever asked him for money without his offering it to me first—when I had asked to redeem my JHS preferred shares as my brother had done. I never begged, demanded, or expected anything else from him, as his eldest son, his wives, my half-sister, and some so-called friends had done.

Somehow, Dad knew that his memory, along with his body, was failing. He needed someone to safeguard what he had built. My father needed to keep his twenty-eight-year promise to me. Who else did he have to shepherd these accounts after he would be gone?

Dad looked again at the documents. He slowly, carefully, and deliberately inked them with his signature. I noticed how much his mark had changed over recent years. It was like the signature of a child. It looked as if my father—his tongue between his lips—were stringing together the letters of his name. His typical big "J" and "S" loops, and the illegible yet profound squiggles for the rest of his last name, had regressed to simple cursive lettering. His signature now would be unrecognizable to any lawyer, accountant, banker, or notary who had done business with Johnny Simkovits from the day he started his Montreal Phono Company forty-seven years ago.

I glanced at Weber. He sat motionlessly, the patient banker he was. I was glad that he was there to witness my father's inking of these documents; otherwise, Dad's mark could have been considered a forgery.

I'm not sure what my father was feeling or thinking at that moment. He acted as if he were performing a simple business transaction, one among the millions he had conducted over his lifetime. He showed no emotion or facial expression. I couldn't detect any jitteriness in his body—like the shivers I sensed in mine as I watched him gradually sign the powers of attorney, one clandestine account at a time.

I looked down at the table. Part of me felt sad. Here was my faltering father, once an influential and revered man in his Montreal Slovak and Hungarian business and social circles, relinquishing a vestige of the power and control that he had coveted so dearly. This money had been his treasure, potency, and legacy. That now became trumped by his inevitable, inescapable mortality. Dad's signature on those POAs meant that what he worked so hard for, making him powerful and robust, would now build his successor's strength and stature.

I continued to watch as Dad signed the last document. I simultaneously felt excited relief and grave dread. My relief was in now having my turn with Dad's money after decades of wondering and waiting. On that brilliant summer day in Zurich, when I was 17, he and I had walked out of his first offshore stash at the *Banque de Genève*, with my following him like a puppy dog behind its master. Now, in a matter of moments, I was becoming the next master of Dad's hidden legacy.

My dread was for the responsibility I now felt, the weight of this underground pile of cash bearing down on me. I needed to bring it carefully above ground and into the light of Revenue Canada. I needed to reveal its existence to my brother, who had been kept in the dark all these years.

My father put down the pen. He employed his able hand to push the documents back to Weber gently. The manager said, "I will fax these to Lux today. Everything should be made official by tomorrow. It should go smoothly. If there is any problem, I'll give both you and Harvy a call."

For the following days, weeks, months, or perhaps years—until my father's passing—I would now be an official co-conspirator in my father's unlawful money maneuvering. My hands were now deep into Dad's concealed cookie jar. I couldn't wait until the day I could break open the container and disclose its contents.

I didn't look forward to revealing to my brother what I now held in my possession. How would Steve look upon me when I told him? Would he be grateful for my honesty, or would my voluntary disclosure to him split us even further? We'd have to work to bring these funds out from the darkness of a Luxembourg bank into the light of the Canadian taxman. I glanced toward the ceiling. *Mom, please give me strength.*

It had taken only a few moments to alter the course of my father's surreptitious gift. I was confident that this money's sordid history wouldn't become its ultimate destiny. The path of the tightrope I had walked for so many years, on which I feared falling to my demise if I leaned too far in either Dad's illicit direction or my brother's righteous course, would now be more of my choosing. If I could keep my eyes on my desired destination at the end of the rope, then my precarious walk might be made easier. And if my path turned out not so easy, I hoped that it would have been just.

Dad nodded to the bank manager but said nothing more. He put his reading glasses back into his jacket's lapel pocket. He glanced at me and motioned toward the conference room door. "Let's go, son."

I stood and walked over to him, pulled his wheelchair away from the table, and pivoted it toward the door. As I started to wheel him out of the conference room, he looked at the bank manager. "Thank you for your time, Weber." Dad said nothing about seeing him again.

Mr. Weber walked over and reached out to take my father's hand, and he presented a small smile. "It has been my pleasure, Mr. Simkovits. I wish you my very best." He turned to me. "And to you, too, Harvy."

I pressed my lips together, kept a soft look in my eyes, and nodded my thanks to the manager. I carefully wheeled my father through the conference room door, past the reception area, through the bank's double security doors, down the elevator, and to his car.

Dad and I didn't say much to each other while heading to his car and then driving back to his home. The careful and gentle way I maneuvered his wheelchair and helped him into the car served as my offer of gratitude for the trust he had bestowed. I was grateful that I hadn't had to yank or even coax those offshore dollars from his withering hands.

On the way back to his office, my father asked, "You'll come to supper tonight with Suzie and me?"

I didn't hesitate. "Sure, Dad, I'd be happy to."

Having me join him for supper was now more important than all his dollars and euros in Luxembourg. Tonight would be a night for a quiet celebration—Dad with his one daily vodka on the rocks, and Suzie and I with our regular glass or two of wine. We'd offer "To your health!" in Hungarian, French, and English. Suzie would have no suspicion as to why Dad and I were lifting our glasses. Our usual conversation about her daughter and grandkids would provide a distraction from the bestowed burden I now fully bore.

As I drove back to my father's apartment, I made sure to keep both of my hands on the steering wheel and both of my eyes on traffic. Today, my life has become more precious; I didn't want to cause a fatal accident.

Tomorrow, I'd start to think more about my Elliot Trudell lawyer, the Canadian government, and my brother.

* * * *

Reclaiming Precious Property

A few weeks after my father had bestowed on me a power of attorney over his Global Trade Bank accounts, I spoke with him during one of our regular Sunday evening calls. There was one more thing I wanted to get out of the way before I spoke again to my lawyer at Elliot Trudell.

I said, "Dad, can we go to your safety deposit box at your bank?" I spoke softly and calmly. "I'd like to remove my items from there and put them into a different box." I kept my voice steady. "After you're gone, I'd hate it if Steve and I would fight about what items in there belong to me."

Dad was well aware that Steve and I rarely agreed on anything. There was a twinge of sadness in his voice. "Okay, son. When do you want to go?"

"I'll be in Montreal next week for my regular monthly client trip. How's then?"

"Sure, anytime," he said.

The following week, without Steve or Rob knowing, I drove Dad to his company's bank for nearly fifty years. During that half-century, the outside of the bank's stone block structure hadn't changed. The inside now sported security glass between the tellers and the customers. Similar security precautions had replaced the bank's previous windows and doors. Several robberies in the area, including at this bank, had compelled such measures.

Every time I had been here before, I had seen Hassidic Jews—wearing long beards, black garb, and black hats—walk up and down the streets carrying on their business. In the last decade or more, a Greek community had formed in the area. Many of the bank's employees, even the most recent manager, were Greek immigrants. It was interesting that Greek Canadians now worked here. As far as I knew, Hassidic Jewish Canadians never had.

The moment we walked in, the head bank teller recognized my father. The Greek woman motioned us toward her as she stood behind a customer counter. Dad approached her, and I followed.

"Hello, Mr. Simkovits," she offered with enthusiasm. "We haven't seen you here in a long time, perhaps over a year." She looked at me. "I see you have brought your son!" She quipped, "Is this handsome fellow your eldest or your youngest?" She looked back and forth between us and smiled. "I see where he gets his good looks."

Dad and I smiled back, but my father couldn't offer her more than a three-quarter grin. Though it had been many years since I had been here with him, I found it both amusing and irritating that his service providers, like his friends and colleagues, couldn't keep my brother and me straight. "Yes, Roberta," my father said, his voice garbled. "You remember my youngest, Harvy?"

She reached out her hand. "It's a pleasure to see you again, Harvy. You must be the son that lives in Boston."

At least she had that right. Dad answered before I could. "Yes, and he's not around Montreal much. He comes to visit only once in a while."

It was amusing how I had become the focus of this conversation without having said a word. I put out my hand. "Good to meet you, Roberta." We shook hands, and she offered another smile.

She turned back to my father. "So, what can I do for you today?"

Dad answered. "Harvy wants to open a safety deposit box, and we want to get into mine."

"Certainly," she said. "Did you bring your key to get into your box, Mr. Simkovits?" It sounded as if Dad had come here once without.

"Yes, yes; I have my key." He pulled it out of a small, leather key pouch that was probably as old as I was, and he showed her the key it contained.

"Okay," she said. "Allow me to fetch the paperwork and get Harvy started." Within seconds, she had walked briskly to her desk and returned. She looked at me. "I see from my list that the location next to your father's box is free. It's the same size, the second largest we have here at the bank. It costs $125 per year. Would you like that one?"

I suspected I'd have a box here only while my father was alive. Not wanting to sound uncertain, and wishing to indicate that I may have more to deposit, and desiring to make today's transfer flow smoothly, I responded, "Sure. That's fine."

Roberta led us to the back of the bank. We walked into a room-sized safe that housed over a hundred deposit boxes of various sizes. It wasn't a grandiose space like the ones seen in the banks depicted in James Bond movies. Dad liked modest service-provider ponds where he could be a big customer fish. Being among the bank's largest and longest patrons made him feel he'd obtain better attention and service. Certainly, Roberta was proving that today.

Using her master key and our box keys, she unlocked the two safety deposit boxes, Dad's full box and my empty one. We headed for a private room. I carried Dad's chest, which felt as heavy as a contractor's toolbox. Roberta brought my new container.

After she left, my father opened his deposit box. Sitting on top was a stack of folded legal documents with blue paper covers. Dad picked up those papers and put them to one side.

My eyes suddenly opened wide. Underneath were dozens of boxes, cases, and pouches. Dad talked as he rummaged through his treasure. "Half of what's here are gold coins; the rest are silver. I used to have many 5-ounce gold bars too, but I traded them over the years to buy other things."

I knew he had, years ago, traded a few gold bars for the Rolex he had subsequently given to his grandson in Slovakia. I didn't say anything about that. Instead, I asked, "How long have you been collecting coins, Dad?"

He spoke slowly, trying to annunciate his words. "I started collecting when you and Stevie were kids. I first bought Canadian silver dollars through the '60s and '70s. Then, into the '80s, I got Canadian $20 gold pieces, and then I collected $100 gold coins afterward. That's what most of these are." He opened a few of the small boxes. "Today, the gold coins are worth at least ten times their face value."

I had no idea if Dad was exaggerating or not.

He grabbed a pouch and dumped the contents on the small table. Forty or fifty quarter-ounce and half-ounce gold coins tumbled out. He spoke slowly, his voice raspy. "These are old French francs and Hungarian forints and other baloney like that. They're all pure gold."

He raised his good hand to make his point. "You never know when a government will change, and you'll have to run for your life." He worked to form his words. "Before and during the war, people escaped with coins like these." He pointed to his feet and then tugged at his jacket. "They hid them in the bottom of their shoe or sewed them into their coats."

Though Dad had told me those things when I was a teen, I didn't interrupt him. There was no reason to trample on his teachings.

He opened a couple of the bigger cases, with each housing multiple gold and silver coins. Dad pointed. "This one contains a set of Chinese panda coins, and that one is from Iran." He gestured toward the image stamped onto the coins. "That's the last Shah and his wife." I looked but did not touch.

I pointed to an object that attracted my attention. "What's that, Dad? Another gold watch?"

He retrieved a silver metal watch with a matching bracelet. "It's a solid white gold Omega. I bought it in Switzerland a long time ago." He turned it over. "You see the band? It's integrated with the watch case as if it's one long piece of gold."

"I remember it now," I said. "You once showed it to me in your office when I was a teenager, but I never saw you wear it."

I could make out his garbled words. "It's out of fashion, but it's still worth its weight in eighteen karat gold." He shook the watch slowly in his right hand as if he were gauging its mass.

I nodded my understanding without showing exuberance for the heft of the gold in that timepiece. With Dad's Rolex now gone to Igor, my brother might want this Omega because I had gotten the Patek. *We'll see when the time comes.*

I pointed to some smaller boxes and cases at the bottom of the deposit box. "Could those be mine?"

Dad put them into my hands. "I think all these are yours, son."

I opened them one by one to confirm that they were indeed mine. The boxes held coins from The Bahamas, Bermuda, Greece, Jamaica, and other West Indies islands, places I had travelled with Dad or Mom when I was in my teens and early twenties. Dad had bought most of those coins for me when we had visited those lands, though I had purchased a couple of pieces myself. I was glad and impressed that he remembered. I was appreciative that he had brought me here today to make my life easier with Steve.

I placed my coin cases into my new deposit box. I retrieved my possessions from my jacket pockets that I had recovered weeks earlier from my father's office safe and placed them alongside the other items. Compared to Dad's box, mine looked pretty empty, but neither he nor I said anything. I could return later to downsize.

Dad came forth with something I didn't expect. "Harvy, what if I give you power of attorney over my deposit box here, just as I gave it to you at my bank over there?"

I thought for a moment. Maybe Dad thought that, with such a move, I wouldn't have to wait until probate was complete before I could have access to his box after his death. Perhaps he also didn't trust Steve with these precious things as much as he trusted me with them. I looked at him. "I appreciate your thought, Dad, but what about Steve? I'd hate for him to feel bad that I had power of attorney, and he didn't."

My father looked at his box and then turned partially toward me. "You're right, son." He added nothing else. He then picked up a couple of the documents he had put aside and put them into my hand. "These are old land purchase and sales agreements and contracts I did over the years."

I glanced at the blue covers of the documents in my hand and the ones still on the table. Dates went back twenty and thirty years. The street names of Dollard, Hochelaga, Thompson, and Monte de Liesse popped out of the ragged blue covers. Those names referred to the apartment and industrial buildings Dad had owned over the decades. I looked at him. "Has everything here been sold, or are there any properties that are still in your or JHS's ownership?"

His eyes shifted back and forth as if he were racking his brain. He spoke again without looking at me. "Everything has been disposed of a long time ago."

"So why do you keep these papers?"

He thought for a moment. "We don't have to, son. We can throw them out." He grabbed the pile and placed all the documents into my open hands.

Suddenly, there was dead airspace in the cramped room in which we stood. My father stared for a moment at what he had given me. He said, "No, son; leave them in the box for now. You and Stevie can throw them away when I'm gone."

I said, "Okay, Dad," and placed the documents back into his box. There was no need to pitch his petite collection of property papers. He seemed connected to what he had placed there for more than a generation.

Dad had never maintained a museum of the myriad record players and console stereos he had produced over the decades. I now realized that he might have been more proud of collecting properties than spending thirty years in manufacturing. Maybe he kept these deeds and contracts because they could easily fit into a bank safety deposit box rather than fill a warehouse of antiquated console models.

I took a long breath. Steve and I would rummage through these papers when Dad was gone. I smiled inside. Maybe we'll put them into our father's coffin so he could show St. Peter his real estate success here on earth.

Dad and I closed our respective boxes and exited the room. I carried both containers and placed them into the lockers from where they had come.

Steve and I would have the solemn chore of divvying up Dad's pile of precious metal after his passing. That task might now be made easier with my smaller collection tucked away elsewhere. It was hard to fathom that my father's accumulation was as old as I was. It demonstrated his faith in gold and silver, based on his long-standing belief: *Anything could happen with the government.*

That statement echoed in my head. I wondered what I would be facing with our Canadian government after my father would no longer be with us here on earth.

* * * *

Hungarian-Slovak Lion in Winter

Steve and I had rarely confided in each other as kids or young adults. After dropping out of Harvard Business School, I tried to rekindle our relationship during the years we worked together at JHS, but my efforts didn't last. During the cross-Canada trip that we had taken together, Steve abandoned me by the side of a Vancouver Island road. At JHS, he left me to fend for myself while he went globetrotting to East Africa and Israel, after which he turned Mormon. From then on, our lives split once again.

After the proliferation of email in the mid-1990s, Steve and I could air some issues long distance. It started with my mentioning his chronic lateness. I wrote: "Steve, when Dad gets agitated about your being late to friends and family suppers, he complains to everyone around him, and they get upset too. But when you finally arrive, no one says anything about it because Dad is again smiling."

Days later, my brother typed back: "My priorities are to my church and family."

In return, I typed, "So aren't we family too?"

Days later, he responded: "Not as important as mine, but I'll try to do better."

Afterward, he was only fifteen to twenty minutes late to family events instead of thirty minutes or more.

As time passed, Steve and I confronted weightier issues. He once typed: "You were always Dad's favourite. I felt I couldn't compete."

I responded: "You always fought with him and disagreed with everything he said or anything he wanted to do. At least I tried to find a middle ground."

Before pushing "send," I added, "I get it. It must have been hard for you. No wonder you were closer to Mom."

Nothing came back from him in return.

On another occasion, I became peeved at Steve regarding a JHS issue. I typed: "Why is it you never give in to what Dad or I want? You can be as stubborn as him. I know you don't want to be like him, but you are exactly that way sometimes. What the heck is that about?"

A couple of days later, I received: "I do what I think is right for me."

I thought for a day and then responded: "Yes, what's important to me is never important to you. But you always want Dad and me to bend to or accept what's important to you. Do I have that right?"

A day or two later, I got a response: "Don't sweat it, Harvy."

At least he was reading my messages, and we were communicating somewhat. Neither of us mentioned our email exchanges when we saw each other in Montreal.

After airing a few things over the internet, Steve and I became more cordial with each other. When we met, our quick hugs lasted a few tenths of a second longer, as if a tenuous truce had built between us. We stopped shunning each other, and we talked when we had to, especially about Dad.

* * *

One weekend, about a month after Dad had returned from Florida, Steve called me in Boston. His voice showed concern. "Dad is writing all kinds of cheques. Some are for tens of thousands of dollars."

Months before Dad gave me power of attorney over his offshore accounts, Steve had shared his concerns regarding our father's untethered spending. It now seemed that our father's writing of cheques from his legitimate personal bank accounts was getting out of control. "Who are the cheques going to?" I asked.

Steve spoke matter-of-factly. "Dad gave $25,000 to the Slovak Church for a new church roof a while ago, plus another $10,000 for religious statues. When he was in Slovakia last fall, he transferred $25,000 to the Archdiocese there so that they would send a new priest to Montreal."

Suzie had mentioned that the Montreal Slovak Church's previous priest had retired. It then became difficult for the church to find a replacement cleric. Multiple letters from the churchwardens to the Slovakia Archbishop in Bratislava had yielded promises but no pastor. It seemed that no Slovak preacher wanted to come to Canada on a multi-year stint or perhaps for half a lifetime. But shortly after Dad had made his cash donation, the Slovak Archbishop sent a new priest to Montreal, a Father Novak.

Steve continued to speak matter-of-factly. "I have no influence over Dad's U.S. account in Florida. But with his bank accounts in Montreal, I've now stepped in several times to stop his uncontrolled giving. I call his bank manager and ask him to cancel the new big cheques that Dad writes. The manager there knows that we have the Quebec Mandate."

Thank goodness Dad had signed a Quebec Mandate—as recommended by his notary, Peternik—a couple of years after Dad had completed his will. The Quebec Mandate was like a durable power of attorney. It permitted my brother and me, together, to take over Dad's health decisions and his financial affairs if he were severely disabled, either mentally or physically. Officially, the mandate required two independent doctors to declare Dad incapable. But Steve was able to leverage that document in other ways.

Our father's bank manager knew firsthand about Dad's growing absentmindedness. He allowed my brother to cancel any suspect cheques, but only if Steve got to the manager in time to issue a stop payment. Perhaps it wasn't above board for the manager to do that for Steve, but I was glad he understood and could curb our growing predicament. Dad was losing control.

I asked my brother, "So how do you know when you need to step in and stop a cheque Dad has signed?"

Steve spoke dryly. "Rob and I have a signal. If someone comes to Dad's office looking for a donation, Rob calls to give a heads up." He took a long breath and continued. "I then rush down there. Thankfully, I live only fifteen minutes away." He inhaled deeply again. "I pretend I'm in the area and just dropping in. I ask questions of the people that have come to see Dad. If I feel they are looking for money, I quietly pull them aside and tell them, 'I'm sorry, but my father is not in control of his giving. Please leave him alone and not ask for any donations.'"

Steve's tone remained matter-of-fact. "Knowing I'm standing in the way, they leave. But if they've already left with a cheque by the time I get there, then Rob fills me in. I call the bank and issue a stop payment."

Though it was good that my brother was around to stop our father's money bleeding, I couldn't believe what was going on. "Who are these darn people who are asking for money?" came bursting out of my mouth.

Steve ignored my agitation and continued to talk blandly. "It's people Dad knows from the Slovak community or his Slovak Church. He keeps on telling those folks, 'If you ever need anything, then come to see me.' You know how he is, needing to be Mr. Big Shot with his money. The worst offender is that new Father Novak."

"You mean the priest who came here from Slovakia?" I worked to stay calm. "How so?"

Steve motored on. "Novak comes around to JHS every week with another member of his flock looking for a handout. Dad can't stop himself from signing cheques to Novak and whoever the Father brings with him."

I knew from Suzie that Dad was putting $100 bills into the Slovak priest's palm every Sunday morning after services. She had said that both she and other church members were upset at our father for doing so. She then added, "Your father should put that money into the collection plate so that the churchwardens can count and control it."

Irritation was in her voice. "It's not right what Johnny's doing. I told him to stop. But he now takes a $100 bill from his pocket every Sunday and puts it into Father Novak's hand, on top of $100 he puts into the plate." She shook her head. "And the Father takes that money and keeps it for himself!"

Knowing Dad's business history with his countrymen, I started to wonder about this Slovak priest. "Steve, have you talked to Novak? Does he understand Dad's condition?"

My brother's voice elevated a half-decibel. "Novak's English isn't good. I've tried to speak to him in French, which he does seem to speak, but I don't think he understands me. He then comes back another time with the same guy or another flock member looking for a favour."

Steve took another long breath. "Thank goodness Rob is there most of the week to watch out. But he doesn't feel right about stepping in front of these people. Rob calls me to run down to JHS and head Novak off at the money pass." I could feel Steve smile through the phone.

I thought for a moment. "What if we send a formal letter both to Father Novak and the Montreal Archbishop to whom he reports? We can ask that he and the church stop bothering Dad. It might help to put things in writing. Do you think it would make a difference?"

After a pause, Steve responded, "That wouldn't hurt. I can try."

"Let me know if you need any help with that letter; I'm generally good at writing such things."

"Sure; I'll let you know."

* * *

The next time I flew into Montreal, Dad and Rob picked me up at the airport. (Rob was driving Dad's car.) I took over as driver and dropped Rob off at Dad's apartment to retrieve his car and run some errands before rejoining Dad at JHS. I then drove Dad to his office before borrowing the vehicle for the day to see a client. In the car, and out of the blue, my father asked, "Harvy, should I lend money to my doctor?"

What? "What do you mean?" I asked. There was a touch of irritation in my voice. "Your GP is asking for money?" I had met Dad's doctor on several occasions; I had considered him a straight-up fellow. I never before had to wonder about his motives.

Dad was his usual garbled self. "He's having money problems. He wants to borrow another $10,000 from me. Should I do it?"

"Another $10,000? What have you lent him so far?"

"I gave him $25,000, but he signed an IOU for it."

"Okay, what kind of IOU?" I felt like I was peeling back a white onion—the kind Dad used when he cooked his favourite spicy Hungarian food. My eyes stung more with every layer I exposed.

"I have the IOU in the office. I can show you when we get there."

After we had arrived, he pulled a crumpled paper from his desk drawer. It was hand-written:

> *For consideration of $25,000, I will name John Simkovits as a beneficiary in my insurance policy for that amount.*

The doctor's scratchy signature, hardly legible, was under it. I looked at my father. "Dad, this is not a proper IOU. There's no interest amount stated; he doesn't have to pay you back until he's dead, and there are no witness signatures."

Dad ignored my comment. "Do you think I should lend him more?"

Dad rarely asked me what he should do with his money lending or charitable giving. If he was asking, then he had reservations about loaning more cash to his doctor. During his business days, I had known my father to ask for solid collateral for sizable loans, like a mortgage or lien on a property.

A fire grew inside my gut. Dad had, for decades, told me never to be irresponsible with money, to be careful about both what I spent and to whom I lent or gave. He was now reckless, unable to say no to his doctor, and not protecting himself with a formal loan agreement. *What was happening to my businessman father?*

I raised my voice. "You shouldn't give your doctor another penny!" I took a breath to keep control of my voice. "I can't believe he's asking you. And what proof do you have that he has put you on his life insurance policy?"

My father stared at me blankly and didn't answer. Maybe he didn't know how to respond to my confrontation. By lending money to friends and associates, perhaps he was trying to hold onto what manhood he had left after losing half of it to a stroke. But he was getting out of control.

I looked at my father, pointed at him, and spoke as calmly as I could. "Unless you promise you won't do it, Dad, I'm calling your doctor right now. I'll demand that he give you the money back right away, or sign a better loan agreement, or give you some proof of the insurance death benefit he had promised you." I went further. "There may be grounds to report him to the Quebec medical board for taking advantage of a patient."

Dad batted his hand. "Okay, okay, son. You don't need to say anything to anybody. I won't do it. I'll say I don't have any more money to lend." He returned the crumpled loan agreement into his desk drawer and offered nothing more.

Though my father never made a second loan to his physician, I didn't know if he'd see a dime back from the first. I decided not to create trouble for his doctor. Steve and I might need the physician's signature if we had to exercise Dad's Quebec Mandate. Others in Johnny Simkovits's world wouldn't be as gracious as his bank manager in allowing Steve and me to exert limits on our father's check-writing.

* * *

It wasn't only Dad's church and doctor who were working to tap into Dad's assets. After our father had left for Florida in January of 2000, my brother disclosed, "One of Dad's distant relatives from Bratislava, Slovakia, a Mikal Dula, came to Montreal last November to visit him."

"What was that about?" I asked.

"He and a colleague flew here for a couple of days to see Dad about a business deal in Slovakia. I happened to be at the office when Dad met with them." Steve spoke in his serene monotone. "I didn't understand their conversation because they all spoke in Slovak. Dad later told me that he was helping Mikal start a business over there."

It was good that Steve had a flexible volunteer schedule with his church and could drop in regularly to see our father. My brother's voice showed concern, unusual for him. "Before Mikal left for the airport, Dad handed the guy a stack of $100 bills. It seems as if Dad paid for their plane tickets from Bratislava and their hotel in Montreal."

"Hmm," I said. "Let's keep a watch on this, Steve. I'd hate for Dad to get entangled in something else in Slovakia, even if it involves a relative. I wouldn't want him to get screwed again." My voice grew with apprehension. "You remember what happened with Canexco?" I didn't mention my brother's failed SBP spinoff.

"Yes, Harvy, as clear as yesterday. But if Dad has a written agreement with Mikal, I'm not sure what we can do."

I didn't say a word. Unlike my aboveboard brother, I didn't care if our father had signed a contract. Dad's former Slovak partners hadn't cared about intellectual property and legal protections when they stole Canexco's patent.

The following March, I visited Dad for a long weekend in Deerfield. One evening, Suzie came to me after Dad had gone to bed. Her face and voice expressed concern. "Harvy, this guy Mikal Dula keeps on calling your father."

Her eyes looked worried. "I don't let your father pick up the phone here anymore, and neither do I. Instead, I let the messages go to the answering machine." She took a breath. "I'd like you to hear some and see if you can make any sense of them."

"Is Mikal speaking in English or Slovak in those messages?"

"It's Slovak, but maybe you can understand a few words."

I listened while Suzie played a few messages. The man's deep voice sounded as if he were pleading. What I could make out was, *"Prosím, Janos* [Please, Johnny]" repeated several times. It seemed the man was desperate.

I turned to Suzie. "How long has this been going on, and how much does Dad know about these messages?"

"Mikal's been calling several times a week for the last few weeks. As I said, I don't let your father near the phone or the message machine. Frankly, he shows no interest when the phone rings."

I thought for a moment. I wondered what Dad might have promised this distant cousin. I suspected that my father (and maybe my brother too) wouldn't leave a family member in the lurch, but I didn't consider this man to be my family.

Dad hadn't mentioned anything about Mikal to Steve or me. He didn't tell us what he had promised his kin, so I felt no obligation to the guy. I had to protect Dad in the same way Steve had stopped some of his bank cheques. Right or wrong, I felt no qualms in rebuffing money-begging phone calls.

I shook my head. "Suzie, you're here in Florida for only another few weeks." I pushed the erase button on the machine. "Keep on doing what you are doing, including erasing these messages." I looked at her. "I don't know what business my father has with this Mikal guy, but Dad's in no shape to do anything for anyone anymore, especially for anybody overseas."

Suzie nodded her understanding and acceptance.

I continued. "Eventually, Mikal will get the message that Dad's no longer interested in whatever they had going in Slovakia."

After she and Dad had returned to Montreal, Suzie said that the calls from Mikal had stopped. Neither she nor I said anything to my brother about the unilateral decision I had made.

* * *

Though I knew my father had many millions stashed offshore and was spending only the annual interest he made from those funds, I wondered how much legitimate money he had left onshore. If he spent that down, it could mean he'd have to take more funds out of JHS.

According to my rough calculations from our company statements and my limited knowledge of property values in the area, JHS's cash, building, and land properties were worth several million dollars. Outside of Dad's preferred shares and his few controlling shares, my brother and I owned most of JHS's assets through our common shareholdings in the company. If Dad ran out of his own money, might he take from his sons again via our holding company?

I had to dig deeper into my father's finances. I wanted a firsthand view of what damage he was creating to his bank accounts. If the situation looked dire and Dad was bleeding cash, Steve and I might have to exercise the Quebec Mandate sooner than later. I loathed the thought of having to take financial control away from my father. *How might he react?*

Later that week, I walked into my father's office when Suzie took Dad to a doctor's appointment. I didn't tell Rob that I was coming. If the bookkeeper expected me, he might defend himself better against my questions.

I considered that Rob must know what was happening with my father's bank accounts. *Wouldn't he tell Steve or me if he saw a problem?* I hoped he would have shouted a warning if he saw Dad's legitimate money ship running aground.

I didn't tell Steve about my pending investigation into Dad's cash holdings; I wanted to look at Dad's accounts first. I didn't want my brother to know that I was snooping around if there were no issues.

After initial greetings, I looked at the bookkeeper. "Rob, can you please show me my father's Montreal and Florida bank account statements for the last few years?"

I suspected I might get resistance from JHS's 20-year employee, now more of a paid office companion. But he seemed relieved that I was taking an interest in my father's accounts. Within minutes, he placed three banking files in front of me. Each was many centimeters thick. These were Dad's Florida account and his Canadian and U.S. dollar accounts in Montreal. The statements went back for more years than I had requested.

I nodded at Rob. I took the thick pile and went to sit at my father's desk in his private office. I wanted to examine the status of each account to understand how much my father was spending monthly and annually. I also wanted to see how much he had started with years ago and what remained now. I dug in, starting with his Florida USD account from five years earlier.

After seeing many months of five to fifteen thousand dollars in that account, I found a $120,000 U.S. deposit made about three years ago. *That makes sense.* That amount was the difference between the sales price of his Boca home and the purchase price of his lesser-expensive Deerfield condo.

I paged through the subsequent statements, jumping a couple of months at a time. I could see that from January to April—the months that Dad spent in Deerfield—his Florida account dropped steadily by about $40,000. That pattern repeated every ensuing winter. *How is he spending $40,000 in a little over three months?* Suzie had said that Dad was putting $100 bills every week into the Catholic priest's hands when they went to mass in Deerfield. That was pocket change compared to the big bucks that were flying out of this account.

I jumped forward, getting to the most recent statements. Only a few hundred dollars remained in the account. *Oh, God!* I felt a tremble down my spine. Dad had consumed all the U.S. cash he had had in Florida.

I turned my attention to Dad's Montreal bank accounts. I looked at the U.S. dollar account first, looking for the $185,000 deposit he had made on selling the furniture in his Peru, NY house. There it was, deposited over five years earlier. The only income he had in that account was the interest on that amount. It also looked as if he hadn't deposited any cash payments he had received from the Global Trade Bank—probably a good thing.

I quickly paged through the U.S. dollar statements to see how the account balance went up and down during the years. To my chagrin, it showed a steady downhill slide. I jumped forward to the most recent statements. There was little left in the account. His legitimate U.S. funds in Canada were exhausted. *God!* I felt sweat under my arms and a shudder in my ribs.

I sat for a moment to catch my breath. My father had burned through all his onshore U.S. cash. *Why the hell had I not taken a closer look earlier?* I shouldn't have trusted either Rob to raise a red flag or my brother to look closely at Dad's spending. I should have paid more attention. *What idiots we are!* I couldn't believe we had let this happen.

I took a long breath and paged through Dad's Canadian-dollar account, again starting five years earlier. I prayed the story would be different there.

In the oldest statement, Dad's Canadian dollar account showed over $200,000—that money mainly reflecting the $175,000 he had redeemed of his JHS preferred shares when Geoff Levi had been JHS's accountant.

As I again paged through each subsequent month, I could see several similar direct deposits coming into the account. Those deposits totaled over $15,000CAD per month.

Okay, that makes sense. Those were Dad's monthly insurance annuity payments, private pension withdrawals, and social insurance payments. Those vehicles would give him a steady income for as long as he lived. Because I suspected the insurance company, like social security, paid withholding tax to federal and provincial governments, much of that money was after-tax. *Thank goodness he's getting money monthly on which to live.* Those payments were guaranteed for Dad's life.

I sat back and took long breaths. I knew that Dad had over three-hundred-fifty thousand dollars remaining in his retirement pension—Elaine hadn't gotten it all. From his Canadian-dollar bank statement, I gathered he was taking the money out of that pension fund according to the rules: the minimum required payments each month until the funds were exhausted when he'd turn 90. But at his current level of spending, he might need to take more money from that private pension. That money was meant to last ten more years but could become exhausted much sooner.

I jumped forward to Dad's most recent Canadian dollar statement. There was only $10,000 left in the account. Dad had spent everything that had come into it, including the $200,000 he had started with five years earlier. My heart raced; my armpits got wet. *On what is he spending all this money?*

I could tell from the Canadian statements that one of his highest monthly bills was his AMX card payments. Suzie had mentioned that Dad could spend $750 in one night at the Troika with her and his friends. *I bet the restaurant still loves him.* I paged backward through the statements. I saw cheques of $10,000, $15,000, and $25,000 jumping off the pages. Some of those were the donations he made to the Slovak Church, both in Montreal and Bratislava. *His church must love him too.* I figured that one $25,000 cheque had to be the loan to his doctor. *Dad must have his whole world loving him!*

I remembered the years when Dad wined and dined his friends at the Troika, Tokay, and other swank Montreal joints. He loved to be the grand host by paying the tab. Why hadn't any of his friends protected him from himself these last few years? Were they taking advantage of him now that he was gradually becoming disabled? Were they all freeloaders like his *Schmack* lawyer had been? It seemed as if they had closed their eyes to his untethered outlays. Or maybe Dad had bragged to them about having more assets than he did; thus, they felt that he could afford his enormous expenditures.

I took more deep breaths. *All this is Dad's money!* None of us, even his friends, had a right to supervise his spending. But this was well beyond normal! I made a quick calculation. Dad had been spending or giving away about a quarter-million after-tax Canadian dollars each year for three to five years. That amount didn't include the cash that had floated out of his offshore accounts—a quarter-million U.S. dollars in just the past year!

Dad lived in an assisted-living apartment, with many of his and Suzie's meals included, for only $2000 per month. I knew he wasn't lighting his 25 daily cigarettes with $20 bills, so where was the cash going? The money that was flying out of his accounts was unfathomable!

On the other hand, Dad had been generous to me, paying down my home mortgage and often putting cash into my hands. (And he had done similarly with my brother.) But those gifts didn't account for more than a million dollars that had disappeared from his legitimate and illegitimate bank accounts. His legit accounts were now virtually empty. Shivers jolted through me, and sweat oozed out of me.

I have to confront Rob about this! He's been watching this money drain and, for years, hadn't uttered a word about it to my brother or me.

I took another deep breath and walked into the main office. Dad's bookkeeper still sat where I had found him. He hadn't run out the front door, never to return. I looked directly at him. "Hey Rob, what's going on here with Dad's money and bank accounts. I see that he's spending everything he takes in. Hardly anything's left. Can you tell me what's going on?"

Rob's voice was meek. "I'm glad you're looking at this, Harvy." I could see his body shaking a bit. But was he stressed about seeing that money pass through my father's hands or about my asking questions?

I kept my voice calm. "What do you think is happening to the cash?"

Rob took a breath. "Your father spends it or gives it away. I think you know that Steve comes in here almost every week to stop cheques your father signs. But Steve can't put the brakes on everything. Johnny still has his credit cards and can go to the ATM. These last few years, anytime he sees money in his accounts, he thinks about who he could give it away to."

Dad's recent behavior didn't resemble that of the tight-fisted businessman I had known. Though he had been generous when entertaining, it was never to the level of giving all his money away. My head began to ache.

Rob added something I hadn't expected. "From somewhere, your father gets a bag of cash every month. He turns around and gives it away to different people. Then he goes back to get another bag."

It was clear that Dad was tapping his offshore accounts at the Global Trade Bank. Perhaps he was obtaining that cash with the help of the mysterious Hungarian Montreal friend he had once mentioned to me.

Rob wasn't letting on what he knew or didn't know about my father's offshore assets. I didn't ask or say anything more about those bags of money. I figured that the less I comprehended what Rob knew, and the less he understood what I knew, the better it would be for us. Instead, I asked, "So my father's annuity and pension income—the over $15,000 he gets every month since he retired—he's been spending that too?"

The bookkeeper shrugged. "It's all working to maintain your father's lifestyle and his desire to give his money away." Rob's face seemed relieved about getting the situation off his mind. He added, "I had to transfer money from his Canadian account to his Florida account because he ran out of cash there this winter." He took another breath. "I'm glad you are looking at this, Harvy. There's nothing I can do to stop your father."

I screamed at Rob in my mind. *He's been doing this for at least the last three goddamn years! What about a heads up to Steve or me?* But those words did not come out of my mouth.

Sweat formed on Rob's forehead as I eyed his face. Though he looked uncomfortable, he seemed to have been straight with me. I realized that he was no police hound for this boss's son; he was only an obedient bookkeeper dog.

Though Rob was an honest guy, he probably didn't know what to do besides blindly continue the accounting and companion jobs that Dad had hired him to do. He was trying to be loyal and trustworthy to his employer. *It's Steve and me who have been the idiots these last few years.* Though I wished Rob would have said something, it wasn't his doing that there was no money left in my father's bank accounts. *God help us all!*

"Okay, Rob," I said. "Please keep Steve and me informed if you see Dad get into serious money problems. We'll have to figure out how he can support himself in Florida next winter."

I berated myself once more as I drove back to my father's apartment. I had had a secret hope that Dad would have drawn down his offshore funds and leave his legitimate assets intact for his estate. *Son-of-a-bitch!* I once again had been utterly naïve about my father's ways. Though I tried to play well the rummy cards I was given, Dad always seemed to have an extra joker in hand.

That evening, I had supper with my father and Suzie at their home. After the meal, while Suzie went to put things away, I spoke to Dad privately. I didn't reveal that I had looked at his bank accounts, but I stated what I had heard from my brother and Suzie. "Dad, why are you giving away so much money, especially to the Slovak Church and their priest here in Montreal?"

He paused for a moment. He looked into my face as he pointed toward the ceiling. His voice was gruffer than ever. "I pray to God every day that I can live another day to give money to the church."

Wow! I hadn't expected that. Was my father now at the mercy of his religious beliefs, negotiating with his God to let him live a little longer? It became crystal clear that Dad was trying to stack the deck with St. Peter.

I pressed on, keeping my voice low. "Dad, why aren't you giving away your money *over there* rather than what you have *over here*?"

He looked quizzically at me and announced, "What's the difference which money I give?"

I looked away and left the conversation there.

* * * *

19

Wrenching the Pen Out of His Hand

My brother had written a letter to the Montreal Archbishop about Father Novak. He also spoke to the Slovak Church's churchwardens about the Father, who was still coming every week to Dad's office looking for donations for flock members. During one of our now weekly phone calls, Steve updated me, "The churchwardens are saying that they too are upset with Father Novak. They're trying to get him replaced through church channels."

I was stunned. "What's the wardens' beef with the guy?"

Steve responded matter-of-factly. "It seems the Father is trying to bring to light the money that the churchwardens have been keeping in separate trust accounts, money that they are trying to keep out of the diocese's view."

"What's that about?"

"You know those church Christmas and Fall Harvest parties and the other fundraisers they do? Some of the wardens keep those accumulated funds hidden in separate accounts that are not transparent to the diocese. If the church's balance sheet would reflect those funds properly, then the diocese would want their cut every year, something like 6 or 7%."

Son-of-a-gun! Johnny Simkovits is not the only tricky Slovak. "How much money are they hiding from the church?" I asked.

"I'm not sure. People I know there are telling me it's hundreds of thousands of dollars. Father Novak is trying to bring that money out into the open. It's irking the wardens and trustees who are trying to protect those funds by keeping them hidden."

"These Slovaks do know how to finagle," I huffed. "Sometimes, I don't feel proud of being connected to our family's heritage." I knew many honest Slovaks, including relatives in my father's family, but others seemed shady.

"I know what you mean," Steve said.

He continued. "Father Novak is also attracting more francophone people into the congregation. The Slovaks, who have been there for decades, are now feeling like they are in the minority."

Steve spoke frankly. "The churchwardens, all Slovaks, are now trying to obtain another priest from Slovakia who will better work for them, not just for himself or the church bosses." His voice stayed steady. "But you know how tough it was for them to obtain Novak, even after Dad had donated to the Catholic Church in Slovakia. A few of the wardens here feel that the Slovak Archbishop sent over their worst priest."

"What a Slovak 'As the Stomach Churns'!" I said. That was my brother's pun for our mother's TV soap drama, *As the World Turns*. [The Carol Burnett Show had first coined the quip.] "And to think we went to that church when we had been kids."

"Yup!" he retorted.

"By the way, Steve, what happened with your letter to the Montreal Archbishop?"

Steve drew a big breath. "I sent a pretty strong letter. I told the Archbishop that Dad was losing his mental capabilities. I said that our father could no longer hold himself back from giving money directly to Father Novak and the church members who come to see him weekly. I asked the Archbishop to tell Father Novak to stop bothering Dad."

"Okay, any response?"

"The Archbishop answered through one of his aides. That Father said, 'If John Simkovits wants to give his money to the church, then why would the church stop him from doing so?'"

I thought for a moment. *Yes! Who were we to stop Dad from giving his money away?* Certainly, we didn't want our father to run out of savings and be unable to support himself. And we didn't want him to be taken advantage of by distant relatives, so-called friends, or unscrupulous church members. Over the decades, Dad had promised, "You two boys will have everything I have." Yet had he meant "only what I have left"? As far as I was concerned, Dad had crossed a line between affable generosity and absurd giving.

I cursed quietly to myself and then said, "Well, it figures that the Archbishop would be no help. What a racket those Catholics have going in selling eternal salvation."

My religious brother said nothing.

"Did you send Novak a copy of your letter?" I asked.

"Yes, but I never heard back from him."

"That figures too," I said with irritation.

Steve responded. "But Novak has stopped coming around Dad's office. He now knows I'll try to head him off."

"Well, that's something." I took a long breath. "So it looks like you and I have to take matters into our hands to stop Dad's financial bleeding." I took a long breath. "I looked at his Canadian and U.S. bank accounts recently. He's almost out of savings, both here and in Florida."

A hint of surprise came from my normally stoic brother. "I didn't know."

"I didn't either until I had Rob show me Dad's bank statements when I was in Montreal recently."

There was another pause at the other end of the phone. Steve then offered, "Yes, Harvy; I guess we need to put a stop to what Dad is doing."

* * *

In early June of 2000, Steve took our father to his GP. I didn't tell my brother about the dubious loan Dad had given to his doctor—I didn't want anything to interfere with Steve's focus on Dad's mental health. Steve and I agreed that the visit would be under the pretext of a regular checkup. Steve would talk to the doctor about Dad's declining memory and uncontrolled giving.

It was ironic and absurd for Steve to discuss with Dad's GP—someone who had shamefully borrowed money from our father—about our dad's untethered cash handouts. But if the visit resulted in the doctor ruling in our favour, and simultaneously sending the physician an indirect message about not asking our father for more money, then it was worth the gambit.

Steve called me after the appointment. "The doctor heard me out and did some tests. He said he'd send me a letter with his recommendations."

I had a Canadian colleague whose husband was the head of the Neurology Department at one major Montreal hospital. After my father had seen his GP, I said to him, "Maybe there's something my friend's husband can do to help you with your memory." Dad presented no resistance to my offer. Before the appointment, I told the neurologist about my father writing cheques indiscriminately, unlike his normally more discerning behavior.

I disliked my deceiving my father, but he also had deceived or misled me many times. Dad had cashed in Steve's and my JHS shares for Mom's divorce settlement. He hadn't accepted Geoff Levi's recommendations for his JHS preferred shares, after which he cut Steve and me out of JHS's shareholder meetings with his subsequent accountant. My father rarely asked for my opinion ahead of time regarding lending money to my brother or anyone else. He was now throwing away his money to doubtful causes and dubious people. I felt that Steve and I needed to do something, or there might be little legitimate funds left to support him in his waning years.

Dad was quiet and cooperative throughout the neurologist's exam. The physician enacted various physical and mental tests. After the doctor had finished, he turned to me and said, "Since your brother is a Quebec resident, I'll write my letter to him concerning the test results and my recommendations. Expect it in a week or so."

Ten days later, Steve and I talked again. "Harvy, I got letters from both doctors. They concur that Dad has early Alzheimer's and dementia. They recommended that he shouldn't keep control of his assets and health decisions. They said that the government should enforce the Mandate."

It was hard to hear those conclusions, but I felt our father had given us no choice. We had to wrench the signatory pen out of his hand.

"Okay, what's our next step?" I asked.

"I already looked into it, Harvy. We have to tell Dad what we're doing. Quebec law instructs that we need to officially inform him that we will assume control of his finances and health decisions. He would have to agree to our actions in front of a province-appointed social worker that the Department of Social Services will send to interview him."

Now that's going to be a fun conversation! "What if Dad doesn't agree with what we're doing?" I asked.

My brother didn't hesitate. "Then he has the right to fight us in court, arguing that he's still mentally capable. The onus really would be on us to prove his mental incapacity."

I grabbed at straws. "What if we don't say anything to Dad and let the social worker talk to him? Or what if we sit in on the social worker's conversation with him?"

My brother was his matter-of-fact self. "We can't do that. The social worker needs to meet with him privately. They will ask Dad whether we told him what we're planning to do. If we haven't told him, then the social worker's conversation would be invalid."

I felt my ribs shake. "It'll be interesting to see how Dad will react to this," I said sheepishly. "You know how angry he can get when he doesn't get his way."

In his business days, our father's shouts could shiver the timbers of his JHS factory. His bull-headedness could frustrate even a saintly supplier's patience. Steve and I had no clue as to what our father might do when we'd tell him we were taking away his financial control. Would he scream bloody murder? Would he take a bulldog stand against us with the social worker? Would he shake his good hand and grandfather's cane at us in court?

I said, "Listen, Steve. You're in Montreal and will be the one to deal with him day-to-day after we have the Mandate enforced. Let me be the bad guy, the one to tell him that we are exercising the Mandate." I didn't say it, but I suspected our message to Dad might be better received if I delivered it.

"Okay, Harvy. I've already arranged for the social worker to come on Wednesday, June 21, at two o'clock. When should we tell him?"

How about five minutes before two?

I took a breath. "Let's go see Dad in his office that morning. How's eleven o'clock for you? After we tell him, I can grab sandwiches from the deli, and we can have lunch together." I paused and then continued. "Is that enough warning? I hate to give Dad too much time to think about what we're doing."

"I guess that's workable." My brother's voice was docile. "It's hard to believe that it's come to this."

"Yah, it's hard to accept." I took a deep breath. "Dad's always been an in-control person. It might be hard for him to forgo his rights, but we'll cross that bridge if we have to." I paused for a moment and then added. "By the way, can you double-check with Suzie to see that he doesn't have any other appointments that day? And, could you let him know a couple of days beforehand that we are coming to visit him?"

"No problem. And I'll tell Rob to take that day off to give us privacy."

"Good idea. I'll see you then."

Neither Steve nor I were men of many words, at least not to each other.

After I had hung up the phone, I sat quietly for a few minutes. Another Johnny Simkovits chapter seemed to be coming to an unpleasant end. The signs pointed to Dad losing his money senses. He was giving away cash each day so that his God would let him live another day to do the same. The doctors had agreed; Steve and I had their medical might on our side. But how does one suddenly become the parent to their parent, taking away the source of their power and self-worth? My gut wrenched. I now had to take away from the one who had always given to me.

I looked at a large framed picture of Dad, Steve, and me on my office wall. The photo was taken in the early 1990s—a few years after Mom had died but before Dad had his stroke. The three of us had smiled nicely for the camera that day, making us seem like a happy Simkovits family. We had worn our best suits and ties for that photo. Father looked proud of his sons; sons looked pleased to be on either side of their father. He had placed his hands gently on our shoulders.

I looked down at my lap. Maybe, deep down, Dad wanted my brother and me to take command of his affairs. He had given me say over his Global Trade Bank accounts. Then again, it was only a power of attorney; my father still had his hand grasped onto the handle of that offshore pot. Part of me dreaded our dad's ire if he wouldn't accept my and Steve's exercising his Quebec Mandate. *What the hell would we do then?* I wouldn't want to fight my father in court, and neither would Steve.

Photo of Steve, Dad, and me, taken a few years after Mom died. c.1990. Dad is 70, Steve 37, and I 36.

I looked again at the photo. Steve and I had to save Dad from himself before it was too late. How would we feel if little remained of the assets he had accumulated during his fifty years in Canada? From the day our father landed on Canadian shores in '49, after escaping the Soviets who took over his homeland, he had dreamed of making his mark and building his fortune. Dad had succeeded, but now his modest empire—and his oath to my brother and me—was in jeopardy. I couldn't let him squander what he had promised repeatedly to us all these years.

It would be a horrible thing to remove a part of my father's manhood, but he had given us little choice. Dad wasn't the same man he used to be.

* * *

Just *Lassen* to Me!

I arrived at Dad's office a few minutes before eleven on that warm June day. I waited in the parking lot until my brother arrived. *I hope Steve's not going to be twenty or thirty minutes late as he usually is.* Miraculously, my brother came a few minutes past eleven. We shook hands—he and I rarely hugged. "Are you ready for this?" I asked.

He nodded. "As ready as one could be."

We walked down the short path to Dad's office entryway. I opened the door, and we stepped in. We might have looked like a couple of uncertain adult Simbas not quite ready to confront our aging Lion King Mufasa to cut the mane off his back.

Dad greeted us with a big "Hello boys!" in his gruff and garbled voice. He smiled as best he could. Both Steve and I went over to his desk, the desk behind which he had been a factory ruler and real estate wheeler-dealer for many decades. We took turns, Steve going first, bending down to hug our patriarch around his shoulders and to place kisses on both of his cheeks.

"Good to see you, Dad," Steve said.

"How are you feeling?" I said, right behind my brother.

He looked at both of us. "I always feel happy when I see you guys." He offered his customary line. "I just need a little more power."

I smiled the best I could. I knew I was about to take the royal scepter out of our father's ruling fingers and place it in the hands of his rightful successors. I was utterly distressed. If I thought about it too much, my feelings of dread would overwhelm me.

I had to go through with our plan. Whatever wounds opened and Simkovits blood spilled would have to be cleaned and dressed afterward. I had rehearsed my lines as if I were a character in a Shakespearean play, a drama no doubt replayed in countless families from before biblical times. But today's scene would be so present and unpredictable in its finale.

For a few minutes, Steve and I stood and chit-chatted with Dad about nothing important. We soon sat down on the other side of the desk, directly facing our declining patriarch. Steve was a bit off to one side and behind me. I wanted our dad to be focused on me when I delivered my lines, rehearsed over and over in my head during the last few days. I looked at our father, put a serious and concerned look on my face, and said, "Dad, Steve, and I are here to tell you something."

Our dad's glassy eyes stared back at me. I could tell he had no clue as to what I was about to say. He waited quietly.

"Steve and I are worried about you and your memory. We want to take over the control of your finances, enforcing the Quebec Mandate."

There was a long pause. I could see that Dad was thinking, working to take in what I had said. Perhaps he was checking his gut and what remained of his mind. His eyes moved down to his desk and then up to me. He glanced over at my brother—who said nothing—and returned his gaze to me. He raised his shoulders and then his voice. "*What?!* Do you think I'm crazy?"

Our dad's ire was more like that of a tired king of beasts than the fierce, fighting tiger he once had been. What I was to say next would be the defining moment in this conversation. Speaking calmly yet firmly, I looked him in the eyes. "No, Dad. We don't think you're crazy." I took a breath. "We're worried about your memory. You're not able to take the best care of yourself anymore."

I had run the contingencies over and over again in my mind. I had considered that Dad wouldn't relinquish control without a fight. I was ready to unsheathe the letters from his doctors and insist he pass the money reins. If I had to, I would rummage through his drawers, take away his chequebooks, and demand that he relinquish his credit cards.

What happened next was unexpected.

It was as though our father had known that this moment was coming. He looked down again at his desk of forty years, and his voice quieted to that of a lamb. "Okay," he said. Having both Steve and me here to challenge him, and him knowing that he was no longer the capable crusader he once had been, our battle was over within the moment it began.

Steve and I continued to look at Dad. I worked not only to keep my eyes focused on him but also to project compassion. Steve explained that a social worker from the Quebec government would come after lunch to talk to him.

Dad nodded but said nothing. I offered, "Steve and I will stay here with you. I'll get sandwiches from the deli, and we'll have lunch together." I took a long breath. "We'll both be here when the social worker arrives. She'll meet with you in your back office while Steve and I will wait out here."

Dad gazed my way. "Okay, Harvy, get me a lean, smoked meat sandwich, but no pickles—they upset my stomach." He showed no indication of having heard anything else.

I obtained Steve's order and headed for the door. Steve followed me outside, where we stood for a moment. I looked at my brother. "I'm shocked," I said. "I can't believe he's letting go so easily."

"Me too," he nodded. "It was unexpected, yet I'm glad he did."

"We'll see what happens when the social worker comes. Maybe he'll put up more of a fight then."

"Yes, we'll see," Steve offered.

I was back at the office in forty minutes, but a part of me didn't want to return until my next lifetime.

Upon returning, my brother and I sat across from Dad's desk while we had a cordial lunch together. Steve and I talked about our kids, perhaps figuring that talking about Dad's grandchildren would soothe him.

Dad didn't say much as he listened to Steve talk about the challenges with his high school-aged children. He mentioned that his daughter was bright, but she didn't apply herself unless she liked the teacher or subject. They had had to find her a tutor for some of her courses.

I hardly knew my niece or even her younger brother. I remember that she could talk a mile a minute, jumping from topic to topic without much preamble or transition.

"What about your son?" Dad asked Steve, wanting to know about his namesake grandson.

Steve obliged. "He's a good kid and now in junior high, yet classes have been hard for him. We may need to send him to a private school so that he can obtain closer supervision."

I wondered who would pay for my nephew's private schooling, considering Steve and his wife worked only for their church. I figured I knew the answer, so I didn't ask.

Steve looked at me. "What about you, Harvy. How's your son doing?"

My son, my only child at the time, was four years old. "He's in a good pre-school in our town, and he's enjoying it," I said. "He'll start kindergarten next year." I stopped there, not wanting to brag about my precocious boy being ahead of most kids his age in both reading and speaking.

"He's a cute boy," Dad said.

I wondered if our father said that because my son's toddler pictures were the spitting image of my father at that age. My kid's looks were also the spitting image of Gloria's childhood photos. I smiled inside, wondering if I might have married a woman with similar genes to mine.

Dad looked at both of us. "How are your wives doing?"

I again let Steve respond first. He presented a proud smile. "Mine is taking advantage of her elementary school teaching diploma by leading religious education classes at the church."

Though I wished both Steve and his spouse were doing more with their lives than just volunteer work, I stayed quiet while Steve talked. When it was my turn, I offered, "Gloria is doing well in her psychotherapy practice. She recently decided to quit her employee assistance program job and go independent, like I am." I grinned a bit. "She's now doing better working for herself than working for someone else." I raised a hand. "And she works only three-quarter time so she can spend more time with our son."

Dad showed his three-quarter smile. "Good for her!" He seemed pleased about Gloria's entrepreneurial streak. I didn't crow further about Gloria's and my professional endeavours, yet I didn't see Steve's face flinch an iota to what I had said.

Steve turned to Dad and asked about Emilia and Igor. I hadn't seen or heard about those two since we crossed paths in Florida three months earlier. Dad offered, "They're fine."

"What's Igor doing?" I asked.

My father's face looked blank. "This and that," he responded. "I don't know for sure."

A ten-year-younger Johnny would have insisted to his daughter that his grandson obtain a college education, and he would have paid for it. It seemed as if Dad were now disinterested or unaware. He added, "I gave Emilia money so that she could buy Igor a cheap car in Košice."

Okay! I now knew where a little more of Dad's onshore or offshore cash had disappeared. I wondered how Emilia and Igor would react to learning that Steve and I were soon taking control of Dad's assets. I suspected we wouldn't allow Dad's pocketbook to be as wide open with our half-sister and her son.

My brother and I continued to talk about our homes and the towns in which we lived. As Steve spoke, I glanced at the walnut-paneled walls and old wooden desks in Dad's front office. It was hard to believe a quarter-century had passed since Dad had bought this building and moved his factory here. It was hard to gather that his money-making days were fifteen years behind him.

It was harder to fathom that I, on and off, had worked for a decade within these manufacturing walls. In those days, I had perhaps been too afraid to find my independence from my father.

My struggles with both my father's berating ways and my brother's brazenness were still fresh in my mind. That craziness had caused me to leave JHS and find my management training and consulting footing with Moe Gross: my psychologist turned counselor turned employer turned business partner. After nearly a decade of working with Moe, I let go of my mentor to find my way as an independent consultant. I wanted to rely only on myself.

I sighed under my breath. I wouldn't recommend my circuitous and sometimes fumbling path to any other struggling family business offspring.

I glanced at the grandfather clock ticking in the corner of the room, and then I looked back at Dad. His face was as blank as the face of that clock. He nodded here and there but said little as Steve and I continued to talk, our tones subdued. I wondered how many ticks and chimes remained in my father's internal clock. He seemed content to watch his two sons chat back and forth like the clock's pendulum movement. With each of us taking our disparate directions, it was rare to see Steve and me be this courteous and kind to each other.

Thoughts of my mother came to me. Today felt like the day after she had died. Back then, the three of us had gathered to arrange her funeral and call family and friends to tell them the horrible news of her passing. Our focus had been the task before us. We had done it calmly, caringly, and carefully. We had spoken sympathetically and respectfully to each other, as we were doing today. My mother would have wanted to see her family together like this, even with a semblance of love.

I wondered if Mom might be looking down from heaven. If she were, then she'd see us doing what was best for our family. Over these last months, maybe even years, pieces of our father had expired. He was no longer the work-hard-by-day and live-large-by-night man he once had been. A slow and steady hobble had replaced his self-assured and sturdy gait. His searing eyes, stern face, self-confident voice, and strong hands had slowly turned into spacy eyes, sagging face, subdued voice, and shaky fingers. It felt as if we were here today to sit Shiva for the parts of Dad that had passed into the sunset.

I felt impotent in the face of that erosion, like a subordinate son who had watched his sovereign father's gradual and inevitable decline. I could do little about it. Though Steve and I were not close, I was glad he was here to help shoulder this burden.

The government-assigned social worker came right at two o'clock. She introduced herself, and we ushered Dad and her into his private office. Dad walked stooped over, and he ambled sluggishly with his cane. Neither Steve nor I were sure whether Dad would contest our action to enforce the Quebec Mandate.

My brother and I stepped outside to get fresh air. I said, "It's amazing how Dad has changed over these last few years."

Steve responded. "Yes, it seems that the fight has gone out of him."

"I wish I could be a fly on the wall when she asks him whether he agrees to have us take over his affairs."

Steve responded, "Yah, I know."

My brother may have sensed the heaviness in my heart, but he had no idea what else was floating in my mind. So far, I hadn't told him anything about my meetings at Elliot Trudell and the discussions with my lawyers, Jay, André, and Bernard. I had said nothing about the Supporters of Independent University annuity deal or our father's hidden assets at the Global Trade Bank. I figured I should move one Simkovits boulder at a time with my brother. Exercising Dad's Mandate was the first big rock to be shifted. The rest could wait until Dad was on his deathbed or had passed away.

Ten minutes later, the social worker saw my brother and me through the office window. My heart beat fast as she came outside. She looked at both of us and spoke in a business tone. "Your father had heard your motion to take control of his wellbeing. He has accepted that decision, agreeing that the two of you together will run his financial affairs and make his medical decisions."

She must have seen similar family scenes dozens if not a hundred times before. She looked back and forth at our faces. "I'll make my formal report this week, and you two should have a confirming letter from the Quebec government within a week or two after that."

My brother and I nodded. We stood quietly, as if we were stunned mice, our eyes fixed on her.

Dad had been a man we had both revered and feared, one who rarely gave in or let up if he thought he was in the right. He had exerted his might in business and had had his way most of his life. The way he so readily relinquished control of his remaining fortune and what had defined a part of his manhood was both astonishing and sad.

Or was it? Perhaps, at some level, he knew that now was the right time to let go due to his declining fire and wind.

* * * *

Crimp in My Plan

It was time to return to my Elliot Trudell attorney. It was also time to think through letting my brother know about Dad's hidden money. I wondered how much Steve would want to know about Dad's offshore dealings. Certainly, he'd like to know the truth. Yet how would my brother feel and what might he do if he knew I had been, for nearly three decades, privy to Dad's offshore accounts while he had been mainly in the dark?

I don't think Steve would take up arms against me, but he could make my life difficult with JHS after Dad's passing. I was living under U.S. tax law, which had complex rules for foreign company ownership. If Steve got offended, he could hinder me from obtaining the most favorable U.S. tax treatment for my stake in JHS, a Canadian holding company.

I didn't want to smear my favoured son's position onto my brother's face. I needed to protect myself from sibling retribution. Now that Dad was declared incapable, Steve and I had to work as his guardians and eventually as his estate's co-executors. We had been bound together in our father's company since near the time of our birth. Half-dozen properties remained in JHS's asset corral. My brother and I needed to stay on reasonable terms until those assets were developed or disposed of over the ensuing years.

I had to find the right moment to tell Steve about Dad's offshore legacy. I considered letting my powers of attorney run out at Dad's death, allowing our father's last will to govern his hidden money. Because Steve and

I had cooperated well in enforcing Dad's Quebec Mandate, I no longer wanted to hide anything from him. I felt he deserved his fair share of our father's offshore stash. And I didn't want to shoulder the whole Lux albatross on my own.

But I needed to prepare myself. Before I divulged our father's offshore secrets, I had to make sure my voluntary disclosure ducks were in a legal row.

Bernard and I met for the second time in late August, nine months after our first meeting in late 1999. It was a sunny day, but I could feel a cool, dry northern breeze cut through the warm summer sun.

As I approached the Elliot Trudell building, I felt a chill. *Every year, it's always the same.* After mid-August, summer in Quebec could be over on any given day. Though our Canadian days were getting shorter and cooler again, I hoped I wouldn't have to wait too long for warmer days in our Simkovits family's financial affairs.

I waited for Bernard in the same conference room we had first met. I stared at the same dark wood-paneled walls, the same gigantic oval conference room table, the same framed photographs and paintings of the firm's former managing partners. It felt as if I had been there yesterday and as if I were the protagonist in a Canadian crime novel.

I didn't wait long for Bernard. His reserved look and demeanour hadn't changed a bit. I wondered if he could tell from my manner that my entire world with my father had changed since the last time we had met.

He and I greeted each other, and we sat down. I spoke first. "My father was declared incapable recently of managing his money. My brother and I now control his assets. Also, my father has entrusted me with powers of attorney over his offshore accounts."

"That will certainly make everything easier," he said. His tone was as calm and collected as a parish minister. He didn't ask how all those changes had come to be. "We can start with the voluntary disclosure process as soon as you and your brother are ready."

I eyed the attorney. I wondered how much I could trust his high-end firm to shepherd Dad's underground assets into the daylight of Revenue Canada. Would Bernard's advice be dependable and his fees reasonable?

I was my father's son, and I wanted to be careful with Steve's and my inheritance. Steve took the counsel of professionals and priests without grains of skeptic salt, but I wasn't my brother. I wanted to be sure. "Bernard, before I commit to using your help conduct a voluntary disclosure on my father's offshore assets, please take me once more through the rules and process?"

"Certainly," he said. His face stayed lawyer blank.

He started as before, verifying the things he had previously told me. He and his firm would negotiate the deal between Dad's estate and the Canadian government while maintaining identities anonymous. My father (or his estate) would have to re-file his last three years of income tax returns, now including the undeclared income and capital gains from his offshore accounts. There would be no fines or tax penalties involved, only tax and interest charges calculated on money owed from those previous years.

I looked at him. "You mentioned last time that the total tax is typically 35-40% of the offshore assets disclosed."

"Yes," he responded in his lawyerly tone that was noncommittal. "But it can be higher depending on the details of your father's actual investments. It's hard to know before we see his offshore statements—especially the investment income, expenses, and capital gain numbers—and his last three years of tax returns."

"How much higher could it be? And, how much is the government's interest rate on taxes owed for previous years?"

"In the worst case, 50% of the disclosed assets could go to the government." His clear voice was matter-of-fact. "But it depends on many factors," he repeated. "We have to look closely at the actual numbers and work it out from there." He took a breath. "The federal interest rate is currently 18% per annum for taxes owed from previous years. That rate may have been less two or three years ago; I would have to check."

I gulped. I was feeling okay with losing a third of Dad's offshore assets, but half would be pricey. I'd have to share what remained with my brother. *When coming clean about dirty money, the government can take you to the cleaners!*

If my father had remained endowed with his faculties, he would have a Hungarian-Slovak arm-shaking, wall-trembling fit if he knew that I was here and what I was planning. Even in his diminished condition, he might try to cut off my powers over his Global Trade Bank accounts. Alternatively, he might move his money to another offshore bank that would be out of my reach. If he wanted to fight against Steve's and my wielding our Quebec Mandate over his concealed financial affairs, it could lead to a messy lawsuit.

Son of a bitch! For a 50% tax, I might consider not sharing Dad's hidden money with my brother. *What has Steve done for me to make him deserve my generosity?* Without Steve's knowledge, I could perform a U.S. voluntary disclosure on my own some years from now and then obtain every remaining penny.

But I knew there would be a higher cost to my sanity if I didn't do the right thing. It would be hard to keep my knowledge of Dad's clandestine money hidden from my brother. Steve and I would have to sign Dad's final tax return after his death. Though only I'd know that those returns would be false, we'd both be committing fraud.

I didn't want that, and I knew our dead mother wouldn't want me to jilt her other son. If she had any pull with God or my conscience, I'd have to give Steve his fair share. Also, what would I say to my wife, whom I had already confided in, if I didn't come clean to my brother and the government?

I had done some back-of-the-envelope calculations before walking into this meeting with Bernard. I based my figures on what he had previously told me—and now had confirmed—concerning the tax levy I would expect from a voluntary disclosure. I looked at the attorney. "What makes the tax liability so high? How does it get to be up to 50% of the total declared amount?" I lifted my hand off the table. "I've done estimates based on my father's offshore income and gains. My numbers indicate a lower cut to the government."

Bernard revealed something I hadn't known or expected. "In addition to reporting the undeclared income for the last three years, the government would tax half the total hidden capital that existed before those three years. In the tax return calculations, we would spread 50% of his offshore asset value—from three years ago—across the three years of tax re-filings." He spoke matter-of-factly, sounding as detached as my brother routinely did. "Those now artificially inflated annual income amounts would be used to calculate the tax liability, plus the 18% per annum interest owed on the tax for previous years."

My face must have looked puzzled. Bernard further explained, "Your father's income tax return from three years ago would be most affected by three years of compounded interest payments on the taxes owing on the overstated income number. The most recent return would have only one year of interest owing concerning the additional tax."

He stopped there. I looked down for a moment, letting the attorney's information sink in. I made fast calculations in my head: a 53% marginal income tax rate plus 18% compounded interest levied on Dad's inflated income numbers for the past three years could add a massive load to my father's tax burden.

This new facet hit me squarely in my abdomen; it took my breath out of me. *Did Bernard intentionally or mistakenly mislead me in our previous conversation?* I didn't recall his telling me about spreading half the value of Dad's offshore money, from three years ago, over the ensuing three years of his income tax returns. *Could I have missed such a weighty detail when we spoke nine months ago?*

I was confident that I would have remembered a fact that would significantly impact my father's debt to the government. Thus, it would substantially affect what money would be left in his offshore accounts after the government had taken its pounds of tax. I now understood how Dad's estate could lose half or more of what he had hidden offshore. *Had Bernard tried to soft-peddle me when we met previously?*

I tried not to show my disappointment. "Bernard, this consideration would make a big impact on the taxes owing. I'll have to go back and ask my father's offshore bank for three years of statements." I didn't say that I would make calculations to get a ballpark on what my father might owe. I then raised my biggest concern. "Could the government conceivably obtain more than 50% of my father's offshore assets?"

He looked at me for a moment, expressing nothing but his dry lawyerly tone. "Yes, it's possible. But that's not normally the case."

I took a deep breath. "What if we approach the government and make an offer to them for, let's say, 35% of the assets? If they disagree, then we can back out of the deal." I was pulling at straws with that proposal but felt I should make a grasp of it.

Bernard's eyes turned intense. "I'm afraid the government won't do that. They have to go through the detailed tax calculations as per their established rules." He raised his hand off the conference table. "You can certainly back out and take your chances if you don't like what the numbers look like in the end." He gestured toward me. "But then you take the risk of them discovering you on their own, whereby you'd have to pay stiff penalties on top of the annual interest rate."

"How big are those penalties?"

"The fines are worse than the interest rates. In that case, you may remain with close to nothing."

My gut cramped. I needed time to think. I took in another big breath and changed the subject. "Bernard, how would you bill for your work? Do you have a set fee, or do you charge by the hour?"

He stayed calm but firm. "We bill for my time in working on your file and in negotiating the deal with the government." He gestured my way. "You will also need your accountant involved in doing the income and tax calculations and for them to re-file your father's tax returns for the last three years. They would get involved after both you and the government agreed to a deal."

Gee, more professionals to feed!

What Bernard said made sense, yet I again wondered why he hadn't revealed the accountants' role when we had met the first time. I suddenly became skeptical. Maybe my father was right that you can't trust big-firm lawyers. I wondered if there might be something else he wasn't saying. *He's making it sound too straightforward.* I recognized in me my father's mistrust of professionals. I wasn't sure whether or not the Johnny Simkovits housed in me was helping in this conversation.

The attorney worked to be reassuring. "Both my fees and the accounting fees are fully deductible against the undeclared income. Because your father is most likely in the top tax bracket, you'll get more than half our fees back in reduced taxes."

I didn't want to take any chances. "Anything else I should know before I go talk to my brother about all this?"

Bernard shook his head slowly. "That's about it. I'll be happy to sit with the two of you and go over it again—to be sure that both you and he understand."

Yes, I now had the whole picture, and it was much less pretty than I had envisioned nine months earlier. "Okay, Bernard; allow me to digest what you've said and to broach the subject with my brother. I'll get back to you when we are ready to take the next step."

"Okay," he offered. "I'll keep a running account of my time for this meeting and our last one, including them as a part of the project. That way, it will be deductible against the offshore income your father will declare."

I nodded. We stood, and Bernard showed me out. We walked down the hallway that I now had walked a half-dozen times. I once more looked at the pictures of the firm's bigwig lawyers shaking hands with various prominent Canadian politicians. My stomach ached. *These guys certainly didn't build this firm without charging hefty fees.* I wondered if Bernard anticipated that clients like me might be his way to get his picture on these walls.

I wished to keep my father's hidden assets intact as much as possible. I felt I had earned a right to the stash he had promised me. I didn't want to end up with dimes on the dollar. I hoped to clean up the lot and do something worthwhile with the funds. I didn't want to squirrel that money into other hidden bank accounts or indiscriminately give it away as Dad had done these last few years.

I was deeply disappointed that Bernard hadn't shared, nine months earlier, all of the voluntary disclosure details. I wondered if I could trust him and his firm to help my brother and me legitimize Dad's illicit money. The fact that he didn't know the prevailing interest rates on unpaid taxes a few years ago hinted that he had not done many voluntary disclosures. Could other surprises surface later if I let these pass now?

Bernard and I shook hands and said goodbye. *We may never see each other again.* I nodded his way and then walked out of the Elliot Trudell entrance without looking over my shoulder.

* * *

My resolve grew as I left the Elliott Trudell building and entered my car. Whether I was right or wrong about my understandings, Bernard had shaken my faith. I decided not to call him again or follow up with my school chum and Bernard's colleague, André.

I felt that nothing they would say could repair what I perceived was, intentional or not, a gaping oversight. *How could I have overlooked such vital facts or not understood them?* André had said that he was planning to leave the firm at some point, so I didn't see the necessity to inform him of my disappointment.

I made a mental note to call Bernard's office to ask his secretary to send me a statement for his services rendered to date. I'd have JHS pay it down the road and then curtail further work with him.

Both Bernard and André had my business card, but neither of them called me. Had one or the other done so, I would have told them about my misgivings and my decision to part ways with their firm. The fact that neither one of them ever reached out to me suggested that either I was small potatoes for Elliot Trudell or my notion about Bernard's misstep was correct.

But what am I going to do now? Before I divulged anything to my brother, I wanted a game plan for declaring and legitimizing Dad's offshore wealth. I needed a trusted advisor to help carry out the voluntary disclosure to Revenue Canada. I wanted a second opinion to verify what Bernard had told me. I wanted no more surprises. *I hope I'm not overreacting.*

I mulled it over as I went to bed that night in my father's apartment. I had worked to keep a straight face all evening with Dad, not divulging my clandestine intentions.

I was unable to sleep. My chest felt as if it would implode from the weight I was feeling. My gut felt tight, afraid I wouldn't have anybody who could help me. Asleep in the next room, Dad knew nothing about what I was going through or planning.

As dawn came, a name popped into my head.

* * * *

Voluntary Disclosure Plan B

Geoff Levi was a partner in a mid-sized Montreal accounting firm. He had been my friend for almost twenty years. During the previous summer of 1999, he and his wife had been the ones to seat me next to André at their son's bar mitzvah supper. A decade earlier, I had brought in Geoff and his firm to work with our family business.

Geoff had proven himself to be a straight shooter when giving corporate advice. He stayed away from anything that would give the appearance of tax evasion or warping government rules to gain personal benefit. Geoff's integrity was impeccable, maybe even exceedingly so.

To my chagrin, four years after starting with JHS, Geoff was summarily dismissed by my father. The accountant had recommended a corporate dividend transaction that was more to my brother's and my favour than our father's advantage, and Dad didn't like that.

When Dad fired Geoff, I assured my friend that he'd have another chance with our Simkovits family when Steve and I had direct control over JHS. Now that we had exercised the Quebec Mandate, Dad's voluntary disclosure would be the perfect project with which to have Geoff re-engaged in our family's affairs. I hadn't considered him earlier because I thought I needed a tax attorney and not a tax accountant. Bernard had said that I needed both. Geoff could play the accounting role and perhaps guide me to the right lawyer. I felt that Steve and I could trust Geoff to help us.

That morning, I called Geoff. I went to see him that afternoon. I told him about my discussions at Elliot Trudell and my plans to perform a voluntary disclosure on my father's hidden assets. I didn't mention André or Bernard by name. I also didn't reveal that my brother was not privy to my father's offshore holdings. There was no reason for Geoff to know that Steve was only a bit player in Dad's offshore ploys.

Geoff looked at me and said, "Elliot Trudell wouldn't be my choice for you, Harvy. They're not experts at such work, and they have a reputation in Montreal of being costly in the long run."

I nodded. "What alternative do I have?"

He pointed my way. "I know a lawyer from a new and fast-growing Montreal law firm. Their man, Charles Légère, specializes in helping individuals and families with undeclared assets. He does nothing else but voluntary disclosures and has established contacts at Revenue Canada. He's done it many times for people like you."

"How much does he charge for his kind of work?"

Geoff remained matter-of-fact. "Charles doesn't bill by the hour. He's compensated on a percentage of the declared assets. His firm bases that percentage not on the total assets hidden offshore but on the cash you keep after you have paid the taxes." He pointed my way. "You would know your legal costs upfront and not have to deal with unsubstantiated monthly bills. Paying an attorney by the hour is not an incentive for them to get you the best deal as quickly as possible."

My voice got excited. "Okay, let's talk to the guy. When can you arrange a meeting?"

* * *

A week later, I was back in Montreal. I picked up Geoff at his office, and we drove downtown to Charles' firm, housed in a new, shiny glass skyscraper. When I walked through the building's entrance, I knew that Elliot Trudell's office building was viewable a block behind me. I didn't turn around to look.

As with Bernard, I didn't bring my father's offshore statements for this initial meeting. Instead, I had a pad of paper in my portfolio with my questions. I trusted Geoff, but I wanted to know this Charles guy before giving him my business.

The building and offices of Charles' firm were *nouveaux riches* compared to the *vieilles fortunes* I had seen at Elliot Trudell. Office walls consisted of painted sheetrock rather than wood paneling. The conference room had big windows on both exterior and interior walls, giving the place a more open and modern feel. Wall colours were light, and furniture was of light cherry wood rather than dark mahogany. Though Charles was about the same age as Bernard, he was animated rather than stuffy and subdued. His lively tenor voice was in contrast to the baritone I had heard at Elliot Trudell.

Though my first impressions were positive, I had my list of questions. I knew the tax devil hid in the voluntary disclosure details. I wanted to take advantage of the knowledge Bernard had provided regarding the netherworld of government tax bureaucrats. I needed Charles to ramp up my understanding to the next level.

After introductions, Geoff sat off to one side, equidistant from Charles and me. The attorney looked my way. "Harvy, Geoff has told me a little bit of your situation. You should know that I've worked with many children of deceased or dying elders who hold hidden assets offshore." He raised a hand. "Here in Canada, hiding money is a common pastime among older, wealthy Canadians, especially immigrants. Such people who have one to eight million dollars in investment assets do this kind of money hiding in our country. It's often left for the next generation to rectify their predecessor's misdeeds."

I lifted my hand slightly off the table. "What's special about one to eight million dollars in assets?"

Charles spoke confidently. "People with less than one million dollars find it not worth the trouble and expense of hiding their money. Above eight million, it would be more worthwhile for the taxpayer to establish permanent residency offshore, in the Cayman Islands or The Bahamas. The costs of planning and arranging non-residency and living outside of Canada would be more cost-effective at that level of asset holdings."

"My father's offshore assets are definitely in that range." I didn't say where within that range they laid. I did say, "My father sought Bahamian residency some years ago, but my brother and I talked him out of it." I wanted Charles to appreciate that he had a sizable son-of-a-shyster fish on his voluntary disclosure hook. I wanted to see how he'd earn my substantial business.

"I understand," he said. "It can cost severely in family relationships for the offshore account holder to be out of the country for the two years it takes to establish Canadian non-residency."

I was impressed with Charles' understanding, though I felt he was a bit of a talker. I lifted my hand again. "So, tell me the process for performing a voluntary disclosure." I wanted to hear it from the beginning.

I didn't say that I had already heard the spiel from a lawyer at Elliot Trudell. Geoff had told me that he hadn't and wouldn't mention my previous legal explorations.

The attorney outlined the factors and rules. As Bernard had shared, Charles said he wouldn't divulge our father's name to the government until both my brother and I had agreed to a voluntary disclosure deal with them.

But he was less optimistic about the potential tax liability. He looked directly at me. "In my experience, the disclosing party is typically left with 55 to 60 percent of the declared assets after they have paid the requisite tax to the government."

Gosh! That was five to ten percentage points less than what Bernard had indicated. I gulped but worked to keep my face straight. I had no way to know which attorney was correct. *Big bucks could vanish from Dad's hidden holdings.* I took a deep breath. It felt as if Revenue Canada and Revenue Quebec were going to become greedy siblings, taking nearly half of my father's offshore holdings.

Charles confirmed that half the value of my father's undeclared assets as of three years ago would be spread across Dad's last three refiled tax returns. Then he shared a thought that demonstrated his experience. "We can consider the current year, 2000, as one of the three years you'll need to refile your father's returns. This way, you'll only have to pay one year's interest on the taxes owed on the 1999 re-filing and two years of interest on the 1998 re-filing." Like Bernard, he added that his legal fees (to make the government deal) and Geoff's accounting fees (to refile the revised income tax returns) would be deductible from the income in the most recent year.

I thought for a moment. If Dad's 1997 returns didn't need refiling, then we'd save three years of interest charges on the taxes due in that year's returns. That savings could, in effect, cover Charles' fee. My spirits rose, though I tried not to show it at this stage of the conversation.

I asked a question that I hadn't asked Bernard. "How many of these voluntary disclosures have you done?"

Charles didn't hesitate. "Over the last couple of years, I get cases like yours about once a month. I have good relationships with Revenue Canada, and we come to terms reasonably quickly."

"How long does the whole process take?"

"Typically, it's about a year from the time I open a file with the government, negotiate the arrangement, refile the three tax returns, and obtain their acceptance and approval. Revenue Canada may come back with questions or ask for more details after they have looked at the returns, but that's not always the case."

He eyed me carefully. "We try to give them all the information upfront to expedite their process. We don't hide or keep anything from them." He looked for my reaction to his statement, and then he looked away slightly. "But we're dealing with government bureaucrats, so we can't push them. We have to sit and wait for their questions and decisions."

I nodded, but my spirits dropped. A year's wait could feel like forever. On the other hand, one more year was short compared to the twenty-eight years I had sat on pins and needles in anticipation of being bestowed Dad's offshore stash. One year was a small sacrifice compared to the feelings of guilt and anguish I had and still held regarding his hidden money secrets.

I looked at my list of questions. "What about the Quebec government's tax department? Is there a separate process there? Do we have to make a separate deal with them? They'd want their pound of tax, *n'est-ce pas?*"

Charles whipped his hand along the table as if what I had asked was of little concern. "Once we make a deal with Revenue Canada, the Quebec

Department of Revenue follows their lead. They generally accept the deal that the federal government makes with us."

He took a long breath. "We will still need to re-file your father's last three provincial returns in the same way we will refile the federal returns. But when Revenue Canada accepts the returns, Quebec will accept them as they are, few questions asked. They see it as free money without having to do much work at their end. There should be no issues there."

Okay, that's good. But before I accepted, I had another question. "So Charles, tell me how your fees work."

Again, he didn't hesitate. He spoke steadily and deliberately. "Our fee is a percentage of what cash remains after you have paid the taxes owed to the two governments. The fee depends on the size of the assets you are disclosing. It ranges from 3-5% of the assets that are remaining after-tax, so there is an incentive for us to get the best result for you." He looked at Geoff and then back at me. "We can arrange it so that our legal fees and Geoff's accounting fees are made tax-deductible in the current year's return. Our work will cost you less than half our combined fees, considering your father is most likely in the top Canadian and Quebec tax brackets."

Charles paused for a moment and again eyed me carefully. I had a feeling he wanted an indication of the magnitude of my father's hidden holdings. I didn't want to say quite yet how much Dad had placed offshore. This meeting was only an exploratory one. I wanted time to think this through. I didn't want Charles to see quite yet all the dollar signs regarding the potential income to his firm.

Based on the tax formulas Bernard had shared, and after having another look at my father's most recent Global Trade Bank statement, I had done rough calculations. I surmised that Dad's assets and gains were roughly the same over the previous two years as they had been this year. Knowing that Charles could obtain a Revenue Canada deal with fewer years of tax interest to pay, I was optimistic that we would do better than the 55-60% money-leftover-after-tax that Charles had indicated.

But I still needed a full three years of Dad's offshore statements before I knew for sure how much of his offshore money would remain in my brother's and my hands. I would have to call Mr. Weber of the Montreal branch of the Global Trade Bank to get those bank statements. After this meeting, I'd have to cross that bridge without sending any signals to Weber of my real intentions.

I looked back at Charles. My stare met his, indicating that I wanted him to continue from where he left off. He obliged. "I will need to see what your father has as offshore assets before I can quote a fixed fee percentage." He gestured toward Geoff. "Understand that it's the accountants who have to do the tax calculations and to re-file your father's tax returns."

Geoff spoke. "Don't worry, Harvy, our fees will be much less than Charles's." He looked at the attorney and then offered a slight smile. "The accountants do most of the work, but the lawyers make most of the money."

Geoff's face lost its grin. "Charles will be worth it for you because he has a government relationship in place. He'll be able to get a favourable deal pretty quickly. On my end, our fee is based directly on the time we spend. I really can't say how much work it will be until I see what we are up against with your father's offshore income. I'd have to see his offshore bank statements and the last three years of his tax returns to offer a better idea."

I glanced again at my list of questions. "Do we have any other expenses to worry about?"

Charles looked at me again. "Yes, but they're minimal. We'll bill you monthly for any copying and correspondence we have to do, but that's small stuff."

I never understood why lawyers had to bill clients for those meagre incidentals. I never did that in my management consulting business. No matter, I wanted Dad's offshore safe off my back. The government tax and professional fees were the prices I had to pay for not having to look over my shoulders for the taxman for the rest of my life.

I offered, "Okay, Charles, I think I got all the facts and facets. Before we move ahead, I need to speak with my brother. He needs to agree to this." There was no reason to tell Charles and Geoff that Steve still knew little about Dad's offshore affairs. But it didn't serve me well to water down my brother's position.

And, before I talked to Steve, I wanted to obtain the last three years of my father's offshore statements. I hoped I could get them quickly from the Global Trade Bank. Perhaps performing a portion of the accounting on my own could reduce Geoff's work and give me the backup to negotiate a lower fee with Charles.

Charles eyed me and spoke in a dry monotone. "Okay, Harvy, let me know when you and your brother are ready to proceed. For the next time we meet, please have your father's offshore statements with you. We can take a look at them to gauge the extent of this project."

I nodded my understanding, and we ended our conversation.

During our drive back to Geoff's office, my friend reiterated, "Harvy, Charles is your guy for this effort. He knows what he's doing. He can get you and your brother through this with the least amount of hassle and the best deal from the government. You'd be in good hands with him."

I lifted my hand off the steering wheel. "So far, I've been impressed. And I do need to talk to Steve; we can't go forward without his approval. I also need to see if I can get the last few years of statements from my father's offshore bank." I didn't mention the bank's name. "We can't move forward without that."

Geoff turned toward me. "I understand about your brother." He pointed my way. "And you should be able to get those bank statements. No matter what kind of bank it is, it needs to keep those records for its clients."

Our conversation ended there. I dropped Geoff off at his firm's building. I said, "I appreciate your help. I'll be in touch."

He shook my hand, nodded goodbye, exited my car, and headed inside.

I drove around the corner, found a parking spot, exited my car, and hunted for a secluded phone booth. I had my cell phone but wanted no traceable record of my call. I found a payphone in the foyer of a nearby office tower. I pulled Mr. Weber's business card from a hidden compartment in my wallet.

As I lifted the phone receiver to dial Weber's number, I felt as if I were a character in a spy novel. I looked around to make sure that no one was within earshot. I considered holding the phone receiver with my handkerchief—to leave no prints—but thought better of it.

The Global Trade Bank receptionist put me through to the manager. "Hi, Mr. Weber," I said.

"Hello, Mr. Simkovits; what can I do for you?"

"I need something. How quickly can you get annual income, capital gains, fees, and asset statements for my father's accounts starting from Jan. 1, 1997?"

According to Charles, I needed statements going back to January '98. I wanted the extra year if the government wanted to go back that far, as Bernard had implied.

I knew I needed to have a reason for requesting that information from Weber without raising his concern. I kept my voice calm. "I want to know the income and asset growth my father's accounts have had over these years and how much he has been withdrawing from those accounts."

I didn't tell Weber that Steve and I were officially in charge of my father's assets. I didn't want to take a chance that he might say that my brother now needed to be a part of my request. I was hoping the powers of attorney that Dad had bestowed me for his accounts would be enough for Weber to comply with my request.

Weber didn't hesitate. "I have to go to Lux for that information, Harvy; we do not keep it here. Lux has closed for the day, but I can make the request tonight. They can run the reports when they open in the morning and fax them to me when we open here. Is that acceptable?"

I kept my voice calm. "Yes, good, please do that. I'll call you in the morning to see if you have received the documents. I can drop by your office midday to pick them up before I drive back to Boston."

Weber cleared his voice and then expressed concern. "You will need to be careful with such information when you cross the border. No names will be on those documents, only account numbers, but you don't want to raise eyebrows if border officials find such papers with you."

I matched his tone. "Yes, I fully understand. I'll be careful. Thank you for your valid concern." I tried not to come across as edgy or nervous. I hoped I was succeeding.

"Okay, Harvy, I'll be here and available after ten o'clock tomorrow. If I'm not here, our receptionist will have your documents. It'll be in a sealed envelope, and expect a lot of paper."

"Okay, I'll call you a little after ten tomorrow morning."

The following day, the Global Trade Bank's receptionist handed me a five-centimeter thick, sealed brown envelope. The packet had no identification markings on it except for my written name. I was glad that Weber wasn't present to question me or see the guilty look on my face for breaking my father's trust. I was relieved that the old receptionist, Hilde, was no longer there. I wouldn't have been able to smile at her with a straight face. Having Hilde ask about my father would have sent a wave of angst through me.

I thanked the new receptionist, took the package, and left promptly. Perhaps the next time I'd be here, I'd deliver bad news to Mr. Weber—that the Global Trade Bank's seventeen-year relationship with the Simkovits family would be coming to an end. For now, I wanted to leave no clues concerning my plans.

In the empty hallway by the elevators, I unsealed the package and took a look at what I had in my possession. I slipped the documents partially out of the envelope, hoping to keep them from any roaming eyes if anyone unexpectedly passed through the hallway. I thumbed through the pages. The decades of weight on my shoulders came down to this perhaps three-pound package of papers. Nearly thirty years of watching and waiting came down to these thousands of numerical entries on a couple of hundred pages of computer printout.

The millions of fax-machine dots on these pages had been a part of my *raison d'etre*. They represented my collaboration with my father, my competition with my brother, and my mother's premature death. They had caused my continually restless gut and many sleepless nights about my dad's financial shenanigans and his promise of all this to me. These white sheets of black numbers had been a big part of who I was, but damn if they were to be a big part of who I was to become.

I looked to see if the Global Trade Bank's name was on the pages. It wasn't. If U.S. Customs and Immigration searched my briefcase and found these papers, I'd say I was working on a financial report for a client. That scenario was unlikely. U.S. border officials had never searched me during my over ten years of crossing the USA-Canada border by car or airplane. But it paid to be prepared.

* * *

I arrived home late Friday night without a mishap. On the day before my trip to Montreal, I had told Gloria that I was meeting with a legal associate of Geoff's to talk about my father's offshore money. After I had gotten home, I told her, "I'm afraid you won't see much of me this weekend. I've got the statements from my father's offshore accounts going back four years. It will be a massive job to figure out what we will owe the Canadian and Quebec governments in back taxes."

Her eyes showed concern. "Can't you let the accountants and lawyers figure that out?"

I shook my head slowly. "I can, but it'll be a lot more money in fees for them to calculate every bit of interest, capital gains, bank fees, and whatever else from several accounts, and in three different currencies." I looked at her as caringly as I could. "My lawyer has explained the rules the government employs to assess taxes owing on these offshore funds. I need to calculate the numbers for myself so that I can see what I'll be up against."

I kept my voice calm. "My work will help me negotiate the legal fees for getting the voluntary disclosure done. Those fees aren't yet determined fully. And, any work I do will also reduce the accountants' work and costs." My eyes were pleading as I pointed at myself. "I'll be in a much stronger position with my advisors if I do this work first."

Her face frowned. "What about your brother? Could he help you?"

I lifted my palm. "I want to be on top of this before I tell Steve about it. I want him to see how much I've done so that he lets me continue to be the point person with the advisors." I took a deep breath. "All of this has been my burden, not his. I need to get through it for my sake."

She paused and then said, "Okay, honey, I understand." She looked toward our son's room. "Will we see you for meals and bedtime?"

I was glad my wife understood what was at stake. I nodded, and my voice was conciliatory. "Yes, of course; I'll spend time with you at both ends of each day."

Gloria and our son saw me for breakfast and supper that weekend, and I read to him at bedtime. I ate lunch in my home office.

Gloria dropped by my office at noon on Sunday with a sandwich. "How's it going?"

"It's going okay, but it's a lot of tedious work." I smiled. "Thank goodness I never wanted to be an accountant or bookkeeper. That kind of work would put me underground fast."

She glanced at the papers on my desk. "So, what are you doing?"

I pointed to the papers. "I'm going over my father's various offshore accounts, one by one. Each account statement has pages upon pages of dated transactions. I created an Excel spreadsheet on my computer, with separate worksheets for each account, tax year, and currency. For now, I'm calculating and entering rough totals off the statements I obtained from my father's bank, page by page by account." I frowned. "The next time, when Steve and I refile Dad's tax returns, I'll have to log every single transaction by date and amount. That could take me a whole week, but it's better if I do it than being charged $250 per hour by the accountants."

Gloria raised her palm as if she had heard enough. "Okay, I get it, Harvy." She smiled. "Better you than me doing this kind of detailed stuff."

By midafternoon that Sunday, I had aggregate figures logged into my spreadsheets. By that evening, I had run the numbers the way Geoff might run them—according to the deal Charles said he could make with Revenue Canada. I used 53% as my father's marginal tax rate then calculated a 6% combined tax-deductible fee (an estimated 4% for Charles and 2% for Geoff). I applied those percentages to the money left after the Canadian and Quebec governments took their tax cut. I even performed sensitivity analyses—slightly elevating and lowering the tax rate and fee percentages to see how those tweaks might change what might remain in my brother's and my hands.

Though I hoped to negotiate a fee with Charles that was lower than the 3-5% he had quoted, my thinking on that would have to wait. What I now had in my hands would ready me for a discussion with my brother. It was also good enough for getting into the dirty-money details with the professionals.

I studied my Excel spreadsheets. I went over them several times to ensure that I hadn't missed anything in my assumptions or calculations. I had a sense of relief that I now knew what kind of tax liability I'd be up against regarding Dad's hidden assets. I felt ready to take the next step.

Now, when, where, and how was I going to tell Steve about all this?

* * * *

Reign Comes to an End

The pieces to solve Dad's offshore money puzzle were settling into place. I was ready to divulge to Steve what I knew and what he hadn't. But during the same weekend that I had wrestled with my father's offshore accounts, Dad had an emergency back in Montreal. Steve called early Monday morning. "Harvy, are you sitting down? I don't have good news."

My voice became alarmed. "What happened? Is it Dad?"

Steve was his calm-as-a-pastor self. He began, "Over the weekend, Suzie noticed blood in Dad's stool. She called me, and I called Dad's doctor. The doctor said to take Dad right away to the hospital. I picked him up from his apartment on Saturday and took him to St. Mary's Hospital."

St. Mary's was Dad's regular hospital, where his GP was affiliated. It was a teaching hospital where, fifteen years earlier, Dad had received treatment for angina.

I held my breath as my brother spoke. His tone stayed calm and business-like. "Dad was taken right away into the emergency room and then straight into oncology. The head of oncology there knows him. It didn't take the doctor long to diagnose Dad with cancer."

Steve's voice didn't waver. "After having done tests, the doctor told me he didn't want to operate on Dad to find the source of the tumor, though they know it was in his gut. The doctor said that the cancer is extensive and inoperable. There's nothing they can do."

"Oh, my!" My mind and body were beginning to shake. "How much time does he have?"

"The doctor said weeks to perhaps months."

"Should we get another opinion?"

"The whole oncology team at St. Mary's has been on Dad's case. The cancer is very advanced. There are possibly many organs involved. They don't feel it's worth opening him up."

I blurted, "What do you think we should do, Steve?"

He again responded matter-of-factly. "The doctor is advising not to let Dad leave the hospital. The doctor says they could take better care of him there than if he were at home. They gave Dad a private room, and the doctor said he could stay until the very end." He took in a long breath. "Luckily, he's not in any pain. But he can't eat; the cancer makes him feel like he's full all the time. And he barely drinks any water. He's not going to last long."

I placed my palm on my forehead. "Wow, Steve. We knew a day like this would come, but it's still a shock."

My brother's voice remained priestly monotone. "The funny thing is that, with his growing dementia and Alzheimer's, Dad doesn't seem to realize what's happening to him. He can't understand why he can't go home. He can't walk or even stand without assistance. He can't go anywhere by himself, not even to the bathroom." He paused and then added, "How soon can you get here?"

I stood and paced on my office floor for a few seconds. "I need to cancel my appointments for this week," I said quickly. "I can probably drive there this afternoon and be there tonight. I'll go straight to the hospital. How late can visitors be there?"

Steve's voice stayed steady. "For oncology patients, family members can be there anytime. Suzie's with him now. We are trading off being with him. It'll help if you're here."

I kept up my pace. "I'll be there tonight. Please tell Suzie that I'll stay with her at their apartment." I paused for a moment, then I said more slowly, "Dad wanted to live to over 100. Even though we suspected his longevity was limited, this still feels like a big surprise."

A thought came to my mind. I took another long breath. "By the way, Steve, I know it's your birthday in a few days. Let me be the first to wish you the best that's possible under these circumstances."

"Thanks, Harvy. But, with yours arriving in six more weeks, I think both of us will have sad birthdays this year."

I hung up the phone and sat down. My heart and eyes welled, and I put a hand to my temple. I couldn't tell if my tears were compassion for or relief from the man who had played a dominant role in my life. Or was I letting go of my pain that had accumulated because of his decades of finagling? Perhaps my reaction was all those things.

I stood and walked to my office door and, as I had done when my father had had his stroke seven years earlier. I yelled downstairs, "Gloria, honey, I need to get to Montreal today. My father's in trouble."

While I drove to the city of my birth, I thought about Dad's view concerning the subject of death. "When my time comes," he said, "I want a brick to fall from the roof, hit me on the head, and 'Boom!' I'm gone."

Steve had said that Dad wasn't in pain. Maybe this was God's way of granting his wish and giving us time before the boom came down upon him. With the outsized way he had lived his life, it was a medical wonder that he had lasted this long. Living to eighty was a testament to his strength and resilience, though his melancholy about losing his third wife had dragged him down these last five years. His bright Eastern European spirit was now a dwindling light.

I kept both of my hands on the steering wheel as I drove 5-10 mph over the speed limit on the road to Montreal. Twelve years earlier, when my mother had been on her hospital deathbed, my eyes turned wet and my throat constricted as I drove to see her for the very last time. I had glanced into the sky and prayed to God to be gentle with her.

As I drove through the rolling, green mountains of Vermont, I did the same for my father. I pleaded, "God, I know he hasn't been the best example of your work here on earth, but please don't make him suffer. He's a man of his time and place on this planet. He loved the life he had gotten in Canada, and he lived it to the fullest of his ability. Though he has been unkind to some, including his wives and especially my mother, there's no need to make him pay for his sins here on earth." I took long breaths and then glanced upward again. "Please, please make his passing easy." My hand tightened on the steering wheel. "Though I've had my share of angst regarding him, I can't bear to see him suffer."

When I arrived at St. Mary's, Suzie was next to Dad's side. When my father saw me, his eyes widened. He raised his right arm. "I'm so happy to see you, son. Please come and sit next to me."

Suzie stood between my father and me. I hugged her hello first and then grabbed my father's outreached hand, putting my other hand on his shoulder and kissing both of his cheeks. "Hi, Dad; it's so good to see you." I sat down next to him and forced words out of my mouth. "How are you feeling? Are you in any pain?"

He shook his head. "No, no pain. I'm feeling okay. I want to know when I can go home."

Suzie proclaimed, "Johnny, you're very sick, and you can't go home." She looked at me. "He's asked me that many times today." She turned back toward him. "Sweetheart, the doctor wants you to stay here."

"But I want to go home," he said, his eyes pleading.

Suzie responded calmly but firmly, "They can't help you at home. You have to stay here."

Dad looked longingly at me. I said, "Yes, Dad, I know. But you are sick, and you can't leave. The doctors can take better care of you here."

I didn't know if anyone had told my father that he was dying. I wasn't sure he would grasp his situation if we said that to him.

Later, in the hallway, Suzie offered that the oncology doctor had told my father about the severity of his cancer. I decided not to broach the topic of death with Dad unless he raised it. I wasn't afraid of the issue. I figured that if he wanted to talk about his condition and its inevitable outcome, he'd say something about it.

Later that evening, my father asked again about going home. In a compassionate tone, I repeated, "You're not well, Dad, and the doctor wants you to say." My father wasn't about to get out of bed and walk out of the hospital. I figured he would take in what he wanted, when he wanted, and if he wanted.

* * *

During that first week of Dad's hospitalization, Steve, Suzie, and I called our father's relatives and friends. We told them, "We're not sure how much time he has left; it could be weeks or perhaps months. If you want to see him, coming sooner rather than later would be good."

Every day, a parade of people came calling. It was a veritable smorgasbord of ethnicity that one could find in a city like Montreal. Canadians of English, French, Slovak, Hungarian, Russian, Italian, Lithuanian, Polish, and Middle-Eastern descent made up the mix. Former JHS employees, friends from the Slovak Church and the Slovak Business Association, old Montreal Phono and JHS business associates, its customers and suppliers, and myriad past and present JHS advisors ambled in and out every afternoon and evening. They came from Montreal, Quebec City, Ottawa, Toronto, and Vancouver to see the man they respected, even revered.

His closest friends and associates came every week, some twice a week, during the first weeks that Dad lay in his hospital bed. Even Elaine flew in from Florida to sneak in one morning when she thought no one else would be there. (Suzie later mentioned that she and Elaine saw each other briefly.) At times, there were over half a dozen visitors in Dad's small room, two rows deep at the foot of his bed. I imagined a Johnny Simkovits party, with someone opening a bottle of Stoli and passing it around, but no one did.

Though we had told everyone privately that Dad was dying, they acted hopeful. They looked at him and said, "It's so good to see you, Johnny," . . . "How are you feeling, Johnny?" . . . "Get better, Johnny!" . . . "We're praying for you, Johnny."

After hugs and handshakes, Dad nodded, smiled a little, and said, "Nice to see you, too," . . . "Yes, thank you," . . . "I'm doing okay." He raised his able hand and made the best fist he could. "I just need more power." He didn't carry a conversation or invite more chitchat. There seemed to be little gregariousness left in him.

No visitor stuck around for very long. I didn't blame them, for there wasn't much more to do or say to someone who looked at you glassy-eyed.

When Maury Reemer, Dad's insurance agent, came to visit, he presented his big salesman grin. "Now you've really done it to yourself, Johnny." He pointed to himself. "If you want, I can call my people and break you out of here."

I smiled; Dad only nodded. He looked blankly at his colleague as if what Maury had said went straight through his head.

One day, the ninety-year-old Jiri Varga, Dad's long-time Hungarian friend, walked in. He fist-pumped the air and repeated several times, "Johnny, don't give up; hang in there!"

Jiri and my father had come of age together in Canada. They were Iron Curtain escapees, Canadian immigrants, and Montreal entrepreneurs during the same postwar decades. They were the kind of nose-to-the-grindstone, work-hard-and-play-hard, willing-to-bet-the-farm businessmen who helped build their second homeland after the Second Great War.

I could barely imagine what they, and others like them, had sacrificed to create a brighter future for their families. They had come to North America so that they and their offspring wouldn't have to fear war or oppression. They wanted their children to become anything they wanted to be, as long as it was somebody respectable. Their quest for freedom had given them the privilege to criticize our government openly, to live how they wanted, and to provide their kids an education and a step-up in life.

As Jiri departed my father's bedside, he repeated his move and mantra. "Don't give up, Johnny; hang in there!" Dad nodded to his old friend of nearly fifty years, but his arm and fist stayed by his side.

Dad's brusque colleague and drinking buddy, Hans, arrived next. He was weighted down with an arrangement of flowers that completely blocked the top half of his rotund physique. After he had put down the heavy vase, he chuckled as he offered, "Johnny, I can arrange for the Troika players to come and serenade you while you're sitting here doing nothing."

Hans was another immigrant entrepreneur who had started with little. Because of a family connection, he received a sizable business loan from my father soon after the German had emigrated from Europe. Their friendship took off from there.

A rough and tumble guy, Hans built a successful engineering firm. Like Dad, he could hold his liquor into the wee hours of the morning in a crowded barroom. He could also hold his own in a barroom fight when he was bumped into one too many times—and then buy a shot of Schnapps for his gauche opponent after their scuffle was over.

Though Dad's compadres offered well wishes to their long-time friend, I wasn't sure if they grasped his reality. I nodded and smiled at their caring and clowning. As my father would, they'd take in what they wanted to, when they wanted to, and if they wanted to.

I was glad I never saw my father's money-borrowing GP come calling. Perhaps he had come around for early morning rounds, but I never asked or cared. I don't know if I could have held my tongue with that man for having extorted $25,000 from my father and given him an uncollectible IOU in return. Steve and I would have to deal with him after Dad's passing.

I heard from Suzie that my brother prayed with my father during their time together, and he brought his church bishop to pray some more. Suzie shared that Father Novak had come from the Slovak Church to pray with and for Dad. *Novak should be doing hospital shifts by Dad's side for all the money that my father had given Novak and the Slovak Church.*

I made no comment to Suzie about Steve, his bishop, or Novak. I hoped my father was getting comfort from their visits—as long as my brother wasn't trying to convert him. I decided that I wouldn't get in the middle of Dad and his family and friends unless he said something. I was going to be there with my father, my dad, in any way he wanted me to be.

In the hallway outside my father's hospital room, a number of my father's friends remarked, "It's shocking; he's not the same man he used to be." . . . "He had so much more energy." . . . "He was the life of the party." . . . "It's so sad to see him this way."

I looked at them and said, "Yes, I understand." . . . "I know; it's hard." . . . "Thanks so much for being here for Dad and us." I shared a hug and gave a kiss on each cheek, as we European Canadians do, but kept the stiff upper lip of my Anglican prep school training.

All these friends' faces had dropped, or their eyes had reddened, for the man who wanted to live past 100. They had known Johnny Simkovits in so many ways. They had experienced Johnny as a late-night compadre at the Tokay and Troika restaurants. He had been an unpredictable boss who could point his finger at your chest as he shouted orders into your ear. He was a friend who could laugh and slap you on the back or tell you an off-colour joke. He was a customer who could demand better prices on merchandise one minute and then ask you out for drinks and dinner the next. He was a gregarious and gracious garden-party host at his Lake Champlain home. And he was a singer of risqué songs accompanied by his favourite restaurant violin, accordion, or guitar players. But none of Johnny's friends and companions had known my father quite the way I had.

A couple of times, after a visitor had left, Dad looked at me and asked in a soft but hoarse voice, "Who was that person who was here?" When I told him who it had been, he nodded and softly said, "Okay."

While standing in the hospital hallway, one of Dad's Hungarian friends, Mr. Duma, who I didn't know well, asked me, "Does Johnny know he's dying?"

I replied, "I don't know how much of his situation he grasps. The doctor said that he told my father that he has extensive, untreatable cancer." I shook my head. "Dad doesn't ask or say anything about it."

"I see," Duma said. He offered nothing more as his eyes turned away.

Steve and I called Dad's half-brother in Košice to share the sad news of his kin's pending death. After a long pause, Edo offered, "I'm so sorry to hear that. But I can't come to visit because I can't leave Eboya again."

Edo had spent many years helping Dad after his stroke; he had done his kid-brother duty. Steve and I consoled our uncle, "That's okay. We understand. We'll tell Dad we talked to you and that you wish him your best."

Because Steve and I neither spoke Slovak nor thought our Hungarian would be sufficient for a heart-to-heart conversation, we asked one of Dad's Slovak friends to call Emilia in Košice to tell her the grave news about her father. A day later, that friend called back. "Emilia says she sends her prayers, but she can't afford to come and see him in the hospital."

After the cash my father—and even I—had put into her hands over the years, I couldn't understand her decision. Yet, her reaction seemed par for the course for my distant half-sister. Whatever were her unfilled Johnny Simkovits hopes, promises, and dreams, she'd have to find her way to make peace with them.

* * *

Twelve years earlier, when my mother had been on her death bed and later passed away, my brother and I, business-like and matter-of-fact, did what we thought best for her and her estate. We were now doing the same for our father.

Steve and I regularly checked in with the hospital oncologist to see if there was anything new to report on our father's condition or if the doctor knew more about how rapidly Dad's disease was progressing. The physician repeated, "All we can do is let the disease run its course. Your father can stay here in the hospital until the end."

I was surprised that the oncology department would let Dad occupy one of its beds for weeks, maybe even months. Dad's Quebec Health Insurance covered the expenses for his hospital stay, and his supplemental insurance footed the bill for the private room. It didn't cost us a penny—virtually unheard of in the U.S. healthcare system in which I now lived.

Steve and I continued to call Dad's friends and relatives in Canada and Slovakia (those who spoke English) to update them on our father's going on. We called his lawyer, accountant, and other advisors to see what we needed to do in their departments to prepare for our father's passing. We made schedules as to when Steve, Suzie, and I would be with Dad so he wouldn't be alone during the day.

Steve and I planned Dad's funeral service and burial. We allocated priest selection, service configuration, funeral home arrangements, and burial site tasks as if we were in a weekly JHS production meeting. Whatever feelings of pending loss that loomed under our sedate surfaces, those feelings lay stashed in a hospital closet. Maybe it was better that way.

I shared with my brother the scratch IOU that Dad's GP had signed for a $25,000 loan from Dad. Steve and I decided to send a polite letter to the doctor to request the return of Dad's money or for proof that he had placed Dad as a beneficiary in his life insurance policy.

Ten days later, we received a response from the doctor's lawyer, along with bankruptcy papers. It seemed that the "good doctor" was broke, and we'd have to get in line with his creditors. Steve and I consulted our JHS lawyer. He said there wasn't much we could do except use the uncollectible loan as a capital loss on Dad's income taxes. It was yet another loss we'd have to absorb.

Had I been a little shrewder, I might have allowed Dad to play the game of offering another $10,000 to the good doctor (the amount asked for). However, the physician would need to provide absolute proof that Dad was an irrevocable beneficiary of his life insurance policy. I guess I wasn't smart enough back then to have played such a gambit.

Steve and I decided that we didn't want Father Novak to preside over Dad's funeral. We asked another Montreal Slovak priest, a Father Sinal, who served at Montreal's Greek Orthodox Church, to perform the services at the Slovak Church and burial site.

Dad had known the elderly Father for decades—he was the cousin of Dad's former office secretary, Helen. Father Sinal said he'd perform Dad's service for no fee, which we hadn't expected. I was glad that there was at least one responsible and generous Slovak priest in Montreal.

* * *

In the transition times between our hospital shifts with Dad, Steve and I gathered in the hallway outside his room. Both of us stayed calm and respectful. Neither one of us got angry or sad or showed frustration; there was no push or rush. Perhaps because of our turbulent childhood, filled with our parents' angry shouting at each other, it seemed that the last thing Steve and I wanted in Dad's final days was to inflict any unnecessary angst.

We consulted Suzie about what she surmised about our father's condition and what she wanted for him. My brother and I, armed with our Quebec Mandate, made the decisions. It felt odd and unnatural to make choices for Dad, but we did what we needed to do. Other than arranging the funeral and working out our father's financial matters, there wasn't much else that needed doing. We waited for the inevitable.

Both Steve and I wanted to make our father's final weeks as easy and comfortable as possible. It was eerie as to how surreal and cerebral it felt—*Star Trek*'s Mr. Spock-like. It was as if our emotions had been turned off or buried inside. During those weeks that Dad lay dying within the blank walls of his hospital room, I kept on thinking how different it must be for brothers than for sisters when dealing with death and dying. I envied women's ability to express what was going on inside them.

I was glad I had Gloria to talk to over the phone every night. In addition to talking about our 4-year-old—a helpful distraction from my father's illness—she asked how Dad and I were doing. She seemed to understand when I responded, "It feels so unnatural to go through this end-of-life stuff and to work the situation with Steve. Neither one of us is saying much about our feelings or reactions."

For my brother and me, short, calm, informational conversations seemed to work best. Doubt, anguish, and heartache would be dealt with elsewhere and at another time.

* * *

For those trying, final weeks of my father's life, I spent most weekdays in Montreal and went home to Boston for the weekends. I was grateful that Gloria took care of things at home with our young son so I could keep my attention on my father in Montreal. Outside of that, I had long-time clients and friends I could visit in the city of my origin when Steve and Suzie sat with Dad. I told my closest clients that my father was dying. I also offered, "It's good to take my mind off it a bit by coming to see you." They allowed me to work with them and their staff as much as I wanted.

Perhaps I needed those diversions to deflect my deepest feelings about my family of origin. Part of me wanted to put my forbears and brethren behind me as if our self-inflicted suffering had never transpired. I wanted to live my separate life in Boston with my wife and family. I wondered if my father's imminent death would allow me to make peace with my self-conflicted past. Or might my buried feelings come forth to consume me?

My father's visitor crowd thinned as the weeks progressed. Except for a few close friends, it was mostly Suzie, Steve, and me by Dad's side. Each of us took our morning, afternoon, or evening shifts. During those many hours, I considered what more I could or would say to this man, my creator, my predecessor, my Abraham. I glanced at his blank face as he stared at the TV mounted on the wall. Could he take in the hurt I held deep within if I were to divulge my darkest thoughts and deepest feelings about him?

In between the few visitors and regular visits from the hospital staff, there were times when I was alone with Dad for hours. Sitting by his side, our conversations were simple.

"How are you feeling, Dad?"

"I'm okay." He nodded.

"Are you in any pain?"

"No." He shook his head.

"Are you hungry; can you eat or drink anything?"

"No, I can't," he replied in a quiet tone as he raised and shook his palm.

"Is there anything you need?"

He shook his head again.

"Would you like another pillow, or could I adjust the ones you have?"

"I'm okay," he said. Then after a few seconds: "Help me turn over to my other side."

I put my arm under him, and we worked together to turn his body.

"Do you need to go to the bathroom?" I asked.

"No, not now. Maybe you or the nurse can help me later."

"Want to watch TV?"

"Okay." He pointed to the television on the wall. "Whatever channel you want."

As we sat together, watching soaps, I reached over and held Dad's hand. He said nothing as he took mine into his. He then fell asleep in the middle of a program. As he snored—his usual loud elephant snores—I read the paper or pulled out my computer.

At the end of my time with him, as I left him with Suzie or Steve or let him go to sleep for the night, I said, "See you tomorrow, Dad. I love you."

He looked at me. "Goodnight. I love you too." He raised an eyebrow. "How long can you stay in Montreal?"

"I'll stay as long as you want."

"Good," he said.

He nodded, but there was hardly any expression on his face.

* * *

One afternoon, I looked closely at my father's face while he slept quietly. His eyes were peaceful while his breast rose and fell slowly, no snores emanating from him this time. I took a long breath and felt my chest fill with dread.

My father had been a consummate survivor all his life. He made it through a world war as a Hungarian or German reconnaissance pilot flying missions over the Russian front. He risked his life to defect to the Soviet side after the war had turned against the Axis powers. He endured a Russian POW camp where his language skills helped him become a go-between among the prisoners. He avoided potential death again by evading the Czechoslovak First Army's bloody fight against the Germans in northeastern Slovakia.

After the war, he escaped with my mother soon after the Communists had taken over their homeland, walking by night through the woods to get to the American zone in Austria. He arrived in Canada with $50 in his pocket and a dream of creating a thriving company and growing a family tree in a free country. He built a successful business and real estate holdings from the ground up, employing his shrewd mind and strong hands. Could I ever find in myself his optimism, moxie, and grit?

Though Dad's eyes closed as he lay resting in his hospital bed, I could hardly look at them. I imagined they'd open suddenly and stare through me. Though I admired my dad, a growing part of me scorned this man for not being around much during my childhood and abandoning my mother. He had caused her much anguish when he walked out on her, not once but three times. I detested his tolerating my brother's bolshiness and for his many secrets, like hiding his first marriage and daughter from us for decades.

I looked down at the floor. I cursed myself for rarely standing up to my father's bullying and finagling and for staying hushed about his money mischief and late-night escapades.

My throat grew dry and sore. A big part of me revered my father for what he had created over fifty years in Canada, something I didn't think I had the wherewithal to replicate. He had helped scores of his countrymen escape from behind the Iron Curtain, resettle in Canada, and start new lives and businesses here. I admired him for the hugs, handshakes, and hurrahs he got from his Canadian business colleagues and his Hungarian and Slovak compadres. I enjoyed his "eat, drink, and be merry" ways with his chums. He could make people laugh with his racy jokes and funny stories, charm the ladies by kissing the back of their hands, and match any man in a smoky barroom. He had worked hard to amass a small fortune onshore and to stash a bundle offshore.

My eyes began to burn. Another part of me wanted to scream at my father: *I'm pissed at you for what you did to Mom, and for screwing up your marriage to Elaine, and for not telling us about Emilia. I can't believe your offshore money crap took me in.* Maybe I was more pissed at myself for having gone along with his shenanigans or for staying on the sidelines regarding his unending schemes and scams.

I clenched the rail on the side of my father's bed. *I loathed your smoking, drinking, womanizing, and complaining about your wives and partners.* I wanted to bellow, "Dad, you have no idea what it was like to grow up and live as your son. I felt the pressure of your expectations to become a bright MIT engineer, a prominent Harvard businessman, and then a conniving lawyer from who-knows-where. And after I would have accomplished that, you wanted me to come into your business where you'd tell me what to do and how to live." I felt badly bruised and burdened by his "Just *lassen* to me, son!"

Knowing my father, I imagined he wouldn't admit what had been his true desires for me. I presumed he'd shout, "No, not at all! I wanted you to make something of yourself and not be just a 'bloody immigrant' like me; to become somebody and not nobody."

Perhaps, deep down, I was disappointed in myself for not having achieved his high aspirations and for not telling him years ago how I felt. The time now seemed too late for such son-to-father sharing.

I glanced at his face. It was no longer lively, or menacing, or determined, or calculating, or anything. My chest ached, and my gut burned with the thought that he'd soon be gone. Though he had been the source of much of my angst and trepidation since I was a kid, I knew that he had wanted the best for his two boys. Though he wished for Steve and me to reach beyond his business success, he especially wanted me to follow in his finagling footsteps and to build upon his dubious dais. But his triumphs felt tainted.

There had been a sizable cost in trying to rise to my father's bloated aspirations. It led to my feeling alone and scared at MIT after Dad had walked out on Mom for a second time. It precipitated my anguish at Harvard

Business School because I saw myself there more for him than for me. It triggered my depression during my American University graduate program in feeling that I would never measure up to his desires.

I still wondered which I had become in his eyes, somebody or nobody. Part of me aspired to be the man my father wanted; I desperately wanted to make him proud. And, part of me felt I never could reach the goalposts that he kept picking up and moving further away. Could he not have loved me for who I was rather than for what he wanted me to become? Then again, who was I working to become?

As Dad lay limp in his hospital bed, his only manly roars were his elephant snores. I again felt the urge to speak to him, to tell him how I felt about him. I reached out my hand, but my eyes welled, and I turned away.

I couldn't be cruel. I wasn't sure what my father could take in and understand through his diminished mind, his ears perhaps as glazed over as his waking eyes seemed to be. Any dark display would be of questionable benefit, so I held my tongue as my throat grew drier. The time for a heart-to-heart, father-to-son talk had passed away a long time ago. I would feel ashamed if I'd cause him undue anguish at this late hour.

What good would it do? I can't change what he did and what happened years and decades ago. If I blurted out my life of anguish by his hand, I'd have to deal with my complicity, even collusion, in continually striving to be his preferred son. *Is my silence working to protect him or me?* Here I was once again in a Johnny Simkovits double bind.

I surmised that I'd have to struggle with my veiled feelings after Dad was gone. I may need a psychotherapist better than Moe Gross to help me through my lingering anger, angst, and shame.

When my father awoke, he reached for my hand. From the way he took mine into his—holding it gently yet firmly as one would a child's—I realized my importance to him. Without one word passing between us, I sensed his connection to me as much as I felt my tie to him. Our lives were inextricably entwined, no matter how much dirt lay on the floor beneath our feet. For most of my life, that entwinement felt like a choking entanglement from which I wanted to escape and run away. But now, our touch felt like a father-to-son farewell embrace, as if Dad were leaving on an extended voyage.

I looked at my father again and kept my face serene. No matter what kind of connection he felt toward my brother, that comparison didn't seem relevant during these, his final days. I did wonder whether I'd hear an acknowledgement or apology from him about the hurt he had wielded on our family. Maybe he would have asked for my forgiveness had he indeed known how I felt about him. He might have regretted the lifetime of expectations he had placed on my brother's and my shoulders and the pain and hurt he had caused to our mother's heart and spirit.

I showed a smile and said, "Hi, Dad."

He responded, "Hi, son."

From my father's caring look and light touch, I gathered that he and I had held a special bond and trust. And I knew that my time as his successor had arrived. There was no need to hoist, haul, or heave any of our wretched past onto his bed. These last days were to be only for him. My reconciliation with myself would have to wait for another time.

No need to be cruel; be by his side as much as you can.

He'll say what he needs to if and when he wants to.

There's no need to pull your hand away from his.

I numbed and buried my anger and outrage. I spoke with a soft and kind voice. I allowed our hands to meet as Dad reached for mine. I put my other palm on his arm. "Feeling okay?" I said.

He nodded.

I looked at his face. "Any pain?"

He shook his head.

I moved my other hand to his food tray. "Are you hungry or thirsty?"

Another shake of his head.

I pointed to the bathroom. "Do you need to go?"

"No," he said faintly.

I made a circle in the air with my hand and pointed index finger. "Do you want me to turn you over?"

After a moment, he said, "Okay," with a nod.

After we finished, his eyes went back to the television. I sat with him as we had done on many weekends when I was a kid—with my sitting on the floor next to him as he rested on the couch after a long week's work at JHS. With those three letters standing for John, Harvy, and Stephen, Dad had bound the three of us together on this earth. I wondered how much longer my brother and I would maintain that entangled connection. But that was another thought for another time.

When I kissed my father goodbye at the end of the day, I told him caringly, "I love you, Dad." I presented only my most kind-hearted self to him. Dad nodded and mouthed the exact words back to me.

"See you tomorrow?" he asked.

"Yes, Dad, for sure," I offered back.

He nodded his approval.

During his waning days, no acknowledgement or apology of the past came from my father. For those long weeks in the hospital, he never spoke to me about himself, his condition, or his pending death. The only time he initiated a conversation was when he asked, every other day, "Harvy, can you take me home?"

Each time, I put my palm on his arm. "I know, Dad, I know." I shook my head and spoke gently. "Unfortunately, you can't go home; you're too ill. The doctor wants you to stay." I never asked for his reasons for going back home, assuming that he preferred not being in the hospital.

Though I tried, I wished I could have loved my father a little more and shown it by taking him to live out his last days and hours in his bed at home. Perhaps that kind of love, one of choosing compassion and concern for him—and going against the doctor's recommendations—over choosing convenience for us, was too hard for me (or Steve or Suzie) to embrace.

* * *

Dad took in very little food or liquids while in the hospital. He occasionally sipped water from a small paper cup that sat by his bed. My father hardly glanced at his three daily hospital meals. When served, he pushed the trays away from him a centimeter or two. When I asked him, "Why are you not eating," he looked at me and said plainly, "I'm not hungry."

After weeks of the same, his face, arms, and legs thinned as if he were a Holocaust prisoner. His doctor suggested a glucose drip to keep him hydrated and sustained. Not wanting to see his end come quickly, Steve and I agreed.

After a few days on the drip, Dad's body bloated. His skin turned waxy. Every appendage began to look more as if it were a clown's balloon creation twisted into a human shape.

Steve, Suzie, and I talked about hospice care for Dad. We met with a social worker from a palliative care centre nearby. Dad's long-time business friend, Abe, had recommended the place. Abe then made a personal call (and perhaps a personal donation) to have the centre take on Dad as a client.

Early during Dad's hospital stay, none of us had been ready or willing to make a hospice care decision for him. It would have meant a much quicker death unless he was willing to take in some sustenance on his own. His sudden turn from POW to the Michelin Man, and constantly feeling sore in bed, made Steve and I realize there was nothing more the hospital could do for him. We reconsidered the hospice idea.

While Dad slept in his room, Steve, Suzie, and I talked once more in the hallway about the palliative care centre. There, Dad would be made comfortable but not given any medical intervention to sustain his life. There would be no feeding or hydration other than what he took in on his own. Nature would be permitted to take its course.

Steve and I agreed to speak to Dad's doctor one more time. The oncologist repeated his refrain. "Your father can stay here in the hospital for as long as you want. We would make him as comfortable as we can, keep him hydrated, get whatever sustenance we can into him, and treat any pain he might have, and for as long as it takes."

Steve and I went back and forth on the issue for two days, keeping our conversations calm and quiet. We slept one or two more nights on the notion of how quickly we'd let Dad die. I was glad that Steve kept words like "God" and "heaven" out of our conversations.

We talked again to the social workers at both the hospital and at the hospice. Finally, one of us offered, "I guess it comes down to a choice of how we want Dad to die. It could happen here in the hospital until modern medicine runs out of options. Or it could be at the hospice until Dad allows himself to go."

Steve, Suzie, and I spoke of hiring palliative nurses for his home, but that would have put pressure and demands on Suzie and would have been costly. Like the hospital, Quebec health insurance covered the hospice centre, and the trained hospice nurses could better handle a person's last days. Suzie gave her support for whatever Steve and I decided.

In the end, we agreed. We wanted Dad to be as comfortable as possible, to have the least amount of pain or suffering. Prolonging his life only for the sake of extending it wasn't a good option. We wanted him to pass away with whatever dignity we could provide. We wanted to give him and his body some say over the time he had left.

While I drove to Boston to be home with Gloria and our son for the weekend, my brother arranged for Dad to move to the palliative care centre. The month or more he might have gained in the hospital might turn into a week or two in the hospice, but our father and his body would be in charge of his fate.

Dad was transferred via ambulance during the first week of October 2000, just days before my forty-sixth birthday. It was about five weeks after he had entered St. Mary's Hospital, which had been only days before my brother's forty-seventh birthday. Neither Steve nor I mentioned our birthdays while Dad lay in the hospital, and our father didn't say anything about them.

Though we told our dad about his move to a hospice, he didn't ask or say anything about it. On a chilly Saturday morning, the transfer took a little over an hour.

* * * *

To Duma or Not Duma

Mr. Duma, one of Dad's Hungarian friends, came to see my father several times at St. Mary's. While spending time with my father, he'd kindly tell me to go for a walk or take a break at the hospital cafeteria.

About a month into my father's time at the hospital, days before Steve and I transferred him to the hospice, Mr. Duma came to me at the end of one visit. "Harvy, I'd like to meet you privately. Can we have breakfast at Place Alexis Nihon?"

"Sure; what's it about?"

His voice was subdued. "It's a private matter. I can say more when we meet. Will nine o'clock tomorrow morning work for you? I'll wait for you by a table outside of the food court that looks down over the mall."

Though I was hesitant, I said, "Okay, I'll see you there and then."

He nodded, said goodbye, and departed.

The Alexis Nihon Plaza was a complex of buildings linked together by a large indoor shopping mall and multi-screen movie theatre. My former employer, WISE, had resided in one of those office towers. In another was Geoff Levi's accounting firm. In a third was Dad's Global Trade Bank.

The mall unnerved me. I never wanted to see a film at the theatre here. They'd remind me of the dramas that played out in my life on these premises.

I met Mr. Duma as he had requested. He was a gray-haired, slightly chubby man, years younger than Dad. I wondered what he wanted to talk about, and I felt a little apprehensive. Besides knowing him through my father's Slovak Business Association, I knew very little about the guy.

After we had grabbed coffees and breakfast pastries, he motioned to an unoccupied table away from the crowd. We sat down. He began to speak, his accent a deep Eastern-European like my dad's. "Your father told me that you are doing very well as a consultant in Boston. I know you moved there in '89 and got married to a nice girl in '94 and then had a son in '96." He smiled as he spoke.

I was glad he hadn't mentioned my divorce. I wondered where he was going with this conversation.

He continued. "Your father says good things about all of you, especially your boy. He must be almost ready to go to school."

I was cordial. "Thank you, Mr. Duma. That's nice to hear. My son will start kindergarten next fall."

I wondered if Duma's breakfast invitation had anything to do with the Global Trade Bank situated six floors above us. Having my father's imminent passing on my mind, I wanted the fellow to get to the point. "To what do I owe the occasion of this conversation, Mr. Duma, during this difficult time for my family?"

The man's face turned serious. "It's so sad to see your father this way. He and I have been good friends for many years. And we've done some business together." His eyebrows lifted, and his face brightened. "I once introduced your father to a Czech couple that needed money to start a restaurant. Just on my word, he loaned them $15,000 for two years, and I did the same."

He smiled again. "After they had started their operation, your father and I went there for supper one night. The Slavic food was fantastic, very authentic. After we had eaten, your father wanted to pay the bill." Mr. Duma's smile widened. "The owner and his wife insisted that the meal was on them."

Duma was now grinning ear to ear. "But your father pulled out his wallet, took out a $100 bill, put it on the table, and said, 'I want you to take this; you guys would benefit from it more than me.'" He chuckled. "Your father always liked to show his appreciation."

Duma nodded. "After two years, the people repaid our loan, plus interest, and they're still operating today."

I looked at him. "What's the name of the place?"

His eyes stayed fixed on me. "Little Bohemia, in Old Montreal. You should go there sometime."

"I've not heard of it, but I'll look it up," I said. "And I didn't know that story." I nodded. "Yes, my father was that way with his good friends."

I looked intently at Mr. Duma, hoping he would get to his purpose for our gathering. He obliged. "Your father and I have shared much with each other about our personal and business lives. He has told me many things, things that he told no one else..." He leaned forward and pointed his finger my way. "...not even to you, Harvy."

I came back quickly and cocky. "There's probably nothing you could tell me that would surprise me about my father. I've been through a lot with him. He has told me many things too that he never told anyone else."

Mr. Duma eyed me carefully. "I do know that you are closer to your father than your brother is. I know that Johnny has confided in you, but he hasn't told you everything." He took a long breath. "Did you know that before his stroke, he was with another woman while he was still with Elaine?"

For a moment, I was stunned. I looked down at the table then up at Duma. "Is that why you brought me here today?" I felt the heat rising in me and sweat oozing out of me. *Why do my father's friends want to tell me such things?* I blurted out, "Wouldn't it be better to keep such things to yourself?"

Duma stayed calm as if he had expected my reaction. "It's more complicated, Harvy, and the situation is unfinished. There is a promise your father made that remains unfulfilled. I need you to hear me out."

Another Johnny Simkovits mess for me to mop up! "Okay," I said, though I wanted to scream.

Mr. Duma spoke confidently. "One night at the Troika, your father and I were having drinks at a table in the bar area." He pointed to one side. "There were two French women at the next table. Johnny and I got friendly with them; we joked around and had some laughs." He took a breath. "I thought everything would end there, but one woman gave Johnny her number. The next thing I knew, they were getting together."

I raised my voice a tad. "So what's the big deal? My father has met a lot of women at the Troika and has had many relationships on the side."

Duma's voice didn't waver. "But this one was different, Harvy. Johnny got this woman pregnant, and she had a son by him!"

Oh, my God! Did I now have another half-sibling somewhere? If Dad met her before his stroke, the kid must be over seven years old. I kept my hands on the table so that I wouldn't throw them in the air with disgust. "So who and where are these people?" Part of me wished that Mr. Duma wouldn't answer my question. That same part wanted to stand and walk away.

Mr. Duma responded quickly. "Right now, Harvy, it's not important who and where they are. It doesn't matter because the boy died when he was five years old." He pointed away from us. "The kid was in a big car accident with his mother's brother. The uncle survived, but the child went into a coma and later died." He lifted his hand higher to make his point. "The accident was on the Metropolitan Expressway, north of the city. It was such a bad accident that it was in the Montreal newspaper."

My head spun, and my gut wrenched. One second I had a half-brother, and, the next second, he was gone. "So, what does this have to do with me?"

"I'm getting there, Harvy. Please, please listen. I know this is upsetting to you, but you must let me finish." His hand stayed on the table with its palm up and facing me, indicating that he wanted me to remain collected. His face remained kind and caring, his voice calm and considerate.

I nodded for him to continue. He did. "Your father loved that child. He visited him and his mother many times over the years. Though the woman wanted nothing from Johnny, he promised to pay for the boy's education."

That sounded typical for my father. That woman seemed honourable too.

Mr. Duma's voice remained both soft and serious. "But when that boy died, your father went crazy. Even though Johnny's stroke limited him, he went to her home, and they had a big argument. He blamed her for the kid's death. He then hit her again and again." Duma pointed to his face. "He struck her so hard that she needed to go to the hospital."

"Oh, no!" I said. *Oh my frigging God,* I thought. I wanted to raise open palms to put a stop to Mr. Duma's account, but I kept my fists on the table.

He continued. "But that woman was kind, and she cared about your father. She didn't press any charges, but she wanted compensation for what he had done to her." Mr. Duma pointed to himself again. "She didn't want to see him, so your father asked me to negotiate a settlement with her."

I was dumbfounded. I knew my father's ways. Twenty years earlier, he had hit my mother after Steve and I had argued on a trip we took across Canada. Dad became uncontrollably angry after Steve called to tell him that he was leaving me behind in Vancouver and flying home. Dad blamed Mom for not having raised and taught his boys right. He hit her so violently that she had to run out of the house to get away from him. I later felt ashamed that I had not confronted my father about his brutality. It had been easier to blame Mom.

Dad had slapped Elaine too—in the face, twice—when he didn't like the way she had driven them to Florida in the winter following his stroke.

What Mr. Duma was saying about Dad's explosive violence was plausible, but his cruelty to this woman was beyond anything I had known. Had his stroke caused him to cross a boundary he had never traversed before?

My head ached, and I felt my body shudder. I kept myself silent and still as Duma related the rest of this Johnny tale turned bad dream.

The older man looked straight at me. "She and I settled on $250,000 cash, Canadian." He pulled out a folded piece of paper from his pocket and put it on the table, unopened. He pointed upward casually to where the Global Trade Bank branch was situated. "I paid her from my money over there. She then left Montreal and went back to France, where her family lives. I gave her some cash here and transferred the balance to her there."

My mind raced. Might this guy be the Hungarian fellow Dad once said was his Global Trade Bank money mule these last years? My voice quieted. "So you're involved in the Global Trade Bank as my father has been?"

He nodded. "Yes. That's how he and I met years ago, through Mr. Simon at the bank." He smiled. "I had known about Johnny through the Hungarian community in Montreal. But after Simon introduced us, your father and I hit it off. We became good friends."

"So why did you compensate that woman for my father's sake?"

Duma took a big breath. "I still have many property interests here in Canada. I had a bank loan coming due, but I couldn't use my money over there to pay it off, and I didn't have enough capital in Canada to cover the repayment." He smiled. "Your father helped me out. He signed a personal guarantee at his bank for a $250,000 loan to me. At the same time, I paid the woman that same amount. The arrangement worked well for both of us."

My mind was upside down, but I still didn't know why I needed to be involved in Dad's mishigas with Duma. I crumpled my Styrofoam coffee cup. My legs jittered under the table as my voice started to rise again. "So you paid off the woman, and my father guaranteed a loan to you for the same amount. So what's the issue? Why am I here? What do you need from me?" I wished I hadn't been dragged into this abysmal affair better left buried far offshore.

Mr. Duma looked my way again, and his eyes narrowed. "The problem is that I still haven't fully repaid the bank for the loan, and your father hasn't paid me back fully for the money I had given to the woman." He opened the folded paper he had put on the table. "This IOU is from your father to me. Originally it was for $250,000. We later lowered the loan to $150,000 when I had enough money to repay $100,000 to the bank."

Duma paused for a few seconds and then continued. "I can show you the bank loan statements and correspondence if you want to see them. Your father is still a guarantor at the bank. You can ask your bookkeeper, Rob; he knows about it too." Mr. Duma pointed my way. "And your father still owes me $150,000 against what I had given to that woman."

I can't believe this! Into what has my father gotten me?

And Rob knows about this? He hadn't told Steve or me anything. Then again, Rob had never said anything about my father's uncontrolled spending until I confronted him about Dad's empty bank accounts.

I looked at the time-worn paper sitting on the table. I recognized my father's handwriting and signature. It was his more recent stroke-affected scribble, with each cursive letter formed individually and strung together.

The loan agreement looked as if Dad had written it. The $250,000 was crossed out, and $150,000 was marked above it along with the initials "JS."

Below my father's signature, there was a different squiggly signature. Before I could ask about that, Mr. Duma continued. "Harvy, my business now has the money to pay off the rest of the bank loan and to remove your father as guarantor. But your father and I have not had a chance to go to the Global Trade Bank for him to pay back the balance he owes me from over there." He looked away and then back. "Now, there's no way for him to do it."

"Mr. Duma, why should I believe both you and what's written here?"

He leaned forward and looked into my eyes. His voice was quiet but firm. "Because, Harvy, I was the one who, last December, told Johnny and Mr. Weber upstairs," his finger pointed upward again, "that your father should give you power of attorney over his bank accounts over there."

He took a long breath. "I knew your father was no longer able to handle that money himself. I knew he was spending all that he made offshore." His eyes were on me. "I was afraid he was going to give too much of it away rather than give it to you as he had promised."

My face must have been white, for the elder added, "Yes, Harvy, I know about what he has over there and that he had promised it only to you and not to your brother." He took another long breath. "Last year, in front of Mr. Weber, I urged Johnny to give you signing authority. He said he would do it after returning from Florida, and I know he did that in May."

Mr. Duma gestured his flat hand in my direction. "You can ask the bank manager yourself." He pointed to the paper on the table. "This is Mr. Weber's signature on the IOU." He pointed upward once more to the tower that housed the Global Trade Bank. "Weber witnessed our agreement."

My head spun; my heart raced; my gut cramped. I didn't know if I should embrace this man for backing me with my father. Then again, should I banish him from my sight for being a tax-evading scoundrel like my dad? I couldn't help but feel as if Duma were taking me for a rogue's ride, but my father had taken me on many such scoundrel excursions.

Mr. Duma took another long breath. "If you accept what I'm saying, Harvy, then I have already arranged for us to meet with Mr. Weber at 10 o'clock this morning." He pointed to his watch. "He'll be waiting for us in fifteen minutes from now." He pointed to me. "Because you have power of attorney over your father's accounts, you must make this money transfer from his account to mine before the POA runs out upon your father's death."

The man eyed me again. "And this is the time to switch those accounts into your name. Otherwise, your father's last will takes over. And, yes, I know both you and your brother are executors of your father's estate."

I was astounded by how fast this conversation was moving and how much Mr. Duma knew about my father's will, his offshore money, and my part in it. And, Duma was right. If I didn't open new accounts in my name at the Global Trade Bank and transfer Dad's offshore assets into those accounts,

I'd lose my sole control over those assets when Dad died. If I were to mop up my father's mess with Duma, I'd have to make arrangements.

Duma knew nothing of my intent to divulge Dad's stash to both my brother and the government. I looked at him and lowered my voice. "Mr. Duma, I have decided that I'm not like my father. I'm not prepared to maintain his offshore holdings. I want to declare them to the Canadian authorities and pay the requisite tax." I pointed to him. "I don't know how I can give you any money from over there without exposing my complicity in my father's hidden assets. How could I explain to my brother that $150,000 left one of our father's accounts just days before his death?"

Mr. Duma leaned back in his chair. After a moment, he leaned forward again. "Are you sure you want to declare that money, Harvy? I have had my assets with that bank for a lot longer than your father has. When I travel overseas, I use my money over there in my businesses without any problem. It's safe and secure, and it's untraceable to me here in Canada."

I leaned back in my chair and was barely able to meet Duma's eyes. "I'm not a world traveler as you are. I would feel safer and more secure if I'd bring the money into the open. I'm planning to tell my brother about it because my mother would have wanted me to include him in these funds."

Duma placed his hand on his chin. "I see," he said. "I know of your mother's situation, and I understand your decision, even if I disagree with it. It's also good of you to think about your brother that way. I never had a brother, but I know your father wanted you two to be closer than you are."

The air between us stayed still for several long seconds. Mr. Duma looked away for a moment, and then he turned back to me. "So, I have an idea about how we can fix this if you are willing to go along."

I turned over my hands on the table and beckoned him to continue.

"We can make one of your father's accounts disappear," he said.

"What? What do you mean?"

Mr. Duma lowered his voice. "I know your father has a separate account with shares in the Heritage Fund and other mutual funds. The Heritage funds in that account are now worth about as much as what your father owes me. If it's okay with you, you can transfer those funds to me, and we can then call it even." He wagged his finger up and then down. "That venture fund may wind up being worth a little more or a little less than $150,000, but I'm willing to take on that risk to close out Johnny's IOU."

He reached into his pocket and took out his wallet. From there, he pulled out another piece of paper and unfolded it. "Here's my company cheque to pay back the remaining loan amount to your father's bank. When we transfer the Heritage fund, I can give this to you. We can then go to the bank together to cash it or take it there yourself. Or, if you want, I can deposit it myself." He nodded. "Your father's guarantee would automatically go away once the cheque has cleared."

This guy is amazingly fast on the money draw. I thought for a moment. "So, how does that solve my situation with that Heritage account?"

Mr. Duma didn't hesitate. "We can do similarly with the rest of the money in that one account. You can cash in what's left and transfer those funds anywhere you want. You can then close the account and tell no one about it. You won't have to declare it to the Canadian government or tell your brother. It would be as if that account had never existed."

Whoa, whoa! My mind was churning. Was Duma asking me to become a money-hiding scoundrel like him and my father, yet on a much smaller scale?

His eyes were on me once more. "I care deeply about your father; he was like a brother to me. And I really don't need his money, and I don't want to make trouble for you, Harvy. I only want to settle what your father owes me from over there and what I owe to his bank here."

I sat frozen in my chair. My hands were grasped together tightly on the table while my head stayed bowed. *Should I settle this IOU?* The paper Dad signed seemed to be in my father's lending MO of these recent years. He had gotten a similar IOU from his doctor, though without a witness's signature.

Should I trust Duma? He seemed to be on my side, wanting me to gain the best advantage of my father's offshore stash. If I didn't bend to Duma now, then Dad's estate could be on the hook for a hundred and fifty grand to the bank. I would have to explain that to my brother. And, if I dismissed Duma's deal, this man might go directly to Steve to settle this arrangement. How would Steve react to know he had had a half-brother in Montreal?

Should I take some of Dad's hidden money and put it directly into my pocket? My brother would never know unless Duma or Weber told him. Why would they say anything if I settled this matter with Duma?

Should I make the one account disappear? If the account were closed, how would the government ever find out? If Mr. Duma ever told them, then I'd have something on him that Revenue Canada could be interested in knowing.

What will I tell my lawyer, accountant, wife, and especially brother about this? What could I conceivably say to them? I might have to keep my mouth shut and swallow my knowledge of Dad's terrible transgression with that French woman and this foul transaction with Duma.

Maybe I should threaten to report Mr. Duma to Revenue Canada and tell him to leave my brother and me alone. But might he make trouble for us until I had the chance to clean up Dad's offshore assets?

Mr. Duma looked at his watch. "I see it's now almost ten o'clock, Harvy. Mr. Weber will be waiting for us. What do you want to do?"

I continued to look at the table for a moment. I thought of the lyrics of Kenny Roger's song, *The Gambler*. I didn't know whether I should hold onto my cards, fold 'em, walk away, or run.

I sighed, raised my head, put my hands flat on the table, and sat straighter in my chair. I looked into Duma's eyes. Though it wrenched my gut, I knew how I was going to respond to his wretched request.

A short time later, Mr. Duma and I walked out of the Alexis Nihon Plaza. He eyed me graciously as we shook hands and said goodbye. "You know, Harvy; now that you will be declaring your father's money to Revenue Canada, they'll know about this bank." He pointed to the office tower behind us. "I will have to move my money from here and put it elsewhere."

I nodded my understanding but said nothing. I wondered how Mr. Duma would handle his offshore assets as he reached the end of his life. Did he have kids who knew about his hidden money? I asked nothing about it; it was better that I didn't know.

I felt sad for Mr. Weber; he would soon lose two long-time customers. But his Global Trade Bank was in a business I didn't think of highly.

Mr. Duma would come to Dad's funeral to pay his respects to our family. By the subdued way he gazed at me when he said goodbye on that sad day, I figured it was the last time I'd ever see the man.

* * *

Years later, I realized more about the role Mr. Duma played in my father's life.

My father had had various confidants during his years as a Canadian businessman. The first had been his Lithuanian friend, Aras. In 1953, Aras and his uncle had lent Dad money when he started Montreal Phono. Aras was a bon vivant businessman who regularly drank, smoked, dined, and played around with Johnny. They frequented the Hungarian Tokay, Russian Troika, Polish Stach's, Greek Sabayon, and who knows where else.

Then there was a Romanian friend, Ned Meyer, to whom my father confided his distress after fighting with my mother. Dad even lived with Ned and his wife, Mimi, during his and Mom's first separation.

Both Ned and Aras were there for Dad when his forewoman, Magda, took her life after my father's platonic love affair with her had gone stale. (Dad had foolishly slept with her sister.) After Magda's suicide, Ned, Aras, and Dad searched the apartment that she rented from Aras. To Dad's benefit, the three found no incriminating evidence that implicated my father in her suicide.

Then there was Gillian Mozer, Dad's Montreal Phono accountant who had traveled with Johnny through Europe on business. Our two families had vacationed together in Florida during several winter breaks. At my father's behest, Gillian had signed falsified Montreal Phono income tax returns. He also had known about CANEX, my father's offshore Cayman Corporation.

Roger Delliard followed Mozer. He was JHS's accountant, the one who "had an inkling" about my father's offshore accounts. He helped assuage Dad's fears when I had gotten a bank receipt for a $100,000USD transfer that I had made from my Boston bank to my father's Cayman bank branch. I had consummated that transaction on my dad's behalf as I departed Harvard midway through my first year of MBA studies.

And then there was Mack, Dad's corporate lawyer for decades. Mack schemed with Dad about how my father could save personal and corporate taxes. On Mack's advice, my father bought real estate to shelter his income. Mack also had my father spread his business interests across multiple companies to leverage lower small-business tax rates.

There were abrupt endings to all those friendships. When Dad and Montreal Phono got into trouble with Revenue Canada in '75, my father quickly dismissed Mozer—and summarily dropped him as a friend—as soon as the government cleared Dad of criminal charges.

After Dad had left my mother in '80 and moved in with his eventual third wife, Ned kept his distance from Johnny. Mimi, too, felt that Johnny's new love, Elaine, was too American, too independent, and "not her cup of tea." Ned and Dad spoke on the phone occasionally, but they never again vacationed or spent time together.

When I decided to depart JHS for good, Dad didn't want to run the company with only my brother. He then ended his ties with Roger Delliard and his associate Norman. After Dad and Norman had returned from a final business trip to Paris, complete with extracurricular activities at the Moulin Rouge, I never saw those two with Dad again.

Dad's relationship ended with both Mack and Aras when he and Elaine separated in '94. Mack had written a letter to Johnny, fervently disagreeing with my father when he wanted to throw a bunch of assets Elaine's way—to get her back soon after he had left her. Dad separated from his longtime advisor to get back into Elaine's good graces, which failed. I, too, may have precipitated Johnny and Mack's divorce by confronting Mack about inviting my father to the Troika and then letting Johnny pay the tab.

Dad then lost Aras too. Aras' wife became furious at Johnny for bungling his marriage to Elaine, her good friend. Celia stood in the way of Aras going out with his over forty-year business cohort and drinking buddy.

So, who else did my father have left for *tête-à-têtes* about his sordid secrets? The answer seemed to be his most recent compadre in offshore tax skirting, Mr. Duma. Dad needed a companion to crow to, confide in, confess to, or scheme with about his lifetime of finagling.

At least Dad had someone he could talk to and trust regarding his sordid money matters. Yet, I would never come to know whether Mr. Duma had been entirely straight with me about that Troika affair and scratchy IOU.

I did come to understand that, to varying degrees, these sordid chums, cohorts, compadres, and confidants were co-conspirators and clear-cut reflections of Johnny.

Then again, who was I to judge?

* * * *

Moment of Brotherly Truth

A few days after the hospital attendants had moved Dad to the hospice, it was time to reveal to Steve our father's dealings with both the Global Trade Bank and the Supporters of Independent University. Dad's passing was imminent, and I would allow my Global Trade Bank power of attorney to terminate at his death.

My brother needed to know about the voluntary disclosure I arranged for our father's offshore assets. I believed that Steve would have confidence in my accountant friend, Geoff, because of his time as our JHS accountant. With Geoff and his colleague, Charles, in place, I hoped Steve would trust my approach for putting Dad's offshore affairs behind us.

On a cloudy and chilly day in early October 2000, my brother and I met at the funeral complex at the Mount Royal Cemetery to finalize our father's funeral arrangements. Over 150 years old, the Mount Royal Cemetery and Funeral Complex lay on the other side of that mountain from downtown Montreal. It thus gave its Christian patrons the pleasure of being buried "on the mount." The location sported big, lush hardwood trees and tall, thick shrubs, providing the surreal feel of a town for the dead overlooking a city for the living.

Dad wanted to die in style, to rest where his colleagues and friends could visit him, and maybe where he would be a little closer to heaven. He had bought his Mt. Royal gravesite many years earlier—a space ample enough for six coffins. He thought that Steve, his wife, Elaine, I, and my wife would be buried with him one day. (At the time he had bought the plot, I hadn't yet remarried, but that didn't dissuade Dad.) No matter where Dad went in life or would go in death, he liked to do it large and have company.

I arrived at the funeral home on time, at 2 o'clock. Knowing my brother's typical tardiness, I waited for him inside my idling car. I looked out into the frigid day. The leaves on the lush maples were changing into bright gold, green, and red autumn hues. Dying leaves were falling from the trees, and the wind was blowing them about in little dust devils. The wind had scattered those leaves on the ground and against the side of the funeral home.

The scene reminded me of the day, almost exactly a year earlier, when I first met with my high school chum and lawyer friend, André Lefebvre, at Elliot Trudell. His firm was situated right on the other side of Mount Royal from where I stood. As it had been on that day, today was a dreaded day I knew I had to face. I wondered what changes would come forth for my brother and me regarding what I would reveal to him today.

When I saw Steve park, I looked at my watch. *He's only twelve minutes late.* I exited my car and walked to the funeral home's entrance. I wore a heavy trench coat, but the wind still bit into me, making me shiver. I strolled at a steady gait to the large front door. *Take your time, Harvy. He made you wait, so don't rush to greet him.* My chills made me wrap my trench coat even tighter as I approached my brother. "Chilly day, even for Montreal this time of year," I said. I reached out my hand without taking off my glove.

"Winter's coming," he said with a big grin, mimicking one of our father's standard clichés. He took my hand, and we shook quickly.

"Let's get inside before I freeze to death." I didn't realize what I was saying.

"Sure," he said. "Your Canadian blood seems to have thinned since you moved to Boston." His quip roused a twinge in my gut, but I said nothing.

I looked at the funeral home's front door of thick natural wood, perhaps over a century old. It had a large, round iron ring with which to pull it open. "This seems like a very nice place for a funeral," I offered.

"Yes," he said. "Dad wanted to be buried here. I even helped him pick out his big plot about eight years ago. There's room for all of us in there, you know."

I thought of my mother lying alone in the Jewish Cemetery in Montreal's West Island. I was sure a part of her would have longed to be buried next to her one and only husband. "Yes, I know," I said to Steve without looking at him. I curtailed my part of our gallows humour and reached for the door's metal ring.

To reach the main office, we walked down a long wide hallway, panelled in dark wood. Steve looked straight ahead as he offered, "I made an appointment with the director. She's expecting us." His head turned my way. "You know, Harvy, the director of the Slovak funeral home is upset at us."

I turned slightly toward him. "No, I didn't know. Why is that?"

Steve responded with little affect. "It seems Dad is the first Slovak to have services and be buried here at Mount Royal Cemetery, and not at the regular funeral home for the Slovak people in Montreal." His tone raised a touch. "The Slovak funeral home director called the other day to give me heck for not coming to him to arrange Dad's service and burial." He lifted a finger. "I told him that Dad wanted his burial here, and there was nothing we could do to change that."

I felt my morbid humour rise again. "Yah, let the guy go argue it out with Dad," I said.

Steve offered a slight grin. Neither he nor I said anything more about our father's deteriorating condition. We changed our focus to our task.

After quick greetings, the middle-aged woman director ushered us into her wood-panelled office. Steve and I sat on a firm Chesterfield with wide arms while the director sat in a big chair opposite us. My brother and I gravitated to opposite ends of the couch that could probably hold a mourning family of five or six.

"Sorry to meet under these sad circumstances," the director offered. She looked back and forth at Steve and me. "What kind of service and burial do you desire for your father?"

Steve lifted his hand to make a point. "Our father had big events for his friends and colleagues. We need to honour him in the same way."

Though I knew of my father's grandiose ways, I was surprised by Steve's statement. He had never enjoyed Dad's lavish parties. He never liked to "put on a face" for Dad's friends. I retorted, "But this is a family affair,

Steve. Dad was never big and showy with Mom and us. For whom are we doing this funeral?"

The director jumped in. "I'm sure we can find something suitable that would satisfy both of you." She spoke confidently. "We have a large range of options here at Mount Royal."

We reviewed the Slovak Church services, the Mt. Royal Cemetery burial site ceremony, and the Funeral Complex reception. As in all matters regarding Dad's illness and dying, Steve and I approached our task unemotionally. I suspected we had our mixed and veiled feelings, but we talked to the director as if we were planning a JHS end-of-year party.

When it came to the church service, I insisted, "Steve, I would very much like to give Dad's eulogy. You're certainly welcome to say something if you want, but I'd like to be the main speaker." We both knew that I had been closer to our father and could capture his life better than my brother could. I was ready to raise my voice to that point, but Steve acquiesced. "Okay, Harvy, you can do that. But when we do his headstone unveiling at the grave a year from now, I'd like to be the main speaker there."

Though it irked me that my brother never gave me anything for nothing, I nodded my acceptance of his terms. There would be a considerably smaller crowd at the unveiling than at the funeral.

When it came to choosing Dad's coffin, the director walked us through a long adjacent room where a dozen caskets stood along opposite walls. She said, "As you see, we have an extensive selection." Tags marked each coffin's type and price. I saw that they ranged from $2000 to $8000. After only a few seconds of looking, Steve pointed to an ornate coffin of mahogany wood. "I like this one," he said.

I gulped, for the sign next to the coffin said $6000. *Steve wants to play this 'Dad the big shot' thing to the hilt.* I pointed to a less-ornate $3500 casket of dark walnut. "This one reminds me of the console cabinets Dad had built in Montreal Phono. Why not this simple but nice one?"

"Let's keep on looking," Steve said. His eyes stayed on the mahogany casket. "I do like this one."

I didn't look at him as I gestured to the price tag. "But we never spent that kind of money on Mom's coffin."

"But Dad's different," he said without looking my way. "We have to acknowledge his stature in the Slovak community."

My gut wrenched. *Maybe it's your stature you are concerned about.* I turned away and let the decision go for now. I didn't want to argue the point with my persistently stubborn and constantly critical-of-father brother, who now suddenly put our dad on a pedestal. If Steve hadn't heard my point in the Director's office, and if he weren't acknowledging it now, then he never would. Then again, maybe he had the right idea, and I was thinking like Scrooge.

The director pointed to a cherry casket. Its reddish wood looked similar to Dad's back-office desk. "Here is something both of you might like. This cherrywood casket is $4950, reduced from $5500."

Steve thought for a few seconds and said, "Yes, I can go with that. What about you, Harvy?"

Though I thought my brother was still pushing the extravagance, I said, "Okay, Steve." *What's an extra grand or two when I have bigger money issues to discuss with my brother?* When my time came, I'd tell Gloria to cremate me or place me naked in a wicker basket.

Within the hour, Steve and I had completed our arrangements and signed the necessary papers. We headed back down the corridor side-by-side and exited the complex. There was no one else coming into or going out of the building, so I stopped my brother on the stoop outside the enormous doors and said, "Steve, there are some things I need to tell you."

It was now mid-afternoon. The sun was behind the trees, and the air was colder than when we had walked in. *Perhaps this chilly air will work to keep us cool and collected about what I'm going to share, and it might shorten our conversation.* I was beginning to shiver again but worked to keep my shaking hidden. I looked at my brother. "Steve, there are things you need to know about Dad's affairs offshore."

Steve's eyes were on me with interest, but he showed no surprise. "Sure, Harvy; I know some things, and I'd appreciate hearing what you know."

Yah, Steve; you only know what little Dad had told you. I looked directly at my brother's face and spoke calmly. "Steve, I'm willing to tell you as much as you want. I don't know everything about the ins and outs of Dad's offshore money world, yet I'm willing to tell you as much as I do know. But before I say anything, please ask yourself how much you'd want to know about it. You may not want to burden yourself with the sordid details from the past."

I knew that I was presenting a conundrum for my brother. How could he decide how much he wanted to know about Dad's secret dealings and hidden assets without first learning more about them?

If I revealed all that I knew, Steve's first-son ego might become bruised, knowing that he had been in the dark all these decades. I was hoping that he would be happy with the bare minimum of history and focus on the present and future concerning Dad's hidden money. I wanted to let him make his choice after he had reflected on the matter. I hoped that the cold wind would keep his reflection short.

Steve thought for several long seconds, his hand to his chin. He looked at me. "Okay, tell me what you think I should know." I suspected that until he had more knowledge, he'd play along with my little-brother riddle.

I took a long breath. "I think you may know that Dad has offshore accounts at the Global Trade Bank."

My brother nodded.

Forgoing my father-bestowed powers of attorney, I spoke as if Steve and I needed to team up to deal effectively with Dad's illegitimate funds. "With Dad's Quebec Mandate now enforced, and then with his will, you and I have joint control over those accounts."

Outside the funeral home's entrance, Steve and I stood like two frozen popsicles. I was shaking down to my socks, and perhaps he was too, but neither one of us said anything about it. I went on. "I've been talking to Geoff Levi, as well as a lawyer he recommended, about making a voluntary disclosure to the government to legitimize those funds." I pointed to myself and then to the space between us. "I now know the rules to make that happen. We will have to declare the untaxed income and refile Dad's tax returns going back a few years."

Steve nodded. "Dad once told me that he had a small amount left offshore, and it would disappear when he died because he was giving it away."

"Yes, I know, Steve. And he didn't tell you everything." I didn't say why. "It's more than one account and more money than he had indicated."

"How much are we talking about?" His voice stayed as cool as the air around us.

I took a deep breath. "It's in the mid-seven-figures."

Steve didn't flinch.

I continued. "We can make an appointment with the manager at the Global Trade Bank. We'll need to get up-to-date statements, to the day of Dad's death, to file his final tax returns properly and refile them at least for the two previous years."

I didn't mention the bank statements hidden in Dad's private office. I had already removed and shredded those after I had received four years of reports from Mr. Weber. Once Steve and I'd obtain new documents from the bank, I'd destroy the ones Weber had provided me. I didn't want my brother to feel annoyed or disappointed by my having been a step ahead of him.

The wind rustled what leaves remained on the trees and felled many to the ground. Steve stayed quiet, perhaps waiting for me to divulge more. I did, but I skipped to a second topic. "There's also an agreement Dad made at the Independent University of Luxembourg. There he indicated he would give them a one-million-dollar donation after his death."

"Yes, Harvy, I know about that agreement. Dad told me about it years ago." He drew a breath as he looked directly at me. "I suspect we'll have to honor it after he's gone."

I immediately countered. "Steve, I should tell you that the university document Dad signed isn't kosher. I checked it out with a lawyer. We have no obligation to honor the donation because Dad never wrote it into his will."

Fallen leaves blew and scattered around us as Steve looked at the ground and then back at me. "But Dad said he signed an agreement."

From the day I had met Andre Lefebvre the previous year, I knew this moment would arrive. Should I tell Steve that Dad had signed that agreement in 1991 solely for my benefit? Should I divulge that Dad's real intent was to siphon a million dollars of his pension money into a university annuity? That move would save our father's estate over a half-million in taxes and allow me to collect tax-free annuity income for the rest of my life.

I looked directly into my brother's eyes. "Steve, that university donation was based on Dad's having the pension money to fund it. He had arranged it before he separated from and then divorced Elaine." I raised a hand to make my point. "Because she got most of his pension, he no longer has the assets he needs to make the bequest to that university."

I kept my voice collected. "According to Dad's notary, Peternik, he never put that donation into his will. And, according to my lawyer, the donation is not legally binding." I was drawing quick breaths. "We have no obligation to fund it, and frankly, Dad no longer has the legitimate pre-tax money to take advantage of the donation deduction on his income taxes."

In reality, Dad did have that kind of pre-tax onshore funds if one included his remaining shares in JHS, but my assertion was good enough. For now, I also resisted counting Dad's offshore assets as a part of his estate.

Steve eyed me, his face looking intense. "Don't we have a moral obligation to keep Dad's promise to that university?"

There goes my brother again with his resolute morality.

The sun was flashing right into my eyes through the remaining leaves rustling in the trees. I looked at my brother with as much facial intensity as I could muster, and I held myself from blinking too much. I kept my voice as calm and firm as I could. "Take my word for it, Steve. This university donation arrangement was a tax-skirting scheme made for my benefit." I stopped there, not wanting to say more. I didn't want Steve to be angry at Dad or troubled by my being our father's only benefactor of that annuity masked as a donation. But if Steve continued his protest, I'd tell him.

Fortunately, Steve stopped his inquiry. "Okay," he said, "I'll take your and the lawyer's word for it." Maybe he wanted more time to digest what I had said.

My brother's curiosity started to get hold of him. "How did this offshore stuff come to be? How do you know so much about it?"

I stayed calm. "Again, Steve, how much do you want to know about the past? I'm willing to divulge the whole mess if you truly want to know. But please check with yourself first to see if this is something with which you want to burden yourself."

I preferred not to go into the history and details about how Dad chose and trusted me over my brother to know about and benefit from his offshore empire. That knowledge might drive us further apart. We needed to collaborate to sort out Dad's estate and our partnership in JHS. I wanted to let dirty Russian dogs lie sleeping under a Troika supper table. But if my brother pressed, I would pull up the red-on-white tablecloths and reveal the grubby beasts hidden underneath.

Steve looked away for a second or two and then back at me. "Okay, you don't need to say any more about that. What do we need to do now?"

I turned a little to get the sun out of my eyes. I responded. "After Dad has passed, I'll make an appointment for us to meet with the Global Trade Bank branch manager. We'll bring him Dad's will to show that we are Dad's executors. Then we'll ask the manager for this year's account statements up to the date of Dad's death as well as other statements that go back some years."

I took a long breath, but my eyes didn't leave my brother. "At a later time, we'll tell him that we're disclosing the money to the government and closing those offshore accounts. But we should say nothing about that in our first meeting."

I lifted my hand again. "I'll then make an appointment with Geoff and his lawyer associate, Charles. They can bring you up to speed on the voluntary disclosure process." I knew it would be better for Geoff and Charles to reveal those facts. Steve would trust them more than he would me.

Steve nodded again. "I guess we'll have a lot to work on after Dad dies. He'll keep us busy awhile."

I smiled slightly. "Yah, that's for sure." We both knew that the potpourri of properties remaining in JHS's asset corral could take years to dress up and dispose of.

The background around us faded as I looked directly into my brother's eyes. "Steve, please allow me to take the lead on this offshore stuff. I have the people in place to clean up what Dad has created. I want you involved and knowledgeable about everything going forward, but please let me carry the ball. I'll arrange the meetings over the next few weeks, after Dad's funeral."

His eyes looked back into mine, perhaps seeking my sincerity. My eyes were right there to meet his. "Okay," he said.

We shook hands. I said, "As you know, I'm driving back to Boston right now. I'm going to collect my family and drive back here on the weekend so they can say goodbye to Dad." I looked at him. "I hope we'll see you at the hospice on Sunday, or maybe on Monday morning, your Thanksgiving Day here?"

"Yes, I'll be available Sunday after church and Monday too. Call me when you get here. Safe travels to you."

I nodded and started to turn away. Before I could get far, Steve raised his voice. "I know next Monday is your birthday, Harvy. Let me be the first to wish you a happy one."

I turned back to him. "Thanks, Steve. But as you said six weeks ago, when I wished you the same, it's not a very happy birthday season for either one of us."

As I turned forward and walked briskly back to my car, I thought about Dad. Every year since he separated from our mother, he had sent Steve and me large cards and caring wishes for our birthdays. But during his hospital stay, he hadn't said one word about it. Maybe he didn't recall, and perhaps I shouldn't have expected him to remember.

Driving away from Mount Royal, I was pleased that Steve was willing to keep most of Dad's offshore skeletons in a burial casket, at least for now. Though Steve was accommodating, I wouldn't say he trusted me fully regarding the voluntary disclosure. But I appreciated what I did get from him.

I didn't know what swayed Steve to keep ignorant of our father's lifetime of finagling. Only he knew that answer, and I certainly felt he was better off not knowing.

Most importantly, Steve was willing to let me take the lead in working with the advisors to legitimize Dad's offshore assets. That money would be an unexpected bonus to my brother, though it might be a bittersweet one. I hoped that the payoff for my fairness to Steve would be that we could deal amicably with our father's legitimate holdings, especially JHS.

One of my brother's expressions echoed in my head. *Time will tell, Harvy. Time will tell.*

* * * *

End of an Era

Gloria, our son, and I arrived in Montreal late Saturday evening, too late to visit Dad. We went to see him first thing Sunday morning while Steve and Suzie were at church.

Unlike the bustle of the brightly lit hospital, the Mount Sanai Centre was dimly lit and subdued, like a budget hotel's lobby in the middle of the night. There was one nurse on duty, and she told us where we could find Dad.

My father's room looked like a small hotel room with a hospital bed. Behind the bed was a heart monitor. Green lines traveled across a black screen, indicating Dad's heart rate and blood pressure. An intravenous drip was attached to his arm.

When I looked at my father, I became shocked, maybe even scared. Dad's body was as thin as a skeleton. *He's withered away to almost nothing in a matter of days!* His breathing was slow and laboured, coming from his abdomen and not his chest.

I held in my angst. "Hello, Dad. It's good to see you." He nodded at me and glanced at Gloria and our boy. I bent down toward his ear and asked him quietly, "Do you recognize all of us?"

He turned his eyes to his daughter-in-law and grandson. He nodded and whispered, "Yes."

Gloria smiled. "Hi, Johnny."

Dad nodded at her and lifted his right hand slightly off the bed to grab hers. She squeezed it. "I'm happy to see you, but I'm so sorry to see you this way." I could tell she was holding back tears. She bent down to pick up our son. "Come and say hi to grandpa," she said.

Our boy offered, "Hi Papa; see what I have?" He presented a tinker toy car he had brought. Dad nodded again. He then squirmed out of his mother's hands, took his toy, and went to play on the floor.

I asked, "Dad, are you in any pain? Are you hungry or thirsty?" I didn't ask him if he wanted me to turn him; I was afraid I'd break his frail body.

With each question, he shook his head slightly and mouthed, "No."

I looked at Gloria. "Can you stay with him? I want to find the doctor."

She nodded. Her eyes looked sad, but she kept her head up.

I went to the nurses' station and asked for the physician on call. He soon arrived. The fellow was young, maybe 30 years old. In the hallway, I quietly voiced my concern. "Doctor, it looks like my father has lost over half his body weight since he arrived here. What's going on?"

The doctor explained calmly. "We're not giving your father any fluids through an IV, as they did at the hospital." The physician spoke perfect English with only a hint of a French accent. "He's eating and drinking as he wants. But it's not our philosophy to intervene to prolong his life more than he can sustain himself. He has a mild morphine drip to keep him comfortable and calm, but that's all we do." He looked into my eyes. "Did our director not explain that when you arranged to have your father admitted here?"

I searched my memory. "Yes, I guess the director did. But it's shocking to see how quickly my father is withering away. Can't you give him fluids? He's looking so thin."

The young doctor took a breath and stayed calm. "As I said, that's not the way we practise here."

I grabbed another straw. "Does he need the morphine? He's hardly able to talk."

The physician didn't hesitate. "It's for his comfort and protection. We don't want him to get agitated and fall out of bed or hurt himself in any way."

I looked at the floor. "I see." I looked at him. "Are you able to tell me, in your opinion, Doctor, how much time might he have left?"

He paused for a few seconds, his eyes looking unsure, and then he offered, "It's tough to say. Every case is different. He could last another week, maybe two, but it depends on what his body can sustain. If he stops eating and drinking, it will go faster."

My eyes pleaded with the fellow. "Are you sure there is no way to give him an IV to sustain him? He's looking awful and can hardly talk."

The doctor didn't waver. "We only do that if there's a medical reason. If you like, you can talk to the director tomorrow and discuss it with her. There's nothing I can do today." His eyes stayed on me. "You can encourage him to drink and eat on his own."

I knew in the back of my mind that the doctor was right. Steve and I had decided to bring our father here. The hospice wouldn't do anything more than what Dad could do for himself. Other than having said at the hospital that he wanted to go home, Dad had said nothing about how he wanted to die. I didn't know how much he understood concerning his condition.

My heart swelled and ached. *Did I have buyer's remorse for having brought my father here?* When I had stood by my father's bed moments earlier, I could barely look at his face. His cheeks were caved in slightly. His previous straight-back, never-out-of-place, Touch of Grey hair was now entirely grey, thin, and unkempt. It was hard to imagine his youthful, strong jaw and penetrating blue eyes of decades ago.

Part of me longed to have that energetic, live-past-100 man stay alive longer so I could continue to admire him and be his favoured son. Another side of me wished for what was left of this man to go peaceably, allowing his esprit de corps and conniving ways to fade into the background of my life.

I left the doctor and walked back into my father's room. "Hi, Dad," I said softly. His eyes looked at me, but I wasn't sure how much of my presence was getting through. I didn't want to say anything about what I saw of his condition. I was glad there were no mirrors in the room. I held back tears and offered, "We're so happy to see you." I pointed to Gloria. "We came from Boston to be here with you."

Dad glanced toward the floor where his grandson was playing. He eked out a few words in a quiet but raspy voice. It sounded like: "He's a big boy."

"Yes, Dad." I smiled as best I could. "He's growing like crazy. And, he's the spitting image of you."

My father nodded again, but nothing exuded from his face or voice.

Gloria pulled out a photo album and placed it on Dad's torso. Pictures of our son at his pre-school, us at home, and us on our recent summer vacation were in the collection. We talked about his grandson and our family. Dad looked on, keeping his eyes on the pages as we turned them. He offered only the occasional nod.

Gloria and I kept the conversation going while I touched my father's arm and held his hand. Our four-year-old stayed under Dad's high bed. He pushed his tinker toy around and made "zoom-zoom" sounds.

Gloria and I smiled at each other about our boy's obliviousness to what was happening above him. We had told him that my father was very sick, and he would die soon, and that we were here to say goodbye. Our son seemed to have understood.

The noises he now made from under the bed were a relieving distraction from the scene that was taking place above it. I wanted to be on the floor with my son, pretending that everything else in this room wasn't happening. I wished my dad could be there with us too.

Gloria and I kept the conversation going as best we could. We talked about what was happening in our lives back in Boston. I felt dryness in my throat and a growing void in my chest with the realization that my father could die any day or any moment. I fought to keep my attention on him.

The night before, I had slept restlessly. I kept wondering what my life would be like without the effect of this once ruling monarch. Who would I become without him? Would I feel freed from his expectations? Or would memories of our unreconciled father-son drama shadow me for the rest of my days, holding me back from coming into my own?

I turned my eyes toward a blank wall. Images of my mother surfaced from twelve years earlier. I recalled her lying and dying in her hospital bed, her heart giving out. Dad had prevented her from becoming a self-reliant woman. He turned her into his manservant, and then he abandoned her. If she were here, I wondered if she would cry for the pending loss of her ex-husband. Or would she spit on his deathbed for what he had done to her and our family? I hoped her spirit had found peace from her pain.

Around noon, Suzie arrived. She spoke matter-of-factly. "After church services, I had a quick dinner. I'm going to sit with your father for the afternoon." Her voice was caring. "You know, I was through a similar experience with my previous husband."

She seemed stoic and unfazed by Dad's condition. I wished I had her fortitude. She added, "Steve told me yesterday that he would come later this afternoon or this evening. You can go for your dinner now and come back later if you want to."

Gloria turned to me, "Our little guy needs to eat and to have some playground time, or else he'll get fussy."

I looked at Suzie. She spoke before I did. "You go do what you need to. I'll be here until your brother comes."

I smiled appreciatively. "We'll call on the cell phone and let you know." I gestured toward my father. "Do you know if Dad is eating or drinking anything?"

She shook her head. "Not very much; he leaves almost everything."

Gloria and I turned to my father. "Dad, see you later this afternoon. Please try to eat and drink something."

He nodded, but I wasn't sure if he had heard or understood.

My family returned later in the afternoon. Suzie was still there, but my brother hadn't arrived. Nothing had changed in my father's condition. He was snoring softly and looked like a slumbering bag of bones. Suzie said, "He's been like that for most of the afternoon."

We talked awhile about her daughter, son-in-law, and grandkids.

Eventually, Dad woke. I went through my now customary questions with him. After an hour had passed, it seemed as if we had nothing more to say. Steve still hadn't arrived.

My family said our goodbyes. Gloria and I kissed my father, and our son threw him a big kiss from his mother's arms. Dad looked and nodded at us; he had little expression on his face. I said, "Dad, we'll be back to see you tomorrow morning before we head back to Boston." We turned and departed. As we left the room, I couldn't look back at him.

How the hell do families go through such situations? It felt as if a big part of me had been shut down or blocked off. Was I trying to cope with the darkness that was descending on my dad?

I didn't know how to talk to my wife about my feelings. Over a subdued restaurant supper, we focused on how our son was handling what he had seen. Gloria told him, "Tomorrow may be the last time you'll see your papa." Our son looked at her, nodded, and then went back to looking at a picture book.

I was envious of how well our boy seemed to be dealing with the reality around him. We had tried to prepare him for his grandfather's passing. But maybe he didn't know what to say, do, or feel, like I, too, didn't. His grandpa was the first pending death of a family member he had experienced. Maybe he was pretending that nothing terrible was happening. I could understand that reaction.

I called Steve Sunday evening to say we'd be at the hospice the following morning. He offered a church-related excuse about not having been able to come to see Dad that day. I reminded him that he and I had some business to conduct before my family drove back to Boston around noon on Monday. He said he'd meet us at 10 o'clock, and we said not much more to each other.

When my family walked into the hospice centre the next day, the centre's director spotted me. She pulled me aside and spoke softly. "Mr. Simkovits, I know you talked to the doctor yesterday about giving your father hydration." Her voice was compassionate but firm. "As we had told you and your brother, we do not do that here. We only let your father do what he can for himself. We do very little to intervene except to ease any pain."

I nodded my understanding. Without medical intervention, Dad would soon be on his last breath. I resigned and steadied myself for that breath to happen sooner than later. His life now rested between him and his God.

After I went through my questioning ritual, Dad only occasionally looked at Gloria, his grandson, or me. He mostly stared at the wall. We held his hand, touched his arm, and talked to him about anything and nothing until we ran out of words.

My brother walked in at 11 o'clock, an hour late. Minutes earlier, I had said to Gloria, "As usual, Steve's in his own time zone." She nodded but said nothing.

When Steve entered the room, he offered a big, "Hello everybody." It irritated me that he could be upbeat at such a dire and dreary time. Was he trying to be the way Dad had been when greeting supper guests?

I responded coolly. "Hello, Steve."

Steve went up to Dad, said hello, and kissed him on both cheeks. He then turned to me, and we excused ourselves to go into the hallway.

We went straight to business. I said, "Gloria and I have to leave soon to go see Peternik on our way back to Boston. He will notarize the Florida condo's purchase and sale agreement. I need your signature on the document before we go."

Among the few financial decisions that Steve and I had made for our father during these last weeks was a decision to sell Dad's Florida condo. It felt odd to have to enact such a transaction while Dad was lying on his deathbed, but Steve and I wanted to simplify Dad's estate where we could.

"Yes, I understand," my brother said. "Do you have the papers?"

I pulled them from my portfolio and handed them to him. He said, "I trust everything is in order, and you'll keep a good record of the gain and expenses on the property."

I nodded but held my lips together tightly. Perhaps I'd be the same non-trusting way if I were in my brother's shoes.

He signed the document and said, "Leave when you need to." He looked in my direction and smiled. "By the way, happy birthday to you."

Gloria had wished me a happy birthday earlier that morning. Until that moment, I had overlooked it. "Thanks, Steve," I said. "Seems like a very odd way to celebrate. If you haven't sent me a card already, don't worry about it."

I couldn't remember, but I may not have sent him a card either for his event. Sending cards for a special occasion was hit or miss between us.

My brother then asked, "When do you think you'll be back?"

I responded, "Yesterday, the doctor here said that Dad might have another week or more to live. I have things I need to do before I can come back. I'll return by the end of the week."

"Let's hope Dad lasts till then."

"Call if you see his condition suddenly changes for the worst, and I'll get up here right away. I have to be in DC for a two-day seminar—something arranged months ago that I can't change. But I can cut short my part if I have to. Call me on my cell, and I can be here on the next flight."

"Okay, Harv, will do."

I cringed at his use of my nickname, but I said nothing.

Soon afterward, my family and I took our leave. I put my face close to Dad's ear. "Dad, I'm taking the rest of us home to Boston. I'll be back in a few days, okay?" He looked at me and nodded. I didn't consider that a few days might seem an eternity to him. I added, "If I can come back sooner, I will." He slowly nodded again, but no words emanated from him. Maybe I was fooling myself that he would last the week.

Gloria and I gave him kisses on both cheeks. I squeezed his hand once more. We picked up our son and placed his head close to his grandfather's face. "Bye, Papa," he said with a giggle as he gave his granddad's cheek a peck. He put his arms around as much as he could of Dad's blanket-covered body.

Dad rasped out, "Bye, bye," and nodded again in his grandson's direction.

When we walked out of the building, I turned to Gloria, "I hope the doctor is right about Dad lasting through this week."

She gently touched my arm. "I hope so too," she said, her voice filled with care and concern.

* * *

About 7:30 the following morning, Oct. 10, 2000, Steve called me on my cell phone. "Hi, Harvy. Are you sitting down?"

"Wait for a second, Steve. I'm driving to an appointment. Give me a moment to stop by the side of the road."

Less than a minute later, I continued. "Okay, what's up? Something happened with Dad?"

"I just received a call from the hospice centre. The Director said dad died about a half-hour ago."

I took a few seconds to let those words sink in. I felt a sharp shudder in my heart. "Oh, my! How did it happen?"

Steve spoke matter-of-factly. "The Director said that the nurse on duty had done her regular rounds at seven in the morning. Before then, through the monitors, she could see Dad was sleeping soundly. She had even checked on him earlier, and all seemed okay. But when she did her seven o'clock round and checked on him in his room, he had passed away." His voice collected, he offered. "The Director called me right away. It seems he went peacefully."

I cried quietly, "Oh, my! Oh, my! Oh, my!" I kept my voice in control. I felt my heart pounding in my throat. I couldn't figure out what I was feeling inside, but knowing my brother was listening, I held myself together.

I took a deep breath. "Okay, Steve. I need some time this morning to cancel appointments and rearrange things. I guess this means I'm not going to DC, so I've got to let them know. I'll go straight home, pack my things, and be there late this afternoon. When do you think we should have his funeral?"

"There's no big rush now, Harvy. Do what you need to do, and we'll meet later today or this evening at my house." It felt as if he were smiling through the phone. "We'll cook you supper. We can talk about the details then. I guess we'll perform the church services and Mount Royal internment this weekend."

"Okay, Steve. I'll call you when I'm on the road to Montreal."

"Sure, Harvy. Drive safely."

I hung up.

For the next few minutes, I sat in my car, parked along the side of the street. My eyes welled, my throat dried, and my heart beat harder. I felt worse than when my brother called me six weeks earlier to say our father was in the hospital with untreatable cancer.

For the next few minutes, with my face in my hands, I couldn't stop crying. I pulled out my handkerchief and blew my nose, probably as loud as a trumpeting elephant. It was similar to how my father had done during his whole life. I couldn't tell whether my reaction was a compassionate son's grief or a lifetime co-conspirator's relief.

I called Gloria. Through my sobs and wavering voice, I told her the sad news. Though we were surprised at how quickly my father had come to his demise these last days, I could sense her tears for the man who had had an enormous effect on my life. She understood my pain more than anyone else, which helped me feel less alone in my suddenly shifted world.

Like his beloved maternal grandfather, Dad died alone and in his sleep. It was a rapid withering away into a peaceful and pain-free "Boom!" to his mostly gregarious life. That notion gave me solace.

Steve and I had everything set by the end of the next day for Dad's obituary and funeral in Montreal. When we finished, Steve turned to me. "Harvy, there's nothing left to do here until the services this Saturday. Why don't you go to that DC seminar you wanted to go to and be back by Saturday morning? I know how much you had been looking forward to it."

I looked at my brother. "That's nice of you, Steve." I thought for a few seconds. "I know that Dad has airline points remaining in his account. Is it okay with you if I use those points for my flights to DC and for my family to fly here this weekend?"

"Sure, might as well." Like with a skittish cat that comes to you only when it's their idea, my brother could be generous when it was via his initiative.

I departed for DC early Wednesday morning and was back late Friday night. Some of my closest Boston colleagues were at the seminar I attended. I told them about my father's death, saying, "He played such a big role in my life. I have no idea how things will now change for me with him no longer here."

I said nothing about my father's feet of trouble: how I had followed him into dubious business shenanigans and how I went along with his money-finagling, cash-stashing, and blatant womanizing. I was too ashamed to reveal the sordid details. I wanted to put all that behind me as if they had never occurred.

My colleagues consoled me. "Give yourself time, Harvy." . . . "Things will become clearer in due course." . . . "Don't rush to make any big changes." I felt their empathy more than I had ever felt the understanding of my parents and siblings. But I wondered what they might have thought and said had they known what I had done with and for my father over these last twenty-eight years.

I imagined my father on an undertaker's table back in Montreal. Though he might now lay naked and alone on a cold stone slab, many in that city admired his business success and what he had done for the Slovak people in Montreal and Canada. Most of those people knew about Johnny Simkovits's colourful sides. His closest compadres and cohorts also knew about his darker edges. But none of them had lived as close as I had with my father's many shades of grey.

* * * *

Ides of October 2000

Friends and family gathered. Everyone sat still in their seats, hands folded, hardly moving. At the podium, Father Sinal wore in his black cassock. He was completing a quiet prayer in his native tongue. Soft, slow-moving organ music and a Slovak woman soloist finished a sleepy chant.

All became quiet within the bright coloured stone walls and stained-glass windows of the Church of Saints Cyril and Methodius. The only sounds were a loud cough, a shoe scuffing against the floor, and a few bodies rustling to find a comfortable position on the hard wooden pews. Though the high A-frame ceiling was light beige, the sanctuary still seemed dreary and dark. I was relieved that it wasn't damp and dusty here, as it was in many of Montreal's French and Irish Catholic stone churches that waves of Canadian immigrants had built in the first half of the 20th century.

The elderly Father looked at me and nodded. I stood and slowly made my way to the dais. I paid attention to not trip or bump into anything as I climbed the few creaky stairs to the lectern. This church was not much older than I was. The contributions of Slovak Catholic emigrants, who had come to Montreal after both world wars, built this place.

I looked out at a gathering of dark suits and colorful hats. I saw my father's longtime friends—and perhaps a few complicit culprits. My heart beat hard and fast. Many here had known me even before I knew them.

I recognized the people sitting in the front rows. They came to pay their respects to the man affectionately called Johnny, or "Jani" by his closest European friends and family. Those present were pretty much the same entourage of Slovak-, Polish-, Hungarian-, Ukrainian-, Russian-, German-, English-, and French-Canadians who had visited Dad while he lay dying in his hospital bed these last six weeks.

From the podium, it was hard to make out the people sitting in the back. Were any of them ditched friends or jilted lovers?

I hope there will be no trouble here today. I knew much of my father's sordid past and many of his shaded stories, but I wasn't naïve enough to say I knew everything—Mr. Duma had proven that. I hoped that no one here would throw decades of pent-up profanities onto the proceedings. If my mother had been here, or my father's wife before her, there might be blood spilled today—especially if any of Dad's other women had the gall to show.

The heat rose inside my dark wool suit, which didn't feel quite warm enough in this chilly stone church on this 15th day of October. *May the better memories of you, Dad, get me through this.* I retrieved a document from inside my jacket. I slowly unfolded the paper and placed it on the podium.

I cleared my throat; another person coughed. Now was my time.

I proclaimed into the silent void, "Wow! I still can't get over it."

Those words rang from my mouth into this church of colour and light. A previous Slovak priest, Father Billy, had baptized Steve and me here four-and-a-half decades earlier. I had been afraid of that Father because his voice and laugh could be as loud and intimidating as my father's.

Now, we were here to bless and sanctify our dad's life. Johnny Simkovits had given life not only to Steve and me but also to this church and its immigrant patrons. He would be remembered—for good and maybe for otherwise—by everyone he had touched.

I cleared my throat again, caught for the moment by the mixed memories that filled my mind. I looked for comfort in the faces near the front. My eyes moved beyond where my brother and half-sister sat. Next to Emilia was Suzie, my father's last in a long line of partners.

I looked past Suzie to my wife, Gloria. Her face relaxed and eyes compassionate, she looked my way. She knew both what I was going to say here today and portions of the painful family history that had doggedly followed me to this moment in my life. But no one here knew all the Johnny angst that I had known.

Sitting next to Gloria was our son. I had told him that the death of his grandfather was a significant loss not only for our family but also for Montreal Slovaks and Hungarians and many professionals and small-business people in this city. Maybe, one day, I'll tell him why I had insisted to my brother that I should be the one to give my father's eulogy.

I took a deep breath and elevated my voice in the hall of vibrant stone, glass, and wood.

> "My dad's passing marks a significant milestone not only in our family's history but also in the history of the Slovak and Hungarian communities in Montreal."

I thought of Aras, Yasko, and Jiri, the long-time members of Dad's merry Eastern-European Montreal gang. Dad had done business (including funny business and monkey business) for fifty years with these guys who sported hearty *yaytsa*.

Those three immigrant men now sat quietly at different spots throughout the church. Aras sat by himself in the back; his wife had dropped him off so he could pay homage to his long-time friend. Yasko's wife was by her husband's side; they sat a few rows behind my brother. Jiri's wife was already underground, and he was sitting by himself a few rows behind Yasko.

Those wives represented Dad's world of women. Yasko's wife, like my mother, adored Johnny and would do anything for him, though she was deeply devoted to her husband. Aras' wife wanted nothing to do with Johnny, even in death, because of what he had put Elaine through during their separation and divorce. Jiri's wife had died of a ravaging illness before her time. She reminded me of my deceased mother.

I took another deep breath and glanced down to the first row of pews where my relations sat. I then looked back at the crowd and continued.

> On behalf of Steve, Emilia, Suzie, and our families, I want to express our gratitude to all who were there for our family these last six weeks, during my father's dreadful and devastating illness and his final passing.

I wondered how I got such motley kin: a Mormon-convert brother, a hidden-away-for-most-of-my-life Hungarian-Slovak half-sister, and Dad's French-Canadian live-in after his third divorce. Elaine—Dad's only ex-wife who was still alive—had decided not to participate today. She told me she didn't want to take attention away from Suzie, who had been with my father every day for the last five years. It was a mystery as to how Dad had managed to attach himself to such caring and, for the most part, loyal women.

My eyes wandered for a brief moment to the rafters above. *I hope you're in peace up there, Mom.* She had been the one to suffer most under Johnny's hand. She had waited for him every weekday as he came home intoxicated from "making business" half the night with colleagues, cohorts, and customers. Though he smelled of Russian vodka, foul Canadian cigarettes, and French perfume, she had hoped he'd get the wildness out of his system and then come home to her.

Rejected as she had been and devastated by Dad's marriage to another after her, had she survived, she'd be sitting here today right next to my brother. She'd be pining for her one true love. For her husband, she had summarily departed her family in Slovakia and immigrated to Canada. She had completely given herself to Jani. *God only knows why.*

I took another long breath as I looked past the altar to my father's cherry coffin. *I hope you are enjoying it there, Dad. If it had been up to me, I might have placed you into a console stereo cabinet. Thanks to Steve, you got something better.*

I looked back at those gathered. People's eyes were on me, their faces looking patient as a priest in a confessional. I continued my tribute to my father, or might my eulogy be our mutual confession?

> From the time he was young to near the end of his days, my father was a strong-willed man, an independent thinker, a free spirit, and a survivor. While a young man, he made it through The Great Depression and World War II, and he later escaped from the rising Communist regime in his beloved Czechoslovakia.

Everyone here knew my father faithfully loved his homeland. Dad had reminisced about Slovakia's beautiful, rolling countryside, belly-filling peasant food, uplifting and sad gypsy music, and high Slovak Alps. He had boasted of Czechoslovakia being the first democracy in Eastern Europe, a free country between the great wars. I now felt an emptiness in my chest in having lost my second primary connection to my parents' homeland and knowing there would be no more family trips with Dad (or Mom) to the country of their birth.

I looked into the church crowd. I recalled my father's encouragement to stand tall and straight and keep my shoulders down and back. I assumed that position as best I could, and I worked to keep my breathing steady, my voice calm but firm.

> In 1949, my father escaped the difficult, turbulent, and even oppressive conditions in his homeland to make a new home and succeed in a foreign land. He wanted and worked to become somebody.

Many of us here admired him for fleeing Soviet Czechoslovakia and Russian-occupied Austria with my mother and not much more than a couple of stuffed rucksacks. My body shuddered with the thoughts of danger, perhaps even terror, that both my parents must have felt when they crossed the Iron Curtain frontier. They risked deportation to a Siberian work camp if the Soviets had caught them in their escape.

As first-generation Canadian sons, Steve and I were now able to sing praises to Dad's foresight and sacrifices, though I had felt strings attached to his immigrant family wishes. He didn't want us to wander far from the New World nest he had created. I could still hear his continual "Just *lassen* to me" advice.

I imagined that most of my father's contemporaries, like Aras, Jiri, Yasko, and his younger compadres, Hans and Roger, sat here perhaps in awe of their friend. They certainly respected my father's grit and gumption.

But others appreciated Johnny for the business they obtained from him, the sordid deals they had done together, the money Johnny had loaned them and never got returned, or the free drinks, dinners, and devilish delights he had treated them to. *You know who you are!* One culprit was his lawyer, Mack, and I was glad not to see him in the audience today. *Consider yourselves lucky that I don't call out any names. When your times come, may you search your conscience for your complicity.*

I kept my eyes fixed on the crowd and went on.

> Among the immigrants who came to Canada these last decades—having only the clothes on their backs and a few dollars in their pocket—Johnny Simkovits brought his zest for life and a spirit of friendship to this country. He worked fervently and had a nose for an entrepreneurial deal. He loved Eastern European food and had a talent for cooking, and he had an appreciation for lively Hungarian, Slavic, and Russian music. Jani Simkovits was both a gentleman and a character! He lived life to the fullest!

Everyone here knew about my father's preferred venues: the Hungarian Tokay and Russian Troika. He and his closest comrades had fueled up on Montreal's high-life, with my father leading the way of those men-behaving-like-boys good times. Most often, a spirited lady friend had been at Dad's table. *What a bunch of guys they were!*

For years, I, too, had been among the group partaking in my father's festivities. To this day, I still feel shame about what I had been a part of.

I glanced at my father's casket. *Those good old days are now long gone, huh, Dad?*

I looked and gestured toward the end of the first row of pews.

> Today, we are fortunate to have one of my dad's many Slovak friends, Margaret, here to sing one of my father's favorites. Please lend her your ears for the next few minutes.

Margaret stood and ambled to a baby grand piano at the front of the church. Her small, slender frame housed a sizable mezzo-soprano voice. The piano accompanist began his rendition, and Margaret trumpeted a beautiful version of Paul Anka's "My Way."

Yes, Dad had led his life his way. And, for good or bad, he had taken very little input along the way, or he had listened only to the advice he liked. *You were something, Dad!*

Margaret completed her soaring delivery. If Dad were here alive, he'd be on his feet applauding, yet the church was quiet and still. A man coughed, and I took it as another signal to continue. I turned toward the people in their pews. My hammering heart filled my chest as I cleared my throat again.

The other day, my wife, Gloria, pointed out an interesting observation about my father. Whether he sang lively or sad Eastern-European melodies, kicked out his feet to Russian Cossack music, cooked his Slovak and Hungarian favourites, ran his thirty-year Montreal manufacturing business, or turned new acquaintances into immediate friends, Johnny Simkovits added spice to everyone's life.

And not everyone could digest that zest, including me. I had enjoyed the taste for a time, but my father's ways had fueled my bouts of depression when I didn't feel I could attain his aspirations. My brother had also relinquished Dad's seasonings, and he consumed religion instead. Though I wanted to scold Steve for the twisted father-son drama he and Dad had played out over the years, I thought better of that today.

I took a long breath as I retrieved a Canadian silver dollar from my pocket. *Hold steady, Harvy; here comes the hard part.*

A few days earlier, I had found the coin in Dad's office safe, a container for the precious treasure he had worn regularly around his fingers, wrist, and neck. This pure silver coin represented him well.

I lifted the coin into the air and raised my voice in parallel.

> As what's inside every one of us, and like this shiny Canadian silver dollar I now have in my hand, my father had more than one distinct side to his towering personality.

I was oversimplifying. The coin really ought to be a gemstone. There had been many facets to the gem people called Johnny Simkovits. Some of those facets had been clear and brilliant, as in his generosity in helping many relatives and compatriots immigrate to Canada and start a new life here. Other sides had been deeply flawed, like the belligerent tone he could take with his factory foremen and employees, even his wives.

There had been brightly polished facets of Johnny. He dressed in classy three-piece suits and silk ties. He knew the libation every friend and colleague liked to drink or the type of cigarettes they smoked.

There were yet other facets of Johnny that had been rough. When he blew his nose, he sounded like a hyena. When he slept, his snores sounded like a trumpeting elephant. When he ate soup, he slurped it up as his head almost fell into the bowl.

More recently, other facets of Johnny had become discoloured via his physical and mental decline in his last years of life, and his teeth had yellowed by continual smoking. Those stained facets included his clandestine affairs with money and women.

Many of Dad's pals had known of his cheating and deceiving ways. I wondered who else sitting in the church today—in addition to Mr. Duma, who sat alone in the back—knew about my father's parallel life of other women or were privy to his hidden money world. Dad hadn't been the best at keeping his secrets. Perhaps many here assumed that my father carried on a covert life because of the way he lived.

Dad had allowed me to see many of the facets of his gemstone. For decades I had gone along with his dishonest moves with women, in business, and with the government. He certainly had big *yaytsa*. Dad's closest friends might comprehend Dad's complex, contradictory character and double lives. Through my eulogy, I wanted them to know that I had known too!

I took a long breath and lifted the Canadian silver coin a bit higher.

> From one side of this coin—the good side—most of us have fond memories of Dad's lively birthday parties, entertaining Christmas parties, and other social gatherings.

I gestured toward the floor.

> There were many spirited holiday celebrations even here in the basement of this Slovak Church. Jani Simkovits wanted people to feel at home, be with him as an equal companion, and enjoy their moments together.

I looked across the hall and gestured upward.

> I can still hear his deep voice ringing in my head as he laughs heartily or sings his favorite Hungarian, Slavic, or Russian songs. If you close your eyes right now, you might even hear him laugh and sing up there in the rafters.

You were amazing, Dad! Few could maintain your pace. *Astonishing for you to have lived so long.*

I refocused on the crowd.

Johnny Simkovits certainly valued friendships. He told Steve and me, 'It's not only what you know but also who you know that will determine your success.' Dad had many long-time friends who were important to him and, as he would admit, significantly contributed to his success in his adopted country.

Aras knew those people and stories. He, too, had played a part by helping my father get a loan from his uncle when Dad had a record player order from RCA but no factory to build the product. Unlike Aras, other Johnny supporters were already underground. Over the decades, Steve and I didn't stay in touch with any of them, as with most of Dad's contemporaries. Maybe they reminded us too much of our father's absence from our lives when we were growing up.

I paused for a moment to wipe the moisture off my brow. I cleared my throat once more and refocused on the crowd.

> We remember my father's kindness in helping people immigrate to Canada from his Czechoslovakia homeland and giving many immigrants their first job here in Canada.

Georges, Helen, and Rob, who sat right behind Steve and Emilia, could vouch for the veritable revolving door in Dad's manufacturing company. It had led to a smorgasbord of nationalities and ethnicities working there, grateful labourers right off the immigration boat. My father had kept them hustling on his production lines for minimum wage. Some had stayed for years. Others had left the premises as soon as possible, either via their legs or Johnny's foot.

I gestured outward.

> And many here remember my father's generosity to his church, his business associates, his friends, and the Slovak and Hungarian communities of Montreal. He was always ready to contribute when the call came.

Few had given or raised as much money as Dad had for those groups. I more than once heard him call a colleague and mandate, "I'm giving $500 to our Slovak Business Association this year, and you're going to give $500 too."

On the other hand, Dad had exaggerated his wealth. His boasts about his net worth had spurred Elaine (maybe deservedly) to take a bigger bite of his money in their separation.

Perhaps he had also exaggerated his wealth in his mind during his later life, causing him to give away fistfuls of cash indiscriminately not only to the Slovak Church but also to so-called "friends." I looked again into the crowd but couldn't see Father Novak or Dad's doctor. I hoped they felt too ashamed to show their scoundrel faces here today.

I held up my silver coin again, presenting the other side. My hand trembled, but I suspected not enough for anyone else to notice.

> But, like this coin, John Simkovits had a tough side to his complex personality. He had a harsh temper in addition to his tender heart. He could turn hard when things didn't go his way or if he felt that people had let him down. At times, he wouldn't listen, like a boy who wanted things his way.

Most everyone here knew about the death of Dad's natural mother when he was three years old. After being shuttled around to various families for several years, his stepmother raised him, but she later preferred her natural son. Dad had to fend for himself, which led him to develop fierce independence and an entrepreneurial streak.

I raised my voice as if it were a thunderstorm brewing on the horizon.

> Dad had been generous, going out of his way to help many old and new friends. Yet some were wounded by his words, negatively affected by his deeds, or suffered under his hand.

My mother had gotten the most heartache. After she no longer suited him, Johnny continually cheated on her. She was then summarily dismissed for the twenty-four-year younger Elaine.

But now wasn't the time to speak about how you, Dad, had devastated Mom. Now wasn't the time to share that you had never understood Steve or me. Now wasn't the time to say anything about your offshore stash, a twenty-eight-year albatross around my neck that had kept me from standing straight. *Today is your day, Dad.* I'll have to wait until tomorrow to repudiate, rectify, and reconcile your dirty secrets, both onshore and off.

I softened my tone.

An important thing to remember is that we all have two sides to our 'personality coin.' If we can accept that each of us, similarly, has a positive side and a challenging side to our character, then we can better accept the man that Johnny Simkovits was. Dad was not a perfect man (be it husband, father, businessman, citizen, or friend), but he set a vibrant pace that others admired and followed. People got swept up by his good looks, charm, courage, business savvy, and spirit for living every day to its fullest.

I do miss those good facets of you, Dad.

In earlier days, I had felt as if I were your chosen apprentice while you were the master journeyman in the money-making and money-hiding trade. I had admired your business smarts, your jovial camaraderie with friends, and your clever money ways. I had seen myself standing next to you but never in front of you. I never wanted to take anything away from you, only to rise alongside you. I had seen myself as an apprentice horseman learning to take over the master's reins when both of us were ready. I had wanted to stand tall on your shoulders. *But it didn't quite happen that way.* You couldn't let go of your buggy whip. Or maybe I was too timid to take it from you.

I paused for another moment and looked out at the crowd. No participant shook their head or shouted damnation because of my words. No businessperson rushed forward to heave mud onto or into my father's casket. No rejected woman screamed bloody murderer. No jilted colleague wielded a knife to cut out his dead heart. No family member stood and walked out. Everyone remained still as if they were stone statues firmly affixed to their wooden pews. *Might a few here have trepidation about what I have said or even might say?*

Little did they realize that this eulogy not only addressed the end of my father's life but also marked a new beginning for me. I saw it as my defining moment, my time to confront my father's complicated, clandestine legacy.

I looked down at my brother. He was sitting blank-faced in the first row. Only this last week had I begun to tell him what I had known for the previous three decades. But there were other things that not even he would come to know or fully understand, at least for a long time.

After today, Steve and I would have to employ pricey attorneys and accountants to rectify what our father had sheltered in a Luxembourg bank. *How much might we tell our half-sister about her father's offshore shenanigans?*

I raised my voice one more time.

> Dad, we will certainly miss those good parts of you. Steve and I, as well as many others for whom you showed the way, would not be here today if it weren't for your courage, determination, and foresight. We wouldn't have our freedom in this free and great country of Canada if it weren't for you. We will always appreciate and thank you for that. May you be at rest and in peace! We love you, and we wish you well.

I hope I'm sincere.

I looked toward the rafters of the church and raised my hand in salute.

> Oh! By the way, Dad, we expect Saint Peter to know a few more lively Eastern European songs when the time comes for us to join you where you are. And put in a good word for the rest of us with the saint, if you would.

I'm certainly going to need it.

I looked down at the lectern and carefully folded my papers. I glanced once more at the congregation that had hardly moved a muscle or made a sound during my eulogy. I sensed that no one was inconsolable or crying for the loss of our beloved Johnny, but I couldn't tell for sure. I wiped the sweat again from my brow and perhaps a tear from my cheek. I couldn't tell if I felt relief by having finished my presentation without breaking down or in giving witness to the end of my father's rough and rowdy life.

Father Sinal gave me a nod. I walked slowly to my seat, my head held a little higher for having said my piece respectfully. I glanced at my father's coffin. His chapters were now done, yet mine had only begun.

I sat in the pew and got a long hug from my wife. My part in Dad's life and death was now over, but the whole truth had yet to be confronted or told.

* * *

After the service, I stood with my siblings at the back of the church. I looked out across the place where my dad had attended services for over fifty years, two decades longer than he had participated in Sunday services in his Czechoslovak homeland.

Guests talked and milled about while we waited for attendants to wheel Dad's coffin into the hearse. Perhaps symbolic of our separate lives, my brother, half-sister, and I stood at a distance from each other along the church's back wall. Dad's long-time friends and business colleagues mingled around. I sweated and shivered a bit under my suit, and I wasn't sure why.

I saw Dad's coffin ready to be loaded by the funeral home helpers. Neither my brother nor I were there to help carry the load. I wasn't sure why we kept our distance. Maybe we wanted to keep ourselves distinctly separate from the man who had been our patriarch.

The hearse would lead a solemn entourage of cars and maybe tears to the burial site on Montreal's Mount Royal Cemetery—perhaps a fitting place for a father who said his natural mother was a descendant of Hungarian Hapsburg nobility.

Some here traveled a long way to say goodbye to the man who had left an indelible mark on their lives. One, my high school friend, John, approached. When he and I had been nineteen—old enough to drink beer in any Canadian province—we made a cross-country trip to Canada's west coast. We had worked at my father's manufacturing plant that summer to make money before we headed west for nearly a month. "Hi, John," I said. "Glad you could make it from Toronto. How long are you in Montreal?"

"It's good to see you, Harvy. I came here just for your Dad's funeral. I'm driving back tonight." He looked my way but avoided looking directly into my eyes. "My condolences for your loss."

"Thank you, John. I hope you come to our reception at the cemetery, after the burial. We can catch up before you depart."

He nodded. "I'll stick around as long as I can. By the way, I wanted to tell you why I came to your father's funeral." His smiling face looked soft and sincere. "Of all the people I've worked with all my years, your father was the toughest boss. He was also the one I learned from the most."

I smiled back. "Yup! For good or bad, he did rub off on those around him. You'll have to tell me more at the reception." John nodded and left my side to offer his respects to my brother.

My longtime friend Geoff Levi came forward. Having returned as JHS's accountant, he would become a guide for Steve and me as we navigated Dad's offshore affairs. Geoff held no grudge concerning our father's MO of "Do it my way or head for a cold Canadian highway."

Geoff took my hand. "I offer my condolences to you, Harvy." He gazed into my eyes. "It's the end of an era for the Simkovits family, isn't it?"

I wasn't sure if his remark was a question or a statement. I nodded. "Yes, you're very right." Though Geoff was one of my best Montreal friends, and he knew the most of anyone about my father's hidden assets, I still couldn't quite look him straight in the eye. Maybe I felt that neither my brother nor I could hold a candle to a patriarch who had lit up many a Montreal venue. I added, "My dad was one of a kind, much admired by his countrymen."

Geoff kept his eyes on me. "Your eulogy captured the man your father was—the different sides of his character and what he did for many Eastern European immigrants here. Though he had his flaws, he was revered."

"Thank you, Geoff," I replied. "Your interpretation of what I presented is the very best I could have hoped for." I worked to return his look as I continued to grasp his hand. "And considering what you know about my father's world and ways, you hardly know a fraction of the story."

* * *

Dad's burial was nondescript. Guests gathered silently around the gravesite that had no gravestone. That double-sized stone, to be placed at Dad's double-sized grave, was not yet carved. Dad liked to do things big, and his place of burial would be no exception.

Father Sinal offered prayers. The cemetery caretakers lowered Dad's coffin, and more prayers were said. People stood solemnly as the cemetery attendants lowered his cherry casket to its depths. Gloria stood by my side and held my hand. Our son also stood quietly, holding onto his mother's side.

No one from our family, not even my religious brother, spoke or said a prayer, except maybe to themselves. It felt as if a multitude of thoughts were packing the air around us, but I heard no voices. We soon left Dad's body where it had been put to rest, expressing nothing about our memories and experiences. When it was over, I felt pain-numbing relief.

During the reception at the Mount Royal Funeral Complex, attendees approached Steve and me. They told of their shock about how Johnny—someone who acted as if he would live forever—had been so quickly taken away. A few reiterated, "Your father did so much for our people in Montreal," and "During the communist era, he helped many Czechoslovaks get resettled in Canada after they had escaped. He gave them jobs, found them places to live, lent them money, and connected them to the community here." Others acknowledged, "Johnny was a tough businessman but also had a soft heart."

It was as if Dad's hard edges, transgressions, and any other suffering he had caused, were left to hang in the funeral home's cloakroom as people walked in to give their respects. I appreciated the good things people said.

Dad's German friend, Hans, smiled and said, "Your father's done it now! He's having drinks and singing with Saint Peter, leaving the rest of us to fend for ourselves at the Troika."

I smiled and also repeated something I had mentioned in my eulogy. "Maybe my father will put in a good word for all of us." I certainly felt I could use a Johnny Simkovits endorsement when my time came.

My high school buddy, John, came forward again, and I smiled his way. Though he had put on a few pounds, my friend's energy was as exuberant as in his youth. It seemed as if it were just yesterday that we had worked at JHS.

John put his hand on my shoulder and repeated, "Harvy, of all the bosses I've had in my career, I got the most from your father."

I asked him why, and he responded, "Because your father was tough, street-smart, and knew all the tricks. No one could pull anything over on him. He kept employees on their toes, and they worked hard for him. And if they didn't, he took none of their crap and kicked them out on their *toute de suite*."

I grinned. "That's about right."

I didn't hear one harsh, derogatory, or surprising word about Dad that afternoon. I figured we knew that we were speaking to only the "good" side of the Canadian silver dollar coin I had referred to in my eulogy.

What little Steve and I said to each other that day was in kind and gentle voices. Because of the language gap, Emilia remained with her Slovak acquaintances from Montreal. Gloria stayed strong and in the background. She gave me the space to engage with Dad's friends and colleagues while attending to our son.

There were friendly hugs and goodbyes from everyone as the crowd thinned and left the reception hall. Steve, Suzie, Emilia, and my family then headed in our separate directions. Emilia got a ride with a Slovak friend.

Gloria, I, and our son walked out of the funeral home and into the cold mid-October Montreal air. I looked into the sky, with the sun now rapidly heading for the horizon.

I recalled a moment when I had been at the church's podium earlier that day. It was when I had looked out at the faces that had been a big part of our Simkovits family's life and the life of Johnny. Dad had made many strong impressions, both favorable and unfavorable, on the lives of these long-time associates, employees, and comrades. But none of those imprints were placed as deeply as the ones he cast onto his life partners and children.

Before I started my eulogy in the church, I had looked up at the church rafters and mouthed a prayer. Now, while exiting the funeral home, I repeated that prayer in my mind. *Mom, I hope you're at peace, and dancing to the Hungarian Chardas in heaven, reunited once more with your one true love.*

* * * *

Fool Me Once; Fool Me …

Almost a decade after Dad's death, I sent a copy of my parents' war survival and Soviet communist escape story to my 23-year older Cousin Ivan. Ivan survived WWII by hiding in Budapest with my mother and her brother, Lali. He also knew details of Mom and Lali's 1949 escape from Czechoslovakia, when they pretended to be Hungarian Jews heading to Israel. I thought Ivan might have insights or recollections to add to my parents' stories regarding their war survival and emigration.

A week after he had received my manuscript, Ivan called. He spoke matter-of-factly, "You wrote about your parents' escape. You said your father walked through the woods into Austria and to his freedom."

He paused for a moment and then continued. "But I have to tell you something. In the late 1940s, the Soviets cleared residents from their homes and villages close to the Czechoslovak border. The Soviets displaced those people so they could create a border buffer zone." He paused again and then added, "I'm sorry to say, but it would have been impossible for your father to have crossed the border on foot. The only people who could legally leave Czechoslovakia back then were Hungarian Jews. They had the government's permission to immigrate to Israel via Bratislava and Vienna."

Ivan's words surprised me. Dad had told my brother and me that he had engaged a Bratislava "lady from the street." They walked to the border together, pretending to be a couple. He then told her to go back to Bratislava while he continued to Vienna by foot through the woods.

My mind filled with my most pressing question. "So, how did my father get out of Czechoslovakia?" I asked my cousin

Ivan answered. "I remember your mother telling me that your Dad went on the Aliya bus to Vienna with her, Lali, and Martha. Your father pretended to be Jewish like them. They even taught him Hebrew songs so he could sing along with them. That way, the communist border guards wouldn't suspect that he wasn't Jewish."

"My mother never told me that." I retorted. "She had never contradicted Dad's story about his escape of walking overnight through the woods and across the border into Austria and then to Vienna."

"I don't know what to tell you, Harvy, but that's not true." He then added another surprise. "From what I know, your father was never a POW during the war. He also wasn't recruited by the Czechoslovak First Army to fight against the Germans."

I was troubled by what I was hearing. My heart pumped faster in reaction to my cousin's contradiction of the stories my father had told innumerable times to our family and his friends. "So, where was my father during the war?" I blurted out.

"I don't know for sure, but probably somewhere in Košice. I only met him in '48, the year before your parents left the country together in the following spring."

I felt as if I were grabbing at straws. "But my father said that he was a reconnaissance pilot, flying for the Hungarians and Germans. He said he defected in '43 to Russia and was a POW for half a year until the Soviets recruited him into the new Czechoslovak First Army."

Ivan's tone stayed matter-of-fact. "From what I know, Harvy, he learned to fly only after the war. He was not a pilot before then." My cousin took a long breath and added, "If your Dad had been a pilot, and if he downed his plane in the Russian zone, that Russian lieutenant would either have shot him and his military friends immediately or kept them all alive."

There was certainty in his voice. "When the Russians captured people, they either killed everyone or no one. It wouldn't be the case that a Russian

Lieutenant would have spared your father's life and shot only his Hungarian comrades."

"So, do you know what my father did during the war?"

"I suppose your father was part of the Hungarian military and stationed in or around Košice. He may not have seen any action or the insides of that POW camp in Odessa."

I racked my brain. Mom had once let it slip that Dad had been a cook during the war, but I thought she referred to his time as a POW or in the Czechoslovakia First Army. Could my father have contrived the story of being an Axis recon pilot, turning into a Russian POW, and then being recruited and later escaping the Czechoslovak First Army? Had he been only a cook in Košice? He did mention that, during the war, he once peeled potatoes until his hands were raw.

Even worse, might Dad have been a member of the notorious Hungarian Arrow Cross fascist party as some of his birth mother's relatives had been? He had mentioned that his uncles were staunch fascists, one being the mayor of their hometown. Maybe that political connection had kept him closer to home during the war. Also, might he have married a Jew (my mother) after the war for protection—both to hide his fascist background and escape Czechoslovakia?

"Are you sure about this, Ivan?" I blurted out.

"That's what your mother said to me," he replied.

There was no reason for my mother to have lied to her nephew. Then again, she had kept such information away from her sons, even while she lay on her death bed. She may have withheld such secrets for our whole lives and taken them into her grave.

Ivan's words hadn't convinced me entirely. *Am I trying to hold onto my best beliefs about my father?*

After our call, I searched the internet and discovered other Slovaks, like Bohuslav Horak, who had successfully escaped in 1949 from behind Czechoslovak's Iron Curtain. Horak had been escorted across the border by a sympathetic farmer. They passed through the forest that lined the Czechoslovak frontier with Germany.

I knew that my father was prone to exaggeration. But time and time again, he had related the same stories of war and escape to our family and his close friends. Then again, other than the details he had offered, he never explained precisely where and how he had crossed the Czechoslovak border into Austria.

I wondered if my mother had protected her husband by allowing people, even his children, to see him as a more daring and heroic man than he was. My gut turned inside out in learning about yet another Johnny Simkovits exaggeration turned blatant lie and my mother's part in perpetuating it. Could my father have been so convincing in the recreation of his past? It had been as if he had fully believed his baloney.

My cousin Ivan was the last WWII survivor alive from Mom's Tatransky family. I wrote the Hungarian government to see if they had any record of my father's war history. They wrote back and said those military records had been destroyed during the 1944 bombing of Budapest. There was no other source or evidence to corroborate or contradict what Dad had told us.

I may never know the absolute truth. Ivan's jolting revelation may explain how, according to Košice town records that my brother uncovered on a family history trip with our father, our dad had married his first wife on December 28, 1944. That was the month before the city became liberated from the Hungarian Arrow Cross by the invading Soviets. Had Dad been hiding in a Košice neighbour's barn after he had escaped the Czechoslovak First Army in '44, how could he have gotten married without being arrested, jailed, and even hung on the Košice lampposts as a deserter?

Though I was glad that my father had made it out of Czechoslovakia in '49—whichever way he had escaped—I couldn't stop thinking: *If you fooled me once, Dad, then shame on you. And if you fool me twice, then shame on me. But if you deceived me 101 times over half of my lifetime, then ... what?*

* * * *

Part III:

Closing the Book on Dad, Maybe

Cleaning Up After Johnny

Steve and I paid for our half-sister's flight to Montreal for our father's funeral because she had said that she didn't have the money to pay her way. *Yah, right!*

Emilia hardly said a word to Steve and me through our weekend of honouring our father's memory and placing him into the ground. She never thanked us for her plane fare or the funeral we had orchestrated.

Steve and I had offered our Uncle Edo the same flight arrangement, but he turned us down. He said he didn't want to leave Eboya alone in Košice. But I wondered if he didn't want to be on the same plane as Emilia.

The Monday after the funeral service, Steve and I met with our half-sister at my brother's home. We were going to tell her about our father's bequests for her and her son. We asked one of Dad's Slovak friends to act as a translator, so there would be no misunderstanding, if such were possible with Emilia.

Though our dad was Emilia's birth father, I felt a negligible connection and little sympathy for her. In the ten years that I had known her, she never asked anything about my family or me. She never sent a holiday card. She never even offered a warm smile during her and Igor's extended stays at Dad's homes in Montreal, NY State, and Florida. Emilia had laughed and smiled only for our father while she hung unto his arm.

Emilia had used her way with Dad to coax him to purchase a gravesite and gravestone for her deceased mother, in buying Igor a car and computer, and in obtaining numerous gifts for her grown daughters—women I had never met. She never offered Steve's or my kids a Slovakia souvenir or even a chocolate bar.

Elaine had felt Emilia's competition for my father's attention. My half-sister had placed a daughter's eggs into an absentee father's basket, and she'd now find almost empty shells.

A few days before sitting down with our half-sister, Steve and I had gone over our father's will and bequests. I said to my brother, "I feel we owe Emilia nothing more than the value Dad put on his relationship with her, as spelled out in his will."

Steve was more understanding than I. "But look at what Dad has left us in comparison."

I wondered why Dad had given so much less to his daughter. Had he seen through her suck-up-to-daddy veneer? In his Slovak heritage, were daughters meant to be taken care of by husbands rather than fathers? Had Dad's notion of "feeling morally responsible toward Emilia" not translated into many dollars? Perhaps our father had stronger feelings for his sons, especially after what he had put our mother through. Whatever it was, Dad had made his decision about Emilia, and that was sufficient for me.

I raised my hand to my brother's statement. "What Dad bequeathed us has nothing to do with what he left Emilia. She has chosen to be a stranger to us." I kept my eyes intense. "There are others who were closer to Dad, you, and me, thus more deserving, like Suzie and Edo. I'd rather give money to them."

Steve wasn't convinced. "Are we being fair to our sister?"

My back was up. "So what would be fair, Steve? If we gave Emilia a full third of Dad's estate, she'd be getting about as much as Elaine did from Dad in their divorce settlement. How might Elaine, after she had lived seventeen years with Dad, feel about that?"

I put my hand to my forehead. "And such an amount would be more than twice what Mom had gotten from him after thirty years of marriage. She suffered a lot living with him; she'd want you and me to get what she never had. Mom would turn in her grave if she knew we were going to provide a large bequest to Dad's estranged daughter."

I looked down at the floor and then up at my brother, my voice a little calmer. "So what's fair, Steve? Would Emilia be satisfied with $250,000, $500,000, a $1,000,000, or more? Dad might have exaggerated his worth to her the way he did with everyone else. Knowing Emilia, she'd probably be disappointed with whatever amount we gave her." My gut told me there was no real way to calculate fairness with our half-sister.

My brother's hand was at his chin, taking in what I was saying. He then lowered his hand. "Maybe then we should do something more for Igor."

My voice stayed hard. "We know Igor got Dad's Rolex, a new car, a new laptop, and who knows what other gifts. He's now getting money from Dad's estate. And he'll eventually get what his mother has." I raised my voice a tad. "What do you think he'll do with more? I never heard about his applying himself to anything. He's well into his twenties and, from what I heard, barely finished high school."

"What about giving him a college education? Dad's giving money to our kids for college, so why not Igor too?"

I thought for a moment and then acquiesced. Perhaps I felt sympathy for my father's eldest grandson. It wasn't Igor's fault that his mother seemed to care only for herself. "Okay, Steve, I'd be willing to do that. But if you think we need to compensate them further, it'll come from your part of Dad's inheritance."

Steve knew that I had been generous by letting him in on our father's offshore stash. He could relinquish some of his inheritance to Emilia if he wanted. After a moment, Steve said, "Okay. We don't have to offer them any more than that."

Emilia, Steve, and I sat in my brother's living room. Steve and I sat in chairs on one side of the coffee table while Emilia was in a chair on the other side. Our Slovak translator friend, Mary, sat on the couch on a third side.

I talked slowly and calmly to Mary as the rest looked on. "Our father's estate is not as big as he had led us to believe. His divorce to Elaine had cost a lot, and he spent or gave away a good part of his cash these last few years. Even his bank accounts both in Montreal and Florida are just about empty."

I paused to let Mary tell Emilia. Mary did. Emilia's face remained stark and blank.

I continued. "Only this spring did Steve and I see that Dad was getting out of control with his spending. Subsequently, we were able to take signing authority away from him this summer." I pointed to an empty chair on the fourth edge of the coffee table. "Luckily, Dad agreed to allow us to do that without a fight. He probably realized he was losing control of himself and his money."

I took a long breath and pointed to my brother and me. "What's left in his JHS holding company mostly belongs to Steve and me. Dad had arranged that decades ago."

I didn't want to get into too many money details. Mary knew many of my father's friends. Even though she had agreed to keep our conversation private, what I was telling Emilia could get passed around the Slovak community.

Mary shared my news with Emilia. Emilia's eyebrows rose a bit, but she still said nothing.

I got to the bottom line. I told Emilia the modest bequest amount that our father had put into his will for her and Igor. I shared how we would distribute those sums to her over the ensuing years. I said, "What's left in his estate—after making other bequests and paying Canadian taxes—would go to Steve and me."

Steve and I decided to withhold information on the size of Dad's estate. Even if Steve and I had played open book with her, I was sure that Emilia wouldn't have believed us. Dad may have bragged to her that he had millions stashed over the world. He had knowingly or unwittingly set up this situation so that there would be little trust among his kids.

Mary turned again to Emilia and shared my news matter-of-factly. Emilia's face looked pained as she took in my words. I could see she was working to keep her nose from bending. I looked at her and asked, "Would you like a copy of Dad's will?" I knew she understood that much English. I knew that anybody could get a copy of Dad's will by applying to the Quebec registry that held such official testaments.

Even before Mary finished the translation, Emilia looked at me, shook her head, and responded, "No, not necessary."

I looked carefully at my half-sister as Mary explained Steve's and my offer for Igor's education. Mary said in Slovak, "Johnny's last will puts money aside for the college education of Steve and Harvy's kids. If Igor wants to go to college or trade school in Canada, or Slovakia, or anywhere in the Euro Zone, Johnny's estate can pay for his education."

We didn't offer education in the USA because college there could be ten times more expensive. Mary then added in Slovak, "Steve and Harvy feel it would be important for Igor to have a profession."

Emilia looked at Mary and then at me. She pointed to herself. "So would I get that money for him?" she asked in English.

I wasn't going to trust Emilia to invest in her son. She seemed to want Igor by her side continually. I calmly responded. "No, but if he wants to go to school, Dad's estate would completely pay his tuition, books, and expenses."

Steve nodded his agreement.

On Emilia's behalf, Mary asked, "Is there a specific amount specified?"

I turned to her. "Yes, the same amount that Dad put into his will for each of our kids." I threw out the dollar figure. I then added, "What money Dad has left in his company shares will fund those scholarships. Steve and I will be creating trusts to ensure that we use the money only in that way. We can arrange a separate trust for Igor to pay his education expenses." I was glad that Dad had followed my wishes to make such gifts to his grandkids. Emilia couldn't blame Steve or me for how Dad structured his estate.

Emilia's face stayed blank after Mary had translated. Emilia turned to Steve and me and said, "I'll think about it."

We ended our money conversation there and soon said our goodbyes. Emilia shook our hands but said nothing more. There was no "Thank you," no "See you sometime in Slovakia." Nothing!

Though I hoped she wouldn't, I imagined her bitching back to Košice about how she got shafted by her Canadian father and half-brothers. But it hadn't been Steve or me who had scripted Dad's bequests. Emilia was welcome to have it out with her father when she got to where he now was.

* * *

I was again in Montreal weeks after Emilia had flown back to Slovakia. Steve offered, "It seems that Emilia is telling her Slovak friends here in Montreal that you and I got most of Dad's money and that she and Igor got next to nothing."

Par for the course for my half-sister! I looked at my brother. "Steve, I thought you didn't care much for the Montreal Slovak community and what they think." I didn't feel a strong connection to Dad's Slovak friends and colleagues, especially after being raised speaking my parent's Hungarian. Over the years, I was the one that had gone to the Slovak and Hungarian Balls and Slovak church events with Dad and Mom, then Dad and Elaine, and then Dad and Suzie. Ever since Steve had converted to the Mormon faith, he rarely, if ever, went to any function connected to our parents' heritage.

My brother's voice projected concern. "I don't want the Slovak people here to think badly of Dad. Once in a while, I hear from them, and I'd like to keep it friendly."

It was ironic how Steve had continually disrespected our father, and now he was trying to protect Dad's image. Though he seemed to be a walking Simkovits contradiction at times, perhaps he did feel connected to our Montreal Slovak heritage even though he was not much for it. "Who are the people saying these things?" I asked.

He mentioned three names. He acknowledged that he heard it indirectly through a person in the community who had been close to our father, and that person had heard it from those other Slovaks. None of those people were Mary, our translator with Emilia.

I thought for a moment, then offered, "Steve, what if one of us calls those individuals and talks to them about our concerns and hopes for Emilia and Igor. We don't have to refer to what you've heard, only to say to each of them, 'Because you are close to Emilia, can you talk to her about our wanting to help Igor get a college education.' We then can tell them that we offered that to Emilia, but she hasn't accepted. We can even permit them to talk to Mary and hear from her directly about the proposal we had made."

Steve upped his tone. "But what if those people start complaining about Emilia getting short shrift from Dad?"

I raised my tone to match his. "That's even better, Steve. We can tell them that Dad left a smaller bequest for her, but we are trying to balance things out by giving Igor a college or trade school education—as Dad had arranged for our kids. We can say that we want to help Igor to become self-sufficient." I looked into his eyes. "None of them know exactly how much money Dad has given us. All they need to know is that we are trying to be fair with Emilia and Igor."

My brother had more to say. "But what if they say we should trust Emilia and give her that college money to hold on behalf of Igor."

I pointed to him. "Then say that Dad bequeathed those college funds in a way that we have to put them into a separate trust and spend them on nothing else but our kids' education." That was undoubtedly true, though Steve and I had the authority to adjust those rules as we saw fit. "We can say that we want to play by the same rules for Igor."

Steve thought for a few seconds, his hand to his chin. "Okay, Harvy; it's worth a try."

He and I called Emilia's three Montreal friends. We asked them to talk to Emilia on our behalf. They mentioned how our Dad might have been unfair to his daughter, and we acknowledged that point. We told them we wanted to correct the wrong to the extent we could. We explained our education offer for Igor. They admitted that Emilia never mentioned that part to them. They accepted the fairness of Steve's and my terms, and they offered to speak to Emilia on our behalf.

We later heard back from one or two of them. Those friends said that they had had a conversation with Emilia, but they didn't know what she would decide regarding our offer for Igor.

* * *

Months later, Helen and Georges invited Steve and me for supper. After thirty years of service to JHS, they never received a pension from Dad, and Steve and I wanted to correct that wrong to some extent. We offered them cash from Dad's estate. It was on the order of what Emilia had gotten, but we gave it to them in one lump sum.

Over a delicious stuffed cabbage meal that Helen had cooked, Georges spoke. "You boys were generous with Helen and me. Though your father employed us for most of our working lives, and we built a home and had two wonderful children, we never had a lot of money to spare. What you gave us will certainly help through our retirement. We deeply appreciate it."

The Slovak-speaking Helen pointed our way. "You know, your Košice sister talked to me after she had found out what she got from your father's estate. She didn't say how much, but she complained about how little she received from Johnny. She wondered how her father could do that to her."

There was Emilia again playing the wounded victim. I wondered if her upbringing or culture or a Johnny Simkovits gene made her that way.

Steve and I stayed silent as Helen continued. Her voice elevated. "I usually keep my mouth shut in such family situations. But I became peeved at her when she said that about Johnny. I told her, 'Steve and Harvy are Johnny's rightful children.'" She gestured as she said, "I pointed my finger at her and told her, 'You had a father when your mother remarried after Johnny had left Czechoslovakia. I'm sure you got something from him when he died.'"

I came in. "Steve and I offered Emilia more than what Dad had put in his will for her and Igor. We were willing to provide Igor a college education."

Steve added, "She hasn't yet agreed to our offer."

Helen didn't hesitate. "That's so nice of you two. Your father would be proud of you."

Helen rarely had an axe to grind with Johnny Simkovits, even though she and her husband had worked under Dad's heavy hand for many years. I was grateful that she saw my half-sister the same way I did.

Steve and I didn't hear another word from the Montreal Slovak community about how Emilia felt shortchanged. And, we never heard back from Emilia about our education funding offer for her son.

* * *

Steve and I had tried to think of every loose money end before Dad's passing. My U.S. tax lawyer suggested that we sell Dad's Florida property while Dad was still alive (to make U.S. tax reporting easier), and we did. I attempted to put some of our father's assets into a charitable trust to save on taxes and do something benevolent with a portion of our inheritance. Steve could then gift money to his church, having his donation come from pre-tax assets. Our Canadian lawyer soon told me that having power of attorney over our father's finances didn't give us the authority to rearrange his estate, so my idea became shelved.

No one mentioned, not even Dad's insurance agent, to declare a change of beneficiary for Dad's registered retirement pension. According to Suzie, Dad had promised her that money, which amounted to hundreds of thousands of dollars, pre-tax. But Dad hadn't made the arrangements to change his pension beneficiary from Steve and me to her. That would have allowed the monthly pension payments to be transferred directly to her, on which she'd then have to pay some taxes.

It wasn't until after Dad's funeral that Steve and I realized that oversight. The government would tax our father's pension at a hefty 53% in his final tax returns. Realizing our omission, Steve and I looked at each other and shrugged. "You can't win them all," he said.

"Might Dad not have wanted Suzie to get anything?" I asked. "Years ago, I remember him saying that he had paid thousands of dollars for this and that for her." I took a long breath. "He didn't appreciate her, as with every other woman he lived with."

"Whatever Dad intended, we should take care of her," Steve said.

"I agree with you on this one, Steve. Suzie did a lot for him. She deserves what Dad had promised her."

Suzie had taken care of Dad for five years with few complaints. She cooked and cleaned for him, and she massaged his legs every night before bed. Dad's last partner had stayed loyal, though she scolded him for smoking too much or not exercising his arm and legs every day. Suzie would sometimes say with a stern voice and wagging finger, "Johnny, you should know better! You need to take care of yourself."

Knowing my father's way of neglecting himself, I held nothing against Suzie for her occasional reprimand, though her words never changed Dad's behavior. He would smoke more at his office and less at home, or he'd say he did his exercises when he might have done them for only a few minutes.

Steve and I put the after-tax cash from Dad's pension, plus tens of thousands more, into a lifetime annuity for Suzie. It would give her a steady annual income until she died. Suzie also had other pensions from Canada, Quebec, her former employer, and her late husband. We felt she'd be okay. We gave Suzie Dad's car, apartment furnishings, and whatever she wanted from his personal belongings.

Suzie never had any big aspiration for our father's money, and she was a frugal person like our mother had been. She appreciated what we did for her. When we told her about the arrangements we were making, she gave us hugs and a big "Thank you, boys."

For nearly twenty years, Suzie continued to collect her annuity and pension incomes into her late eighties. She continued to live independently in Montreal, unattached to any other man. As she closed in on 90 years, dementia crept into her mind, and her body failed. My wife and I held her as a step-grandmother to our kids. We continued to visit her and invite her out for supper when we came to Montreal. We did that until the time came when she barely recognized us.

The one thing I did feel a loss for was Dad's diamond tie pin. The one-carat stone in that pin was the only diamond remaining from Dad's mother's brooch. Suzie kept the piece, saying, "I want to turn your father's diamond into a ring for me."

Though I felt a pang for not having the jewel, I had no good reason to ask her for it. She deserved the memento, perhaps even a pseudo engagement ring, from her late partner.

The sad part was that all the original cut diamonds from Dad's mother's brooch were now forever gone, scattered in the wind as the ashes of a deceased might be.

* * *

In the following summer of 2001, my family and I travelled to my parent's hometown in Slovakia. I wanted to reconnect with Edo and others from my father's family in Košice.

I felt sad while walking the streets of my parents' hometown. All my mother's relatives and extended family from there had passed away or moved to the USA, Canada, or Israel. Slovakia, like most of the Slavic countries, had become nearly devoid of Jews. At the beginning of WWII, over 12,000 Jews had lived in and around town—then a small city of 65,000. By 2001, perhaps 3000 Jews remained in the whole country of perhaps five million inhabitants.

Steve and I didn't want to tell Edo that his big brother had left him nothing in his will. Steve and I felt that our uncle shouldn't be forgotten or punished because of our father's failings. Dad had many times foisted his "*Lassen* to me!" onto his kid brother. Leaving nothing to Edo hadn't been right.

Steve and I agreed to give Edo an annual stipend on the scale of what Emilia and Igor were getting. It would help Eboya and him have a little better life in Košice. Slovakia was still an inexpensive place to live, about a quarter of what it cost to live in Montreal, the least expensive city in Canada.

Over Eboya's tasty chicken paprikash, I promised Edo that he would get those payments for the rest of his life. Privately, my brother and I had agreed to monitor Edo's situation and offer him more money if he needed it in the coming years.

I didn't appreciate having to be a decider in Edo's inheritance, but Steve and I had to be prudent and measured with our uncle. As far as I knew, Edo was still in touch with Emilia. Better they commiserate about holding the short end of Dad's money stick than for them to bicker or boast about who had received how much. I suspected that many families get upset, even up in arms, around sharing a sizable estate, no matter how much care goes into dividing its holdings. Steve and I probably couldn't make every relative happy, no matter how much we gave them.

I added a perk for Edo and Eboya. "If you ever want to come to visit your friends in Canada, Steve and I would pay for your trip."

Edo and Eboya offered their acceptance with a nod and a smile. At the time, they seemed appreciative of the modest bequest we provided.

I later heard from one of Edo's Košice cousins. "Eboya is not happy that Edo got so little from Johnny." She went on. "But what you and Steve did for them was the right thing. Eboya would give all their estate to her relations if she could." Though I had never met Eboya's family, Edo's cousin said that Eboya had an elder brother and a grown niece and nephew over whom she doted.

A few years later, Eboya became ill with cancer. She pressed Edo to bequest their assets only to her niece and nephew. When Steve and I found out, we were okay with their decision. We certainly didn't need Edo's money. After Eboya had passed away, and on another one of my trips to Košice, Edo confirmed that what he owned would go to Eboya's niece and nephew.

I later felt Edo was shortchanging his closest cousins in Košice. There were two in particular who remained close to him and had helped him over the years. One had dinner with Edo every week and kept tabs on him. The other helped him organize and do his paperwork, including writing emails to Steve and me on his behalf.

When I returned home, I wrote Edo a letter asking him to reconsider his estate decision and to include his close Košice cousins in his will. "They have done a lot for you, and you shouldn't forget about them," I said.

My uncle's cousin emailed a month later, saying, "Edo said he never received your letter."

I consoled myself. *One can only do what one can do.*

On that same family trip to Slovakia, now nine months after Dad's death, I reached out to Emilia. Some days before my family would depart my parents' hometown, I asked Edo to call her. I wanted to reconnect and see if time had given her a different perspective on Dad, Steve, and me.

I heard nothing back from Emilia until the morning of our last day in the city. She called early that morning to our hotel room, saying in her meagre English, "I do not feel good. I not meet. I still sad about Daddy's death."

I told her, "I have presents for you and Igor that I brought from Boston. Can you at least meet for coffee this morning?"

"I too sick to meet," she responded. We ended our conversation there.

In retrospect, it may have been a good thing we didn't meet. Gloria and I had gotten her a box of assorted fragrant soaps, a product we thought wouldn't exist in Slovakia. However, I later found out that such a gift in my parent's home country could infer that you thought the gift receiver to be dirty and in need of a bath.

For the next three years, Steve and I sent Emilia and Igor their yearly inheritance payments as Dad had bequeathed them. Over those three years, those two never reached out, not even sending us a holiday card.

Steve and I then made another decision. Not to prolong the inevitable, we sent Emilia and Igor the remainder of their inheritance in one lump sum. I told my brother, "I don't know about you, but that's probably the end of my connection with our half-sister and her son."

That Christmas, Emilia did send cards to Steve and me, thanking us for the money. But I felt her gesture too little too late. I never received another card or note from her, and I never sent her one either. I walked away from another muddy mess that our father had left at our feet from his grave.

Thanks, Dad, for another unhappy ending.

* * *

Years after Dad's passing, I visited Father Sinal in the Catholic Church's home for retired priests in Montreal. I wanted to ask the Father—the Slovak priest who had officiated at Dad's funeral—about his perspectives on the money dealings between Father Novak and my father. Sinal gave me an audience at his retirement home. His hair was short and gray. Though his body was thin and frail, his handshake was firm, and his smile reflected deep compassion.

After we had talked about how he knew my father through his Cousin Helen, I asked him about the money dealings of the Montreal Slovak Church.

Sinal stood up for Novak. "Novak was trying to do his job to the diocese. He wanted to bring into the open the money that some of the churchwardens were hiding from the church." He raised an arm. "Novak did nothing wrong in wanting those finances to be transparent."

"What about the money my father was putting into Father Novak's hand ever Sunday? Was it right for Novak to accept that?"

Sinal looked at me with caring eyes. "What was he supposed to do, say no? Your father was a big donor; Novak didn't want to insult him."

"But Father Novak came every week to visit my father and ask for money for this person and that person."

Sinal was unmoved. His voice stayed quiet and calm. "Your father was encouraging him to come. A priest is there to help his church members, and your father was a big help in assisting others."

I surmised there were multiple perspectives regarding any egregious situation, yet I was surprised by Sinal's view. My voice may have turned slightly hard. "But it was getting out of control. My father was giving his money away indiscriminately."

There was no judgement in Father Sinal's voice. "How was Novak supposed to know that? He was only trying to be caring and helpful."

Father Sinal pointed to himself. "On the other hand, I never went to your father to ask for money." His voice elevated slightly. "Your father called me many times to ask for my blessing and advice, but he never offered me money. He gave to Novak and everyone else, but never to me."

Sinal raised a finger and looked past me. "Maybe I should have asked for something for my parish, but I never felt right about doing so."

* * * *

End to a Father's Burden

Four seasons had to pass for my brother and me to complete Dad's tax re-filings for his half-a-lifetime of money hiding.

We had started with Mr. Weber at the Global Trade Bank. We gave him a copy of our father's will, indicating that we were Dad's estate executors. We then asked him to provide a set of Dad's bank account statements that went back three years. I had called Weber the previous day to tell him not to mention the statement printouts he had given me previously, and he complied. For the moment, Steve and I said nothing about declaring Dad's offshore money to Revenue Canada. Only I knew that Weber and Steve were keeping secrets from each other. It felt strange but necessary.

Soon after Dad's passing, the Supporters of Independent University sent a letter asking for payment according to the agreement Dad had signed in 1993. Steve and I ignored their advances. Though we heard nothing more from them, we later found out that a lawyer had applied for a copy of Dad's last will from the provincial registry. Steve and I figured the lawyer represented the Supporters of Independent University. Nothing came from that registry request because Dad's will had not included the Friends donation.

I wondered if Steve and I had done right by jettisoning the university gift and annuity. Indeed, Dad hadn't kept his end of the bargain. He gave most of his pension to Elaine, and he never put the Friends bequest into his will.

Steve and I still could have honoured the donation. We would have become the legitimate benefactors of the annuity's annual income and then declare it in our tax returns each ensuing year. Over our lifetimes, Revenue Canada and the IRS would have accepted the deferred taxes on the one million dollars.

But our least complicated choice had been to make the university agreement disappear. Discarding that agreement was as if we were jettisoning an irritant half-relation from our lives. I certainly didn't want the likes of the Global Trade Bank and the Supporters of Independent University to be a continual reminder of my father's non-legit dealings, like the illegitimate offspring that Mr. Duma had mentioned.

Steve accepted my wish for that university gift. Had he wanted us to do differently, he would have asked me to divulge everything straight and not hold back on what our dad had intended. But he chose to tacitly go along with my stance regarding the legal and moral dilemma we faced with that money-hiding, tax-evading agreement.

I don't know if we had been right or wrong about discarding that deal like a bad card in a gin rummy hand. Our action of ignoring that annuity bothered me for years. My inner Johnny Simkovits tempted me to make the prearranged donation to the university. I could take the tax-free payments myself for the rest of my life, not saying anything to Steve. But my conscience wouldn't have allowed that privilege.

Perhaps what Steve and I did was good enough. I knew my mother would have wanted her children and grandchildren to have the most benefit from Dad's estate. In a bitter moment after Dad had left her for the third and final time, she made a fist and blurted out, "If I can't have your father's love, then I want us to have his money."

In the end, Dad had signed that illicit Friends agreement, not my brother nor I. Our father never made it binding by putting it in his will. Perhaps Steve and I were morally bound to honour our father's initial wishes, but his intention had been blatantly tax-skirting. Why should we dignify a contract made by and with any devil but ourselves?

* * *

With Steve's consent, I took the lead with Charles and Geoff regarding the voluntary disclosure to Revenue Canada. I would negotiate Charles' fee and arrange Geoff's accounting work.

Steve and I met with the pair at Charles' office. We brought copies of Dad's offshore statements and three years of tax returns. While Geoff and Steve sat to one side of the conference table, I sat across from Charles.

Besides being interested in the total assets Dad held offshore, Charles pushed the documents over to Geoff. "The accountants will take care of refiling your father's tax returns once I have formalized the arrangement with Revenue Canada." He looked at Steve and then at me. "For now, Geoff should file your father's final returns for this year as if the offshore assets didn't exist."

My eyes widened to Charles' notion of continuing to deceive the government, but I let the lawyer continue. He spoke assuredly. "It could take a year to complete the voluntary disclosure process. We should initially act as if your father's offshore money isn't a part of his estate. Once we finalize the deal with Revenue Canada, we'll refile your father's last three returns, including his offshore earnings at that time."

Steve nodded, and so did I. I then looked at Geoff. "I've put together spreadsheets that show estimates of our father's income and capital gains from his offshore money for the last three years."

Geoff returned my look. "Estimates won't be good enough, Harvy. We'll need to account for every income and expense transaction from your father's bank statements going back for those years."

I didn't want the accountants to do calculations that I could do myself. I offered, "Geoff, what if I create detailed spreadsheets of the income and expenses from my father's offshore accounts, by currency and by year?" I didn't say that I had already started on that project.

Geoff nodded slowly. "That would certainly help regarding the tax returns, once we receive a confirmation from Revenue Canada about the refiling rules they will accept." He pointed to the statements. "However, my tax preparer will have to verify your spreadsheet entries against the Global Trade Bank statement you are providing us here."

"That's understandable," I said. *More damn costs,* I thought.

Just *Lassen* to Me!

The weeks and months progressed. There were more meetings with Charles. We continued to sit in our same spots—my brother at the end of the conference table while I faced Charles across the table.

Steve kept his promise to allow me to do most of the talking. He leaned back in his chair, holding his right hand to his chin with fingers over his mouth. His right elbow was on his left arm that lay across his abdomen. It was as if he were in deep thought. Occasionally, he asked a question, which Charles or I answered without hesitation. I figured my brother was okay with my having most of the discussion with Charles.

I believed I especially proved my worth when we negotiated Charles' remuneration. Charles waited to clarify his fees until later down the voluntary disclosure road. I was okay with his delay because it offered me more time to confirm the disclosure rules and my calculations regarding Dad's offshore accounts. A month or two into the process, as Charles was preparing to present his proposal to Revenue Canada, he called for a meeting with my brother and me.

At JHS, before that meeting, I showed Steve my spreadsheets with the initial estimates I had produced based on our father's offshore accounts. I told him, "I want to try to get the best fee deal we can from Charles. Let me go it alone with him for now, acting as an agent for both of us." I smiled. "This way, he can't corral us at the same time, and I can say that I need your acceptance of any fee proposal he makes." I looked intently at him. "You and I will then have another chance to think through his proposal before accepting or rejecting it."

Steve agreed. He and I then arranged to meet at JHS right after my pending conversation with Charles.

Charles and I met again at his firm's conference room. I allowed him to set the pace of the conversation. I knew the negotiation adage: "The first one to talk money is often the one to become disadvantaged in the deal."

After pleasantries, Charles offered, "My firm needs me to finalize our fees with you."

I said, "Okay. What's your specific proposal?"

He stared at me, his baby blues eying me carefully. "My partners are expecting a 5% fee on the money retained after your father's estate pays the taxes on his offshore assets." That percentage was at the high end of the 3-5% range he quoted when we first met.

I sat still in my chair. I had done my homework. I had an informed idea of how much Steve and I would retain once we struck our deal with Revenue Canada. I looked at Charles' face, and I said flatly, "My brother and I cannot agree to that percentage." I stopped there.

The room was silent for a moment. Charles leaned slightly forward. "So, what's your proposal, Harvy?"

I spoke calmly, my tone clear. "You had mentioned that the voluntary disclosure rules are pretty standard with the government." I shot for under Charles' low end. "My brother and I are willing to accept 2.5% on the bulk of the assets saved from the tax authorities. Also, we'd consider a bonus if we retain a larger than expected percentage of my father's assets." I kept my face straight and eyes firmly on the attorney.

Charles knew that he had educated me well on the voluntary disclosure tax rules. By now, I had shared that I had explored the voluntary disclosure option with another lawyer before coming to him. Charles knew I had the opportunity of going back to Bernard if he and I couldn't agree on a fee.

The attorney thought for a moment, his fingers to his chin and his back against his chair. "Okay, our firm can accept a 2.5% fee on the first 50% of the assets we secure for you." He leaned forward. "But we'll expect twenty-five percent of every additional dollar we get for you above that percentage."

I was surprised and pleased that he consented to my proposal on the first 50% of retained assets. That was a significant saving. But I wasn't quite finished negotiating on the other 50% of my father's offshore money.

My face didn't flinch as I leaned slightly forward and put a hand on the table. "Charles, let me show you some numbers." I opened my portfolio, retrieved my spreadsheets, and put them on the table. I placed a palm on the documents. "I've done calculations based on the tax guidelines you have shared with me. I figure we can easily do much better than retaining 50% of my father's offshore assets."

I pointed to my papers with my other hand. "In two of the last three years, my father had fairly low income and capital gain amounts in his accounts. My calculations show that we could be left with 70% of his offshore money after we have paid the taxes."

I could see Charles' eyebrows rise, but the rest of him stayed steady. I leaned forward further and slowly pushed my documents in his direction. "These are my figures based on the offshore bank statements I have given Geoff. What helps is that one of my father's accounts shows capital losses in the Euro currency because of that currency's depreciation over the last few years." I pointed to some numbers on my spreadsheet. "Those unrealized capital losses will limit the tax liability to the government."

Charles glanced at my documents, and then he looked at me. "So what are you proposing, Harvy?"

I kept myself steady. "Our fee breakpoint should be 70% of the assets retained. According to my figures, it will be easy to reach that level. My brother and I would be willing to pay a higher percentage if we can surpass that much asset retention." My voice stayed firm and spine straight.

Charles eyed me intensely for a long few seconds, putting his fingers to his chin once more and leaning back in his chair. He then leaned forward and spoke firmly. "If it's 70% breakpoint you want, then my firm will expect fifty cents on the dollar beyond that."

Perhaps I responded too quickly. My voice elevated. "Fifty cents on the dollar!? Isn't that kind of high, Charles?" Had my father been here, I'm sure he would have yelled, "Do you think I was fucking born yesterday?" and then he'd storm out of the room. But I didn't do that. I didn't want to let go of what I had won so far from Charles.

His tone remained resolute. "We have never had a situation where a taxpayer has retained such a large percentage of the assets in a voluntary disclosure." He looked down at my spreadsheets. "I trust you have done your homework. Nevertheless, I have to go back to my partners with the potential for a big bonus if we clear a certain percentage for you. If you want to set the line at 70%, then it has to be fifty cents to my firm on each additional dollar retained by you beyond that percentage."

Now it was my time to think for a few seconds. I took my time. I turned my head away slowly. I held my hands steady on my lap. I kept my face expressionless as I turned back to the attorney. "Okay, Charles. I'll share your proposal with my brother. We'll get back to you by tomorrow."

The attorney opened his portfolio and pulled out some papers. "I'll fill in these contract documents between our firm and you with the breakpoint and percentages we just discussed. We'll need both your and your brother's signatures." He signed his name to the document. "If any changes occur with these figures," he glared at me, "and I can assure you there won't be any reductions from my end, then we'll rewrite and initial next to the changes." His eyes stayed on me. "I can't take another step with your voluntary disclosure with Revenue Canada until I get these papers back from you."

I put my palms flat on the table. "Okay, Charles. I'll get back to you tomorrow as to where Steve and I stand."

I didn't say that I already agreed with what he had put in the document. If we exceeded the 70% asset retention figure, then we would have performed a minor miracle. I'd be happy to share half of anything above that miracle with our lawyer.

I later met with Steve at JHS. We stood as we talked. He asked, "How confident are you with your calculations, Harvy? Are you sure we can get away with paying the government only 30% of Dad's offshore money?"

I pointed to my spreadsheets. "I closely examined Dad's income and capital gain numbers from the Global Trade Bank statements, as well as from his tax returns for the past three years. I've spent hours re-examining my spreadsheets, plugging my aggregate numbers into the tax formulas that Charles and Geoff have provided." I turned the page. "Look, I've even done some simple sensitivity analyses, varying the expected tax rates and government interest rates."

I pointed to my results. "According to my overall analysis, we should clear between 69.6% and 70.8% of Dad's offshore assets after we have paid the tax to both governments. That doesn't include the fees to Charles and Geoff's firm, which will also be deductible against the income in the most current year." I looked at my brother. "I'm very confident about this."

Steve glanced at my spreadsheets and then returned his gaze to me. "Then let's give Charles what he wants. You got him down on his overall fee. Let him feel good about getting a bonus at the high end if there's something to be had there at all."

"Okay, Steve. And I'll let him sweat about it tonight; I'll call him in the morning and tell him we agree to his terms. We can sign his agreement now, and I'll deliver it tomorrow."

* * *

Charles presented his proposal to Revenue Canada in the spring of 2001. It was over a month until the government came back with a response. They acknowledged the parameters of his plan. Steve and I then accepted their terms.

Charles subsequently divulged to the government that he was representing the children of John Simkovits, and we were going to submit updated tax returns from 1998 to 2000. In Boston, I held my breath that whole day. I imagined the RCMP waiting at my doorstep, but no one was there when I arrived home.

Per my agreement with Geoff, I sorted and logged every transaction of Dad's offshore investments, putting in forty hours that next week to get it done. Every piece of income, capital gains and losses, bank costs, and management fees were considered for our father's various accounts, in three currencies, for the last three years. I entered every bank fee down to the "no-name fee," which the bank charged such that an account would be identified solely by a number and not a name. I made thousands of numerical entries onto pages upon pages of digital spreadsheets.

I preferred to do this work myself rather than have the accountants do it. Perhaps it was my penny-pinching father in me who didn't want to spend more than necessary on professionals. Or maybe I wanted insight into the detailed comings and goings of my father's offshore money. Or perhaps I wanted to impress my brother with my diligence. In any case, after I completed my work, Geoff told Steve and me, "Harvy saved at least $10,000 in accounting costs by the detailed work he did."

I jumped in, looking at Geoff. "And, for the thousands of entries I made onto those spreadsheets, your tax preparer only found two small discrepancies, which we were able to clear up in five minutes."

I hoped my brother appreciated what I had done for us.

Steve said nothing.

Before Revenue Canada approved our tax re-filings, a new government bureaucrat took over Dad's file. After Charles had submitted Dad's updated returns, the woman official kept on asking for more information and additional bank statements regarding Dad's offshore accounts. At a meeting with Charles, Geoff, and Steve, I raised my voice. "We gave the government everything that Charles outlined in our deal, as well as what they wanted in their initial request for documentation. Now, this new woman is nagging us for more documents. Why should we give in to her?" I banged my finger on the table, as my father might have done. "It'll be more work for the accountants and me. I thought a deal was a deal, and now she's nitpicking at us." My father might have yelled, "Screw the bitch!" but I didn't.

Charles stayed calm. "It's a new government person who's in charge of the file. She wants to make sure that everything is clean and nothing is missing. I did tell you that it's unusual for the government to get only 30% of the hidden assets as tax revenue." He took a long breath. "Her boss might be having a fit that they're going to get less than a third of your father's offshore money. Or maybe she's trying to make her mark as a new person in that department." He looked at me. "She also may be fishing around to see if you two are hiding anything."

Steve looked at Charles. "Let's give her what she wants." Though my brother didn't look my way, I knew he was talking to me. "We have nothing to hide, do we? Let's do what Hillary Clinton should have done with the White House travel department during the Clinton administration—to throw those travel-gate files onto the front lawn and allow the prosecutor to pick up what he wanted."

I thought for a moment. I hated to acknowledge my brother's bursts of wisdom, but he was right. Even though it would mean more work for me and Geoff's tax preparer, we gave the new government hound dog what she had wanted. It felt odd to be at the mercy of a federal bureaucrat who I had never met and would probably never see in my lifetime.

For the ensuing month, every day felt as if I were living one of Dad's expressions: "Sitting on pins and needles."

After those additional weeks of worrying and wondering, Revenue Canada came back to Charles. They approved the refiled tax returns.

Charles offered, "They found no irregularities." He pointed our way. "Though their cut was lower than expected, they anticipate that both of you will deposit the remaining funds into a Canadian bank or trust company so they can obtain future tax on the earnings."

Steve and I planned to put what remained of Dad's offshore assets into a Canadian bank or trust company. Because we had filed the voluntary disclosure under Dad's name, Revenue Canada didn't know that I paid only U.S. taxes. They'd see negligible future tax revenue from me.

It took nearly three more months until formal federal and provincial government assessments arrived. They confirmed accepting Dad's tax returns and our paying all his back taxes. Dad's estate was now scrubbed clean, and my conscience as well.

My many hours of tax estimations turned out pretty darn good. In the end, the government's tax take worked out to 29% of Dad's total offshore assets, a tad better than my most optimistic estimate. It felt odd for Steve and me, never having had so much money in our possession, to co-sign cheques to Revenue Canada and Revenue Quebec totaling over $1,500,000CAD. That was on top of another nearly half-million dollars we had sent in with Dad's final tax returns before we enacted the voluntary disclosure. My brother and I also cut other cheques to Charles' and Geoff's firms for over $160,000CAD, though those dollars had been tax-deductible.

I felt a little disheartened that all that money could have been mine had I kept my father's hidden empire intact. But I preferred to give the taxman his rightful due rather than having to evade him for the rest of my days. What would I have told my son, or any other child of mine, if I had continued on my father's crooked course?

Charles was happy that our fee deal netted his firm a bit of a bonus. As I handed Charles his check at a follow-up meeting, I found myself curious. "Charles, how does our case compare in size to the other clients you've served these past years?"

He first pointed out his capabilities in having gotten a good deal with the government. Then he shared, "The size of your father's offshore estate is about average for us."

I found myself a little disappointed with his "about average" response.

Then he added, "Yet your situation resulted in the lowest percentage that I've seen the government obtain from anyone conducting a voluntary disclosure in Canada."

I smiled inside regarding that one.

* * *

Until Revenue Canada completed our case, Steve and I kept Dad's offshore stash at the Global Trade Bank. After we had received the confirming letters from the federal and provincial governments, we interviewed a handful of Montreal money managers who Charles introduced to us. After presentations from each firm, Steve and I quickly agreed to go with a top-notch fellow at a big Canadian bank.

After securing our new money manager, Steve and I made an appointment with Mr. Weber at the Global Trade Bank. We sat in the same conference room we had occupied a year earlier. It would be for the last time.

I pulled no punches. "I'm sorry to tell you, Mr. Weber, but my brother and I have decided to take our father's money out of the Global Trade Bank. We are repatriating the funds to Canada." I pushed a sheet of paper toward him that held our new bank account and routing numbers. "How quickly can you sell everything we own and make the transfer to this account?"

Weber looked down briefly into his folded hands and then lifted his head. "Your father is our biggest client here. It will reflect badly on me at our head office if you close his accounts during my time in Montreal. Was there something we did to have you make that decision?"

I spoke calmly, my spine straight and my palms flat on the table. "No, Mr. Weber, it has nothing to do with you or the bank. We have decided to declare our father's offshore assets to the Canadian government. You can tell your head office that a part of our deal with Revenue Canada was to move the assets back into a Canadian bank." I fibbed a little about that. I didn't want Weber, a friendly enough fellow, to feel responsible for our decision.

"Okay," he said, looking at both of us. "I'm sorry that you are leaving us. It seems there is nothing I can do to change your mind." His statement sounded like a question.

My brother offered, "It's nothing against you or the bank. We need to bring the money back to Canada."

Weber looked at me and spoke slowly. "We can dispose of the assets and make the transfers within four or five days. Would that be okay?"

"Yes, Mr. Weber," I said. "Thank you so very much."

Webber added, "Okay, then. I'll get the paperwork."

Steve and I hardly said a word to each other as we exited the Global Trade Bank a half-hour later and walked toward the building elevators. We stood for a few minutes waiting for the elevator car to arrive, both of us facing its metal doors. Steve spoke without turning my way. "Harvy, I appreciate everything you've done around Dad's offshore money." He glanced my way. "And I do hope you won't hang any of this over my head in any way, especially now that we will work together to deal with JHS."

I felt my brother's request a little odd, but I said, "Okay, Steve." I figured he didn't want me to lord over him regarding my gift of sharing Dad's hidden assets.

I would keep my commitment for five years.

My brother and I met with Geoff at his office later that day to give him a cheque for his firm's accounting work. I also thanked him for his referral to Charles. Near the end of our brief meeting, I pulled out a small box from my briefcase and handed it to my friend. I said, "My father had a custom of giving gifts to those who helped him significantly in his life in Canada. Here's something from me for what you have done for our family."

Geoff took the box and opened it. Inside was a Canadian $100 gold coin, worth many times its face value. He looked at it and then at me, "That's nice of you, Harvy. Thank you very much."

I hadn't told my brother I was going to give Geoff a gift. The coin had come from my half of our dad's collection of precious metal. Geoff was my friend; I felt it right to provide something to continue building our bond. If Steve wanted to give Geoff a gift, or not, that was up to him.

I suspect my brother couldn't deal with coming empty-handed. He said, "It was the least we could do for your efforts."

I growled inside. The nerve of Steve to pretend my generosity was also his. I bit my lip and said nothing. It wasn't the time.

* * *

A year after Steve and I had gotten out of the tax woods with Revenue Canada, Geoff and I had dinner. After we had ordered, he lowered his voice and said, "Your voluntary disclosure made history at Revenue Canada. Because of your case, they are changing the rules for such disclosures."

I leaned forward in my chair. "How so?" I asked, matching his tone.

Geoff responded. "Charles' deal with Revenue Canada resulted in their getting less than their customary 40% or more of the undeclared assets." He blinked a few times. "Charles told me that the government wasn't pleased with their take from your father's offshore money. They're now changing their policies. They'll be going back five years instead of three for the refilling of tax returns."

Geoff took a long breath and continued in a low tone. "And now, the Quebec Department of Revenue also wants to get into the voluntary disclosure act. They used to sit back and let Revenue Canada make the deal for both governments. They're now building a voluntary disclosure department that will have to be dealt with separately. They may even have different rules and ask for different backup information." He took a long breath. "With both governments now in the hidden money game, it could take two years to do what you and Steve did in only one."

"Wow," I said. "I guess our timing was good."

Geoff nodded. "It could have been a lot worse. You not only made it under the gun, but you and your father made Revenue Canada change their firearm too."

Two decades earlier, I had heard from a former tax lawyer acquaintance that the Canadian government's corporate tax department changed its rules on handling obsolete inventory. It was after the government concluded its 1975 tax case against Dad and his Montreal Phono Company. Now Johnny Simkovits was leaving his mark once more on the Canadian tax system. But this time, he did it in death.

I wondered what indelible marks Dad would leave on my brother and me.

* * *

Over a decade later, at the funeral of a Hungarian friend of Dad's, I bumped into Mr. Duma. I didn't expect him to be there, and I hadn't seen his smiling face until he approached. He put out his hand and said calmly, "Hello, Harvy. I hope you and your family are well."

I knew nothing about Mr. Duma's family. I smiled, took his hand in mine, and said, "Yes, thank you, Mr. Duma. I hope you, too, have been keeping well. It's been a long time since I last saw you." It had been at my father's funeral.

"Yes! Much has happened since that time, and I'm glad to see you." He motioned for us to take a few steps toward a spot that was away from other people. He lowered his voice. "I wanted to tell you that, for the sake of my children, I'm following in your and your brother's footsteps."

My eyebrows rose. "What do you mean?"

He didn't lose a beat. "I, too, am declaring everything I have 'over there' to the Canadian government." His face became long as he kept his voice down. "I'm already a year into it, and it's probably going to take another year to complete. Both governments have been sticklers with me. They want detailed documentation of transactions going back ten years. They want to make sure the money I have had all that time in Canada is clean."

I took a breath. "I'm sorry for your trouble, Mr. Duma. I guess my brother and I were lucky to declare my father's hidden estate when we did."

"Your timing was perfect, Harvy. I haven't been so lucky, but my kids will be happy when it's complete. I don't want to leave a burden on their shoulders."

I looked into his face. "I understand. By the way, if you need a good lawyer, I can refer you to the guy who helped us do our voluntary disclosure."

He stared at me for a moment, then replied, "That's okay, Harvy. I have a lawyer I've been working with."

For a moment, I wondered if Mr. Duma was entirely straight about his actions. It crossed my mind that maybe he just wanted me to believe that he was no longer a money-hiding and tax-evading bandit.

Though I would never have said anything to Revenue Canada about Mr. Duma, I had once asked Charles, "Would the government be interested in knowing how tax-skirting people like my father hid money offshore?" I had been specifically thinking about the Independent University annuity agreement Dad had signed. Charles had responded without hesitation. "The government wouldn't be interested, Harvy. Unlike in the U.S., Canada has no law or benefits at this time concerning whistleblowers."

I looked at Mr. Duma and kept my voice low. "Your children are lucky you are doing this for them; that's very good of you." It didn't matter if he was telling the truth or not. My years of carrying my father's offshore albatross were now long behind me.

It then came to me that I had questions for Mr. Duma concerning the woman he had told me about when we had met for breakfast at the Alexis Nihon Plaza, the woman with whom Dad had had an illegitimate son. I wanted to know her name and the years in which the son had been born and then tragically died. I looked at Mr. Duma, "Can I ask you something?"

"Sure, Harvy. What is it?"

I hesitated for a moment, took a deep breath, and then said, "Actually, it's not important."

I had suddenly concluded that, concerning my father, it might be better if I didn't know some things.

* * *

My Abraham's Precious Legacy

Steve and I gazed into Dad's safety deposit box at our father's bank. My brother's first words were, "Since you got the Patek Phillipe from Dad, Harvy, can I have the white-gold Omega?"

I had expected the question. I nodded, "Sure, Steve." I felt the watch was reasonable compensation for my having gotten the Patek. Then again, Dad had given me the piece nearly 25 years earlier, but I didn't say that.

Earlier that day, in Dad's back office, I had claimed the brooch from Dad's mother. Steve took our mother's gold jewellery for his daughter. I took Dad's two gold rings, one of which was missing its diamond that wound up in a snowbank in front of his office—after Dad lost it when he threw a snowball at a black cat.

Now, in the cramped safety deposit box room of Dad's bank, Steve and I sorted what remained of our father's precious possessions. We created small piles of silver and gold coins that we figured to be of equal value. We flipped one of the valuable coins and took turns claiming individual stacks for ourselves. These Isaac and Ishmael brothers received rightful portions of our Abraham's precious treasure.

* * *

Two years after Dad's passing, I took my Patek to several high-end watch dealers in Montreal and Boston. I always thought that the watch's small face and thin alligator leather band didn't suit me. I was considering replacing it.

I anticipated an "ooh" or an "ahh" from every store owner and manager. I expected them to beg me to trade or sell it.

Over and over again, the proprietors said, "Mr. Simkovits, your Patek Philippe is a very exclusive piece." Though it was one of the thinnest watches in the world, it was among the plainest models available, not even significant enough to be featured in comprehensive catalogues of antique gold watches. Various store owners offered $1,000 to $1,800USD for the timepiece. They told me that Dad might have paid $500 for it in the 1970s, not the $5,000USD he had boasted of its value.

My heart hung heavy. Could Dad have been led to believe—or was he fooled to think—the Patek was worth much more than it was? His tendency for exaggeration now lingered past his death, resulting in my disheartenment. *There he goes; he did it again!* It hurt to know that he, intentionally or not, had played me once more. It irked me that the solid white-gold Swiss watch that my brother got may have been the more valuable timepiece. *I should have known by now that this was Dad's way.*

I never went back to Steve with my sour grapes about the watches we had received. I had made my bed with that Patek as I had done with Dad, and there was no point trying to change it.

Many years after Dad's death, the Patek still sits in my bank deposit box, again rarely seeing sunlight or starlight. Every year, I visit it on my father's birthday. It shares good company with the more modest gold coins Dad had bestowed on me over the years, along with my take from his safety deposit box. As I open my deposit box, I take a deep breath to try to recreate my father's affection for precious metal, though I never reached his level of collection, admiration, or portage. Outside of my wedding band, I only wear my MIT graduation ring—a symbol of my academic achievement.

There, in my box, also sits my grandmother's brooch. Its ruby-laden flower petals and zirconium centers remind me of my father's affection for the mother he hardly knew. I wonder how Dad might have been different had she not gotten ill and died when he was a toddler. Would her overt nurturing have balanced out his overbearing nature?

I, once again, open the long and slim, blue felt watch case that housed my ultra-thin timepiece. Once more, I attach its black alligator strap to my wrist. I twist my wrist around to see the watch from different angles. I think again about how Dad and I were the same and how we were different.

Living a life of hard work by day and being a gay reveler by night, my father enjoyed wearing the trappings of his success on his fingers, wrist, and tie. He was his best when he entertained his customers and compadres, buying drinks, meals, and songs for them at places like the Tokay and Troika.

Unlike Dad, I preferred to have my precious things tucked away. I was home for most suppers and in bed by eleven. I met colleagues and friends for coffee or lunch rather than for drinks and late nights. I became a kid-shuttling basketball- and soccer-Dad rather than a habitually absentee father.

My father's continual absence from our family's life made my younger heart yearn for him. I had wanted him to feel proud of my winning soccer record in high school and my academic achievement at MIT. I had wanted to gain his "Good boy, son!" and to breathe in the festive and self-confident air that surrounded him. As a professional, I now obtained pleasure from helping clients turn around challenging company situations. Maybe I wanted to impress them with my smarts as I had wanted to impress my father.

I look again at the Patek on my wrist. I frown. *Its small size still doesn't suit me.* As I now remove the watch from my wrist, I could hear my father say, "Be smarter than the rest." . . . "Don't let anybody take advantage of you." . . . "Become somebody, especially your own boss and man." . . . "Be generous to your friends, for you never know when you might need them." He might also add, "You can't trust anybody, even someone you know." . . . "You have to screw SOBs before they screw you."

I hope the Patek would continually remind me of my father's admirable qualities and how I might better express my love and appreciation to my wife and kids. Though Dad had sounder advice and portrayed a rigorous work and play ethic, I didn't want my children to emulate him. I'd never want my kids to have blind adoration for and unquestioning loyalty to me, especially if it sacrificed their belief in themselves. I'd never want to see them sheltered or locked in my shadow but to discover their natural light.

I trust that, deep down, my father would have wanted that too.

* * * *

Pelé Sunset

Nine years after Dad's passing, in the summer of 2009, Edo still lived in Košice. He was 78 years old and living alone. Eboya had died from cancer a few years earlier. On one warm late-August day that year, my third cousin, Dr. Alec Šimkovič, found Edo passed out on the floor of his condo. Alec immediately took him to the hospital, but Edo died that night.

I had planned to be in Košice that October to visit Edo and his relatives. I arrived there six weeks after Edo's passing, too late to participate in Edo's funeral. I met with Beatta, one of Edo's cousins from Dad's stepmother's side of the family. Beatta said that Edo's funeral had been lovely, and Dr. Šimkovič had paid for it.

Sadness was in her eyes when she added, "Edo's body was taken by Eboya's niece and nephew to be buried next to Eboya. They now lie side by side in a small village far away, the place where Eboya's family is from."

I never got to pay my respects to my uncle. I couldn't meet Eboya's family because neither Beatta nor I had a way to get in touch with them. All she knew was that they lived a day's train ride from Košice.

I wanted to hear more about what had happened to Edo. Beatta and I met Dr. Šimkovič for late afternoon tea. I had first encountered the doctor in 1993, on a trip I took with Dad, Elaine, and Steve to Czechoslovakia six months after Dad's stroke. Alec became Edo's physician and friend after my uncle had returned to Košice after living for twenty years in Canada.

When I had first seen Alec, I thought he resembled my brother. Now, sixteen years later, Alec still looked like Steve. Not only were his face and smile similar, but his gestures—the way he gently raised his hand when talking and placed his hand lightly on his chin when thinking—also mimicked my brother's motions.

Alec understood English but was shy to speak my language. He explained in Slovak what had happened to Edo. Beatta translated.

"I called Edo every morning just to see how he was doing," he started. "I phoned him that Friday morning, and there was no answer." He raised a palm. "When I got to Edo's condo, I found him on the bathroom floor. His face, still full of shaving cream, was contorted. It was clear that he had had a stroke." Alec looked at Beatta. "He was still breathing, so I got him to the hospital." He shook his head. "But Edo was gone by that evening."

I was surprised that Edo didn't last as long as Dad had. Though my uncles kept trim and fit, maybe his rich Slovak diet of kielbasa and dumplings, and his long-time propensity for the brew, cut short his life. Also, he had lived most of his days in Košice—primarily a steel-manufacturing town during and after the communist era. Then again, maybe strokes ran in the men of Simkovits lineage, though I knew Edo's father, my grandfather, had died of heart disease in his early 60s.

Soft-spoken as my brother, Alec added, "Sometime before he died, Edo told me that he wanted to be buried in Košice and not in Eboya's hometown. He said that his family is here and not there." Alec shook his head again. "But Edo never got to rewrite his will before he passed away." He looked my way. "At Edo's funeral, I asked Eboya's niece and nephew to bury Edo in Košice as he wanted. But they cited Edo's will and moved him halfway across the country. There was nothing I could do."

"That's too bad," I said. I leaned back in my chair and looked at Alec and Beatta. "I suspect that Edo's friends and relatives here will never go visit his grave there."

Both Alec and Beatta nodded.

Alec pulled an envelope out of his jacket. "Harvy, I did get permission from the niece and nephew to enter Edo's apartment with my key. I was able to retrieve this for you."

Alec handed me a thick package, and I opened it. It contained a mélange of photographs taken in Canada and Slovakia of Edo, Dad, Elaine, Steve, and me. The photos spanned thirty years. "This is all the photographs I could find," he added.

"That's so kind of you to get those for me. Might you still have access to the apartment? There are several photo albums and souvenirs from Boston that I had given Edo over the years. I'm wondering if I could get those back by which to remember him."

The doctor shook his head once more. "Very sorry, but the niece and nephew have changed the lock. I can't go there anymore."

"How do they have that right?" I asked. "You and I are more Edo's relations than they are."

The doctor shrugged. "They claim to be his legates. They had keys to his apartment and are now in control. It will be up to our Slovakia probate court to decide the ownership. There's nothing we can do until then."

I shook my head and again said, "That's too bad."

I looked into my third cousin's eyes. "My brother and I appreciate your taking care of Edo's funeral and service arrangements. We would like to contribute to those costs if you'd accept."

Dr. Šimkovič lifted his hand and responded, "It's not necessary."

It looked as if he were going to say more, but I interrupted. "If you don't want anything from us, then allow our government to help you."

I explained how Canada's pension plan paid $2500CAD toward a citizen's funeral expenses. The doctor's eyebrows rose. He said that he'd provide me receipts so that Steve could make an application on his behalf.

Beatta and I walked back to her apartment. As we talked along the way, I had an epiphany. I stopped in my tracks and turned to Beatta. "What's the process here in Slovakia for dealing with people's estates when they die?" I moved my hand toward my head and looked at her. "You and I know that Edo wasn't good at complicated things."

In reality, Edo had been a little simple-minded. He could sit for hours at a party and hardly say a word to anyone, that is, while he was sober. After having a couple of drinks—sometimes Dad putting that loaded handgun into his half-brother's hands—Edo staggered around the room. He'd say, "You're my best friend" to every man he knew, "I love you" to every woman, and "I'm now the big boss" to my brother and me. Only Dad or my mother could take the drink out of Edo's hand, sit him down like a child in the kitchen, and get strong coffee into him.

After Edo had returned to Slovakia twenty years ago, and his mother had passed away, Eboya straightened out her man. Beatta may not have known about Edo's drinking, but she must have known that Edo wasn't the brightest Simkovits. She had helped Edo with his correspondence and paperwork.

I looked at her. "What if Edo made a mistake in his will? Perhaps not everything is written properly regarding what goes to Eboya's relatives."

My short, thin, thirty-something cousin also stopped in her tracks and thought for a few seconds. "I went through something like this when my grandmother died not long ago." She looked at me. "A central office in each region handles all estates here in Slovakia. We have no executors as they have in other countries. When a person dies here, a regional magistrate from the court carries out the disposition of assets as prescribed in the will of the departed person."

"What if the person doesn't have a will or their will is flawed?"

She pointed my way. "Then, the assets are distributed through a prescribed formula that includes the deceased's closest family."

I touched her arm. "Steve, Emilia, and I are the closest family to Edo. How can we find out more about that probate process and have ourselves registered as possible legates?"

I was thinking like my shrewd and scheming father. But unlike Dad, I was seeking a legitimate angle. I looked at Beatta. "I'd like to see if we can put Steve's and my hat into Edo's estate ring. Edo's lawyer may not have written his will the way Eboya had wanted." I knew I was grabbing at a dead man's straw, but it wouldn't hurt to give a pull. "Might you know a lawyer who could help us in Košice?"

Beatta said she knew the attorney who had settled her grandma's estate. She grabbed her cell phone, called, and made an appointment for us to meet the next day.

My mind was thinking, maybe even scheming, but I felt it was for a good cause. For the sake of Edo's closest Košice kin, I was going to do what I could to get them some money from Edo's estate, if there was anything there to get.

The next day, the Košice lawyer heard my concerns about Edo and his will. He said I should register at the office where magistrates probate wills from the Košice region, and that office was only a few blocks away. He would fill out the registration papers for both my brother and me, and I could take the paperwork to that office along with my passport to prove my identity. He added that Steve would also have to confirm his identity, but he could do that later—if there were something in our uncle's estate for us.

I looked at the attorney while pointing at Beatta. "Would you be able to give Beatta power of attorney to act on my brother's and my behalf with the court, assuming a positive result transpires?"

The lawyer nodded. "Certainly!"

I looked carefully at him. "What would your work cost?"

"300 to 400 Euros," he said without hesitation.

My father would have hemmed and hawed about whatever price the guy quoted. I wanted this attorney motivated. "Okay," I nodded. "Let's do it."

When I returned to Boston, I called my brother and shared Edo's death and funeral details. I presented what I had done to register us at the probate court in Košice.

Steve responded, "Okay, Harvy. Good work. But what about Emilia; does she know?"

I responded quickly. "Why should we say anything to Emilia? The last time I saw Edo, he said that she never once visited or called him after Dad died." I took a long breath. "Anyway, she'll probably figure it out herself and go register as I did." My voice turned concerned. "Over there, whoever registers as an estate legate is public information. I wouldn't want to see her face when she sees our names in the registration book."

"I know what you mean, Harvy. She'll be surprised."

I responded, "Yes, I know, yet a part of me doesn't care what she thinks. Edo's closest relatives, like Beatta, deserve something from his estate. I'd hate to see everything go to Eboya's family, who, as far as I know, never did anything for Edo. If we see any money from him, then I want to give the bulk of my share to Edo's closest cousins, Miro and Beatta." I took a long breath. "I hope you also agree, Steve."

Dad had been the one who had created this situation with Edo. If he had left a decent bequest in his will to his half-brother, Edo wouldn't have kowtowed to Eboya's resolve to bequest his assets to her legates. I saw it as my duty to make amends where I could. I hoped Steve saw it that way too.

"We'll see, Harvy; we'll see," my brother said flatly.

I wasn't satisfied with his answer. "By the way, Steve, I spent 350 Euros for what I did with Beatta's lawyer in Košice. I expect you to pay half regarding my efforts on our behalf."

"Sure, Harvy, sure."

A couple of months later, Beatta emailed.

> I received a letter from the magistrate. It's good news for you and Steve. Edo's last will does not leave all his property to Eboya's relatives. In his will, Edo stated that his condo would go to them, but he added nothing about the money in his bank accounts. Those amounts must now go to Edo's closest relatives: you, Steve, and Emilia. And Emilia has registered herself at the court to share in that money.

Damn! She figured it out.
I emailed back.

> That is good news! Would you know how long the probate process will take and how much money Edo had?

A few days later, she emailed again.

> I checked with the magistrate who is handling Edo's estate. He said that most of Edo's money is in Canadian dollars, totaling about $65,000. And it typically takes six months from death for the court to distribute the funds. I also heard that this probate judge is very slow. He makes sure everything is in perfect order before he distributes any funds.

I wondered if the judge might be looking for a handout or gift. Such gestures had been the norm during Eastern Europe's communist days. I had heard my parents once say that some communist-party physicians took bribes from patients who wanted to expedite a physical examination or obtain a prescription.

Would I offer a bribe to this magistrate, as my father might have? I suspect Dad would have found a way to meet the guy and finagle the conversation to see whether the judge wanted a payoff.

But such things weren't my MO. Whether I wasn't skilled at doing what my father could do, or I didn't want to be like him, it didn't matter. I preferred to stay away from anything underhanded.

Weeks later, Beatta emailed once more.

> Eboya's niece and nephew are contesting Edo's will. They are saying Eboya and Edo had a joint bank account and that their aunt and uncle's money should only go to them. They are complaining that they don't have money to pay the monthly expenses on the apartment, and they need Edo's bank funds. The judge says he will have to correspond with Edo's bank regarding Edo's accounts. It could be a month or two before he gets a response. Please understand that this judge is strict with the rules, so Eboya's relatives may not have a case.

I had no idea how Eboya's niece and nephew looked, if they had children, or under what conditions they lived. My cousin Alec had said he met them only once, during Edo's funeral, just before they shipped Edo's body halfway across Slovakia to lie next to Eboya. Alec had provided no other particulars about them, and they never reached out to any of Edo's kin.

Not knowing anything more about them, I remained on my course.

* * *

Fourteen months after his death, Edo's will cleared Košice's probate. Though Eboya's niece and nephew retained Edo's condo (worth over 100,000 Euro) and everything in it, Steve, Emilia, and I were going to get Edo's cash. But there was one hitch, which Beatta wrote over email.

> Harvy, all three of the beneficiaries have to be at Edo's bank in Košice at one time to take out the money. Your brother has given me power of attorney to act on his behalf. Do you want me to represent you too? Or do you want to come to Košice and obtain your money along with Emilia and me?

I bristled at the thought of seeing my half-sister again. I emailed Beatta.

> I want to see you and my other relatives again, so I'm coming. I'll have to put on my best armour for Emilia.

Beatta responded.

> I very much understand.

It was on a sunny but cold morning in November 2010 when Beatta and I met Emilia on the steps of Edo's bank in downtown Košice. The tall and rotund Igor was there too. He followed his mother like a bear on a leash.

I had not seen those two for over a decade. I put on my best smile and reached out for Emilia's hand. "How are you?" I asked.

My half-sister put out her hand and took mine. Her face was as stiff as particleboard. Her hand felt like a cold, dead cod. "Fine, fine," is all she said.

Igor stood to one side and slightly behind his mother. His towering and robust form was like the character Hoss on the bygone TV western *Bonanza*. My half-nephew's face stayed blank as he offered a subdued "Hello."

This reunion isn't going to be a happy one, but I hope it will be civil. I looked at Igor's side to see if he carried a six-shooter, as the Hoss had carried, but saw no gun. *Harvy, stop being so skittish.*

We walked into the bank and up to the cashier. Beatta had come here the previous day to find out who we had to see. In front of the cashier's bulletproof glass booth, Edo's cousin stood between Emilia and me. *I wish I could be on the other side of this glass.* I wondered if a wave of Johnny-Simkovits-like anger would erupt through my half-sister or her son.

Igor had followed a few paces behind. He sat down on a small couch behind us. I looked again to see where his hands were.

During the next 45 minutes, Beatta managed the banking transaction. The three of us faced the cashier's booth. After fifteen minutes of discussion and paperwork with the cashier, I turned my head toward my half-sister and asked, "What's new with you, Emilia?" I kept my tone as pleasant as I could.

She kept her head and eyes toward the cashier and responded in her broken English, "Everything okay." Beatta asked her a few questions in Slovak. Emilia responded with only a few words and no facial expressions.

While the teller counted the money and had us sign forms, I turned to look at my half-nephew. "So, what are you doing these days, Igor?" I glanced at his wrist to see if he was wearing Dad's Rolex. He wasn't.

Igor looked at me with cold eyes. "A *leettle* of *dis*, a *leettle* of *dat*." I felt as if I were talking to a member of the mob.

Dad had a way about him in stressful situations. He could bribe people with his charm or his money. He could be humorous, offer a cigarette, or show his big Johnny grin to break the tension. Most people responded well to his advances. But I had neither his innate talent nor developed skill, and I sorely felt its lack today. Maybe Dad's malicious treatment of my mother— and the way he threw away friends when they no longer suited him—caused me to shun my father's best faces. Here at this bank, I wanted to finish the transaction and get out of my half-relations' sight.

I ended my inquiries and resigned myself to the cold shoulder coming from my closest kin in Košice. I didn't blame them. It wasn't their fault that it was this way. Before his death, Dad had probably promised Emilia and Igor an overstated chunk of his money. But he never told Steve or me about it or made such bequests in his will. Emilia probably thought she'd get all of Edo's cash, though a good part of it had come via the stipend Steve and I had given Edo after Dad's death. *The awful family web a failing father can weave!*

Then again, might Emilia have a rightful claim to all of Edo's money? If I had been in her shoes, might I feel cheated out of another inheritance? Did it make a difference that I was acting on behalf of my other Košice relatives?

Part of me felt sorry for my half-sister. She had expected a lot from her natural father, but he had fallen short. She may have felt jilted, but she had offered no voice to Steve or me regarding any claim to our father's estate.

If Emilia thought she was entitled to a larger share of Dad's assets, wouldn't she have told us what our father had promised her? Our mild-mannered Suzie had declared what our father had pledged to her, and we obliged her claim. I'm sure Steve and I would have listened to any reasonable plea Emilia would have provided, and we would have given her more.

Another part of me felt Emilia and Igor were getting what they deserved. I never saw her demonstrate any gratitude for what she received from our father. I suspected Emilia obtained money from her deceased mother, step-father, and husband, besides what Dad had given her over the years. She hadn't had to work for a living for the last two decades, from before the time I had met her.

My half-sister should feel lucky she didn't have to live her whole life behind a dark Johnny Simkovits shadow the way my brother and I had done. If only Emilia had hung less onto Dad's arm and shown a little more interest in Steve and me, then we could have felt more connected to her. Maybe Dad, in the end, had seen the greedy daughter in her and bestowed a rightful due. Then again, she probably saw me as covetous as I saw her.

Thanks, Dad, for bequeathing your unfinished family business. If you had shown a little more forethought regarding your kin, I might not be in this tense situation at this Košice bank. I kept thinking I was fair and just to those who deserved the most from Edo: his closest cousins in Košice. Or was I deluding myself?

When the money distribution was complete, Emilia, Igor, and I nodded at each other, said goodbye, and they walked out of the building. Beatta said she needed to talk to the manager—to transfer my brother's share to his bank in Canada. So she and I hung back.

After my relations exited the bank, Beatta turned to me. Her jaw was halfway to the floor. "I'm glad that's over. Did you see their faces? Like stone, both of them!"

After that day, I never saw or heard from Emilia or Igor again. If Beatta ever reencountered them in Košice, she never told me.

* * *

In the hours after that banking exchange, I created two gift envelopes and stuffed two-third of my newfound Euros into them. I gave one envelope to Beatta for the help she had given to Edo over the years and for the work she had done with the probate court. She immediately said, "No, you should take that for yourself. Edo was your uncle. It's rightfully yours."

I pushed the envelope into her palm. "No, Beatta, if Edo had been straight in his thinking, he would have wanted you to have this. You were a big help to him." I shook my head. "I don't need this money; it's for you."

She gave me a big hug. "Thanks so much, Harvy." She thought for a second. "I can use it for my honeymoon when my fiancée and I get married."

Later that day, I gave the second envelope to Edo's first cousin, Miro. Miro and his wife, Anastazia, were retired school teachers and lived off small pensions. They lived a few buildings away from Edo's condo. From the time Eboya had died, Miro called on Edo or had dinner with him every week. They had been as close as brothers from the time they were kids.

Miro, Anastazia, and I went through a similar ritual as Beatta and I had performed. I had to insist that they take the money. They gave me big smiles and hugs. I said, "Next year, I'll bring my whole family to Košice to see you."

Anastazia offered, "When you come, we'll cook supper—chicken paprikash!" They knew it was one of my favourite Hungarian dishes.

I smiled, "For sure."

I didn't know how my father would have handled this situation. Would he have carried out what I had accomplished? Or would he have allowed the money to go to his daughter? Would he shake my hand or shake his fist at me for what I had done?

My brother later told me that he had given Beatta 1000 Euros for her work with the probate court. He took the rest, saying, "I need the money. I've put most of my inheritance into my new business, and I'm down a lot since the Great Recession."

Same old Steve story. "That's too bad, Steve," I said. "Hope you can get out from under it."

I hoped I had done the right thing with Edo's cash. *Thanks, Dad, for placing another family conundrum at my feet.*

I utilized the final third of my portion of Edo's inheritance to bring my family to Slovakia the following summer, in 2011.

We reunited with my Košice cousins, and I got to see Dr. Šimkovič once more. Other than buying him dinner, I didn't offer him any of Edo's estate. He was well-to-do in Košice. I believed I would have hurt his pride if I had given him any cash. By now, he had received a check from the Canadian government for Edo's funeral expenses, and that may have been enough.

Unlike Dad, who offered handouts indiscriminately to his relatives, I wanted to be more mindful of my giving. Over dinner, I looked at pictures of Alex's daughter and grandchild. The smile on Alex's face was priceless.

Anastazia cooked that chicken paprikash for my family. It was delicious—as good as my mother's. My kids devoured her cooking and mopped up the creamy sauce with clumps of rye bread, and asked for more.

As my father had done for his extended Košice family, I took Miro, Anastazia, Beatta, and her fiancée out to supper with my family. We went to a traditional Slovak restaurant on Košice's main street.

Before we headed to the restaurant, we walked around town. My parents' city had changed immensely since the Soviet communists left the country twenty-two years earlier. Košice was now a popular tourist destination that sported cobblestone sidewalks and sidewalk cafes. Taverns stood against the old, thick stone walls that had protected the city from the Ottoman invasions of centuries ago. Before WWII, my mother's family had lived in a brick house that stood against one of those walls, in a Jewish section at the edge of the inner city. When the family fled Košice for Budapest during WWII, the Nazis turned their abandoned dwelling into a horse stable.

After my mother and her kin had returned to Košice post-WWII, their home was no longer livable space. They moved into an apartment next door, a building abandoned by fleeing fascists. Today, their original brick home was a storehouse. The apartment building had been renovated and turned into a city school.

In the ensuing post-WWII decades, Košice shuttered its synagogues. It made me melancholy to think that Košice now had very few Jews and a dwindling population of Hungarians. There was no one left here from my mother's family. They had died during WWII, escaped the country during the Soviet era, or passed away before the end of the communist regime.

After the Communists had departed Eastern Europe in '89, Košice went through significant gentrification. Rows of dull grey concrete apartment buildings—that I remembered from my childhood—were transformed into bright buildings with colourful exteriors. The city's downtown now boasted a beautiful fountain by the old Opera House, where my uncle had worked.

That artistic fountain displayed a sound and light show that played at the strike of every daytime and evening hour. The water danced to chamber music coming from speakers strategically hidden in the surrounding shrubbery and trees. After dusk, lights flashed in sync from beneath the fountain and through ground fixtures around the pool. It was a grand display for what previously had been an unassuming city. The mayor of Košice had initiated the city's revitalization, and he leveraged that accomplishment a few years later to become the President of Slovakia.

Knowing how the Communists had allowed everything here to deteriorate, I was impressed at what my parents' hometown had become. But it was sad that neither of my parents had gotten to experience their city's revival. I imagined them smiling in the heavens because I had once more come to visit the place of their birth.

Over supper, my kids had crispy Wiener Schnitzels, doused in the juice of half a lemon—also my favourite dish when I had been their ages. When the waiter served the main course, everyone raised their wine glass. "Thank you, Harvy, for bringing us together."

I raised my glass to them. "No. It's Edo and my father who we should thank." I then told everyone how Edo's close Canadian friends called him "Pelé" or "Brazil" because he liked to play soccer and tan his body to a deep bronze. My relatives smiled; they also knew Edo's summer habits.

I lifted my glass a little higher and pointed it toward the reddening sky and setting summer sun. I spoke in Hungarian. *"Köszönöm nagyon szépen Edo bácsi, Pelé, és kedves apa.* [Thank you very much, Uncle Edo and dear Dad.]"

Everyone grinned as they said, *"Egészségedre!* [To your health!]"

Had I been my father, I might have kept my glass in the air and responded with the almost indistinguishable, *"Egész seggétre!* [To your ass!]"

Instead, I looked at the sky and smiled.

* * *

A couple of years later, Elaine and I had supper together during one of my winter trips to Florida. Out of nowhere, she said, "It took a long time, Harvy, but I've been able to forgive your father in my mind. I'm finally at peace with that man and all that led to the end of our marriage."

It's good that someone who had been close to my father was over him.

She continued without prompting. "However, of all the people, I still have difficulty with that Princess Emilia. The mention of her and Igor's names makes my blood boil." She took a deep breath. "The way that woman hung onto your father's arm, and the way she never lifted a finger to help when they visited our home, she was so spoiled. And the way she cut the meat on her teen son's plate, she did the same to him."

Elaine looked away and then back at me. It was now twenty years since those events, and she recalled them as if they had occurred yesterday. She went on. "Talk about them being opportunists! Emilia had your father wrapped around her little finger. We were always shopping for her, her kids from her two marriages, and her mother—be it slippers, bathrobes, or who knows what else. And that woman was getting cash from Johnny too. I guess it was good for her while it lasted."

Elaine was a good barometer for me. I looked at her. "I get it, Elaine." I pointed her way. "Did I ever tell you what happened with Edo's will?"

Her eyebrows rose, and she looked at me with deep interest.

I told her what had transpired with Edo's estate in Košice.

Glaring at me, she said, "It's a never-ending story with your father. I'm glad Emilia didn't get all she wanted. I'm pleased that you were able to put her in her place in her not getting more money than she did."

As we finished our meal, Elaine added a spicy observation. "One person I feel a little sorry for is Suzie. I understand your Dad's other Slovak friend, Kate, had tried to steal Johnny away and get him to marry her, though she professed to be Suzie's friend."

For many winters, Kate had visited my father and Suzie at their Deerfield condo. She had been a big help to Suzie because Dad never liked to be left alone for more than thirty minutes at a time. He'd get anxious and peeved, and then he'd badger Suzie for being gone for so long. Kate accepted the sitting-with-Johnny responsibility while Suzie went grocery shopping. Yet Dad told me, "*Dese* two *vivem* yackety-yack all the time!"

I couldn't refrain from chuckling at Elaine's declaration about Kate wanting to make moves on my father. "Where the heck did you hear that, Elaine? Did my father tell you while he was still alive?"

"No," she said. It was another Slovak woman friend of Johnny's who had told me. Her name is Marie."

I smiled. "I don't know Marie, but I think she's mistaken. From what I saw when I visited Dad in Deerfield, it was the other way around. Dad was the one who was making the moves." I took a swig of my drink. "He told me he was getting fed up with Suzie and wanted to leave her for Kate."

My hand made a fist for the anguish that my father had created for his women. "One time, while Kate, Dad, and I were in the building's elevator, he propositioned her right in front of me. He told her how much he loved her; he went on and on like a schoolboy." I sighed. "I finally stepped in and changed the subject to stop him from acting like a fool, embarrassing all of us."

Elaine's eyes glared at me. "That's funny. Marie first told me that Johnny had proposed to her about living with him after our divorce." She sighed too. "After Marie had said no, Johnny asked Kate. But Kate also told him she wasn't interested, so your father found Suzie. Marie later told me that Kate changed her mind and wanted to be with your father."

I shook my head and smiled. "I don't believe it. Kate was too smart to get herself involved with my father. She knew what Suzie was going through with him." I laughed. "Anyway, it's nice of you to give me more to write about. It goes to show, no one knows the whole story regarding Johnny Simkovits."

More years later, it occurred to me that, at that Košice bank with Emilia and Igor, I hadn't asked my nephew why he never wanted to go back to school on his grandfather's dime. His reaction would have told me whether his mother had even told him about Steve's and my offer.

Chalk it up to a lost opportunity. I'd never know, but I guess I hadn't cared.

* * * *

Sibling Setup

Long before Edo's passing, and one year to the day after Dad's death, my father's closest family and friends gathered by his gravesite in their Sunday best. Steve came with his spouse; Suzie came with Kate; I was there with Gloria.

Abe, a close business associate and a good friend of my father, was there too. He had spent much time with our father during the last decade of his life. Abe and Dad had gotten together in Montreal almost every week for lunch, and Abe had visited Dad every winter in Florida.

Abe was one of the few people who could take my father and Suzie out for supper and be permitted to pay the bill without a protest from Johnny. After Dad had died, Abe accepted without hesitation to become JHS's third director, in case my brother and I had disagreements.

Though we were a small group at Dad's gravesite, we seven had been the ones closest to my father in the last years of his life, except maybe for Mr. Duma. We gathered for the gravestone unveiling.

The fall day was cold and windy. *Why is the weather always dreary whenever I have to deal with something regarding you, Dad?*

Steve stood next to our father's new grey granite headstone. Its size was over two coffins wide and nearly two high. My brother had wanted the massive monument to cover the six-person plot (two wide and three deep) that Dad had bought for himself and our family.

I looked down at the otherwise barren gravesite. *Hell, if Gloria and I would be buried here with Dad and Steve.* That wouldn't be heaven for me.

We stood in a semicircle around Dad's site. Steve unfolded a piece of paper. He was cashing in on my promise to allow him to perform our father's headstone unveiling, considering I had done Dad's eulogy a year earlier. Other than Steve saying some words today, there was no other service planned.

Steve closed his eyes and recited a prayer. I looked at my father's large gravesite and massive headstone. *I guess you like to be the big shot even in death, huh, Dad? Your other son wanted to present you that way too—he was the one who ordered this stone for you. I might have left you with a pile of cracked rocks.*

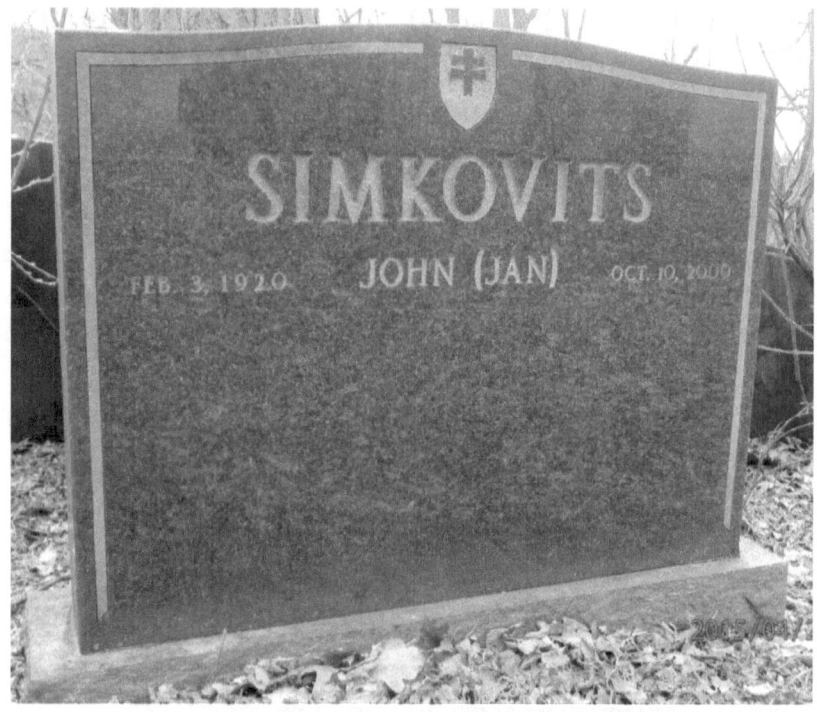

Our father's headstone was as stark and incomplete as the feeling in my heart. It was different from our mother's gravestone in the Jewish cemetery. Other than Dad's full name and the dates he lived, we had no words on his stone to describe who he was, his personality or achievements. Only the Slovakia crest was situated at the monument's apex, above his name, to indicate his heritage.

Steve and I couldn't conceive of anything to write about our father, or maybe we wanted to leave lots of space under his name where we would write names of those who would lie here with him. For me, the open space on that monument symbolized our dad now being alone, something he hated in life. Outside of Steve and maybe his wife, the rest of us weren't planning to join him here. But if Steve changed his mind, our father's remains might lie here forever alone on Montreal's Mount Royal hillside.

After saying his prayer, my brother glanced at his paper. He seemed unprepared, his eyes searching for words. For the next several minutes, his speech meandered. He spoke of our father's survival of WWII, his escape from communism, and his immigration to Canada with our mother with nothing more than $50 in his pocket. Steve offered how Dad had made a big success of himself in business here in Canada.

My brother spoke disjointedly, as a jittery corporal might speak of an esteemed general. He mentioned Dad's devotion to the Slovak Church and community. He added how our father had helped many immigrants from his country. He said how Dad was a gregarious entertainer, generous to his friends. As Steve had done at Gloria's and my wedding seven years earlier, his talk became a ramble, with many "ahs" and "ums" rolled in.

I couldn't believe my ears. Gloria and I looked at each other. We were astonished at my big brother's tender tone and his sticky-sweet sentences. One would have thought our father was Pierre Elliott Trudeau or Jean Drapeau (a former mayor who brought the '67 World's Fair and '76 Olympics to Montreal). From my brother's repeated hesitations, which flickered on the edge of his river of praise, I guessed that he held conflicted feelings about his forbearer. He was going on like a guilt-ridden Hamlet.

I bit my tongue at Steve's display. I didn't want to break my assurance to let him take the lead at this unveiling. After over ten minutes of us standing with stone faces and jittery feet at my brother's long-winded accolades, Abe broke in. "Steve, your father wasn't perfect. He had his difficult sides too."

I was grateful that Abe came forward. I continued to keep my mouth shut, and so did Gloria. I stared hard at Steve. *Stop your damn overcompensation! Dad was successful, but he was no saint.*

For the next few seconds, Steve said nothing. I didn't know whether or not he would say more, but I didn't hesitate. I grabbed Gloria's arm, and we turned to walk back to our car. We'd wait there to say goodbye to everyone.

My wife, a psychotherapist, held my arm tightly. She spoke quietly into my ear while we walked away from the gravesite. "It looks like your brother is still holding onto a lot of stuff regarding your father."

I nodded. I surmised that my brother's constant torment of our father in life (and the other way around) had gotten the better of him today. Dad was still living deep in the psyche of his first son. And I didn't want to fool myself about my father still living in this son too.

May our respective saviours help us survive you, Dad.

* * *

If my brother and I were to deal effectively with what remained of JHS, we had to get along. There were still five properties that the company owned, Dad's factory building plus four sizable land acreages around Montreal and Ottawa. It could take years for us to dispose of raw land in the current down market or develop those acres if we went that route.

Over the decades, Dad had systematically placed those properties under JHS's corporate roof. Years before his death, my father and his accountant, Roger Delliard, had told Steve and me, "There's no personal estate tax in Canada. But when people die here, their estate has to pay a final income tax as if everything they own had sold on the day of their death."

My father looked at us, his eyes narrow and intense. "If my properties would stay in my possession, then you might be forced to sell some of them to pay my final income taxes. If they remain in JHS—a corporation that can live forever—then you can defer capital gains taxes until you dispose of each property, one by one."

He gazed our way with soft, fatherly eyes. "I hope you two will stick together after I'm gone. That way, JHS can be a bank of assets for anything you want to do in business." Though Dad knew that Steve and I were not friends, he still hoped we would maintain the legitimate property legacy he had conceived and built.

Over the ensuing years, while at WISE and in my independent consulting practice, I worked with many owner-managed companies, including family-owned businesses as ours had been. I had helped many business partners, including siblings and cousins, mend their differences. Having learned well from Moe Gross, I enabled owners to work together to leverage their businesses in supporting their privileged lifestyle and giving them stature in their community. The most successful companies were those whose partners laboured to make their relationships work and business last.

In my situation with Steve, I wasn't sure that I wanted our sibling partnership to continue. Dad had placed a wedge between his sons, and he might have lodged it too deeply.

Soon after Dad's passing, Steve and I were at our corporate lawyer's office. We were there to restructure JHS's ownership into our names. My brother turned my way. "Harvy, can you allow me to be the big brother, letting me be President of JHS?"

Our attorney, Sam, was our contemporary. (Dad's business friend, Abe, had recommended Sam after Dad had let go of Mack.) The attorney looked at me and said, "Technically, Harvy, it would be better for Steve to be President. That way, JHS can look more like a Canadian-owned company."

He pointed my way. "If you were President, then JHS would appear more like an American-owned corporation. JHS then risks being taxed at a higher rate, as a foreign corporation operating in Canada." He pointed our way. "Even though you and Steve are 50-50 partners, you want to demonstrate to the government that JHS is Canadian owned and operated."

I thought for a moment. "Okay. Then let's make me both Vice President and Secretary-Treasurer of the company."

My brother turned briskly to our lawyer. "Can he do that, have both those positions?"

"You can do anything you want," Sam said. "One of you could have all three positions, but that's not common or recommended for your corporation's size. And, if Harvy has both those positions, I'd advise having a third corporate director in addition to the two of you. It should be a person you trust, someone who could help settle disputes. As your corporate attorney, I wouldn't recommend it to be me." Had Mack been our lawyer, I'm sure he would have written himself in wherever he could.

Steve and I nodded. My brother looked my way again. "But why do you want to have both of those positions, Harvy?"

I looked at him, my eyes intense. "It's simple, Steve. A vice president carries no real power in the corporation. They're only there to act on the president's behalf if and when the president can't fulfill his role. On the other hand, the secretary-treasurer has signing authority over some of the company's financial affairs." I turned to our lawyer. "Isn't that right?"

Sam nodded. "Yes, that's true. But the president can commit the corporation to contracts during its business operations. Only if there are major structural changes in the company, like issuing or redeeming shares, would the secretary-treasurer carry any real clout." He looked at my brother. "The secretary-treasurer must sign off on those kinds of corporate changes."

I figured that structural changes would be a rare occurrence for JHS, considering it was a holding company of just cash and property assets, and it had only two common shareholders. But my carrying of both the VP and Secretary-Treasurer positions was better than having only one of them. I looked at my brother, "I accept you being JHS's President. And outside of my taking on the other positions, we can ask Abe to be our third director."

Steve didn't hesitate. "Yes, I agree with you regarding Abe." Steve was as aware as I that we didn't always agree on things. Abe would be someone neutral to go to if we had a severe conflict. Dad, too, had wanted that for us.

My brother's voice stayed flat as he gave a half-smile. "And I can accept your being both JHS's president of vice and treasurer of secretaries."

Sam and I half-smiled back. Though Steve's humour was a little off-key, my wife had told me, more than once, that mine could be that way too.

I had one more condition on my mind. Steve might have trouble with it, but it was important to me. "Steve, I'd like to set a limit on the size of cheques you can sign as President. Any cheques larger than, let's say $5,000, should have a second signature from either Rob or me."

Steve's eyebrows rose as if I had unexpectedly slapped him in the face.

We had earlier agreed that Rob should remain part-time with JHS. As Dad's almost third son, Rob was the most knowledgeable about our JHS properties. I felt he'd inform me if Steve planned to make a foolish move with JHS's money. Steve had loaned money to friends and never got repaid. He had also overly trusted a business partner, and it had burned him.

My brother glared at me. "Isn't $5,000 kind of arbitrary, Harvy? Is there a reason you don't trust me?"

I was unfazed. "There's never a concern about trust when there's a system of accountability in place. You know that, Steve." Neither of us said it, but we both knew what had happened in my brother's previous ventures.

Steve thought for a few seconds. "What if we make it $10,000, Harvy? I don't want to have to come to you or Rob for every little thing."

Steve did have to pay many bills to maintain our JHS properties. "Okay, Steve, as long as you keep me up to date with the goings-on in the company. As President, you have a responsibility to your equal shareholder."

"Okay, Harvy." His words sounded hollow, but I said nothing about it. Being sons of Johnny certainly didn't instill unwavering trust and confidence between us. I was glad Sam was there to witness our agreement.

Our attorney said little during our conversation. That was good because Steve and I seemed to be working things out. After we had signed updated corporate minutes that included our new positions, Steve turned my way once more. "So, what's your hope for JHS and our future together?"

I had to hand this one to Steve. He hit the family-business nail on the sibling-partner head before I did. I had been thinking about that question for years. Could Steve and I have a future together in Dad's holding company? Could he and I work to develop the properties that JHS had in its asset corral? If I had a brother I respected and felt he also valued me, then I might have enjoyed doing property development projects with him for years to come. We had a valuable asset that we could put to work for our benefit.

But many things were working against us, even beyond my personal feelings about Steve. Though he saw himself better than Dad, I knew that neither he nor I were the shrewd and tenacious businessman our father had been. Given our distant and tenuous relationship and living under two different tax regimes, continuing a Canadian partnership might become onerous for an American resident like me.

I didn't want to say it, but could I even trust my brother? There was much patriarch water under our family bridge. Could we continue our brotherly truce as we had done in managing our parents' estates? Could we overcome our Simkovits history? I didn't think Steve would steal from our company—he took the Ten Commandments too seriously. But there was nothing in his religion that would stop him from doing something senseless.

I avoided answering Steve's inquiry directly and turned to Sam. "What would be the options for Steve or me to separate ourselves from JHS? If I decide not to stick it out in the company, I want to know what we could or should do in that case."

I pointed to my brother and then myself. "It's unlikely that Steve and I will have the kind of money to buy each other out. And we don't even know the fair market value of most of the properties that JHS retains. Other than JHS's old factory building, the rest is a hodge-podge of land in the outskirts of Montreal and Ottawa."

Steve nodded his agreement. Our father had left a motley crew of assets. He had been trying for years to sell off many if not most of those properties, zoned commercial, residential, one even as green space. There was an old family idiom that I felt applied: "If you want your children to spurn your legacy, then leave them property."

Sam looked at me, his voice calm and collected. "The best way for one of you, perhaps even both of you, to get your money out of JHS would be for JHS to redeem your shares. Based on the current book value or fair market value, the corporation could offer what your shares are worth. JHS can pay you outright from its cash reserves to redeem those shares, subsequently cancelling those shares in your corporate books, as we did with your father's preferred shares at his death." He glanced at Steve. "What remains in the company would then be the property of the remaining shareholder."

Years ago, when Dad's lawyer Mack was still in the JHS picture, he had drafted a "shotgun" buy-sell agreement between Steve and me. That simple contract stated that one of us could offer the other a specific price for their shares. Thus, Steve could contractually say, "Harvy, I'd be willing to buy you out for $X." If I refuse to accept that price, thinking the number was low, then I would be automatically obliged to pay him that amount to purchase his shares. Either one of us could pull the trigger on that shotgun, forcing one to buy out the other.

Though the shotgun buy-sell had sounded intriguing, my brother didn't want to sign that agreement. He didn't want a legal firearm to our heads, especially when the value of JHS's property holdings would be hard to calculate. I, too, stood with my brother regarding that onerous arrangement.

Steve and I would be better off maximizing JHS's assets' value and then share equally in that higher value. Our father's foresight and hope regarding JHS made sense in that regard. Neither Steve nor I wanted to feel disadvantaged by selling out of JHS early and at an arbitrary shotgun price.

Sam looked at me with intensity. "As a Canadian non-resident, you would have to pay a 15% Canadian withholding tax on your shares' capital gain when you take your money out of JHS." He pointed to the company minute books sitting on the table. "I know that your cost of ownership was negligible. Thus, you'd have to pay Canadian withholding taxes on the redemption value of your shares. And you might have additional federal and state taxes to pay in the U.S."

"You Americans don't pay much in taxes down there, right?" Steve quipped as he grinned.

I cringed inside. My brother and father had many times kidded about my paying lower tax rates in the U.S. Though there was some truth to that, I felt they never took in the bigger picture. There were high social security and Medicare taxes, state taxes, and onerous tax rules for ex-pats living stateside. Since I moved to Boston, I had to pay a tax lawyer every year to perform complicated reporting to the IRS and the U.S. Department of Treasury regarding my foreign corporate holdings. My shareholdings in our little Canadian holding company compared to holding significant ownership in an American multinational corporation.

There was so much extra reporting for resident aliens holding foreign assets that it could feed an army of tax lawyers. Dad might complain, "That's the problem when most politicians are lawyers; they work to feed their kind." Those onerous U.S. tax rules would also restrict how Steve and I could retrieve our money from JHS, but I didn't want to traverse that cross-border tax bridge today. Steve and I needed to focus on the status and disposition of JHS's properties to raise enough cash to buy me out from the company.

I sidestepped my brother's tax quip and looked at Sam. "What if we don't know the true value of the company's assets? We own properties where we can only guess their worth."

The lawyer responded. "Then you may have to wait until you sell those properties, pay the requisite tax within the corporation, which nets to 25% of the capital gain, and then redeem your shares when you turn enough of your JHS assets into cash."

I had heard enough. I turned to my brother. "Listen, Steve. I don't think you and I are the types to develop property; at least I know I'm not. Maybe we should work to sell (or just partially develop so we could more effectively sell) the properties JHS owns, and then we can pay ourselves the proceeds from that." I looked him square in the eyes. "It could take years to get that done, considering the recent dot-com bust that's affected both Canada and the U.S."

It hadn't been considerate of Dad to die right in the middle of an economic downturn. Maybe his ghost and the ghost of our mother would enjoy seeing her sons tied together awhile longer.

I continued. "I think it would be my long-term goal to get out of JHS and see us separated, but we have a lot of time to talk about that. Let's focus on monetizing our JHS properties. Maybe we could develop them to a point where we can reap a bigger return."

Steve nodded. "Okay, Harvy. I'd be happy to see us out of these various holdings. Maybe we should start by putting Dad's old factory building on the block. I'm developing some business ideas and could use those proceeds."

You'd better not drag JHS and me into anything sour.

Steve looked at Sam. "As you know, JHS is having trouble with its current manufacturing tenant who is leasing our factory building. Our building expenses are growing, and our tenant isn't paying his rent. He owes us many months, but he is claiming poverty. He says he's expecting a big contract to come in, after which he can pay us. But so far, he offers only promises."

That was a good segue out of our talking about Steve's and my eventual split. I didn't want to say anything about not trusting my brother. Who knows, we might build a tenable trust if we worked together to sell our JHS's properties for a decent gain.

But the thought of being tied to Steve for the rest of my life soured my stomach. Dad had carried Tums lozenges in his jacket pocket to calm his acidic stomach after a hearty meal. Tied to my brother, I didn't want to pop Tums like candy for the rest of my life.

I looked at Sam too. "Okay, so what can we do as landlords to deal with this tenant who isn't paying his rent?"

* * * *

Day of Redemption – The Beginning

In late 2002, two years after Dad's death, Steve called. He was jovial. "Hi, Harv! Did I tell you that I found a partner, and we are going into business?"

Of course, you didn't tell me. "No, what's it all about?" I said.

Steve was exuberant in his low-key way. "We're going to import and distribute motor scooters and ATVs [all-terrain vehicles] manufactured by a Korean company. Our company will be called Canadian Motor Sports."

Typical for my brother, and like our father, Steve never asked for my advice or opinion before jumping into something. My voice didn't quite match his enthusiasm. "That's interesting, Steve. How did you get into this? What's your arrangement with your partner, if you don't mind my asking?"

Steve obliged. "I know Andrew from our church. He approached me because he heard that the Canadian distributorship was available for the Korean product. He knows I've been looking for a project to get into."

For sure! My brother had been advertising himself to his church friends like our father had done with his Slovak community, telling them how he could help if anyone needed money to borrow. Steve had "put on the drum" (as our father used to say) his desire to find a business venture.

Steve continued. "Andrew and I will be 50-50 partners, with each of us putting in startup capital. He'd handle the outside marketing and sales while I'd handle the inside purchasing, warehousing, and company accounting and financing. The bank and I will be financing the inventory, but that should be no problem."

"How is that? Motorized vehicle inventory can get expensive. You'll need warehouse space to rent too."

"That's the great thing, Harvy. We'll be buying from our Korean supplier via a letter of credit, payable thirty days after the product lands in Canada. However, we will be pre-selling the product to dealers who will have their inventory financed through GE Capital." He was as exuberant as ever. "We'll only sell to solid dealers who can get approved financing, so we'll know they are good for the money. When our dealers get delivery, then GE will pay us before we have to pay on the letter of credit to Korea."

I could sense Steve smile through the phone. "We'll have our money from our customers before we have to pay our Korean supplier. Thus, our business won't need much financing, except for maybe our spare parts inventory and other start-up costs."

Smells too good, my father might have said. "I do hope it will work out that way, Steve," I offered. "By the way, what will make your business better or different from your competitors, like Honda or Kawasaki? Won't you be selling into a marketplace that has a lot of dominant players?"

Steve had an answer. "We'll start by coming in at the low end of the product line, with scooters and ATVs. We aren't going head to head with the big guys' bread-and-butter lines." He was on a roll. "Our costs from Korea will be such that we can undercut our competition by a couple of hundred dollars per unit wholesale. As we become successful, we'll move up the food chain to small gas-powered motorcycles and maybe electric scooters."

He took a long breath. "Also, we will have one big advantage that none of the competitors have."

I played along. "Okay, Steve; what's that?"

"If our customers commit to using special engine oil that CMS will recommend and provide, then we can offer them a two-year product warranty instead of only one year. We will be the first ones to do that in Canada."

My voice rose a tad. "Wouldn't a two-year warranty be expensive? And can't your competitors do the same?"

His voice didn't falter. "As I said, Harvy, the special oil we'll use will cut down on any engine problems, the largest source of warranty issues. Andrew says our competitors won't do the same because they'd have to do it for their whole motorcycle line, which would be too costly for them."

But companies like Honda aren't stupid. They could do what they want to undercut you if you get uppity with them. I worked to poke other holes into my brother's bright business balloon. "But aren't scooters a seasonal business, selling only in the warm months. What are you going to do for the rest of the year?"

Steve came back. "Andrew and I have done a preliminary plan. We figure we'll have to sell 600-800 units per year to break even, including paying our salaries and the interest on my loan to finance the company's initial inventory. I feel we can do even better, and it'll be money in our pockets."

It seemed as if my brother had had the angles covered, or was he fooling himself? Though Steve now had his executive MBA, I wondered how much of this business talk was coming from him rather than Andrew. "Okay, Steve. I wish you luck with it. And I hope you'll be careful."

"Thanks, Harvy, and I will."

Then something came that I didn't expect. "By the way, Harvy, remember how Dad arranged for us to get a quarter of his estate every five years, starting from when he died?"

After Dad's passing, my brother and I put Dad's cash assets into a John Simkovits Trust. Steve and I would get the trust's income every year, plus a quarter of the capital every five years. I had suggested that arrangement with Dad when he had asked my help with his will, seven years before he died. "Yes," I said cautiously.

"Well, I need the second installment now, a few years ahead of schedule. Can we do that for both of us? You know, I haven't been working since Dad died. This opportunity is my chance to do something with that Queens University MBA I received years ago."

Steve had been waiting in the wings with his diploma since the mid-1990s. He hadn't had a job after getting his degree. I didn't know why he hadn't considered working for another company before spreading his business wings on another private venture. Maybe my brother was too independent to find a regular job, as I had strived for in my own consulting business.

But I had worked many years at WISE to learn the consulting ropes before going out independently. Was Steve trying to skip an internship before taking the plunge with Dad's money into another business gamble?

Maybe he thought he had what it took, having worked over a decade for our father, plus a few more for a couple of other small manufacturers in which Dad had placed him. Dad had many times said, "Work for yourselves so you can get all the benefit." But one could also get all of the losses. I was glad I was in a professional service business that required little capital investment. The kind of business Steve was thinking about needed significant outlays.

"I thought you didn't need much capital for your business, Steve." I stayed away from confronting my brother's true motivations. He'd never listen to me anyway. "And can't your new partner chip in more?"

"Unfortunately, Andrew has no more money to put into this besides his initial investment. He has a big family to feed."

I guess there are no big Mormons pockets in Montreal other than yours, Steve.

My brother continued. "We have startup costs that I'll be financing, in addition to our inventory. Andrew and I have agreed that our new company will pay me 8% on the money I'd put into the business as working capital. We're not taking any salaries until we can sell our products when the season starts next year, but I need cash now. We'll get a bank line of credit too, but that'll take a little time to arrange."

I kept on poking at my brother's idea. "Don't banks want to see two or three years of profitable operations before they provide financing?"

Steve took another long breath. "We'll see, Harvy; we'll see. We are working on a financial plan to take to the Bank of Montreal. But for the interim, I'm sure you don't want me to borrow from JHS, so I'll need my next installment from Dad's trust."

This situation was what my father had feared—that Steve would sink money into questionable projects and then come up short. As trustees of Dad's estate, Steve and I could do anything we wanted with Dad's money as long as we agreed. We were three years away from the second payout from Dad's trust. *Too bad Dad didn't agree to have his notary, Peternik, be our executor. I then wouldn't be put in this precarious position with my brother.*

I realized this was a defining moment in repairing my relationship with Steve. If I said no to his request and cited Dad's will, or if I questioned him on what happened to the first payment he received from Dad's trust (perhaps he gave much of it to his church), he could make my life more difficult regarding JHS. In Canada, he had certain tax advantages that I didn't have in the U.S. regarding taking capital gains out of our company. If I said no to him now, he could later make it harder for me to ease my U.S. tax burden regarding my extrication from JHS.

There was another consideration. Dad had wanted me to be my brother's keeper, a watchdog to prevent Steve from losing the money our father had left us. I detested having to play that role. It wasn't my job to keep my eyes on my brother's affairs, be it in business, church, or family. Let him give all his money to his church or waste it on a fool's venture for all I cared.

I wondered whether my sarcasm—even ire—toward my brother was indeed mine or something Dad had implanted. I didn't give it a second thought for now. If Steve wanted to sink his half of our father's estate into a pot of fool's gold at the end of a business rainbow, then who was I to stand in his way? He was an adult and not a toddler; he'd live or starve based on his decisions. Would Steve even listen if I tried to sway him away from a business I wouldn't touch? Then again, he might become a big success in his circles. *Should I give him the opportunity to prove me wrong?*

The money Steve wanted from Dad's estate would eventually be his. There were two additional installments to come in eight and thirteen years. "Okay, Steve. I don't mind giving us the next installment early, as long as we don't involve any of JHS's money in your venture at any time."

Steve almost chuckled. "Sure, Harvy, sure. I won't touch JHS assets for any project of mine."

From your Mormon mouth to God's ears.

* * *

Our father's aura continued to hang around Steve and me like stinking Hungarian salami in a butcher shop. Steve wasn't the only one with something to prove. Each of us sought acknowledgement from the other, with both of us standing in for our father.

I wasn't fully aware of my motivations at the time, but deep down, I wanted to show my older brother that I, too, was capable. I desired his respect and acknowledgement that I had never received from him. From the moment Steve and I took over JHS, I exerted my opinions about how Steve and I should market and sell our JHS properties.

When Steve and I formally took over JHS, we listed Dad's factory building for sale. That move made it easier to extricate our non-paying manufacturing tenant, who was now squatting in our building. We had little legal recourse to get him out. Steve and I were not ready to walk over to his office next door and punch him in the nose like our father might have done. Sam, our lawyer, warned that any hostile maneuver could stimulate a lawsuit from the guy who had little to lose because of his failing business.

Though our father had bought his factory building twenty-five years earlier, he later said he had grossly overpaid. He shouted, "That schmuck real estate friend of mine, Vidor, screwed me good with this building. I trusted that bastard too much." He raised a fist. "When I found out what he did, I kicked his ass out of my sight." Vidor's hoodwinking of my father probably embarrassed Dad more than his paying too much for the building.

Steve and I wanted to be more thoughtful about the real estate agent we hired. We interviewed several agents and engaged an experienced guy who specialized in industrial buildings.

Once we had the agent in place, I may have exerted my will too much over our sales negotiations. From the onset, I told my brother, "Steve, I taught negotiation skills in McGill's MBA program, so please listen." I raised my index finger. "First, we can't pull a sales price from our stomachs." That was another expression our father had employed, except he'd say "ass" instead of "stomach" when he didn't want to be polite.

I went on. "We have to do research and see what the selling price would be for mid-sized factories like ours." I raised a second finger. "We also have to set a minimum price that we are not willing to go below, no matter what." I raised a third finger. "We can't tell our agent what our minimum is, for he might communicate it inadvertently to a buyer to get a quicker sale."

I was trying to work for both of our benefits. I also acknowledged my brother's good ideas when he had them, and he certainly had some. But underneath my helpfulness, I tried to prove to Steve that I could do things better than he could, just as he had done with our father. I wanted him—as I had wished for Dad—to recognize my intelligence and worth.

Steve seemed to accept my suggestions. After researching comparable properties, we decided to list Dad's old, tired building at $1.5 million. We knew our asking price was high, but the agent assured us that it was a reasonable starting point. Steve and I set a minimum sales price of $1.2 million, which we privately agreed we wouldn't ever go below.

A few months after listing the property, our agent found a bonafide buyer after getting a few low-ball bids from bargain hunters. His initial offer was $1.25 million, $50,000 above our minimum!

Steve and I were pleased, but my brother was ready to rush into substantial concessions to close the deal speedily. I may have responded too quickly or harshly. "Steve, even though this potential buyer has come in above our minimum, don't we still have to work to get the best result? We should make our concessions slowly, waiting until the last day before the buyer's offer goes off the table." I raised a finger again. "And, our first concession should be our biggest one, with each subsequent price reduction being smaller and smaller. This way, the prospect gets the message that we are coming close to our minimum, though we know he has surpassed it."

I suggested we talk to our agent about the prospective buyer to get his view of the fellow vying for our property. I arranged the call and asked Steve to let me take the lead in the conversation. He listened while I spoke over the speakerphone—I never wanted to go behind my brother's back regarding JHS. Before I made the call, I asked Steve once more not to reveal anything about our strategy. He accepted with a simple "Okay."

On the call, I asked our agent, "What's your read on the prospect; why does he want our building? Is he motivated to buy, or is he just kicking tires?"

The agent responded openly, calmly, and professionally. "The buyer is looking for a bigger industrial building for his operation. Your property could be a good fit for him. It offers expansion possibilities if he needs additional space." His tone stayed steady. "The guy is an importer and distributor. He needs space for warehousing and simple production. He doesn't need state-of-the-art systems or very high ceilings like you'd get in a newer industrial building. That's why he's looking at older buildings like yours."

"Okay," I said. "That's helpful." I took another breath. "And what's his personality like? Is he a negotiator type or a quick decision-maker?"

The broker thought for a moment before he spoke. "He's an importer who buys and sells consumer goods. He's a consummate negotiator." His voice turned serious. "You should know that I don't think he's in any rush. He said that his current space, though tight, still works for him."

I thanked the agent for his input. I then looked at my brother, "Steve and I need to discuss this, and we'll get back to you within a day."

The agent accepted, and we ended the conversation there.

I hung up the phone and turned to Steve. "It sounds like this buyer wants our building." I raised a finger. "But what our agent said about the prospect not rushing, it could be a negotiation tactic to get us to lower our price quickly. But I suggest we tough it out with this guy, doing the opposite."

I took a long breath. "We have to be prepared to go back and forth with this prospect for the next weeks or even months until we get a price we agree on. The final price may be close to the middle of where he and we are now." I raised my flat hand to make my point. "The good thing is that our back and forth with this guy may give us time to see if we can get a better offer elsewhere. Let's not rush with the size and timing of our concessions." I closed my fist. "We want to give the buyer a message that we won't sell unless we get closer to our original price."

Steve looked at me. There was no telling expression on his face or in his voice. "Harvy, are you sure this buyer will stick it out with us? Wouldn't it be better if we tried to get a quick sale?"

There may have been a tinge of annoyance in my voice. "You heard the agent, Steve. The buyer is a consummate negotiator and isn't in any rush. We should be the same way with him. Both the buyer and our agent will understand that approach."

I tapped my index finger on the desk in the way my father had done. "If we make our concessions too fast or too deep, he'll think there's something wrong with the building and then hold firm to a lower price. We need to give him the impression that we have a good building to sell and that we're not willing to go lower than what we feel it's worth."

Steve said, "Okay," but I couldn't get a read on his face. He and I then set a new minimum price of $1.3 million for the building, a number we wouldn't go below. We again agreed not to divulge that number to our agent.

We must have gone back and forth with the prospective buyer over a dozen times over six or seven weeks. Steve and I made our concessions smaller and smaller at each round, and so did the buyer. Near the end, we were only $25,000 apart and $30,000 higher than Steve's and my revised minimum.

In front of Steve, I called our agent once more. Again, I didn't tell him that Steve was overhearing our conversation. I held my voice firm and serious. "Before Steve and I agree on any more concessions to your buyer, are there any other potential prospects for our building?"

The broker was calm. "Not at this time, but you never know what can show when." He took a breath and added, "On the other hand, often your first prospect is your best one. You guys are so close that I hope we can strike a deal."

I took a long breath. "I have a crazy idea if you are willing to hear it." I had said "crazy" for effect.

"Okay," the agent said.

I went on. "What if you ask the buyer if he's willing to split the current difference between us? Don't tell him I said that, but make it your suggestion. You also might tell him that he should take pride in having gotten us down a little closer to his initial $1.25 million initial bid rather than our original 1.5 million dollars asking price."

I kept my pace. "Between you and me, if the buyer isn't willing to split the difference, then I'll tell my brother that I'd rather wait until we find another buyer rather than go any lower." I raised my tone. "This guy has pushed us far enough! Our back and forth has been a royal pain."

Little did our agent know that I was working to create a price barrier. Unlike my father, who would have yelled at the broker by now, I stayed calm and collected. Yet, like my father, I wanted to communicate my displeasure and steadfastness. Dad had taught me a thing or two.

The agent said, "I like your ideas, Harvy. I'll give them a try. I'll call you back as soon as I hear from the buyer."

We hung up. I turned to my brother and employed another one of our father's expressions. "Let's see if the buyer will bite." Steve nodded his acceptance, but his face again looked blank.

A few hours later, the agent called back. He said, "The prospect agrees to split the difference. Will you and your brother be good with that?"

I kept my voice flat. "I have my brother here with me. Please wait a moment, and I'll ask him."

"Okay," he said.

I put my hand over the receiver, and I turned to Steve. "We got the prospect to split the difference. Are you still okay with that?"

I knew that Steve had already agreed with my approach, so it didn't matter what he'd say. I wanted to kill a moment before going back to the agent. I wanted to create an impression that this last concession was, even now, a painful one for us. I needed the broker to make the buyer feel good about making the final and winning gambit, though it had been my idea.

Steve nodded, yes. I took my time to take my hand off the receiver. When I did, I said, "Steve accepts; it's final then."

And it turned out that it was.

I was proud of having orchestrated the deal for our father's factory. I expected my brother to say, "Good negotiating, Harvy." Instead, he looked at me stone-faced. "Did our agent say when the closing might be?"

Perhaps I had been cocky. Or maybe Steve couldn't acknowledge that I made a good deal. Though I had won the battle with the buyer, I may have lost any hope for our sibling partnership right then and there. Both of us desperately wanted the other's acknowledgement, which made it unbearably hard for either of us to provide it.

Thanks, Dad, for what you had bred in your sons.

* * * *

Day of Redemption – The Muddling

Through the early 2000s, I was still travelling to Montreal once a month to see clients. Each time, Steve and I had supper to go over the latest happenings regarding our JHS properties. I seldom asked Steve about his new business, but he shared news once in a while. I suspected he wanted to demonstrate to me—or whom he saw as our father in me—that he knew what he was doing.

By the fall of 2005, Steve had completed three years of selling motor scooters, ATVs, and dune buggies. I had no sense of whether his company was making or losing money. Though I was curious as a competitive brother might be, I preferred not to know. Steve was always upbeat about CMS, but the details weren't my business. I didn't want to make him feel like our dad was looking over his shoulder, even if Steve had placed me there.

At one of our suppers, Steve was particularly cheerful. With no preamble, he offered, "I'm planning to write a book about my life."

I nearly spit out the water that I had just sipped from my glass. I cringed and held back a chuckle. Months earlier, I had told Steve I had started to write a memoir about our parents. I guess he had to meet me there, maybe even try to one-up me. "That's great, Steve," I said with little emotion.

He spoke confidently. "I'm going to write about my overseas travels and my experiences in business." He smiled. "Even with CMS, anything that could go awry for us has gone wrong." He was practically giddy.

Because Steve had provided an opening, I asked, "How so, Steve?"

He shook his head. "From the time of our first product shipment from Korea, things haven't gone the way we had expected. It's been comical."

He grinned as if he were ready to script a bestseller. He looked my way. "Do you remember how our Korean supplier had to reroute our first shipment of scooters? It had been originally heading for the U.S., but our supplier was able to divert it to Canada."

"Yes, I do remember your mentioning that a while ago."

"Well," he continued. "Canadian customs wouldn't allow that shipment to enter the country. Our supplier built those scooters for the States, so they didn't have the CSA sticker." (The Canadian Standards Association [CSA] was like Underwriters Laboratory [UL] in the USA.)

"But didn't you say that your Korean supplier makes the identical bike for both U.S. and Canadian markets?"

My brother raised an open palm. "That's right, Harvy. The only difference between the U.S. and Canadian bikes is that darn sticker. Because of that, we had to reroute the whole shipment from Montreal to Champlain, NY."

Steve was as animated as I had ever seen him. "It took over a month to have those scooters approved by CSA. Andrew and I then had to go down to Champlain and open every container and put the new sticker on every scooter."

He sighed. "We were seven weeks late with our dealer shipments and lost half our selling season. By the end of the year, we sold only 400 units and were lucky to break even, though we took no salaries."

I could hear my father's *"Hesus Maria!"* from his grave. I nodded slowly, my elbows on the table, my hands clasped in front of my mouth, my index fingers on my lips to keep myself from saying anything deprecating.

Steve kept talking. "Thank goodness that Andrew and I orchestrated things better after that. We doubled our sales in our second season, and we increased it again to 1000 units this past year. We are now paying ourselves a salary. We have sales reps working in both Quebec and Ontario, and we plan to expand across Canada for the next season."

My consultant's radar felt a blip. "Steve, I would think with that few units per year, you probably haven't come close to saturating the Quebec or

Ontario markets. Why are you going to spread yourself thin across the whole country when you still have a big marketplace closer by?"

My brother had an answer. "It turned out that only a portion of the bike dealers here are strong enough financially to meet our terms of GE Capital financing. We don't want to sell to any weak guys, so we'd rather go far and wide to find the right dealers to carry our line. They pay for transportation anyway, so it doesn't matter where in Canada they are."

He raised a hand like a professor talking to a student. "Andrew figures that if we can't find enough of our type of customers across the country, we'll move up the product food chain to bigger bikes and all-electric vehicles with the few good dealers we have."

"Okay, Steve," I said, though I was skeptical of their plan. I didn't want to say anything to make Steve believe I was against his startup's growing success. I prayed that my brother wasn't going to get over his head as he had done before. Knowing that Andrew was from Steve's local church, I didn't think the guy would cheat my brother. But that didn't mean that they were seasoned businessmen.

I changed my tack from business strategy to corporate finance. "So, what's going on with your bank financing?"

He grinned. "Now that CMS has three selling seasons under its belt, we have approached the Royal Bank for a loan for next year's inventory. We have to commit to our supplier soon so we can have the product on hand for spring. As our inventory grows, I can't carry the whole cost by myself."

"I see," I said, nodding at my brother. "I thought you had everything presold and needed little bank financing."

Steve lifted his hand again. "Yes, that's true in theory, but it hasn't worked out that way completely. Our best dealers are well-financed and don't want to pay the high interest rates to GE Capital. They'd rather pay a slightly higher price instead, or we give them a one to two percent discount if they pay within 30 days—like Dad used to do with his suppliers at JHS. Thus the bank financing we need is very short-term."

Mon frère shook his head. "But those people at the Royal Bank were tough on me. Before they'd give me a penny, they wanted a lien on all my assets, including what I still have left in Dad's trust. As collateral, I had to sign over nearly everything I owned." He gazed at me across the table. "But I drew the line in keeping my JHS shares and my house out of their claws." He offered another smile. "CMS was able to obtain 80 cents of financing for every dollar I put in as a personal loan to the company."

Excellent negotiating on your part, Steve! Other entrepreneurs I knew got one to two dollars of financing for every dollar they committed to their company. My all-cards-on-the-table brother got eighty cents. I didn't say a word.

Steve smiled as if he had drawn a money rabbit out of a bank hat. He repeated, "I stood firm on saying no to my JHS shares and home as security against the loan. They eventually gave in on that stipulation."

I remained curious. "Did you go by yourself to the bank, or did you bring an accountant with you?" From what I heard from Geoff Levi, he worked as the accountant for Steve's company.

Steve offered a puzzled look. "Harvy, I went by myself." He pointed to his chest. "I'm an honest guy and played open-book."

There's your problem, Steve! I learned from my clients—even those with the highest integrity—that one should never lie to their banker, but one should also never tell the whole truth. Unlike our father, who had known his limitations and would bring his accountant or lawyer to any critical business negotiation, my brother wanted to prove that his open and honest ways would overcome any business or banking obstacle.

May God be with you, my brother.

At our next JHS financial meeting, our very up-and-up Geoff chastised my brother. "You should have brought me with you to your bank or let me find the right banker for your company. I know many of those guys and could have gotten you a better deal."

Steve ignored Geoff's comment and moved to another topic.

I later shared my concerns privately with Geoff regarding my brother's business acumen. To my surprise, my friend responded differently than I had expected. He offered, "Steve's grown immensely since your father died. He's come from under your dad's shadow to do something useful and productive."

But I don't think you know my brother. I nodded but offered nothing more. I trusted that time would reveal if I was right or wrong about Steve's growth, acumen, and business prospects.

After telling me about his CMS bank negotiations, Steve stopped eating his supper. He looked at the table, his face serious. He put a finger to his mouth as he finished chewing and swallowing his last bite. My brother then said, "Harvy, I might need to tap into my half of what's left in Dad's trust. Could we do the same thing we did three years ago, taking the next installment out early?"

I thought for a moment. The same sibling forces were at play for me as had been before. Steve and I had only a couple of parcels of land remaining in JHS. On the horizon, I could see us parting ways. I needed my brother motivated to allow me to separate from JHS in a tax-efficient manner.

I looked at him across our supper table. "You know, it costs three thousand dollars a year for Geoff's firm to file taxes on Dad's trust. If we took all the money out of the trust now, we could save $30,000 over the remaining ten years. What if we distribute everything to us, and then we can close the trust? That way, you'll never have to bother me again about Dad's estate."

Steve's face lit up. "Great idea, Harvy!" It was his turn to borrow a line from our father. "It would be nice not to have to feed the accountants."

Yes, and I hope you don't blow the money. I could feel my father turn again in his giant Mount Royal grave, for I was letting go of a money tie that might bind my brother's loose ventures. But Steve was a grown man, and I wasn't his keeper. He still had half of JHS's assets to fall back on if he lost his inheritance from Dad's estate.

I wanted to be fair with Steve, and I had my needs to consider regarding our holding company. I hoped that Steve would give me a fair shake when it came time to deal with the American complexities of redeeming my portion of our JHS's shares.

I hoped I wasn't fooling myself on how accommodating my brother would be when it would be my turn to request a concession from him.

* * *

I didn't know it at the time, but from the day we sold Dad's old factory building, it seemed that Steve's attitude toward our partnership changed, but maybe it had always been that way. He stopped informing me as to what was going on at JHS.

Every six to nine months, Steve and I had yet another sibling talk. Over a quiet restaurant supper, I'd say: "Steve, why didn't you tell me about…?" . . . "Don't you think I, as your brother and partner, should know what you are doing regarding…?" . . . "What obligation does the president of a company have to his equal shareholder?"

I never raised my voice but kept an inquisitive tone, as Peter Falk did in the Columbo television detective series. I wanted us to work together. I couldn't understand why he excluded me from important JHS matters, like saying how he was marketing our remaining land parcels.

During those sibling chats, Steve never looked me in the eyes. He kept his hands folded on the table and eyed the opposite wall. He'd calmly say, "I'm sorry, Harvy. I'll try to do better to keep you informed." After each conversation, Steve did keep me more abreast of things for a while, but his improved behaviour never lasted.

Our overarching goal remained the same: to dress up each JHS property to make it more valuable to a prospective buyer. Steve never wavered off that path. But outside of our face-to-face meetings every month or two, he excluded me from most of his activities as JHS's President.

In one case—our most complicated land project—JHS owned land on the South Shore of Montreal that had six conjoining neighbours. The neighbours banded together to put forward an over 1000-acre, multi-phased development plan to the local municipality. Steve and Rob participated in many meetings with the property owners and town committees. Negotiations dragged on for years.

As the town was coming close to approving the combined project, Steve called me. He was a touch more exuberant than usual. "Harvy, I was able to play one of our neighbours against another. I talked to our two closest neighbours about buying our lot that's situated right between them."

Steve was pleased with himself, and rightfully so. "Our neighbour to the east didn't want our land," he said, "but I didn't divulge that to the neighbor to the west. The west neighbour thought he was bidding against the east guy."

Steve added that the west guy was motivated because buying our land would make him the biggest property holder in the whole project. He'd then have greater leverage in negotiating with the other landowners and the town, as well as have one less neighbour to deal with—us. My brother took a long breath and then offered what that neighbour was offering for our plot. "Are you okay with that?" he asked.

Though Steve had excluded me from his thinking and those negotiations, he had conferred with other landowners he knew in the area to learn what would be a fair price for our property. The offer was decent, and no agent commission would be involved. "That's great, Steve," I said.

I was pleased about the pending sale and about Steve having gotten a reasonable price, but I felt uneasy about his having kept me at arm's length. I kept my mixed feelings to myself. *Harvy, allow your brother to win this one.*

JHS had another plot of rural farm acreage that Steve figured was worth a million dollars. I had no idea how he had determined that number. Before he listed it on the market, I told him, "A million dollars sounds good, Steve, but we should do some research to find out what comparable properties are selling for in that area."

Steve agreed initially. He called back weeks later. "Rob has approached me. He says that he might have a customer for our property; he knows a prospective buyer. If Rob can make a deal, he wants a sales commission. Would you be okay with that, Harvy?" He didn't slow down. "Rob says he would be fine with 2.5 percent, half of what a real estate company would get on selling our lot."

I took a long breath. "I guess that's okay, Steve. But let's set a time limit of 30 or 60 days before we officially list the property with a broker. If Rob has a buyer on the hook, it doesn't hurt to tug on that line and see what surfaces. But let's not give him the impression that we'll wait forever."

Had I sounded too much like Dad again?

Steve paused for a moment and then said in a subdued tone, "Okay."

I repeated what I had said in our previous call. "And let's try to research property prices in that area—even if we have to pay a real estate agent for an assessment. Or try the town clerk's office to see if there have been any recent sales." I felt like my father; he always had to plead with Steve to do straightforward stuff.

Steve retorted, "Land in that area is not moving very much. It's still a recession here in Quebec, you know. There won't be recent comparables."

I kept my voice calm. "Wouldn't it pay to find out what we can, Steve? Don't you want to be certain about our asking price, not just pull a number from your stomach?" There was Dad in me again!

"Okay, Harvy," he said flatly.

Weeks later, Steve called again. He said, "After thinking about it, I told Rob that I'd consider 1.1 million dollars for our property. Rob went to his source and came back with a verbal offer. Do you accept?"

I became miffed that my brother made that decision without me, but I again tried to say collected. "Sounds good, Steve. But how did you determine that specific price?"

"It felt right to me, Harvy." Steve's stomach was speaking loudly. He added, "I also told Rob that we'd give him just $25,000 as a bonus for brokering the deal." (That was a little less than the commission Rob had asked for.) "I feel right about that as well," Steve said.

The property horse seemed to be out of our JHS asset corral. I offered, "Alright, Steve." I held back my disappointment with my brother's unscientific methods. I wasn't about to go to Montreal and do that land research myself. Perhaps Steve had performed a minor miracle in selling our property via Rob. I asked, "Might you know anything about that buyer? Why does he want our land?"

Steve spoke in his matter-of-fact way. "The buyer wants the land for his two grown sons who are contractors. Someday, they'll build homes there."

I thought for a moment. It could have been Steve and me building houses there if we had gotten along better and been interested in and talented for land development.

I couldn't hold back my frustration. "Steve, I'm wondering why you continue to keep me at arm's length about your negotiations. In one breath, you accept my input, and in the next, you don't act on it."

It felt once more as if Dad were in the gap between us.

There was a long pause, and then he offered, "You're far away from this, Harvy. You're in Boston; I can't stop in the middle while things are moving forward fast."

"But all it takes is a 10-minute call. What holds you back from picking up the phone?"

After another pause, Steve added, "I guess I like to do things on my own."

There was Dad in my brother again! Steve had to counter my "Let's slow down and think this through" with his "Let's get it done and do it my way." I don't think Steve could put his finger on what bothered him about me. If he knew, he didn't say.

Our conversation again reminded me of when I was ten years old. Steve and I had been riding our bicycles around our Montreal suburb, where we had lived as kids. Some distance from home, he sped up and left me behind. I could see Steve wave goodbye, a smirk on his face, as he rode off to visit a school chum. He didn't want his little brother tagging along, especially one *who* he saw as our dad's goody-goody boy.

Steve left me in the dust again on Vancouver Island when he got mad at me for being bossy. He stranded me there as he merrily drove to Vancouver. Steve couldn't engage with his words. Instead, he made his little brother impotent, even disappearing in his mind. He was doing such again with these JHS land deals.

I had tried to make our sibling partnership work for five years—though perhaps not as adeptly as I had hoped. Steve continued to assert his "I can do it better without you" big brother approach over a sibling he perhaps resented, even despised. I painfully pondered what else I could do to break the Simkovits mold that had us solidly shaped in our ways with each other.

That night, I couldn't sleep; my stomach was churning. As I had done times before, I churned things over in my mind about my brother. Our tormenting sibling ways, in part, had been of our father's making.

From the time we were kids, Dad had bound us to Montreal Phono and JHS. For over forty years, he had bestowed upon his sons the financial growth of his company, telling us, "JHS is more yours than mine. When I'm gone, I hope the two of you will get along and do something with it."

I certainly appreciated my father's foresight and his financial generosity to Steve and me. But I wondered if his promised legacy was also a collar around our necks, with Dad holding tightly onto the leash. Though the value of Steve's and my JHS shares became worth many times more than Dad's ownership, he rarely bestowed upon us any say over the company's finances. He never trained us to work together. Dad had been the boss, and that was it.

As I lay in bed, I kept my eyes closed and slowed my breathing to try to relax my mind. During Dad's manufacturing days, Steve and I had been able to join forces awhile at our father's company, but our efforts hadn't lasted long. Now, he and I didn't have the desire or wherewithal to redefine and recreate JHS. Because of our mutual distrust and disregard, our only reasonable option was to liquidate JHS's assets for our mutual gain.

Those financial profits perhaps were Dad's penance to Steve and me for his not having been around when we were kids. Or were those benefits his money enticement not only to keep us glued together but also to ensure that we'd remember his generosity?

I shivered in my bed. I felt my father's noose around our necks and attached to his grave. In the darkness of my bedroom, I imagined him chuckling in his cherrywood casket as he kept one hand on the leash.

I opened my eyes and looked at the ceiling. *Why can't Steve and I get along?*

I reminded myself of how Dad had incessantly complained about my brother, saying, "Steve doesn't care about earning a living for he's lost in his religion," . . . "I don't know what he would do if I didn't feed him and his family," . . . "He never listens to me nor has time for me."

Dad blustered to anyone who'd listen rather than put his foot down with his first son or talk to him as an adult. Dad felt stymied by Steve's continual contradiction that all he could do was rant and rave about it. Maybe Steve intended to make his father feel impotent.

I shared the blame regarding my brother for having been overly loyal to Dad. I had vied for my father's acknowledgement and his hidden offshore money. I could very much understand Steve's lack of trust.

But Steve had made it easy for me to become our father's confidant. Predictable as my Patek, my brother gave Dad *agita* about every little thing, seemingly even the time of day. The disrespect Steve levied on our father fueled my disgust for my brother, even in the face of my growing distaste for

Dad's money-hiding ways. Perhaps I also held a metric ton of jealousy as to what Steve had gotten away with while our dad had been alive.

I tried to put all that behind us after our father had died. I never raised my voice to my brother. I talked to him openly and rationally whenever I had an issue with him. I sought out win-win solutions. I strived to obtain the most we could from our JHS assets. I acknowledged Steve where I could, though he never again said, "Good work, Harvy," after mentioning it in connection to our voluntary disclosure.

I closed my eyes and tried to get to sleep. *Was I not able to bury my need to be our father's preferred son?* Then again, I was sure Steve had gotten signs of Dad's aces for me, causing my brother to harbour his jealousy of my having more of our father's favours.

Steve had to prove that he knew how to do things better than Dad or me. Thus, he resisted my influence as much as he fought against our father's wishes. Could our being born thirteen-and-a-half months apart, and Mom dressing us as twins, have precipitated my big brother's need to be so steadfastly distinct?

Should he and I see a business therapist, someone like Moe Gross? Then again, Steve abandoned his therapy with Moe for communion with his God. I expected that if we had counseling together, I wouldn't stand my brother wielding his moral self-righteousness, probably as much as he wouldn't fathom my exerting my professional know-how. Could we ever break the sons-of-Johnny die that our master craftsman father had forged?

I turned again in my bed and pleaded for sleep.

Steve and I, like Dad, were far from perfect in our ways with each other. Could we ever accept our deficiencies and forgive each other for our parts in this tumultuous and tormenting father-son triangle? Could we ever break the mold and end the awful drama in which Dad had cast us?

* * *

I went to talk to our accountant and my friend, Geoff, about my concerns regarding Steve. By now, our reinstated JHS auditor knew us well.

Geoff and I met alone at his office. The conference room furniture here was more austere than at Elliot Trudell or Charles's firms. Like my father, I preferred our regular professionals to be tasteful but not extravagant.

After Dad died, I considered it ironic that Steve and I convened at Geoff's office rather than JHS. Our father had managed to get his accountants to make the commute to his company.

Maybe Dad had given them the line that he was too busy with his business to come into the city. Or perhaps he paid them enough to make it worth their while to make the trip to JHS. Or maybe it was the spiked coffee or tea that Dad served when they came his way.

Then again, Steve and I could have been wimps not to insist that Geoff make the hike to us. I saw it as a professional courtesy, and possibly saving money, to have Geoff not drive to JHS for our generally brief meetings.

I looked at my friend of nearly twenty-five years as he sat at the head of his long conference-room table. Geoff's small stature and prematurely balding head made him appear non-threatening. Over ten years ago, when I convinced my father to hire Geoff, I figured my brother would get along with my friend. At the time, I didn't realize how true my notion had become.

I leaned forward, folded my hands on the table, and got to the point. "Geoff, Steve's not keeping me in the loop about things he's doing at JHS."

I saw Geoff as a good listener and a fair judge. I explained a recent altercation to him. I added, "I talked to Steve several times about his tendency not to inform me. Things get better awhile, but then he goes back to holding me at arm's length." I looked closely at my friend. "Can you talk to him? Maybe you can find out what's preventing him from treating me as his equal partner."

I knew my father had employed his accountants and lawyers as envoys between himself and his colleagues, even his sons. Dad never quite knew what words to use when it came to difficult subjects, or he just wanted sympathetic reinforcements. I was annoyed whenever JHS's professionals talked to me on our father's behalf.

But now, I believed I was engaging Geoff as a sibling envoy for a legitimate cause, and I hoped with more finesse than my father had done. I had made good-faith attempts with my brother and felt that we were no better off. Geoff might be a good intermediary.

Geoff leaned back in his chair and nodded while I spoke. After a few minutes, he leaned forward and gestured my way. "Don't be so hard on your brother, Harvy." His eyes were on me. "You know Steve had been under your father's thumb for many years. He's come out of his shell and has matured a lot since your father died."

Geoff spoke assuredly and in his usual quiet tone. "Steve's managing his business well. He's shown good initiative and is acting responsibly in both CMS and JHS. I don't think you should be overly concerned about him."

Geoff glanced down and then back at me. "Though I have to say that his partner is a stickler for our accounting fees—he scrutinizes every dollar."

I mulled over in my mind what I had just heard. Geoff hadn't addressed my issue. Had I been sitting where he was, I might have first empathized with my concerns. I would have asked more questions before providing an opposing opinion. Could it be that Geoff's accounting work for my brother's CMS business now competed with his loyalty to me and JHS? Or was I overreacting as my father might?

I kept my hands folded on the table and changed my tack. "Eventually, Steve and I will have to talk about our division of JHS. Before we enact our separation, we've been waiting until we sell our remaining land properties. What would be the best way for us to separate eventually?"

Geoff thought for a moment and then responded. "I assume you know that it will be you who would have to redeem your shares in JHS. By living in the U.S., you'd have tax disadvantages if you were the one to buy out your brother and become the majority shareholder of a Canadian corporation."

I nodded. "Yes, I know, Geoff." I had heard this before from JHS's corporate lawyer and my U.S. tax attorney. JHS would have to redeem and cancel my common shares, giving Steve full ownership of Dad's holding company. I felt that the transaction would have to happen in one fell swoop, for I didn't trust my brother to pay me out over time. Having now sold a majority of JHS's properties, Steve and I were at the threshold of the company having enough cash to purchase my shares.

Though my concern grew about Geoff's manner, I pressed on. "JHS still has a couple of properties left in its stable. Because of the weak market for land in Montreal and Ottawa, we won't have a good idea of what they're worth until we find a buyer who is willing to purchase them. It could take another year or two or more before we can dispose of them."

Geoff came back, perhaps a little too quickly. "Land is just land, Harvy; there's always a price for it. Can't you just put those plots on the market and see what you get? It shouldn't be too hard to sell; it's only a matter of price."

I leaned back in my chair to better take in my friend's seeming lack of sympathy. *Is he working to push me out of JHS?* It felt as if he were standing up for my brother's interests more than mine.

I glanced out of the room's picture window. We were high enough to have a good view of the city that generations of immigrants, like my father, had built. Those settlers had made Montreal their second home. I realized that Geoff didn't understand Steve's or my financial aspirations as sons of Johnny. We would never sell our JHS property at a fire-sale price.

During the four decades of amassing his Canadian holdings, Dad probably made as much money in real estate as he did in running his record player and console stereo business. He had churned his Montreal Phono cash cow into parcels of property. Dad liked the look and feel of brick and mortar and to look upon landscapes on which he could build the same.

During my youth, Dad had owned five large industrial and apartment buildings in addition to his Montreal Phono factory. Though he often complained about unreasonable and non-paying tenants, his motto was: "There's money to be made with properties as long as your timing is good."

After Canadian tax laws had changed, creating less advantage for wealthy individuals to hold real estate personally, my father worked to sell his diverse collection of motley buildings. He then invested the proceeds in annuities for his retirement.

Then, through JHS, Dad purchased tracts of land—hundreds of acres all told. They were everything from grain and vegetable plots to tree-overgrown lots and commercial spots. One couldn't even walk through some of the acreages because of dense shrubbery and fallen trees.

Dad had speculated on new developments coming to Montreal's South Shore and north of Ottawa, but his speculations didn't turn out quite right. Then again, time could spur development, and the Quebec and Ontario economies were improving as we were moving into the middle of the first decade of the new millennium.

I stayed another moment in my meditation, staring out the window as Geoff waited patiently for my response to his statement about trying to sell JHS's remaining land properties quickly.

Dad had seen that Steve and I were not interested in being landlords or developers. I don't know about my brother, but I shunned going out with our father to visit his timeworn buildings and overgrown land. After years of listening to my father yell about "bastard tenants" who messed up their apartments and complain about "fucking city governments" that tightened property regulations, I had no appetite for real estate.

Buying and selling properties was my father's sandbox, not mine. I rarely showed interest when he pulled out a table-covering land map or building blueprint at his office to "toss around ideas." I tuned out whenever he boasted about projects that didn't get off the ground more often than not. Every time Dad sold another holding, I felt relief, anticipating less drudgery for my brother and me after his death. My father's random buildings were now long gone, the profits churned into life annuities that expired when he died.

Dad's factory had been the last building that JHS had owned. Our father had kept that old, tired edifice to have a place to park his degrading body during his retirement years and to make rental income for JHS. Because it was hard to find a suitable manufacturing tenant, our factory building was the first thing Steve and I sold after Dad's passing.

As for JHS's landholdings, Dad had sat on those assets for decades, becoming stuck with them. Though he had tried to market those properties in the years before his passing, he would never "dump them on the market." He held on patiently, even stubbornly, until better times would come or "until he could find a sucker for it."

Steve and I were left to wrestle with what Dad had called "Quebec farmer's fields" and "Ontario bushland." Because of my disinterest, I never even laid my eyes on those parcels. But, like our father, neither my brother nor I were about to give away any part of Dad's land legacy unless we could get a decent dollar. It wasn't "just land" to us, as Geoff had expressed. Those plots, lots, and spots represented our financial future and the independence we yearned for in life and from each other.

Goff leaned forward and asked, "Harvy, are you listening?"

I snapped myself out of my thoughts and leaned forward too. "Geoff, you know how real estate hasn't been moving much in the areas north of Ottawa and south of Montreal, where JHS has its remaining two properties."

I looked directly at him. "It's taken Steve and me four years to sell two of JHS's landholdings, plus our factory building. We were lucky to get out of those with moderate gains. I think we'd want to wait until we could put a good story behind each of the remaining two acreages so we can get out with a decent profit." I put my hands flat on the table. "We have little idea what their fair market price would be. That price could dramatically increase if we can develop a compelling sales proposition and find the right buyer."

Geoff looked skeptical. "Harvy, land is land," he repeated. "There's always a price at which one could sell it. In reality, you two could separate at any time. You don't have to drag it out the way you are."

I didn't know if Geoff's "you" meant "my brother and me" or only "me." I wondered if Steve had said something to Geoff that made my friend feel he had to extricate me expediently from my sibling partnership.

I ended our conversation that didn't seem to be going my way. "Okay, Geoff. I'll talk to Steve and let you know."

I respected Geoff, but I wondered if he understood my perspective or was even on my side. *For whom is he working?* Wouldn't our long-time camaraderie buy me some sympathy, at least initially?

When I'd redeem my JHS shares, Geoff would be working for Steve at JHS and CMS. Was Geoff buttering that other Simkovits loaf before its time? *Or am I the problem child here?* I couldn't understand what I might have done to get a cold shoulder from my comrade.

I didn't follow through on my talk with Steve. Because I didn't have Geoff on my side, I decided to stay the course that Steve and I had set years earlier. No matter how much my brother wanted me out of his JHS hair, I wouldn't address my separation until the last lot of our father's land was on its way out of our holding company's door.

* * *

In December of 2005, five years after Dad's death, Steve and I had good fortune. We passed papers on the third of JHS's four land properties.

All told, JHS amassed over $2.5 million in after-tax proceeds from these land sales and the sale of JHS's old factory building. The combined capital gain amounted to about $1.8 million—exceptional results in slow times for land sales on the outskirts of Montreal. Steve and I owed our father much for having, as he had said decades earlier, "bought that land for peanuts."

We felt proud of our accomplishments, though we hardly patted each other on the back. We might have felt like wealthier men, but our father had locked that wealth within our JHS holding company. Steve and I now held the money leash on each other rather than Dad holding that leash on us. But with JHS's corral nearly vacant of properties, my extrication from our company was becoming foreseeable.

There was one property left, a hundred-acre plot north of Ottawa. I had never laid eyes on it, though Steve quipped, "That piece of bushland is so dense with trees and swamps that it has winter beaver dams and spring fish ponds." I didn't know if he was kidding or not.

Because the city had rezoned that plot as green space, Dad had tried to sell it as a prospective golf course. He had even paid for a golf course study and plan, designed by a Hungarian golf course architect who lived in Ottawa. Though there had been lookers upon that story, there had been no takers. Steve and I might have to wait for years until the city would rezone that area when the city's housing expanded in the direction of our acreage. Like our dad, neither Steve nor I wanted to discard that property for a loss.

In mid-December of 2005, Steve and I started envisioning our JHS separation beyond our remaining Ottawa property. My brother was eager to get the conversation going because he needed money from JHS for his family. The growth of CMS's operations and inventory had tied up his inheritance.

Steve and I talked over the phone and via email about effectively separating myself from JHS. I explained my U.S. tax situation, especially how certain tax-free corporate capital gains for Steve in Canada would be taxable for me in the USA. I then suggested, "You have a big Canadian tax advantage available by my having left Canada for the U.S. So let's work to equalize the Canadian and U.S. taxes we'd each have to pay in redeeming our company shares."

I took a breath and added, "If you don't think my idea is equitable, considering our different tax circumstances, please offer another way for me to separate myself from JHS that you think would be fair." I left him to sit with my thoughts.

A week later, two days before Christmas, Steve emailed Geoff, copying me.

> Dear Geoff:
> JHS is a Canadian federally chartered holding company with two equal partners, one residing in Canada the other in the United States. My U.S. business partner is requesting concessions from his Canadian counterpart because he chose to live in another country where he cannot enjoy the one tax advantage open to Canadian residents. My partner is not asking for a concession from me but, in fact, a tax subsidy. I'm insulted. If he wants to have the same [tax] benefits enjoyed by Canadians, I suggest he pack his bags and move back to this country.
>
> I have heard about Harvy's U.S. tax situation for the last five years. JHS has spent thousands of dollars attempting to assist my partner in his U.S. tax considerations, and to no avail. Any way you slice it, the bottom line is that I doubt he can 'have his cake and eat it too.'

Oh, my frigging God! My heart raced, and my gut shook. Though I had wondered when I might see a belligerent Johnny Simkovits come forth from my brother, I was still taken aback by his resentment and sarcasm. Like our father, Steve couldn't confront the person who peeved him; he had to complain to somebody else. My brother couldn't merely address me with his sibling displeasure, saving us from embarrassment. I had told him that I'd be open to his ideas on my fair extrication from JHS, but he had to take control of the conversation and complain about me within the same keystrokes.

Though Steve sounded off in his Johnny Simkovits way, at least he was copying me on his rant to Geoff. I read on.

> With JHS's most recent property sale, there are now sufficient funds in our company's coffers to repurchase my partner's shares. I propose that we move in that direction. I request that, in the coming year, we work with you to

> complete this transaction. Otherwise, it may take ten to fifteen more years before we can touch any JHS funds. I shudder to think how much personal tax my partner will have to pay on the gains in our millions in JHS assets.
>
> Could I have said it more plainly?
>
> Wishing you and your family the season's best,
> Stephen

Steve may have been exceedingly right about my wish to see a concession from him, but he was enormously wrong about my intentions of shortchanging him. I knew he didn't see things with the broadest tax picture in mind. Like Dad, my brother only saw things in how they affected him. He didn't want to look at the larger view of us together. I felt my head bouncing off the hard wall my brother had created.

Father, forgive him, for he knows not what he does.

Unlike our dad, I wasn't going to fight Steve's fire with mine, though I wanted to slap sense into him. If I were to survive my corporate separation from Steve, I needed sound logic, a professional tone, and not channel my father's bickering and bravado. I responded immediately to my brother's flame, copying Geoff:

> Steve:
> I'm astounded by your remarks and only wished you had said more to me before making such strong words public. Sadly, it appears that we have now gone beyond the point where you and I can talk through this situation civilly.
>
> I suggest that Geoff speak to both of us in the new year and see if we can find a principled way out of this 'tax box' that would be acceptable to us. Alternatively, we do have a Board of Directors' forum with our third director, Abe. We can bring him into the conversation if need be.
>
> I'm sorry that our conversations about my equitable separation from JHS have generated such an adverse reaction in you. I can understand it, yet I believe you may be misinformed about our total tax picture and its nuances.
>
> Respectfully, Harvy

I didn't think Steve fully understood or wanted to know how he was personally benefiting from my U.S. tax situation and its complexities. My leaving Canada for the U.S. fifteen years earlier would allow him a significant tax advantage with JHS's capital gains asset, but only if we played the Canadian side of the tax game right. But before I'd let him take any gains out of our company, I wanted him to agree that we would share in those cross-border benefits.

Conversely, Steve saw my stance as his paying a portion of my U.S. taxes. And he saw me as his only obstacle in taking his share of our money out of JHS. I wondered how I could open my brother's eyes about these and other advantages to him by having me out of JHS, including his not having to deal with his irritating little brother any longer.

* * *

Steve and I spoke briefly late on Christmas Day. Our voices stayed subdued as we wished each other a Merry Christmas. I said matter-of-factly, "We'll work to figure out JHS after the New Year."

He offered a standoffish, "I hope so, Harvy."

Though I was bothered by the tension between Steve and me, I kept it from my wife and family. I didn't want to spoil our holiday celebrations because my brother and I were squabbling about how to end our partnership.

A few days after Christmas, over an early breakfast with Gloria, our kids still in bed, she looked my way. Her face expressed concern. "Harvy, you seem to be preoccupied. What's going on?"

I hesitated for a moment and then offered, "Steve and I are disagreeing about how to divide JHS's assets so that I can get out of our company."

She looked quizzically at me. "Isn't that an accounting matter? Can't Geoff and his firm help you?"

I looked into her face. "I wish it were that simple, honey. There are options available to Steve and me in taking money out of JHS. Both he and I have to agree on the method we want to employ."

I lifted my hand off the table. "I've asked Geoff to talk to Steve and me to see if he can get us to agree on the best method by which to extricate me from JHS." I took a long breath. "I've proposed a solution to Steve, but he's totally against my idea. He thinks that I want him to subsidize my U.S. taxes. But what I want is to equalize the tax payments we both have to make to our respective governments."

Her face looked perplexed. "That sounds complicated. Can you explain it so I can understand it?"

I combed my thoughts. How could I easily explain a complex corporate tax problem that had started sixteen years ago, the day I had left Quebec for happier career hunting grounds in Massachusetts? Back then, Dad had hired Roger Delliard's accounting firm to look at what JHS should do to prepare the company to handle my move to the U.S. Roger's firm produced an over 20-page report, which cost Dad thousands of dollars.

The report's recommendations were complicated and unwieldy, as if Roger had written it for shareholders of a large public corporation. I got a severe headache when I tried to digest both the new corporate structures and the personal holding companies that the accountants had recommended for my brother and me.

Not able to get our heads around the report, Dad and I ignored them. Instead, Mack drafted a simple buy-sell agreement that Steve and I signed.

I looked at my wife across the kitchen table. "Steve and I have a buy-sell arrangement that says we can't sell our JHS shares to anyone else before offering them first to each other or to JHS itself. Thus, for my getting out of JHS, he and I need to be in 100% agreement on how we would do it."

"Okay, that makes sense. So what's the problem?"

My eyes looked back and forth between her and the kitchen table. I took a moment to organize my thoughts, and then I looked at her. "Not until I left Canada and hired an international tax attorney here did I appreciate the tax complexities I have in the U.S. concerning my ownership in a foreign corporation. The issue now is that Steve has certain capital gains tax breaks in Canada that I won't get here in the States."

Gloria put her hand on mine. "I still don't see what the problem is for you and your brother and why you can't work it out with Geoff."

I looked back at her. "Give me a chance to tell you a few things, and then you'll better understand the fight that Steve and I are having." If I could win over my wife, I might have a better chance to convince my brother.

Though Gloria's face looked a bit skeptical, she nodded. "Okay, honey, but I guess that it isn't the tax technicalities that are holding you guys back. There's something more personal behind it."

Perhaps my psychotherapist wife was right, yet I wasn't quite willing to go there until she understood more technicalities. I raised my open palm. "Please allow me to tell you some things."

Seeing her offer no resistance, I took a deep breath and continued. "The big issue for Steve and me is the difference in the way the U.S. IRS handles capital gains from a Canadian corporation as opposed to how Revenue Canada handles it. In Canada, half of the capital gains that JHS has made over these last five years are tax-free," I raised a finger, "but those gains are locked into what's called the company's Capital Dividend Account or 'CDA'"

Gloria nodded. "So taxes work differently in our countries. So what?"

I raised my palm at her. "Please bear with me another minute, honey. You need to know a couple more details to understand what's going on."

"Okay, Harvy, get there fast, or you'll lose me to a romance novel."

I nodded, smiled a little, and continued. "Because of JHS's recent profitable property sales, JHS currently has $900,000 of such CDA money that's tax-free in Canada, which Steve and I, as the company shareholders, equally own." I pointed north and then to myself. "As long as he and I agree, we can take that CDA money out of JHS tomorrow."

Gloria's eyes opened wide. "Okay, then do that! What's the point of having that free money sitting in your company?"

I responded quickly. "There's exactly where the problem lies. If I still lived in Canada, then Steve and I could do exactly that. JHS would give $450,000 to each of us tax-free, and there would be no problem."

Gloria was nodding, but she still held a quizzical look on her face.

"But here's the rub." I tapped my index finger on the table. "Because I'm now living in the U.S., the IRS and Mass Department of Revenue don't recognize that Canadian CDA money as tax-free. My tax accountant here says that I would have to pay 21 percent in federal and state tax on my half of that CDA while Steve would pay nothing in Canada for his half of that cash."

I stopped for a moment to let that information sink in. My honest and fair-minded wife's eyes looked a little glazed over. "Isn't that just what it is, honey?" she asked. "Haven't you always said that our U.S. tax rates are less than what you would have had to pay in Canada? Can't you grin and bear this one benefit to your brother?"

My eyebrows lifted, amazed at how much Gloria was channeling Steve. I interjected. "That's precisely his position. He's saying, 'Harvy, you pay your damn taxes in the U.S., and I'll pay mine in Canada.'"

Gloria looked like she would say more, but I raised my palm again to stop her. "There is one last important quirk you need to know if you want to understand my take on this. It changes the whole picture from what you just said and what Steve has been telling me."

Gloria hunkered down in her chair, arms folded and mouth closed. I went on. "Geoff told us that we could work the CDA distribution such that Steve gets all the $900,000 CDA money tax-free while I get a $900,000 company dividend that would be taxable both in Canada and the U.S." I looked straight into her eyes. "In other words, I'd thus have to pay $190,000 in combined Canadian and U.S. taxes for my $900,000 JHS dividend while Steve would pay nothing in Canada if he got JHS's CDA cash." I looked intensely at her and put my fist on the table. "That's a huge benefit to him and disadvantage to me." I took a breath. "I don't consider that fair."

I raised my hand once more, not giving Gloria the chance to respond quite yet. "It would be good if Steve took all of JHS's CDA money, but Geoff has told him that he's not entitled to it. I'd have to agree to allocate that asset completely to him. So I want Steve to compensate me if he is to get my half of JHS's CDA." I didn't think I was greedy to level the tax treatment between us, especially for the gift of Steve obtaining that entire asset.

I looked again at Gloria. "Steve sees my request as my wanting a tax subsidy from him. But I don't think he understands the whole tax picture."

Gloria put her hand on my arm. "So what are you looking for from your brother, Harvy? How can you help him see things your way?"

I took a long breath. "None of us knows yet what the right amount should be for Steve to compensate me. I'm open to working it out as long as it's rationally based. But I first need Steve to acknowledge that my way of seeing our tax situation is more appropriate than his way of seeing it. Unless I can get him to accept my view, he'll think my withholding the distribution of our CDA cash is my way to extort blood money from him."

Gloria eyed me carefully, a psychotherapist's look in her eye. "So it seems that what you're looking for is Steve's acknowledgement that you're more right about this than he is. Do I see that correctly?"

I looked down at the table and thought for a moment about her point. My wife had hit a Simkovits sibling nail on its head.

I looked directly at her. My voice might have elevated, but I worked to stay calm. "Look, honey. You know I've been fair with Steve concerning my father's offshore money. I've been accommodating in giving him all of the money in our father's estate ten years before Dad wanted him (and me) to have it. This past year, I even let CMS borrow $200,000USD from JHS at the lowest bank loan rate to help him fund his damn scooter business—because CMS maxed out its bank line. And, I've given Steve and his wife full control over the assets that we put aside from Dad's estate for his kids' college education. I've bent over backward for him again and again."

I lifted my hand off the table. "Yes, Steve has been accommodating regarding my U.S. tax situation. But other than JHS paying a few thousand extra bucks to our accountants to coordinate with my U.S. attorney around these cross-border tax issues—those costs being 100% tax-deductible to JHS—there's been negligible impact on our company holdings." I raised my voice a tad. "The only thing I've ever held back on was not allowing us to withdraw cash dividends from JHS until we figure out this CDA issue."

I took another long breath. "Just as Steve did with Dad, he doesn't want to kowtow to me." I put my hand back on the table. "I do want to get out of my brother's hair and let him do what he wants with what's left of JHS." I looked at her with intensity in my eyes. "But I'm not going to do it without an accommodation that I think is fair and equitable."

I looked down again and then back at her. "This is one instance in which I'm taking a stand because Steve has never made anything easy for me. And time is on my side because I don't need JHS's money to live on the way he does." I hesitated for a second, and then I continued, my voice calmer. "But I don't want that kind of pressure to be the deciding factor for him. I need Steve to see that I have a rational case. I want him to accept my way of looking at JHS's CDA assets and to see it as being fair to both of us."

My wife presented a long face. "So, how are you going to do that, Harvy? Is Steve willing to hear you out?"

My back slumped, and my face turned glum. "Well, that's the other problem. Steve and I are now at the point where he's stopped listening to me. I've tried to explain my CDA perspective to him, but he refuses to see the situation the way I do. So I've asked Geoff to step in. He will talk to Steve and me in January and then come forth with what he recommends."

I took my eyes away from her and looked out the kitchen window. "Unfortunately, there's one more twist to our little sibling drama. In one of Steve's recent emails, he said he doesn't trust Geoff to represent his best interests. Steve's retaining a separate accountant. He wants a second opinion as to what he should do to take the best advantages of JHS's assets, especially before he becomes the sole owner of the company."

Gloria's eyes were on me. "What do you think about that?"

I nodded. "I understand Steve's need to protect his interests, but I'm confused by his move." I shook my head. "I'm not against Steve getting such advice, but I always felt as if Geoff were more on my brother's side." I paused and then added, "Maybe he has been playing devil's advocate with both of us. Maybe each of us feels that Geoff's standing more with the other."

I looked back at Gloria. "I emailed Steve saying that I understood his wish for outside advice. I told him that he had a right to get a second opinion. I also said that I'm okay with his accountant talking to Geoff to understand the facts of our JHS situation."

I upped my tone a touch. "I also requested that Steve's accountant speaks to my U.S. tax attorney (or me) so that he can get the full picture of our different tax regimes." I tapped my finger on the table again. "Without that, Steve's guy may only see Steve's Canadian half of the picture. And if JHS is paying for Steve's second opinion, then I want my U.S. two cents in there."

Gloria looked into my eyes and put her hand on mine. "It sounds very complicated, honey, and it does sound like you are trying to do the right things, especially involving Geoff."

I put my hand to my forehead. "I've been having sleepless nights over this, though I do believe I see things more clearly than Steve does."

She put her other hand on the table close to mine. "I do hope you won't be harsh with your brother. Even though he may be misguided or ill-advised, he's a caring and gentle soul."

A voice rose in my head. *Why does even my wife think I'm the mean brother and that Steve's a saint who needs to be understood or protected?* All my life, I felt only Steve's my-way-or-no-way resistance. No one had ever stood with me.

Though I became peeved, I didn't say another word. I nodded, rose from my chair, and walked into another room. *Was Gloria, like Geoff, seeing a sinister part of me that I couldn't fathom or wouldn't face?*

I had more restless nights. *How the hell was I going to have my obstinate, not-fully-informed brother see my view on JHS's CDA?* I hoped that Geoff would understand my perspective and then talk tax sense into Steve. I hoped that my brother's new personal accountant wouldn't muddy our JHS waters. Maybe it would be up to me to figure out the JHS money maze where my father had placed us.

It was not a Happy New Year for me that year.

* * * *

Day of Redemption – The Ending

I soon found out that it was not just my brother that I was fighting.

In a phone conversation with Geoff during the first week of January, I presented my perspective on JHS's CDA. Before I could finish, Geoff cut in. "Harvy, you have many tax advantages as a U.S. resident; why not let your brother win this one? Steve will pay his rightful Canadian taxes, and you'll pay your rightful American taxes. It should be nothing more than that."

It felt as if I were speaking directly to my brother. I was once more astonished that my friend would hardly consider my point of view. I reiterated, "For me to relinquish my half of JHS's CDA asset to Steve, I want some fair compensation from him."

Geoff was matter-of-fact. "Normally, Steve's tax rate on regular corporate dividends is 33%. It's only on the CDA money that his Canadian tax would be zero. Your dividend tax rate in the U.S. is 15%, less than half of what your brother has to face here."

I jumped in. "Don't forget, Geoff, that I have to pay another 6% tax in Massachusetts."

My assertion didn't faze him. "That still makes your overall American tax rate a third less than Steve's combined federal and provincial rates."

His words didn't deter me. "Look, Geoff, JHS has $900,000 in CDA assets, which is about 30% of its total value. Steve can get all of that CDA money tax-free in Canada while Uncle Sam would make me pay a 21% tax here in the U.S. on the same asset" I kept my voice firm but in control. "If I took my half of JHS's CDA money, $450,000 in this case, I'd be facing about $95,000 in taxes here. But if Steve would take my CDA money instead, he'd pay absolutely no tax on it. Shouldn't he then pay me something for that benefit? Getting my half of JHS's CDA, instead of his getting a taxable dividend from JHS, has to be worth something to him."

Geoff took a deep breath. "So, I guess that what you are expecting from Steve is something in the range between $0 and $95,000."

I was annoyed at Geoff's consideration of "$0." *Why isn't he getting my argument?* I hardened my voice. "Geoff, anything near zero is not an option. To bestow Steve with my half of JHS's CDA, I'd need to get close to that upper limit unless there's a rational reason as to why I shouldn't."

Geoff's voice didn't waver. "But you get so many other tax advantages by being a U.S. resident that Steve doesn't get here in Canada. Your income tax rates there are so much lower than here."

I was miffed. "Geoff, we've had this conversation before. Maybe my U.S. federal and state tax rates are lower, but not by that much when you add in U.S. Social Security and Medicare tax, which is another 12.5% net."

Geoff kept grabbing for handles. "But Social Security and Medicare benefits are something you pay into now to get a benefit later. You can't count that."

I began to feel as if I were fighting a Canadian tax myth about the American tax system. Perhaps I was also disputing some Canadians' negative perception about people like me who departed my country—chased away by Quebec's Separatist movement and attracted to better U.S. prospects.

I was annoyed at Geoff for not acknowledging my point of view. I raised my voice, but I didn't get angry as my father might have. "Doesn't Steve's tax rate include the Canadian and Quebec pensions and Canadian Medicare too? We've got to talk apples to apples regarding taxes, don't we?"

"Okay, Harvy. I get your point though I may disagree with it. From another perspective, who says the CDA money is yours or Steve's? It's JHS's."

There he went again, making an argument for my brother's benefit. "Yes, Geoff, but that CDA is assigned equally to its shareholders unless they agree to allocate it differently. As an equal shareholder to my brother, and as JHS's Secretary-Treasurer, I won't sign off on giving the whole CDA to my brother unless I get fair consideration for it." I was glad I had insisted on that corporate title when Steve and I had restructured JHS after our dad's death.

Though Steve and I were sitting on approximately $1.5 million each in JHS, I still thought I was making a fair point. He and I always said we would be fair to each other. For me, this CDA situation was a part of that fairness.

Geoff pressed on. "If I accept your argument on the CDA assets, Harvy, then what about other types of income that you and Steve have been getting from JHS? Should we work to equalize your and your brother's tax payments on those as well? And should we go back into the past to make sure you both would have paid the same percentage of taxes over the years? How far should we go?"

My hand closed into a tight fist, but I worked to keep my voice as loose as I could. "Your argument is a red herring, Geoff. JHS's CDA asset has nothing to do with Steve's or my earned income over the years. If it weren't for the CDA's $900,000 size, I wouldn't be concerned with it. There's only one reason why all of JHS's CDA money could go tax-free to Steve, and that's because I walked out of Canada sixteen years ago. There's no other way he would have otherwise gotten my half of that asset."

I took a breath and threw out my bottom line. "If Steve can't agree to fair compensation for his obtaining my half of the CDA, then let him have his half, I'll take my half, and we'll call it a day. I'd be ready to pay 21% in U.S. taxes on my portion rather than giving it to him for nothing." My voice turned snarky. "Then Steve will have to pay a full 33% tax on that and the rest of his JHS money."

Geoff went on. "Aren't you being narrow-minded on this, Harvy, perhaps even punitive?"

I held back my Johnny Simkovits anger but held onto my edginess. "From where I stand, Geoff, you could say the same thing about Steve." I took a deep breath as I banged my hand on my office desk, though I worked to keep my voice calm. "Why do you seem to take my brother's side, Geoff? What's going on with that?"

There was a pause on the other end of the phone. Geoff then offered, "It's funny, Harvy, your brother has said the same thing to me about you. With both of you, I work to poke holes in your stance with each other." He took another breath. "Steve seems to be feeling as strongly about this CDA situation as you are. I don't know if he'll give in to you."

Certainly not if this is the way you are working this situation between us. I worked to tone down my edginess and cut back to my bottom line. "Geoff, unless we come to a dollar figure that Steve and I can consider fair compensation, then we'll play it by the customary rules. Steve and I will split the CDA 50/50. He'll then lose the tax-free benefit of having my half of that asset."

After another pause, Geoff spoke calmly, "I'm not sure I agree with you, Harvy, but I will relay your stance to your brother and see what he says."

"Very well," I said.

We ended our conversation there. I put down the phone with little hope that Geoff would get my big brother to bend.

Geoff called back a few days later. "I'm sorry, Harvy, but your brother says he's not willing to subsidize your U.S. taxes."

Steve was continuing to play his only negotiating card. The fact that Geoff was mimicking my brother's language verbatim made me wonder if he was representing me well with Steve. I asked, "When Steve said that, Geoff, how did you respond?"

There was hesitation in Geoff's voice before he said, "I told him exactly what you said, Harvy." Geoff didn't elaborate, and I didn't press further.

It looked as if Steve and I were stalemated. *How can Geoff not see my side on this CDA money matter? Could I possibly be in the wrong here?*

Deep down into my bones, I felt I was more right than Steve. Over these last five years, I had bent over backward for him with everything JHS. It was time for him to yield to me. Though I wished Steve would understand and agree with my view, I knew that the longer we waited, the longer the money pressure would mount for my brother. Thus, time was on my side.

My only concern was that Steve might write JHS cheques to himself without telling me. I didn't think he was the type to screw me the way his former Ottawa partner had done to him in their home construction business. I was glad that I had insisted that any JHS cheques over $10,000 would require two of three signatures from Steve, Rob, and me. My brother couldn't go far over a money edge without my finding out about it. Or could he?

* * *

Geoff had been of no help. I struggled through more sleepless nights. *How can I prove to Steve that I have a compelling case for him to compensate me?* I kept my sibling struggle away from Gloria. My predicament with my brother, bestowed on Steve and me by our father and then perpetuated by us, was solely mine. I had to find a compelling way to sway *mon cher frère*.

After several wide-awake, pre-dawn mornings, there came a series of brainstorms. After the last one, I rose from my bed while it was still dark outside. I went to my computer and sent my brother an email, copying Geoff:

> Steve:
> After both of us talked to Geoff, it seems we are no further along in agreeing on how to split JHS's Capital Dividend Account. If it's okay with you, during my next business trip to Montreal, in February, I'd like us to meet with our third JHS director, Abe. If you agree, I can call him and arrange it.
>
> Also, I'd like to ask Geoff to prepare a statement of precisely what JHS is worth based on our most recent financial statements. I will ask him to assume that I will redeem my shares and take my money out this year, in 2006.
>
> We can ask Geoff to assume that we'd sell JHS's remaining (Ottawa) property for a nominal amount of $300,000 this year. He can use that figure in his calculations for JHS's asset value, including its CDA asset. That property sale may not happen this year, and my $300,000 number may be off, but Geoff's subsequent calculations will give us a chance to see what JHS is worth, both before and after each of us pays our respective taxes.
>
> I hope you agree with this approach.
> Harvy

A day or two later, Steve wrote back that he accepted my next steps. He added that he was going to talk to his accountant once Geoff provided the JHS valuation.

I called Abe and gave him a cursory understanding of what had transpired between my brother and me. I asked if he could meet with us over dinner in Montreal in early February and act as a mediator.

Abe agreed.

I arranged for us three to convene at noon at a restaurant equidistant from JHS and Abe's office. I also scheduled, with Steve's permission, a meeting with Geoff for the subsequent morning. No matter what came out of our conversation with Abe, I didn't want too much time to pass before Steve and I moved forward with my extrication from JHS. I was fed up with him as much as he seemed fed up with me.

Five days before our meet-up with Abe, my brother emailed. He confirmed our time of gathering and added, "If you have an agenda for our meeting, please email it to Abe and me."

There goes Mr. President Simkovits! He's expecting his VP brother to do the planning and arranging for him as if he were the Johnny Simkovits king of our JHS castle. I immediately wrote back:

> Steve:
> That's a funny request, considering you were the one in December to bring our JHS issues to a head—which we needed to do. For me, the purpose of our meeting with Abe is to talk about what caused our flurry of angry emails last December. Then we should talk about options to generate an equitable, fair, and amicable separation between you and me regarding JHS.
>
> By the way, what's *your* agenda for our meeting?
> Harvy

Steve never responded.

Later that morning, I sent Abe a private email.

> Abe:
> You should know in more detail what's been happening between my brother and me.
>
> Since late December, Steve and I have gotten angry with each other and have not spoken much, except through email. I tried to reach out to him weeks ago about figuring things out between us (regarding redeeming my JHS shares and separating from him), but he is not comfortable talking with me alone, though he agrees that we need to talk.
>
> Starting early this month, Steve and I have had numerous one-on-one conversations with Geoff Levi, our JHS

accountant. Geoff has tried to mediate between us. But because Geoff is my friend, Steve does not see Geoff working in his best interest. I, too, have been disappointed in the advice we have received from Geoff. I don't believe he and his firm have presented our JHS accounting, tax issues, and options well, such that Steve and I could make better decisions for my effective and amicable extrication from JHS.

Most importantly, during our upcoming dinner together next week, perhaps the best thing you can do is allow Steve and me to hash out our differences. Indeed, I'd appreciate your perspectives, but all I ask of you is to make sure that we have a civil and complete conversation about the personal and tax matters we face in having me depart JHS. I believe your presence alone would allow for that.

Thank you so much, Harvy

I attached the emails between Steve and me from the previous month to show Abe what I was up against regarding Steve.

Abe wrote back, saying, "I understand, and it's a shame that the two of you are fighting."

* * *

Abe had been a good friend to my father. He was a Lebanese Jew who had built successful garment manufacturing and distribution businesses in Israel, Japan, other parts of the Pacific Rim, and Montreal. Abe, a dozen years younger than my father, saw my dad almost every week. They had many meals together or shared office visits.

I had once asked Abe what he liked about my father. The short and burly man thought for a moment and then responded. "JHS's bank manager introduced Johnny to me, and we hit it off right away."

Abe put his hand to his face as if he were thinking. "I was an only child in my family and never had a big brother. Your father was like that for me. He helped me in business, even lending my company hundreds of thousands of dollars for some years when the banks wouldn't give me the time of day."

He spoke appreciatively. "Your father has also been a good sounding board, especially in dealing with overseas suppliers. I appreciated the business connections and the advice he has given me over the years." Dad's helping of Abe was similar to Aras's Uncle Chasen having helped my father when he started Montreal Phono in 1953.

I was impressed with their relationship. Abe repaid his business debt to my father and never had his hand out for anything more than friendship. When I was in Montreal to visit clients, Abe invited my father and me to several suppers. Steve had never become as close to Abe as I had, but my brother respected the man enough to allow him to be JHS's third director.

Abe very much knew, both through my father and from me, that Steve and I were very different people, never close as adolescents or adults. Like Dad, Abe wanted Steve and me to get along, but he understood that Steve's oil and my water didn't mix.

I assumed that Steve would email or call Abe in preparation for our directors' meeting, but I don't believe he did. Maybe my brother felt that his God in heaven would be on his side as he faced his brother on earth. I felt that God only helps those who help themselves. Though there was a risk that Steve might see Abe flatly in my camp, I hoped my brother would at least listen while in Abe's presence.

* * *

For four decades, the Ruby Foos gourmet Chinese and seafood restaurant squatted on the northeast corner of Montreal, next to the Decarie Expressway. That highway—built two stories below ground level but not underground—was so congested at rush hour that many Montrealers called it "The Decarie Depressed-way." I hoped I wouldn't get depressed after being with Abe and Steve at the Ruby Foos Motel.

Starting after WWII, the former Ruby Foos Restaurant had been a Montreal hot spot in its heyday. There, one could have one's picture taken and see it soon appear on the restaurant's match covers. During daylight, Ruby Foos was a watering hole for the three-martini business types. By night, it was considered a gathering place for the diverse likes of Pierre Eliot Trudeau, NHL hockey players, and Montreal's upper-class Jewish community members who wanted to see and be seen.

When my father's business had been in full swing through the sixties and seventies, he had taken many an out-of-towner to Ruby Foos. They enjoyed dinner or supper at one of its four restaurants of various Asian cuisine, or they listened to live combo music in one of its three lounges. Upon arriving for a meal, Dad liked to kibitz with the restaurant's pretty hostesses. He may have kissed their hand gracefully, bantered with them amusingly, or tipped them handsomely to obtain a table when patrons packed the place. Dad had known how to do such things.

In 1984, a few years after Quebec's first sovereignty referendum had failed, and the same year that Dad closed his business, Ruby Foos Restaurant shuttered its doors. Its demolition made room for an expansion of the adjacent Ruby Foos Motel, which now sported a high-end French café, the Tulip Noir. It was more appropriate for Montreal's francophone business set.

I chose Ruby Foos' Tulip Noir Café for our gathering of JHS minds because it was halfway between JHS and Abe's company and because I knew Dad had very much enjoyed the long-gone restaurant. He and one of the pretty French Canadian hostesses there were long-time friends—platonic, I heard, but one never knew for sure with my father. Today, I hoped that his ghost would be present here and on my side.

I arrived early and found a quiet table in the back of the café, far away from other patrons. I had brought Geoff's summary of the value of JHS as of the end of 2005. That document showed JHS's current value, assuming its remaining Ottawa property would sell for a nominal $300,000.

Using Geoff's work, I created spreadsheets to present to Abe and Steve. I felt well-armed with the facts to battle with my brother about JHS's CDA asset. My only risk was not being able to explain my case clearly for Abe and Steve to understand. If they didn't interpret my numbers correctly, they'd never see things my way. I hoped that Abe's presence would keep my brother's mind open and his Simkovits heels out of the ground.

Based on Geoff's valuation, the good news was that our company was worth considerably more than had been written into our JHS balance sheet—$700,000 more than I had expected. A week earlier, I had asked Geoff about a funny asset line on his pro forma valuation labeled RDTOH Recovery, with an amount of $725,000 written next to it.

Geoff had responded in his matter-of-fact manner. "That recoverable RDTOH money comes from the capital gains taxes JHS has paid over the years. JHS can get that money back from the government when the company issues cash dividends to you and Steve. It's the government's way of preventing double taxation, where both the corporation and its shareholders pay taxes on the same capital gains. When JHS pays out sufficient dividends, the government will send JHS a cheque for that RDTOH money."

Though I was happy about that government windfall to my brother and me, I found myself miffed again at Geoff. "Geoff, for these last five years that you have been doing JHS's statements and tax returns, why is it only now that Steve and I know about this RDTOH thing?"

He came back quickly. "I thought you did know about it. It's standard corporate stuff."

The strikes were building against my friend. "Geoff, I asked Steve if he ever heard about it. He said he never did. And, I never saw it written into our JHS statements."

Geoff's tone remained accountant monotone. "RDTOH appears in your company's tax returns every year that JHS has a capital gain. It'll show up in JHS's balance sheet only after JHS pays a dividend to its shareholders. So if JHS redeems your shares this year, then an RDTOH line will be seen in this year's statements. The government will then send JHS a cheque some months after the company officially files its returns for this year."

Count on the accountants to throw in a bunch of technicalities.

I had never examined JHS's tax returns. As President, Steve signed them. I trusted that he would look at what he signed, but I now gathered that he didn't. Perhaps the tax returns were too unwieldy, or Steve trusted our professionals too much, or he was too busy with CMS. By now, Dad might be yelling at Geoff for this oversight, but I stayed calm. "What does RDTOH stand for anyway?"

He responded quickly. "Refundable Dividend Tax On Hand. It's a term the government created that applies to private corporations like yours."

As my father had often said, the government complicated the running of small businesses such that it took an army of accountants and lawyers to wade owners through the minutia. Wouldn't it be better if those professionals employed their time and energy to help business owners strategize their corporate future and deal with complex shareholder issues, like the CDA issue with which Steve and I were now dealing?

My tone elevated a notch as I looked at Geoff. "Steve and I should have both known about and better understood this RDTOH account in our books." I was looking for him to take responsibility.

He remained his reserved and firm self. "Again, Harvy, I thought you guys did."

Our conversation ended there. Because this oversight had suddenly made JHS $725,000 richer on paper, I didn't pursue it further.

Because Geoff had disappointed me once again, I'd use his name in vain in my Ruby Foos' presentation to Abe and Steve. It was one of the several points I was going to make to my brother today. I was hoping to leverage Geoff's oversight to my advantage concerning JHS's CDA asset.

Abe arrived on time. I stood up partially and took his outreached hand in both of mine. "It's good to see you, Abe. How long has it been?"

"Good to see you too, Harvy," he said in his high-pitched tenor voice. "It's been too long." He pointed my way. "And why haven't you come to see me since we had your father's gravestone unveiling?" He raised his voice in mock ire. "It's only now that you call when you and your brother are in trouble?" That last sentence could have been both a question and a statement.

"I'm sorry, Abe. I should have come to see you sooner. You have always been a good friend. By the way, how's your wife doing?"

"She is good; she sends her regards."

"Tell her the same from me, and send the same to your son as well."

"Thank you, Harvy." Abe sat down across from me. He gestured my way as he said, "You know, my son is now doing almost all the international travelling for my business. I've been doing less and less every year." He smiled as he pointed to himself. "Pretty soon, all I'll have to do is count the money."

I smiled back. "Your son is lucky to have you as a father. You're better than my father was at passing on the business reins."

Abe looked my way. "Yes, and my son has proven that he can do it better than me. And, unlike your father, I know I'm not going to live forever and must make room for the next generation. What other choice is there?"

I was impressed with Abe's foresight. I pointed to him. "You're lucky that you have only one son in your business and not two."

He pointed back. "I was lucky with all my three children. My first son became a big orthopedic doctor in the U.S. My daughter is in the hotel business, flying worldwide as a consultant for a big chain. And my youngest son was both interested and capable of working with me."

I was envious of Abe and his brood. I wished more of his ways had rubbed off on my father, but they hadn't.

Abe looked directly at me and wagged his finger. "Brothers like you and Steve, who grew up together, shouldn't fight about money. Steve is your only brother, and it's not right that you and he can't agree on important things."

I looked down at the table as I felt the disappointed father in Abe. I raised my eyes and looked at one of my dad's genuine friends. "I understand, Abe, and I know my father would have said the same. But Steve and I have never been good friends, and he hasn't given me any other choice. I tried to work things out with him, but you saw the emails he sent."

Abe nodded, and his voice quieted. "I know, Harvy, I know. Your father said many times how stubborn your brother could be." He lifted his hand off the table as he raised his voice. "But it's still not right that you two are fighting."

I smiled. "Maybe you could say that to Steve; he won't listen to me."

Abe nodded. "Yes, I understand, and it's too bad."

Suddenly Steve was at our table. I glanced at my watch. My brother was only seven minutes late, a near-record for him. He hardly glanced my way as he reached out his hand to our father's friend. His voice was sickly jubilant. "It's so good to see you, Abe. You're looking well. How are your wife and son?" I cringed at his exuberance that was a little forced, a little too much.

Abe responded, "Very well, Steve, very well. And they send their hellos to both you and Harvy." He gestured in my direction.

Steve turned toward me as if I had suddenly shown up on his radar. "Hi, Harv! I hope you had a good trip here and are enjoying our winter weather." He smiled. "If you stay long enough, we'll thicken your blood again."

"Nice to see you too, Steve," I lied. My brother's digs about my living in the U.S. irritated my skin more than any dry, cold Canadian weather.

Part of me wanted to get down to business quickly and get our meeting done. But through my professional training, I knew that the first party to talk about business and money was frequently at a disadvantage. I said, "Have a seat, Steve, and we can order. We should eat before we get serious."

Steve did, we ordered, and then we chatted about our families. Abe broke the ice. "What's going on between you two that you need my help?"

I motioned my hand toward my brother. "You're welcome to start."

Steve turned in his seat to face Abe. My brother's presentation was short and to the point. "It's simple, Abe. Harvy wants me to subsidize the higher taxes he has to pay in the States if I obtain all of JHS's CDA assets."

I wanted to yell out: *It's our joint CDA money, Steve!* Instead, I held my hands together under the table and kept myself quiet and still.

Steve stayed focused on Abe. He raised an open palm, like a priest ready to speak to his flock. "I'm not willing to pay Harvy on the side for assigning all of JHS's CDA to me, a move that makes common sense. Harvy should pay his rightful taxes in the States on his JHS dividends while I pay my rightful taxes here in Canada. His U.S. tax rates are lower in general, so I can't accept his wanting a subsidy."

Steve was hammering the same nail he had been hitting for the last two months. I intended to demonstrate one of Dad's favourite Hungarian expressions: *There's nothing in your hand that you are holding onto tightly.* It had taken many restless nights of wrestling with my arguments to refine the ones I believed would open my brother's fist.

I looked at Steve. I made sure I stayed a little bent over so that my head was a touch lower than his—at least for the moment. "Anything more you want to say, Steve?" *Stay small and hang back, Harvy, so he can feel his big-brother oats before you work to cut them down.* My years as a student of Moe Gross, and the negotiation techniques I had learned and taught at McGill's MBA program decades earlier, were going to come in handy today.

Steve continued to look at Abe. "That's it from my perspective."

Abe turned to me. "So what do you have to say, Harvy?"

I had readied myself for this moment. I went to my briefcase and pulled out Geoff's JHS valuation plus other spreadsheets I had created. As I placed the documents on the tabletop, I prepared the table for Abe and Steve.

I looked at Abe, but I was speaking to Steve too. "To fully comprehend my position on this, Abe, I need you to understand the facts of what Steve and I are arguing about." I glanced over to my brother. "I need both of you to bear with me for the next few minutes while I go through the JHS valuation from our accountant as well as spreadsheets that I have created based on that valuation. You can then better judge whether what I'm asking for from Steve is fair."

I turned my head and shoulders toward my brother. "Steve, I think it's important for you to have a better handle on these numbers before passing judgment on our CDA situation. I believe these are important figures that will inform us as to what is a fair price for my JHS shares."

I looked carefully at my brother and worked to tamp down any ire in me. If Steve sensed my deep frustration with him, it would stimulate his stubbornness. Steve was merely uninformed, acting on a Johnny Simkovits gut impulse and not solid rationale. I looked intensely at him. "Steve, are you willing to take a close look at what I'm going to show you?"

He looked surprised by my question, then grunted softly. "Okay, but it's going to be hard to change my mind on this."

"That's fine, Steve. I can accept that for now." I kept my face serious and my eyes on him. "For the next few minutes, please allow these valuations, spreadsheets, and calculations to do the talking."

I handed Steve and Abe the first set of documents, just two pages. "The top page here is Geoff's Pro Forma Liquidation numbers for JHS. Steve, I believe you saw it when he emailed it to us last week. It states what JHS was worth at the end of 2005, assuming we sold our Ottawa property for $300,000 net." I pointed to specific lines. "As you can see from his analysis, JHS has about $725,000 in RDTOH and $940,000 in CDA money included in its value of $3.7 million Canadian, or $1.85 million to each of us, before tax."

Steve and Abe nodded. I continued. "Before we turn to the second page, do you have any questions about this one? Depending on what we get for our Ottawa property, the 3.7 million dollar figure could be higher or a little lower, but I think it's good enough for our purposes today."

"It's good enough for me," Steve said. "I did briefly look at this after Geoff had sent it."

Unlike me, Steve rarely dug deeply into stuff from the professionals.

Abe stayed quiet, carefully perusing what was in front of him. I continued. "If you now turn to the second page of this document, you'll see a simple spreadsheet that I created. It shows how much money Steve and I would have in our pockets, both before and after paying taxes, if we liquidated JHS today based on Geoff's valuation."

I looked at Abe and Steve to make sure they had their eyes on the second page. They did, so I continued. "This spreadsheet looks at two share redemption scenarios. The first, Scenario A, is based on my never having left Canada; or with my coming back this year to get the tax-free benefit from my half of JHS's CDA money."

Steve's face tightened, perhaps thinking I was throwing a red herring on the table. Though I knew that a return to Canada wasn't realistic, I wanted my brother to believe that I might do it. He had mentioned it sarcastically in one of his emails, so I might as well milk the notion.

I went on. "In Scenario A, Steve and I would split JHS's $940,000 of tax-free CDA money and then have to pay 33% tax on the rest. Each of us would then obtain 1.395 million dollars after taxes. Do you both see that?"

Steve and Abe continued to nod. I pointed to the other side of the page. "Now look at Scenario B. In this case, Steve stays in Canada and gets all of JHS's CDA money tax-free. He then pays 33% tax on the rest of the money he gets from JHS, while I pay 24% in the U.S. on my half of JHS."

Steve came in strongly. "Why 24%, Harvy?! I thought you told Geoff that your dividend tax rate down there is only 21%."

"That's correct, Steve, and it would be 21% on the Canadian-tax-free CDA money. But because JHS's CDA funds would go to you in this scenario, I'd have to pay a 15% Canadian withholding tax on my dividend from JHS before paying my U.S. federal taxes."

I took a breath and placed my palm on the table. "According to my tax attorney in Boston, I could claim those Canadian taxes as a credit against my U.S. taxes, but I wouldn't get them all back." I raised my hand off the table. "It's a complicated formula that only the tax professionals can work out. You can ask Geoff's tax accountant about it; she has talked to my tax attorney in Boston to confirm that percentage. They calculated that my effective U.S. tax rate would be about 24% on my non-CDA dividends from JHS."

I looked at Steve's face. "You're certainly welcome to call my tax attorney in Boston if you don't believe me." I knew my brother wouldn't make that call; Steve never liked talking to the professionals. Maybe he felt his executive MBA couldn't trump a law or accounting degree.

"Okay, Harvy," my brother barked. "What's the rest you have here?"

He sounded so much like our father.

I went on. "According to my calculations, if I pay 24% in taxes on my $1.85 million, then I'm left with $1.405 million, or about ten thousand more dollars than if I had resided in Canada." I worked to keep my tone even-keeled. "That's good for me, but look at the next column, Steve. If you get all of JHS's CDA money tax-free and then pay your expected 33% on the rest of JHS's assets, then you are left with $1.550 million, which is $155,000 more than if I had resided in Canada."

I came to my climax. I raised my hand and mock waved. "By Steve just waving goodbye as I invested the time and expense to leave Quebec for Massachusetts, he's now going to get a $155,000 net-after-tax bonus from JHS. It's $145,000 more than I would get by having crossed the border to be an American resident." I took a deep breath. "I'm wondering if that's fair."

Steve spoke. "I didn't push you out of Quebec, Harvy. You left on your own." That again sounded like what our father might say.

I responded quickly. "Okay, Steve, please hold that thought. You had your opportunity to talk. Unless you have any specific questions about these hard facts, let me finish my presentation before you offer an opinion."

Steve looked at Abe. Abe looked back at him and calmly said, "Let Harvy finish. You can speak again afterward." My father's friend stayed on the course I had set for him. Big brother had had his chance to state his case, and now it was little brother's turn.

I pulled out the second spreadsheet and gave copies to Steve and Abe. "Let me explain this spreadsheet that's a little complicated. It answers the question, 'What if JHS would have sold its land properties to Harvy and Steve at a nominal yet acceptable value soon after our father's death?'"

I looked up again to make sure Steve and Abe were following my lead. They both had their eyes on the second document. I continued. "In that scenario, Steve and Harvy would have owned those properties personally until they sold them years later for a profit." I then cited my brother's line. "Steve then would have paid his rightful capital gains taxes in Canada on his half of those property gains, and I would have paid my rightful taxes in the U.S."

Steve's tone remained a touch harsh. "Okay, so what's the difference as to whether JHS owned those properties or if we owned them individually? JHS is yours and mine anyway." Though our father was resonating clearly in my brother, at least Steve wasn't swearing like a Slovak.

"If you look at the spreadsheet closely, Steve, you'll see that, with the capital gains on those land sales coming directly to us, there would have been considerably less CDA money in JHS." I repeated, "You would have paid your taxes in Canada while I would have paid mine in the U.S., and that would have been the end of it."

I came to my point. "The money that would remain in JHS's CDA—by JHS having sold its properties to us years ago—would have been small, perhaps one to two hundred thousand dollars, not the $940,000 it is now. That CDA cash wouldn't have been worth arguing over the way we are doing now. I would have gladly signed it over to you because it would have been a much smaller amount. I would have dealt with my capital gains treatment in the U.S. while you would have dealt with yours here."

While Steve took in my words, I leveraged my Geoff Levi argument. Geoff hadn't supported me with Steve, so why should I back my friend now?

I pointed to Steve and then to myself. "You and I got bad advice from Geoff and his firm. He knew years ago that I was going to separate from JHS one day. We could have taken those land holdings out of JHS and sold them to ourselves personally, each of us owning half. That way, the capital gains would have gone directly to us, resulting in a much smaller CDA asset in JHS. You would have paid your net 26% tax on your capital gains on those sales, and I would have paid my 24% in the U.S., *and*," I stressed, "we wouldn't be fighting about anything."

I took a very long breath as I raised my hand again. "Frankly, Steve, I would have been far better off by having done that back then. It would have been better than the solution I'm going to propose now, as to what I see as a reasonable and equitable fix to this problem."

Now it was time for me to raise my voice a tad to display my disappointment, but not with Steve. I shoved my finger down on the table. "It's like with JHS's RDTOH money. Geoff has been lax about that, and I don't blame you for not trusting his advice. Even though he's my friend, he hasn't done us any favours regarding planning for our eventual separation. It would have been much better for the both of us had we taken the land out of JHS and owned it personally, way before we sold those properties for the sizable gains that we obtained."

There was dead silence at our table. After a moment, Steve spoke. "I'm not sure about this, Harvy. I need to speak to my accountant." He was waffling, deferring to people who were not in the room. But his wavering told me I had loosened his grip on what he felt he had held convincingly.

I looked at Abe and then back at Steve. I put my well-prepared solution on the table. "Steve, I think that what I'm going to ask you is very fair to both of us. I'm not looking for the whole loaf from you, but to share the loaf we have both gotten from my leaving Canada. It's not the full $155,000 bonus you'd get, nor the $145,000 difference between us that I'm seeking from you. I'm asking that we split the lower amount by you paying me $72,500 in cash. Then we both win on account of my having moved to the States. It would compensate, in part, for Geoff's oversight."

I wouldn't let my brother obtain the full $155,000 after-tax benefit by my having left Canada. He hadn't done anything for it, except to be my brother. And hell if I was going to let him believe that what I was asking of him was unjust. I'd be happy with the $72,500 to win my argument.

I had laid out my logic as plainly and methodically as I could. I was ready to argue Steve to Dad's grave if I had to. I felt I had the god of sibling fairness on my side. Though $72,500 was small compared to what I expected from my JHS share redemption, it wasn't chump change. Better the added amount be in my pocket than in my brother's. I didn't believe I was greedy. Steve was not getting cheated out of anything. He'd walk away with more than equal money in his own pockets for not having done any more than to say goodbye in 1989 when I crossed the U.S. border.

Dad once told me, "You need to know when it's time to shut up." I did so now and stayed quiet, allowing my brother to feel the weight of my arguments. I had one other gambit left that I mulled over. *Should I say it?*

Had my father been the one across the table, he might have become belligerent at this juncture, standing up and storming out of the restaurant because someone had gotten the better of him mentally. Dad wanted to show that he was the boss, especially in front of a close colleague.

But I knew that Steve prided himself on not being like our father. He wasn't going to get upset in front of Abe. He wouldn't show his suspicious, skeptical, or sarcastic Simkovits side that he had shown me in his emails.

My brother looked at the papers on the table. He took off his glasses so he could bring the documents closer to his eyes. It seemed he felt the strength of the logic that I had put between those eyeballs. He was taking his time, looking at everything, perhaps seeking a place to puncture my presentation.

I knew what else I wanted to say would be risky. Five years earlier, I had promised Steve that I'd never lord over him regarding my sharing Dad's offshore assets with him. (Legally and morally, he was entitled to that hidden money, but Dad had wanted only me to have it.) I had made it easy for him to obtain half of Dad's offshore stash—unlike what he had been doing these months regarding JHS's CDA asset. I now felt I had to remind him of my open-handedness and even-handedness so that he would do the same today.

I spoke softly yet assuredly. "Steve, since Dad died, I believe I have been very open and equitable to you concerning his estate, both onshore and off. I'm asking, this perhaps one time, that you be as equitable to me."

Steve lifted his index finger as a gesture of "hold on for a moment." He continued to reexamine and reshuffle the papers in front of him. His shuffling went on for an eternity but was maybe a minute or two. Abe turned toward him. "Steve, Harvy has made an excellent analysis." His voice was assuaging. "I think you should settle with him and not drag this out."

I had little idea of what was going on in my brother's mind. I had put forth ironclad arguments that would result in sibling equity. Maybe, like our father, he wanted to be sure that I wasn't taking advantage of him. For decades, Dad had hidden many things from his first son. So maybe he was seeking anything that might be missing from or hidden in my numbers. But I had played open-poker with him, and it was now time to lay down his cards.

After another moment, Steve looked up from the documents. His voice was calm and quiet. "Okay, Harvy. Let's work to equalize what money we end up with after we have paid our taxes to our respective governments."

There were a few seconds of silence at our table. The tension in my jaw fell away. Abe disappeared from my view. I looked down at the table and then up at my brother. I spoke quietly. "Okay, I'm glad you accept my proposal."

Steve asked, "But what do we do with JHS's Ottawa property? It may be worth more or less than $300,000. How can we rightfully know both the total worth of JHS and the right CDA compensation from me to you without knowing the exact value of that property?"

I smiled inside and offered, "That's a good question, Steve." And I had an answer. I lifted my hand. "It's relatively simple. We don't have to know the exact value of our Ottawa property right now." I kept my face from smiling. "We can do a version of what Geoff should have done with us years ago."

I land forward. "Let's pick the smallest number we think the Ottawa property could sell for today. Maybe it's the $300,000 as in my analysis, or it may be less. We can seek a *bona fide* assessment from an Ottawa realtor and use that value for the land. Then, with their number, we can calculate the value of JHS, which we can use for the company to redeem my shares."

I took a long breath. "And then, immediately after JHS has paid me out, I can buy my half of the Ottawa property from JHS at half of that assessed price, or $150,000 as per my analysis."

I kept my eyes on Steve. "We can then continue to work to sell our Ottawa property, but now it will have two owners, you via JHS and me personally. It changes nothing for you because you'll be the sole owner of JHS." I put my hands flat on the table. "Would that be acceptable to you?"

Steve thought for a moment. "Yes, I guess that'll be fine." He looked my way. "As long as you pay the costs of the property's transfer."

I almost smiled at how much Steve was like our father, despite how hard my brother tried to be different. "Sure, that's fair." That was fine, especially if it made him feel he won something.

Abe came back into the conversation. "It looks like the two of you have made a good arrangement."

Steve and I nodded, and we ended our negotiations there. I felt great relief and knew that it was time to stop negotiating. The more face I'd allow my brother to save, the less the chance I'd stimulate his stubbornness.

At the end of our dinner, Steve picked up the bill. "I'll put this through the company," he said. I allowed him to be pseudo magnanimous, for the two of us were the company. "Thank you, Steve," I responded.

Steve looked at Abe. "Thanks for coming out and spending time with us today."

I looked at my brother. "I want to thank you, Steve, for hearing me out." I turned to Abe. "Yes, thank you, too, for your time."

Abe was perky as if he had been the deciding factor in this battle of the brothers. He nodded and showed his open hands. "It was my pleasure, Harvy—anytime for you and Steve." He had played his part perfectly. What he had said had been well timed and precisely what I had hoped.

On the way out of the restaurant, Steve turned to me. "That was a good argument, Harvy." My ears perked as he continued. "JHS's CDA asset would never have been a big problem if Geoff had advised us years ago to sell the company's land properties to ourselves."

"Thanks, Steve." It was rare for him to acknowledge my perspective or capability. And I now knew what had tipped him into my camp. I felt our negotiation had been a boulder-moving struggle, with no help from Geoff. I added, "Geoff never made us aware that such an option existed. I'm as disappointed as you are. It has cost both of us."

It certainly had cost me greatly.

* * * *

36

There's Dad Again!

The morning after we met with Abe, both Steve and I reconvened at Geoff's firm. Geoff and his tax-preparer, Howie, led us into a small conference room that had no windows, as bland as an accountant's tie.

After we had sat down, I turned to Geoff. "Steve and I have decided on how I will extricate myself from JHS. We agreed to get an assessment for JHS's remaining Ottawa property that you'll use to calculate JHS's total value and the value of its CDA and RDTOH assets." I pointed to myself. "After my share redemption, I'll buy half the Ottawa property from JHS. We have an Ottawa lawyer lined up for that transaction."

I reiterated the side-deal that Steve and I worked out for my brother to have JHS's CDA assets. Other than raising an eyebrow, Geoff asked nothing about how I could convince my brother of that consideration. Neither Steve nor I said anything about how, the previous day, I had used Geoff's name disparagingly to close our deal.

I didn't say anything to Geoff about how Steve and I might have been better off had JHS sold its land holdings to us years ago. Though that hindsight was now 20/20 for Steve and me, Geoff might have pointed out a technicality that wouldn't have allowed the transfer of JHS's property assets to us—like how we would have come up with the cash to make those purchases. I was glad that Steve, too, said nothing about it.

Our conversation turned to the timing and process for JHS redeeming my shares. "How quickly can we get it done?" I asked. "Both Steve and I are biting at the bit to get me out of JHS. I want my shares paid out, and Steve wanted his CDA money yesterday."

I was channeling Dad. I looked back and forth between Geoff and Howie. "Could we backdate the transaction paperwork as of the beginning of this year, with JHS paying me out as soon as everything is signed?"

The ordinarily slow-reacting Howie jumped in. "We'll have to complete JHS's year-end for last year, 2005, to get the most accurate value of the company. If I can get JHS's books from Rob right away, then we can be ready to finalize JHS's 2005 statements and tax returns in perhaps one month." He looked at me. "There will be additional government paperwork to file for Harvy's share redemption, and we'll have to instruct your lawyer to prepare the corporate legal documents."

Howie took a long breath then continued to speak in his deep, monotone voice—ideal for a back-room auditor. "We can work to have JHS statements ready by the end of March. We can complete the share redemption the next day and file the necessary government documents in the first week or two of April, along with submitting Harvy's requisite 15% withholding taxes to Revenue Canada. JHS then can pay out Harvy for his share redemption, and Steve can get the CDA assets right afterward." He looked at Steve. "How quickly can Rob send me your accounting files for last year?"

Steve had been quiet up to then. He leaned forward in his chair, put one arm on the table, and spoke to Howie as if the auditor were the only person in the room. "I have to say that JHS won't have the money in April to pay out Harvy."

The room became deathly silent. Everyone's breathing stopped, including mine. All eyes were on Steve, whose eyes were still on Howie as if Geoff and I weren't there. Howie responded, "What do you mean, Steve? Why won't JHS have the money?"

Steve continued to speak in a muted monotone. He repeated, "JHS right now doesn't have enough cash to reimburse its shareholders. For one thing, CMS isn't yet in a position to repay the $200,000USD it borrowed from JHS last year." He took another deep breath and stayed focused on Howie. "Also, late last year, the Royal Bank decided to pull CMS's $1 million credit line as of the first of this year. When we found out, CMS immediately opened loan negotiations with the Bank of Montreal for a $1.5 million line there, but they haven't come through as of yet."

I glanced at Geoff. As CMS's accountant, I wondered if he should have known about CMS's banking problems. He was glaring at Steve, his face as puzzled as I suspected mine was.

Steve looked down at the table and then up at Howie. "I was hoping we'd have that credit line by now, but Bank of Montreal may not approve it until May." Steve kept his eyes only on Howie. "CMS had to finance its 2006 inventory, so I borrowed $900,000 from JHS, which was the proceeds from the two property sales we made last year."

He took a long breath. "I won't be able to pay that money back to JHS until the Bank of Montreal line is in CMS's account." His tone elevated a touch. "CMS will pay JHS interest on that money, at the prime rate."

Steve, you took JHS money for CMS? screamed in my head. *How could that be?* You had promised that JHS would never be involved in any project of yours. *Why didn't you or Rob tell me about it?* I held my emotions in check the best I could. My heart felt as if it were going to beat right out of my chest.

I worked to control my tremors. I said, "I'm sorry, Steve, but I don't understand." Had I been my father, I might have raised the roof and made the walls shake with my anger. I kept my voice collected. "How could you have taken that much money from JHS without Rob or me co-signing the cheque?"

Steve glanced my way and spoke matter-of-factly. "I asked Rob to sign." My brother's demeanor seemed calm as a Buddhist monk. I sensed he was holding himself tightly together. "Please don't blame Rob," he offered. "He wanted to tell you, but I asked him not to."

Why didn't Rob tell me? My voice started to rise. "Steve, it's his job to tell me such things!"

Steve could hardly look my way. "Again, Harvy, I told him I would handle it with you. Please don't be hard on him."

I glanced over at Geoff and Howie. They were opened-mouthed and dumb-faced as accountant deer in client headlights. I couldn't believe they weren't scolding Steve for his irresponsible action, and Rob, too, in absentia, for his collusion. I didn't know what to say. I didn't want to scream at my brother as my father might have, though I felt the urge to do so. Instead, I shut my mouth, stood, and walked out of the room and into the hallway. Geoff stood too and followed me, leaving Howie to deal with Steve.

I turned to my friend after the conference door had shut behind us. I spoke quietly, though I was shaking with rage. "I can't believe what my brother just said. How dare he do such a thing?"

Geoff tried to be disarming. "Harvy, you should have seen your face when Steve said what he had done. I thought you were ready to explode."

I stared for a moment at my colleague. I wondered why he wasn't inside the conference room to defend my shareholder interests with my brother. If Dad were here, he'd be screaming at his accountant, kicking his behind to do something, anything, to try to get the upper hand on the situation. I felt as if Geoff had placed another nail in the casket of his and my friendship. "What can we frigging do?" I asked.

Geoff looked at me. "We have to get Steve and CMS to repay those loans so that you can get your money out of JHS."

Well, thanks for stating the obvious. "But do I have any recourse for what Steve did?" I pointed to myself. "He took JHS money without telling me, his partner."

Geoff thought for a moment. "Steve did obtain a second signature for that cheque. You can't do anything about his not having told you. He is the President of JHS and acted within his bounds."

"But he had no moral right to take JHS's money without my permission. And what about Rob? He's supposed to tell me about and protect me from Steve doing such things."

Geoff showed an open hand and shrugged. "Rob has never been a bright light. He was perhaps following President's orders."

I recalled how Rob couldn't handle ethical dilemmas with my father. He hadn't told us about our dad's uncontrolled spending in the years before his death. But I had explicitly asked him to inform me if Steve ever tried to pull a fast one with JHS's money. I now knew whom Rob was working for—indeed, not me!

It crossed my mind to leave the premises and go to JHS directly to give Rob a piece of my mind, the way Johnny Simkovits might. Instead, I raised my voice with the hope that it would reverberate through the closed door between my brother and me. "How dare those two do this?" I felt my father's profound outrage and disheartening disappointment in my brother's dishonesty and Rob's disloyalty. I looked at Geoff. "Steve would never consider doing such a thing with his CMS partner. How am I, his brother, lucky enough to be treated this goddamned way?"

I wasn't sure if Steve was more aboveboard with his CMS business cohort, but he professed to be "Honest Abe" with everyone, even to a fault.

Geoff's voice stayed quiet and calm. "Harvy, let's focus on getting that money back from CMS and then getting you out of JHS. There's no benefit in creating more animosity between you and Steve."

Though my friend may have been correct, I again felt unsupported. I wondered how many more nails we had left to hammer into our friendship. Geoff then offered words that made me feel understood. "Steve's still seeing your father in you, Harvy. He may never get past his not trusting you."

There's Dad again, working to create animosity between Steve and me!

I took a deep breath. Geoff finally made a point I could accept. Steve had always blended me with Dad, seeing us as plotting against him. Why should things be any different today? I felt my father's fate befallen me again, re-lived once more between my brother and me. I soothed my voice. "Okay, Geoff. I need a second to calm down, and then we can then talk to Steve."

Geoff nodded and put his hand on my shoulder. "When you're ready."

A moment later, I nodded. Geoff led the way back into the small conference room, and we sat down. Howie looked back and forth at both of us while Steve's eyes remained down. Howie offered, "Steve says that he'll be able to pay back JHS in May or June."

Steve lifted his hand. "As soon as CMS obtains its Bank of Montreal line, I'll repay JHS."

Everyone nodded. Howie continued. "We'll have to create a new year-end for JHS, perhaps June 30th, so we can calculate an accurate value for the company at that moment in time. We'll then redeem Harvy's shares."

Geoff interrupted. "June is a tough time of year for our firm. We'll be busy with corporate tax returns; July 31st or Aug 30th would be better."

Steve offered, "CMS's year-end is Sept 30th. If we create a new JHS year-end at that same time, then the two will coincide. Considering that CMS might still be using JHS as a bank, having the same year-end might make it simpler for us."

Once again, Steve was considering his needs first. He had done the same with our father, as our father had done the same with our family.

Everyone turned toward me. Geoff spoke. "Would a new September 30th year-end be okay with you, Harvy? That will provide plenty of time to complete last year's statements and get everything ready and done for your share redemption by early October."

I looked at the three fellows. Only Geoff looked back at me. I said, "Will the government let us change JHS's year-end that easily?"

Howie replied, "As long as you have a reasonable reason, which I think you do, the government will allow it. They get such requests all the time and rarely say no."

Though it seemed an eternity away, September 30th was better than December 30th. I needed to give Steve no reason to withhold anything from me again, especially my JHS money. I turned to my brother. "Do you promise the three of us that there will be no more surprises? And, until my JHS shares are redeemed, I want to see the company's ledgers each month."

Steve turned my way, a startled look on his face. But I had been given cause to make my request for JHS's accounting records. "Okay, Harvy," he said softly. "Rob is converting JHS's ledgers into QuickBooks. He can email you the files after he has completed each month-end." Steve nodded. "And, yes, I promise; no more surprises."

I turned to Geoff. "It's decided then. We'll go with the new September 30th year-end for JHS. We'll work to have me completely out of JHS, my money in my hands, as soon as humanly possible after that, and not a day later than necessary." I turned to my brother. "Any issue with that?" It would be my 52nd birthday by then, and I hoped it would be a happy one.

Steve responded, "No issues here, as long as I can get JHS's CDA money out too, as soon as humanly possible."

Howie came in. "You guys need to be realistic about the timing." He pointed our way. "Remember that you need to pay a dividend to shareholders, either to one or both of you, before you can apply to get your RDTOH recovery money. We can consider Harvy's redemption as a dividend, but the RDTOH reimbursement may not come until late this year or early 2007."

He looked intently at Steve and me. "I have to do calculations to see if the redemption amount for Harvy's shares will get all JHS's RDTOH assets refunded in one fell swoop. My first thought tells me that the dividend to him may not be enough. Steve would have to take another dividend down the line to get back the rest of what JHS is due from the government."

As my father used to say, *Government bureaucrats, lawyers, and accountants rule the world.*

Steve said, "We might have to withhold an amount from Harvy's share redemption and pay him the balance when the RDTOH money arrives."

This ending with my brother was going to take forever! I stared at the ceiling for a long second. *Dad, you're like the government and the professionals; you never made anything simple. And Mom, I know you wanted Steve and me to stick together, but your other son hasn't made anything easy for this one.*

I looked back at Geoff and Howie. "Is there an alternative here, guys?"

Geoff looked at Howie. Howie offered, "The government will double-check your company's RDTOH numbers. They will reimburse you what they believe is the right figure. You won't know what you'll get until their assessment and cheque are in your hands." He raised a finger. "You can appeal if you think they made a mistake, but it can take many more months to get a decision, and their word is final."

As opposed to the previous day, little was working in my favour today. I looked again at our accountants. "Okay, okay, guys. Tell us what we need to do next and what you need from us by when. I'll get my money when I get my money. Let's hope it won't take until I'm underground like my father."

Geoff smiled. "Don't worry, Harvy. It'll be behind you in less than a year from now."

From your mouth to my father's ears in his grave. One hell of a way to end a sibling marriage I never created. Thanks, Dad!

We proceeded to work out an action plan.

Though I felt I was entitled to my disappointment and anger, I never displayed it to Steve while in our meeting. I'd wait for an opportune moment to have a word with him concerning what he had done behind my back.

Will our sibling relationship survive the blows that our father and my brother have laid on it?

* * *

The previous day, before we departed Ruby Foos, Steve had given me a JHS cheque. It was for JHS bonus money, dubbed a "management fee," a partial payment from our 2005 land sales. Steve had given himself a cheque for the same amount, all blessed by Geoff.

On the ground floor of the building that housed Geoff's firm was Steve's and my Canadian bank. After we had met with Geoff and Howie, Steve came there with me. We stood in the teller line to make our deposits.

The mood between us was subdued. Steve acted as if nothing arduous had happened between us. We spoke about our kids and didn't say a word about what had transpired upstairs with our accountants.

After some moments of waiting in line, I couldn't stop staring at Steve. I was seeking a place to start, to get to my point obliquely. I took a big breath. "Steve, how did you set the terms of the loan from JHS to CMS?"

He answered point-blank. "I made the loan a variable prime rate. It follows the bank's prime lending rate, month by month."

"And what was the rate CMS had been paying your bank?"

"Prime plus 1%." He looked at me. "But isn't it better for JHS to get 5% from CMS rather than 2% in a short-term certificate-of-deposit at the bank?"

"But doesn't CMS pay you 8% on your personal loan to your company?"

"That's a long-term loan, Harvy. JHS's loan to CMS is only for some months."

Steve's answers were logical to him, but it was yet another time he had made a JHS decision in his favour without conferring with me, his partner.

I cut to the chase. "So why did you hide that loan to CMS from me?"

Steve looked uncomfortable as he searched his mind for an answer. It was as if he had not expected that question. He didn't quite look at me. "Harvy, I guess I didn't want to give you any advantages in our negotiations concerning JHS's CDA money."

I was impressed by Steve's honesty but deeply disappointed with his thinking. It seemed that if he had asked my permission for the loan, he'd feel in a weaker position vis-à-vis our CDA negotiation.

I took another breath and responded a little facetiously. "That was certainly an honorable thing to do, Steve. I'm working on playing open-poker with you, and you're withholding cards."

Steve looked down and away. "I'm sorry, Harvy. I feel bad about what I did. In retrospect, I should have told you."

I hear you, but I don't believe you. I didn't press my point and wondered if Steve's remorse was genuine. He had said similar words before, as sincerely as Canadian pumpkin pie, but it never changed his ways. Dad showed up smack dab between us no matter what we said to each other. I now realized that Steve never trusted me, as he never had faith in Dad, and he never would. There was no hope of his ever considering my interests equally with his regarding our father's legacy.

There are defining moments where one gets to know exactly where one stands with another person. Because of my brother's calculated duplicity, something broke in me that day regarding our family bond.

Perhaps there never was any potential for trust between us, but now I knew for sure that there never was and would never be. My pious brother had gone behind my back. He had manipulated Rob like a Johnny Simkovits pro; thus, *mon cher frère* had forever betrayed my confidence.

Could I and would I ever forgive him?

Even if I would forgive, I would never forget.

* * *

That weekend, I wrote Abe an email.

> Hi Abe:
> Thank you for your assistance last week with Steve. Even though you didn't need to say much, your presence was important, and what you did say was helpful.
>
> I want to let you know that Steve dropped a bombshell the next day at the accountants' office. In the middle of planning for my share redemption, he told us that he had siphoned $900,000 of JHS's money to CMS in January. He said he needed the money to buy motor scooters from Korea for his business until his new bank line came through. The accountants and I were astounded that Steve had done such a thing without ever mentioning it to me. It will affect my being able to be paid out by JHS promptly. Rob colluded in this act because he co-signed the cheque for Steve without telling me.
>
> I'm deeply disappointed in Steve, and I have told him such. We talked about it after we had left the accountants. He now feels bad about his behavior. Though my father may have wanted it differently, this is another reason why I cannot remain in JHS with my brother. Because Steve failed to honor our partnership, I can no longer trust him to act in both of our best interests.
>
> It's regrettable; I thought you should know. Maybe you can have lunch with Steve sometime. He needs to understand why he withheld such information and the implications of breaking a business covenant with his brother and partner. I'm sure he would never treat his CMS partner that way. His behavior is a carryover from how we were with each other during our days with our father.
>
> Be well, and thanks,
> Harvy

As I pushed "send" on that email, I looked at the ceiling of my office. *Mom, now that your devout first son has sealed you in Mormon heaven, when the time comes, maybe you, too, could have a talk with him about how he treated your second son here on earth. And while you are at it, give Dad a piece of your mind for me.*

Just *Lassen* to Me!

Though Steve asked that I not blame Rob for co-signing a JHS cheque to CMS, I still held our bookkeeper responsible for his lack of consideration and negligence. That same weekend, I crafted an email to him but held onto it until Monday. My human resource development training told me that I shouldn't reprimand an employee during a weekend or when angry.

I also wrote to Geoff, recounting my conversation with Steve. I asked him if I should reprimand Rob. That Monday morning, he wrote back:

> Harvy:
> I am in total agreement with you regarding Steve's timing. What he did was in bad faith, especially coming from a person who prides himself on always taking the high road.
>
> For Rob's role, wait a few days before sending the email and see if you still want to send it. I find that time can add sobriety. Then again, his actions shouldn't go unnoted. I think that you are entitled to express your disappointment. He was on the payroll for the sake of all JHS shareholders, not only Steve.
> Geoff

Wednesday morning, I reread my letter to Rob to make sure it said what I wanted. I then pushed the "send" button.

> Rob:
> I've debated for several days on whether I should send this email or not. Geoff Levi agrees that I should express my reactions regarding what happened between Steve and me recently.
>
> Last Friday, in front of our accountants, after negotiating my pending departure from JHS, Steve said he had taken $900,000 from JHS for CMS. He also said I should hold him directly responsible for that act and not blame you. After much urging from you to let me know about the withdrawal, he added that he promised that he would "handle the situation" with me.
>
> However, I find myself deeply disappointed in your behavior. Your action to sign that cheque to CMS without my knowledge disregarded the trust and confidence that JHS

shareholders have bestowed upon you. You were supposed to act as a buffer between us and not enable actions that could adversely impact any JHS partner. Sadly, you broke your covenant, which you had reiterated to me not long ago, of acting in the best interests of both Steve and myself. No matter how much pressure Steve may have put on you or how much he assured you that he would make it okay with me, you set aside your obligation to this shareholder. That saddens me.

Unfortunately, your collaboration with Steve on this matter, no matter how much unintended, has precipitated a further rift between my brother and me, which we will have to repair over time, if possible. I can no longer trust him on money issues. You had the option of saying to Steve, 'Before I sign this large cheque, let's give Harvy a call, so he knows what's going on, and it doesn't damage your relationship.' For whatever reason, you chose not to do that.

Rob, I'm not angry at you about this, just profoundly hurt. I think you try to do the right things, yet this time you failed. For me, it has become another reason why I cannot remain in partnership with Steve, nor trust your looking out for my interests in JHS. You were supposed to watch my back, and you didn't. And Steve played on your loyalty to him such that he would not be disadvantaged in his negotiations regarding my separation from JHS.

I'm sorry that it has come to this. At least with my being out of JHS within the next year, you won't have to deal with such mixed loyalties or ethical dilemmas again.
I wish you well,
Harvy

Rob never responded to my email. As with Steve, something broke in me regarding our 25-year JHS bookkeeper. I didn't blame him entirely for his transgression, for he was only working to protect his JHS and CMS jobs with Steve. Though I understood why Rob had done what he did, I could no longer have faith in him. After my JHS share redemption was complete, I anticipated our paths might never cross again.

Yet another unhappy Johnny Simkovits ending.

* * * *

Day of Redemption – The Aftermath

It took eight months to reach my day of JHS share redemption. Geoff's people had to finalize the company's annual statements and work with our JHS lawyer to prepare the redemption documents. Steve and I had to obtain an assessment for our Ottawa property to determine what number to plug into Geoff's valuation of JHS. Steve and I had to work with the Ottawa real estate lawyer, who would transfer half of that property from JHS to me right after my shares were redeemed. Revenue Canada allowed JHS to change its year-end to September 30.

At every month end, Steve had Rob email me JHS's ledgers to check his bookkeeping. I didn't say more to Rob about his disloyalty. But I checked his entries in every account, so there'd be no errors in calculating the company's value on our redemption day. I was following the Reagan doctrine of "trust, but verify," but I no longer trusted.

Hundreds of emails and phone calls occurred between and among me and Steve, Rob, Geoff, Geoff's staff, my U.S. tax lawyer, and JHS's corporate lawyer. We worked on calculating every number down to the dollar. The noose that Dad had placed around Steve's and my neck was not easy to untie.

Five weeks before our redemption closing date of October 1, I emailed my brother. Rob was not providing timely JHS statements at the end of every month, and errors and omissions filled the ones he had provided.

Steve:
Rob hasn't delivered end-of-month statements since we talked about fixing the previous month's numbers. I don't see him using you as a resource to help him. Can you speak to him and figure it out?
Thanks, Harvy

Unusual for him, Steve responded in a few hours instead of a few days:

Harvy:
I reviewed the recent statements today. There is a hiccup in the foreign exchange account. Instead of what should be a foreign exchange loss in our JHS ledgers, there's a $10,000 gain. When JHS lent funds to CMS, there were many transactions as funds were dispensed a portion at a time. JHS bought U.S. dollars on behalf of CMS. In retrospect, I should have transferred Canadian dollars and let CMS worry about buying U.S. funds. I complicated the bookkeeping by having JHS buy U.S. money on behalf of CMS. In a nutshell, Rob is investigating how we got this discrepancy of a foreign exchange gain versus a loss.
Regards, Steve

I wrote back within the hour:

Steve:
Sorry, but I guess this is one more example of how you and Rob do things without consulting our advisors or me on the best methods. I'd like Geoff's assistant, Howie, to come to the office and see what Rob has done in the bookkeeping; or for Rob to email Howie the QB files and me the statements. Let's get on the phone and figure this out so that our accounting makes sense.
Harvy

Steve responded a few days later.

Hi Harv:
Howie is most welcome to come anytime and bring along a $500/hour forensic account. By the way, Rob did locate the discrepancy over the weekend and will make the proper adjustments. I hope to get the statements out to you soon.

As for your comment, it's a pity. It seems that you're acting as the judge and jury, or you enjoy making a mountain over a molehill. You didn't live the day-to-day drama of CMS waiting for funding from the Bank of Montreal last winter while our Korea supplier requested payment daily. They delayed shipping CMS the containers of motorcycles that we needed desperately for early spring sales. That's where I lost my sleep. Thank goodness my half of JHS's money was there to save CMS. CMS would be dead now if I had waited for the bank. JHS is now benefitting with a 6% interest rate on the $900,000 CMS borrowed. And the loan is fully guaranteed by me. As you know, CMS has repaid the $200,000USD loan from JHS.

You raised the backs of my hair this time. Chill out. I apologized once for "going behind your back." Had I discussed these issues before borrowing those funds, you would have used the situation to your advantage in our buyout discussions. As brothers, I wonder if we care about and understand each other's interests, needs, etc.
Stephen

It wasn't only Steve's neck-hairs that were on end. Somebody had to wake up my brother about his projections, and I put myself in charge of that. Dad couldn't shake Steve from his self-focused ways, so I now made it my duty to do so. Though I felt pent-up anger, I communicated calmly and collectedly. I had to point things out to my brother. I wrote him back.

Steve:
The back of your hair seems to be getting much exercise this year. Please consider the following. On your right hand, feel free to count the times in the last 5.5 years (since Dad died) that I have gone behind your back and made any decision or taken any action regarding JHS or Dad's estate without your consultation and consideration. Then on your left hand, count the times you've done the same with me. What do you get? Yes, it's true, and maybe understandable, that I may be oversensitive, overreacting to these minor situations with you. But the math on your fingers continues to add up.

I do work to understand your interests and needs if you tell me about them. I don't appreciate your continued assumption about my taking advantage of our negotiations in

February with Abe had I known the truth about CMS's need for financing. You had a moral and ethical obligation to share JHS's loan to CMS with me, your business partner and brother. (Does your CMS partner get the same treatment from you? I think not.)

You pride yourself on your honesty and integrity, yet you fall short of that with me. I wonder why. I suspect that you continue to see me as the sort of perpetrator that Dad was. I am not perfect, yet I believe I work to be open, fair, and reasonable with people who are that way with me. Other than my sometimes judgmental or harsh reactions, what substantial tangible harm have I ever acted out on you? What have I done that caused you to lose trust in me and feel that I'm working against our mutual interests?

Why do I continue to feel that Dad is with us every time we interact? (I do include myself in co-creating that.) I guess both of us have a hard time gracefully admitting when we are wrong, and we find it hard to make it up to the other when we transgress. Dad never took responsibility for his bad behavior and threw the blame on others for his mistakes. His bad manners seem to live in us with each other.

It is rare that you and I ever bestow acknowledgement and approval on each other, which perhaps fuels the damaging discourse between us. I've tried, over the years, to acknowledge when you do things well on our behalf. (I hope that you have felt that, and it's not my fantasy.) But I find it exceptionally rare for you to acknowledge my strengths and capabilities or that you work to recognize and repair your errors or omissions with me.

Maybe we are a pair of jerks looking for approval from our father through each other, but then never offer it because it makes us feel 'lesser than' to the other. Isn't that crazy-making? So when I don't get acknowledgment from you (as we both rarely did from Dad), I can get sensitive and judgmental, which might cause you to hide things from me (like dad did all his life with his wives and family). What a negative cycle of hurt and pain! Both of us are responsible for continuing this pattern.

The bottom line is that it's about acknowledgement and respect, which builds trust. When one of us doesn't feel it from the other, he does not offer it in return. I guess we have fallen into a hole of denying or withholding such good things from each other. And I'm afraid that we may have gotten too far down into that hole to get ourselves out of it. We have not been able to build a solid foundation for respectful discourse.

For that reason, I think it necessary that we disassociate ourselves from anything that would continue to bring Dad into the space between us. In part, it's a shame that it has come to this, for when we put our collective minds to the business situations we've faced together at JHS, we do much better than either of us would have done by ourselves.

At this juncture, if we can finish our business relationship with win-win intentions and mutually fair outcomes, it might (might!) help us both move beyond our poor patterns of behavior with each other. Let's hope so.

We both still have much work to do! May next year be a better one for us.
Harvy

Maybe I was channeling my psychotherapist wife that day. I wrote that memo without anyone's assistance. I went over and over it to ensure that it said what I wanted without anger or blame, just calling out what I saw.

It helped to focus a concave mirror at my brother's "Johnny Simkovits" MO. My father couldn't do that with his first son without yelling at him or complaining to everyone else when he felt powerless with Steve. I had tried to help Dad employ other methods to deal with Steve, but my advice may have been too self-serving.

Into what kind of box had Dad locked the three of us?! Our father had created that box, and his two sons continued to hold up its sidewalls well past our dad's lifetime. Because our father was no longer here, I felt it was my lot to confront my brother more appropriately. But I wasn't sure if I was doing that for Dad's sake, Steve's sake, or just for me.

In typical Steve fashion, he didn't respond to or even acknowledge my email. Like our father, he couldn't admit his flaws or failings, especially not to his little brother. Maybe, fundamentally, I was the same; but at least I had given it and us a try.

After sending that message to my brother, I promptly received JHS statements and responses from Rob. I had productive conversations with him and Howie to rectify myriad mistakes in JHS's books. There were so many errors in our ledgers that it made me wonder why Dad had kept Rob employed—maybe it had been for his gin rummy playing. My father certainly didn't retain Rob for his bookkeeping acumen and accuracy.

I could only hope that such things were going better for Steve at CMS.

Another hundred emails flew in every direction in the days leading to and just after September 30th. Steve and I finally met at Geoff's office on Friday the 13th of October to sign papers. I didn't know if this was my lucky or unlucky day, but it was six years—almost to the day—since Dad had passed away.

The mood was subdued as Steve handed me both U.S. and Canadian dollar JHS cheques totaling two-thirds of what JHS was paying me. We signed those cheques quietly in front of Geoff and Howie.

Steve then handed me a postdated cheque to cover my 2006 JHS management fee. I was to deposit that cheque only after I had paid JHS for half of JHS's remaining Ottawa property. That transaction was in the works and was going to close early the following month.

The last third of my JHS money was to come after Revenue Canada would approve JHS's September 30, 2006 tax returns, and they'd reimburse JHS a rightful portion of its RDTOH money. I had no choice but to trust my brother on that future payment.

After we had signed all cheques, I signed my ownership of JHS over to Steve. When we finished inking the papers, Howie turned to Steve while pointing to a document. "Steve, JHS will need to submit this six-figure amount along with this form to Revenue Canada for Harvy's Canadian withholding tax. You need to do it no later than Monday."

Howie looked intensely at my brother and spoke in a severe tone. "Don't screw around with that submission, Stephen. It will come back on you and JHS harshly if you do." He kept his eyes on Steve. "You'll need to deliver the cheque to the Canada Revenue Agency here in Montreal and have this paperwork stamped by them to prove the cheque's receipt."

Steve nodded, smiled, and chuckled a bit. "Okay, Howie, okay. I get it. I'll do the submission myself on Monday."

Howie pointed to a number on JHS's most recent statement. "Technically, Steve, as of tomorrow, you can issue a cheque to yourself for JHS's CDA assets." He took a breath and pointed his finger at my brother. "And once JHS receives the RDTOH reimbursement from Revenue Canada, later this year or early next year, you will immediately provide Harvy another JHS cheque for the amount indicated here, in Canadian funds."

"Yes, yes," my brother nodded again.

Howie's tone lowered. "And as to the CDA compensation for Harvy, that's a private matter between the two of you. I'll do the final CDA calculations for you, but you guys will have to work out that arrangement as you see fit."

I was glad that both Geoff and Howie were here to conduct this financial transaction and all its parts. I didn't think my brother would screw me out of any money, but it never hurts to have a witness or two. Geoff was also CMS's accountant, though Steve had shared privately with me that he was looking for a less expensive option. But that was between the two of them.

I felt much relief in closing my protracted JHS divorce deal. I wondered what I was going to do now that I wouldn't have to spend time—as I had done almost every day this past year—working to extricate myself from a corporate entanglement with my brother. It was an arrangement set up by a father who believed in his generosity and fairness to his sons. But he could also have been considered crass or cruel by some calculations.

Thank goodness I had my consulting work and my involvement in my professional associations to keep me focused on my future. In my professional circles, my colleagues saw me as a competent consultant. I had received awards for my board work from my associations.

Even so, I wondered who I would become now, not being encumbered by my father's burdens bestowed from my birth. I also wondered how my brother's life would be different now that he didn't have me to deal with or answer to, but a part of me no longer cared.

* * *

Once Howie completed the final value of JHS's CDA asset, Steve and I calculated the exact dollar figure to compensate me for Steve obtaining JHS's CDA money. I boasted to no one, not even my wife, about winning my CDA argument with Steve. I didn't consider it a win, just what I was due.

As we neared the day Steve was to pay me on our CDA deal, he sent me an email, copying Geoff. He employed a term he concocted for his payment.

> Harv:
> Abe and Geoff would applaud your even-Harvy-Steven CDA side deal. You're a winner, Harv; you pulled out extra cash. Kudos to you; take a bow; go out and celebrate!
> Stephen

Oh, my dear brother! The next day I wrote back, also copying Geoff.

> Steve:
> For the record, brother, if you check the tax calculations I showed you when we met with Abe, you're ahead by more than that same amount because I stood up fifteen years ago and walked out of Canada. You should go out and celebrate too!
> Harvy

Breaking our entrenched disdain of each other was hard. Though Dad was responsible for implanting our barking rancor, Steve and I were equally complicit in feeding our yowling dogs.

Soon after my share redemption, JHS sold me half of the Ottawa property. The real estate lawyer handled the transaction via fax and courier—Steve and I didn't have to meet.

When I completed the signing and faxing of the documents, I looked at my office ceiling. *Hey again, Dad and Mom. Even when things are over between Steve and me, they're not entirely over. We're still stuck together with this godforsaken Ottawa bushland. Dad, I bet you're chuckling up there about keeping your sons locked in. Mom, I guess you're still hoping that Steve and I will learn to play nice with each other.*

Over the next five years, Steve and I each invested tens of thousands of dollars more into that property to develop the plot to a point where we could sell it to a home builder. The best news was that we got our total asking price for the lot, many times its net cost. For that kind of money, my brother and I accepted the five-year payout the home builder offered, not atypical for such long-term development projects. If everything went according to plan, Steve and I would stay tied at the hip until the buyer made the final payment, when both of us were into our 60s.

For the nearly three decades that JHS had owned that Ottawa property, I never laid my eyes on it. After we had signed papers with the home-builder, I went to see the land to decide if I wanted to purchase a two-acre lot to maintain a footprint in Canada. As I walked down one of the gravel roads that Steve and I had installed, it took less than a minute to decide. *No, thanks!* There were thick and unkempt woods, dead trees lying about helter-skelter that thin topsoil could not hold, and swarms of mosquitos buzzing around my head. They made me wonder what my father ever saw in that godforsaken plot. That place was no promised land from my Abraham.

As in his six-year divorce from Mom, our father had crafted a sibling partnership that was long and hard to unwind, though both his sons were motivated to end it. Part of me loathed our father for having left us a bunch of ragged property assets. The redeeming factor was that there were decent gains in those sales to mask my ill feelings.

Thanks, Dad! I think.

* * *

Steve and I had tried ever so hard to be different from our father. We didn't want to repeat Dad's berating ways. We tried to be reasonable and fair with each other (in theory, at least). We aspired to give to others more than take for ourselves.

Steve had risen in his church to become a Mormon elder and the head of its family history centre. I had taken on board positions in my professional associations. While Steve mentored young Mormon missionaries, I coached both young and seasoned professionals to succeed in their client dealings. Both Steve and I tried to be charitable people, but we couldn't be kind and generous to each other.

Our father never realized the impact of his constant complaining about my brother and his continual showing off of his "MIT son." His words would invariably undermine what he had worked for and accumulated during his over fifty years in Canada. I could imagine Steve seething every time Dad told a business associate with pride, "Harvy's an MIT graduate. He's now a big consultant in Boston." (I had never heard him mention my dropping out of Harvard Business School.)

I know my temperature rose every time Dad confided or complained, "Steve does what he wants and never listens to me." Late in his life, Dad did admit, "I feel responsible for how Steve turned out." But he never comprehended the chronic competition he had created between his two sons.

I understood how Steve's jealousy and mistrust had grown in seeing me as Dad's favourite. I also appreciated how the same grew in me by seeing Steve get away with his chronic tardiness, his continual contradiction of Dad, and his unashamed drinking from our father's money fountain.

Dad so much wanted my brother and me to have life advantages that he never got and for us to carry on his Canadian legacy together. He wanted us to have money (something he didn't have when he walked off the immigration boat in 1949), so we could start a business without being hampered by banks and outside investors.

But Dad's "Just *lassen* to me!" call undermined his sounder fatherly advice. Dad's belligerent ways with his employees and abandoning ways with his wives and other women bred an "I am better than you" resistance from his first son and perhaps "I know better than you" conceit from his second. Steve and I had taken on our variations of Dad's "Just *lassen* to me!"

Steve and I could have done something greater together with Dad's assets, but our mutual mistrust and dislike had stood staunchly in the way. I hoped I would never have to deal with anything financial with my brother again—though I wished we'd each find success after having gone our separate ways.

Once I received my final payments from JHS and Steve, I was relieved, as if Dad's office safe had come off my back. I had survived my "it's nothing to be concerned about" father and my "it's no way but my way" brother. But I didn't know if I should laugh, cry, or grieve about what could have been among the three of us but hadn't.

Then again, maybe I should thank my lucky first-generation stars for being the son of a self-made immigrant. And perhaps I should be satisfied with having played some of my cards correctly along the way.

* * * *

Life after Redemption?

My odyssey of coming clean about my father's hidden offshore assets had started in 1999 with my friend, Geoff Levi, when he sat me next to André of Elliot Trudell at his son's bar mitzvah. It also ended with Geoff in 2006 when I signed papers to extricate myself from my sibling partnership in Dad's holding company.

Geoff had been a big help for the most part. But during the six years that Steve and I had worked to unwind JHS, I rarely felt Geoff's professional friendship. I didn't expect 100% of his allegiance, but I didn't even sense 50% of it. He didn't advise Steve and me effectively for our eventual separation, and he couldn't help us navigate through our differences about JHS's CDA conundrum. Maybe I had expected too much of my friend, but I couldn't relinquish my disappointment in him.

After I had gotten my money out of JHS, I stopped calling or emailing Geoff. I was slow to respond to his outreach. I wondered if I was acting like my father. He had summarily dropped his first accountant, Gillian Mozer, after a 20-year colleagueship. That firing was right after Revenue Canada absolved Dad of criminal charges in his Montreal Phono inventory scam.

In my case with Geoff, it wasn't a single nail that had fastened the door shut on our friendship, but a series of them. I felt I couldn't reopen the door.

As a final act of camaraderie, I suggested to Geoff that he introduce my brother to one of his other partners. "Steve sees you more on my side than his," I told him. "Your firm may be better off with a different point-person handling JHS and CMS from now on."

Geoff agreed, and neither of us said anything to my brother about our conversation. The next I heard, Steve and his CMS partner dropped Geoff's firm for a less expensive alternative. Geoff was heading into the sunset for both Simkovits sons, just as he had when our father had terminated him over a decade earlier.

For years, I continued to wonder as to why Geoff seemed to protect my brother's interests more than mine. Why had he viewed me as a perpetrator with Steve and my brother as the innocent victim? It took nearly a decade for the answer to come as to what might have transpired among us.

In 1993, after Dad and Elaine had separated, Steve had told me, "Beware the wolf in sheep's clothing." Now, years after my separation from JHS, it dawned on me that my brother had well learned to play the innocent sheep himself, victimized by our wolf father and then his wolf-cub brother.

Steve probably told Geoff how I got more of our father's attention and benefits. Steve may have related how he was under Dad's thumb or behind his shadow, that our dad's hand and heart had been more open toward his younger son. My brother played the innocent sheep masterfully with Geoff, projecting "the favoured offspring of a father wolf" onto me.

Beware of sibling wolves in Mormon sheep's clothing.

How did my brother learn to play that Shakespearian-like drama? *From Dad, of course!* Our father had played out similar scenes with his advisors. He bellyached to them about how his wives and business partners were taking advantage of him, wanting his money, and so on. He masterfully made others believe he was blameless.

Steve probably felt victimized in our JHS sibling marriage as much as I had felt that way. But my brother had played the innocent sheep with Geoff better than I had. After hearing my brother's woes, my friend perhaps saw himself protecting or rescuing my brother from the crafty and conniving preferred son that Steve had projected onto me.

Could my unsuspecting comrade have become entrapped by my brother's unconscious cunning? Just as Steve had picked Mormonism to be his salvation from our disaffecting father, might Steve have positioned Geoff into becoming his rescuer from me? No wonder Geoff stood up for my brother and worked to poke holes in my arguments against Steve. I suspect my friend was only trying to help, but he didn't see the devious Johnny-playing-victim in Steve. Geoff saw only the calculating Johnny-perpetrator in this Simkovits son.

Son of a bitch! Geoff's efforts to balance things between my brother and me had worked to turn my friend against me, thus causing my jettisoning of our friendship. I felt terrible for Geoff, and I stung from the loss of our companionship. But I applauded my brother for having so skillfully (albeit semi-consciously) channeled our father's MO of sheep innocence.

And once I nailed the door shut on a person who deeply disappointed me, I found that I couldn't reopen it.

Maybe I threw my brother behind that shut door too.

* * *

Two years after Steve's and my JHS separation, the Great Recession hit the economy. My brother's business was unprepared. In Canada, summer recreational vehicle sales skidded to a halt.

That economic winter provided no shelter for CMS. A year or two later, Steve and his partner looked for new financial investors or merging CMS with a complimentary business. After several unsuccessful attempts, Steve wrote an email.

> Harvy:
> I've sunk over $2 million into CMS and am nearly out of cash. CMS's money is locked into older inventory and spare parts. I need to borrow $80,000CAD for a few months to help finance our 2010 line of vehicles from Korea. We need that new product line to keep our sales going for this year.
> Steve

I was taken aback by my brother's request and his having invested so much into CMS—double what he had once said would be his limit in that venture. I felt sorry for him, and I wondered if I should help. I thought about it for a day and then responded.

> Steve:
> Sorry, but I'm not in a position to lend you or CMS any funds at this time.
> Harvy

The truth was that I didn't think I'd see my money returned. Steve had broken my trust during our JHS dealings. Though I tried not to harbour resentment toward him, I didn't want to give my brother another chance to break my faith. I also didn't want to chase him to repay any loan I'd make to his company.

Steve emailed again a few days later. He had suddenly discovered a $100,000 unused line on his credit cards. He was going to use that to help fund CMS's 2010 line of products.

More good money after bad?

The condition of Steve's business didn't improve. Seeing the writing on the CMS warehouse walls, Steve's partner left the business in 2011. Steve was left holding the whole scooter saddlebag. Over the next year, CMS's salespeople and staff departed, and Steve was left with older scooter inventory to peddle—just like our father had old console stereo inventory to liquidate when he decided to retire in 1984. Only Rob stayed on as the bookkeeper.

It took Steve to the end of 2013 to rid CMS of perhaps a thousand older-model bikes and a contingent of spare parts, all warehoused a little way down the highway from where our father had had his JHS factory building. As it had been with Dad, Rob was the last employee Steve would engage. When Steve closed CMS, Rob retired after over 30 years of working for a Simkovits.

It was the end of a business dream for my brother. He had wanted to prove that he could be a better entrepreneur than our father. Months later, he emailed me, among other friends and relatives, about his business ending.

> Dear Friends:
> I have no regrets about my investment in CMS, though the last few years have been highly stressful. Even though I have used up my inheritance from my father, I would have done nothing differently. It has been a great experience.
> Stephen

I emailed back that I was sorry that things hadn't worked out the way he had hoped. In a later phone call between us, my brother admitted, "I guess I found out I'm not an entrepreneur like Dad was."

I could have told you that a long time ago. I guess Steve needed to find it out on his own. Perhaps it was good that he was living more for the next life than for this one.

Over the years, I wondered why Steve shared so much about his business. I never told him about my venture investments, and he never asked about my consulting business. Maybe my brother needed the same acknowledgement from me that he had sought from our father.

I wondered what Steve was going to do now that he was again out of a job. Would he stay a leader in his church? As long as his congregation continued to look up to him, that might be enough for him. Thank goodness he still had his JHS assets to live on.

I tried not to be judgemental of my brother for his failed business venture. Through my consulting work with owner-managed companies, I knew how hard it was to do what he had tried to accomplish. Only talented, determined, and fortunate entrepreneurs succeed. Our father had had a few failed business attempts before and after he found success in JHS/Montreal Phono. Dad had had tenacity and perseverance that both my brother and I sorely lacked, and sometimes even those had not been enough to help him.

Instead of starting a venture on my own or with a partner, I invested a modest amount of my inheritance in a few socially responsible businesses. After several years of operations, two of those ventures went belly up, losing my total investment. The third one returned dividends over time, but it involved multiple rounds of asking for more cash. Its future was fragile, and its return-on-investment uncertain. My solace was that I had risked a limited amount on those three ventures while other investors in the group had lost or tied up millions.

I tried another approach. I risked another modest amount on a venture firm that raised $5 million to invest in ten socially responsible ventures in New England. The leader of that fund impressed me with her track record and her smarts. I felt she would do much better at picking early-stage ventures than I ever could.

Then the Great Recession hit. After over a decade of working to support early-stage businesses, that venture firm returned 70% of my original investment, and I expected perhaps 10-20% more returned over the ensuing years. I would never be made whole. In a personal call, the fund manager said, "We exceeded our social mission with our fund, creating hundreds of new jobs in Massachusetts and New England. But because of the recession, we fell short of our financial goals."

What else could she say? *Sorry to have lost your father's money?* At least she didn't lose every dollar I had placed with her venture firm.

After I had told Gloria about my latest miss-venture, she looked at me, touched my arm, and said, "You can't sustain too many more of those kinds of losses, right, honey?" At least she didn't yell at me as my father might have. Luckily, we could absorb those failures.

My dream of investing in socially responsible businesses ended there. I could hear my father yell in my head from his grave. *How could you do such stupid things with my money!* As my brother wasn't much of an entrepreneur, I guess I wasn't much of a venture capitalist or what people in the industry call "an angel investor." Unlike my father, who kept trying to make it in business after more than one failure, I curtailed my dream. I still wondered if my self-doubt was mine or a notion my father had implanted. Could I ever be successful without his "Just *lassen* to me!" advice?

I decided to place the remainder of the money I had received from Dad and JHS with several money managers. I had tried to do some market trading myself but never made gains. I had an uncanny way of getting into an investment too late or getting out too early. I fired myself and hired other professionals to do the investing for me. I hated to lose the assets that came from my father. It was as if Dad were still sitting on my shoulder, scrutinizing my every move.

Like my brother, I finally realized my limitations. Fortunately, I had my ongoing consulting work and association involvements to keep me fulfilled.

If I couldn't become a self-made giant like my father, then perhaps protecting what I had inherited from him would be good enough. I created an irrevocable trust, whole life insurance policies on my kids' lives, college plans for their higher education, and a charitable fund. These financial vehicles would allow my family to legally employ the money wisely and with the least tax liability. I wanted both my family and my select philanthropies to get the most from Dad's hard-won assets when I was gone. And, perhaps my less encumbered children would do better than I with Johnny Simkovits's legacy.

Time would tell, as my brother would say.

In the end, both Steve and I had survived our charismatic and conniving father in our separate ways, but I can't say that we thrived. As our father had hoped, Steve and I might have done better by building something together. We could have effectively leveraged the property and cash assets that Dad had left us in JHS and brought it into the next generation.

What potent water Dad had had was now washed away under our Simkovits bridge. At least I knew that my mother would have been proud of my taking advantage of my father's assets to create a life for my family, a life that she had never had.

* * *

Fifteen years after I had consulted with André Lefebvre in 1999, I sought him out again in Montreal. He was working as VP of Finance for a large international company, where he went after departing Elliot Trudell. My school chum had changed much in his face, hair, and physique. He had put on extra pounds and sported grey hair—as I too had developed. I don't believe I would've recognized my high-school chum if we had passed each other on the street, and maybe he wouldn't have known me either.

André recalled our meeting at Elliot Trudell, but he recollected little about our conversation. He didn't even remember the Bernard fellow he had referred me regarding my father's offshore assets. A part of me wondered if these last fifteen years of surviving my father's sordid legacy had been a bad dream or that my imagination had been playing tricks on me.

I reminded André about the voluntary disclosure process his former colleague had explained to me. I told him about the manuscript I had been writing, since 2005, about my father, especially the chapters that involved André and Geoff.

My old friend looked at me from behind his big mahogany desk. "Harvy, you're a smart fellow, MIT graduate and all. I do hope you're not making your life only about your father."

Though his caution may have been a good one, I batted my hand at him. I casually responded, "Don't worry, André," but his poignant comment reverberated in my bones.

My mother's Hungarian family had expressions for nagging problems and dependent people. Many times, she told me, "Don't let that situation break your head," or "Don't let that person hang from your neck." I wondered if my memories of my father might break my head one day or hang around my neck for the rest of my life.

I told myself, *Harvy, you're turning your tumultuous family history into a moving and healing family story. And you're working to leverage that asset for the betterment of yourself and others.*

Though there may be a fine line between visions and delusions, I hoped I wasn't fooling myself.

* * *

Enlightenment can come from anywhere and hit you when least expected.

A year or two after I had reconnected with André, I was close to completing my manuscript. I had started to play golf again. I hadn't played that game since I had played with my father two decades earlier, the last time being some years after his stroke. Dad still attempted to play golf to keep his body moving and to stay connected to his buddies. The day he and I had played, both of us got exasperated with our duffs and slices. Both of us decided to stop playing the sport, though his growing physical disability gave him a better excuse to quit than my mental frustration had given me.

I thought I no longer wanted to play that game, but I started again twenty years later. I hit balls at driving ranges and played at a 9-hole par three close to home to regain my golfing abilities. It helped my hand-eye coordination after I had suffered a minor mini-stroke in my early 60s. *Thanks, Dad, for some of your genes!* Or maybe I had precipitated that condition myself.

One day, I was on the driving range with a friend named Jim. After we had finished hitting, we had soft drinks and shared stories about our lives and families. He and I discovered that we shared much in our family history.

Both Jim and I had older brothers who were in a business started by our fathers. Both of our fathers had hoped and expected that we, as second sons, would get into and stay in the family business, but we eventually went in different directions. Both of our fathers had had critical personalities, berating both of their sons whenever those sons had disappointed them.

As I hit golf balls, I thought of my father in his factory. Dad got mad whenever he caught a guy smoking, kibitzing, or fooling around with others on the job. He'd place his flat hand crotch high and say, "*Lassen* to me! I'll cut off your *yaytsa* [eggs] if you don't stop screwing around." He then pointed to the fellow with a stern finger. "Now, get back to work."

Then it hit me like a clean stroke of a golf ball. That was what my father had done to both my brother and me. He had made us feel impotent if we didn't *lassen* to his ways of doing business and follow in the footsteps he had laid out.

In his reaction, my brother retaliated against our father by working "to cut off Dad's *yaytsa*," making our father impotent in having any influence on his first son. Steve not only resisted almost every suggestion our father made, but he also rejected everything Dad stood for in work, play, and religion.

Conversely, I worked to be more loyal to my father and to show the potency of my *yaytsa* in ways that connected to Dad's wishes for me. (Instead of going to Harvard for an MBA, I went to American University for an organization development degree.) But I continually felt my *yaytsa* compromised and in danger of castration. In my various depressions at MIT, Harvard, and AU, I semi-consciously worked to make myself impotent, fearing my father's disappointment and rejection.

It amazed me how much we three Simkovits males had engaged in fruitless and unfulfilling missions with each other, squeezing each other's *yaytsa* or protecting our *yaytsa* from being compromised.

After Dad's death, Steve vied to disempower the *yaytsa* of the Johnny he saw in me. (He had kept me at a distance from his dealings as JHS President.) On the other hand, I tried to demonstrate my *yaytsa* to the Johnny Simkovits I saw in Steve. We subsequently felt our capabilities unrecognized by the other as we each played surrogate for our father.

Steve then worked to jettison my *yaytsa* out of JHS, repeating what Dad had done to his spouses and other women. (Dad had deluded himself that Mom, and every other female he married or lived with, squeezed his *yaytsa* by putting limits on his life of vices. So he eventually discarded each of his wives and women like a bad card in a gin rummy hand.)

As Jim and I sat, sharing sibling stories and sipping on soft drinks, I felt stunned by my sudden realization of what had happened in my Johnny Simkovits narrative. Part of me felt foolish for the recreated Bible story that Steve and I had played out semi-consciously, reflexively, without full awareness. But I now understood our family drama better than ever, and I felt another weight come off my shoulders in comprehending the age-old storyline that had befallen my family.

I turned to my friend and said, "Jim, I'm feeling good about our play and conversation today." I shared some of my realizations. I smiled, winked, and added, "It seems like playing golf can be good therapy. Let's hit another bucket of *yaytsa* soon."

* * * *

Montreal Funeral, May 2009

Email message from Elaine:

> My mother passed away in Montreal. Services will be held at Mount Royal Cemetery this coming Wednesday at 2 p.m.

Elaine's mother, Jean, had lived in Montreal's West Island, just down the road from my brother. But I never saw or talked to her again after Elaine and Dad had separated and divorced.

There would be other Montreal people I'd know at Jean's wake, many of whom would have been at my father's funeral. Jean's ashes were to be interred in the same Mount Royal Cemetery where my father lay. I cared about Elaine and wanted her to know. Thus I drove to Montreal to attend her mother's funeral, and I told Steve that I was going.

I walked into one of the small chapels of the Mount Royal Cemetery complex as the service started. Dark suits and black dresses packed the place. Hardly a seat was empty. Soft chamber music played in the background. I walked up the center aisle slowly, looking for a place to sit near anyone I knew.

Halfway to the front, I heard a soft voice call my name from behind me. It came from Steve. *My God, he's on time!* Knowing I was driving up from Boston, he had gotten here early and saved a seat for me. I backtracked quickly and sat down beside him.

"Hi, Stephen," I said quietly.

"Hi, Harvy." His voice was quiet too.

"Been here long?"

"Got here a few minutes before you," he replied.

"Lots of people here," I added.

"Yes, from all over."

He and I were never much for profound words with each other.

I looked into the crowd and nodded and smiled at people I recognized from my father's past. I was relieved when they nodded and smiled back at me.

Jean's urn of ashes sat on top of the altar at the front. A Catholic priest offered prayers. The audience recited *The Lord is my Shepherd*, and then we sang a hymn. Elaine stood from the front row to give the eulogy. She had dressed in her black and white best. Her high heels and body-hugging outfit made her look taller and thinner than I remembered. A big black hat was on her head, with the veil placed up over the brim. She began, "I had a whole speech written for my mother, but I can't give it. It would be too emotional for me. Instead, I'd like to share a few stories about her."

Elaine talked off-the-cuff for forty-five minutes, never losing a beat or her place. She spoke about growing up in rural Ontario with her burly father and petite mother. She offered, "With one big squeeze, he could envelop my mum." She smiled. "I was afraid he'd crush her." The crowd chuckled. She continued. "Though she was petite, my mother was never shy about putting us in our place when we needed it, be it my dad, my brother, or me."

In the middle of her talk, Elaine turned to look at my brother and me. "I'm happy to see Harvy and Stephen here. Their father, Johnny, was good to my mother. When we were married, he never excluded her from our life. He invited her to suppers, had her join our social gatherings, and asked her to come on vacations with us." She took a long breath. "On Mother's Day, he'd give her a dozen long-stem red roses, like the ones you see here."

Elaine pointed to the fresh roses lying on the altar next to her mother's urn. They were on the verge of blooming, the way Dad liked to buy them so that they would last the longest time. Elaine smiled again, "And whenever Mum and I would get annoyed at Johnny for this or that, he'd send us two dozen of those things." The crowd chuckled again.

I recalled my father's complaints. "Jean is such a busybody," and "Elaine spends too much time with her mother and not enough with me." Then again, what woman in his life did he not complain about eventually?

Elaine took a long breath and continued. "After concluding the services here and reception down the hall, and for anybody who wants to, I'm going to take those roses and put them on Johnny's grave. That will be my thank you for how kind and accepting he was of my mother."

How nice! I was going to join her for that ritual. Visiting Dad might be good. I hadn't been to his grave since we had unveiled his headstone eight years earlier, a year after his death. I wondered what it might feel like to stand by his side once more.

During the reception, it was as if the years between Dad's friends and me had melted away. Many offered: "Where have you been hiding, Harvy? Still down there in *Bawston*?" . . . "How are you and your family?" . . . "We never get to see you." . . . "When will you come and visit us? We are not getting any younger, you know." . . . "I can't believe it's been so long since your father passed away."

I smiled and replied, "Yes, I know. I'm not in Montreal as much as I used to be." . . . "Boston's keeping me busy." . . . "It's so good to see you too. How have you been keeping?"

Before the reception ended, Steve said he needed to depart. He was never one for Dad's friends, whether they were dark-bread Eastern Europeans or white-bread Canadians. My brother didn't join Elaine, me, and a few others who formed a modest motorcade to travel a short distance up Mount Royal to see Dad's gravesite. I didn't ask Steve why he had to leave, and he didn't offer a reason.

Near my father's site, everyone stopped their cars and exited their vehicles. They stood by the road as Elaine motioned for me to come with her. She carried the dozen bright red roses as if they were a baby in her arms.

Elaine and I walked to my father's plot, located a few gravesites away from the road. She placed the roses in front of the headstone and nodded my way. She bowed her head in reflection, and I followed suit. We stood there in silence for many minutes.

It was early spring in Montreal—the snow had disappeared, but the air was blowing and chilly. The sky was mostly clouded over. The warm sun peeked through here and there. *Why is it cold and drab whenever I'm doing something difficult regarding you, Dad?*

My mind tried to focus on the moment. *Dad, what can I say after all these years? I hope you are well where you are. I hope you are at peace. I hope you're back with Mom, assuming she'll have you. Yes, of course, she would.*

I hope those you have transgressed, like Mom and Elaine, have forgiven you for the stupid and mean things you did. Then again, you were an addicted man and couldn't get past your urges—just as I had trouble with my compulsions regarding you.

I took a deep breath as I looked at Dad's name, "John (Jan) Simkovits," carved deeply into the granite headstone. *It's still hard to think good thoughts about you. I find it's easy to admire you but so hard to respect you. You weren't an evil man, but you surely didn't know how to love those who loved you; you took advantage of us instead. I can't believe how my life was and still feels so connected to you. For good and bad, Elaine and I here are among the few who saw not only the light but also the dark sides of you—though I still wonder how much you still might have hidden from us. Are there any other wives, kids, or broken hearts out there to know about?*

I stood with my hands clasped and my head bowed. I hardly glanced at Elaine. *You know, Steve and I have dissolved your estate trust, and I'm now entirely out of JHS. He's totally on his own, holding onto what's left of his half of your legacy. You were right about him; he's blowing much of what you left him in his trying to be a better man than you. But it's not his fault; you had a part in his making as you had a role in mine.*

I looked into the sky and worked to keep my breathing steady. *Be sure that I won't be my brother's keeper as you wanted me to be. Steve has to learn to make it on his own. Then again, he's not living for this life as you had done. He's planning to be a big man in Mormon heaven as you had worked to be a big man in Montreal. I guess that notion helps him feel better about not having measured up to you down here on earth.*

I took a few more long breaths. *I still wonder if I can live up to the respectable and respected parts of you. I find myself admiring your tenacity in business and your ability to schmooze and entertain into the wee hours. I find that I still revere your accomplishments, for I'm not as natural in my circles as you were in yours.*

I am grateful that you came to North America with Mom, and I didn't have to grow up and live in a deprived communist country or one in continual conflict. You worked hard to be somebody here in Canada. Then again, maybe you were deathly afraid to end up as nobody in your adopted country. Perhaps you had felt such fear while growing up with stern parents and in having lost your mother at such a young age.

I took another deep breath. *Okay, okay! I do owe you for being kind to me: giving me a good education, taking me out to fancy places and on nice vacations, trying to give me a leg up in my life, and leaving me money so that I don't have to beg on the street. Can all that buy you some forgiveness? Yes, maybe a little.*

And, alright! Maybe I'm a good price shopper and a better negotiator because of you. But I try to win with my smarts rather than with your bullying and intimidation—though maybe I could use a little more of your grit and gumption.

I guess you did try to be a good Dad, to teach me things, but it felt as if it were about you and your money. I never felt your interest in helping me discover my future. The things I had to do to gain your attention and appreciation—by keeping your secrets about your hidden assets and hidden away women—were costly to my conscience.

Part of me still loathes myself for having been your "good boy," not divulging your sordid treasure that I had desperately desired for decades. Just as you were devious and secretive, I thought I needed to be the same, keeping things away from Mom and Steve, pretending I didn't know anything. My fear of losing your favour made me clench my teeth, hold my tongue, and gnaw at my psyche.

I stared at his monument. *But I eventually realized that I'm not like you. Your life's trauma, family burdens, and business and money legacy are no longer mine to bear.*

Out of the corner of my eye, I could see Elaine had closed her eyelids. I couldn't close mine, for I feared that I might get dizzy and fall right on top of my father's grave. I worked to keep my eyes focused on the headstone.

Dad, I'm writing a memoir about you. I started it some years ago; I should complete it in perhaps a few more. I smiled inside, thinking, *You and Mom have given me good material.* I focused on his gravestone. *I hope you and she will appreciate it when it's complete, though I'm sure you'll wonder why I'm writing about the dark and distressing sides of our family.*

Yet I suspect Mom would applaud my seeing you more clearly now than when she had been alive. For sure, I'm trying to heal myself by revealing the truth about you and the rest of us. I hope it will make me a better person and more at peace.

My eyes welled, but I held myself back from tearing. I turned my head away so that no one could see my watering eyes. A small part of me wanted to stomp on my father's grave, but I kept my feet still. I thought about what my father might say about my book about him. I could hear him shout, "So, you're *seeting* on your *arsh* all day and *riting bullsheet* about me?" I then smiled as I thought about what he might say next. "At *leest* you *aarren't* costing me money." I hoped that he would be proud of my narration of him.

I looked again at his grave. *Dad, I do hope God has forgiven you because it's still hard for me to do so. But I find that I do love you, and I still want to know that you, deep down, loved me too, and not just for my having kept your confidences.*

Another tear came to my eye, and I quickly brushed it aside. *May the universe help me get beyond you, Dad, so that I can survive your hold on me! I know I can't eradicate all of you in me, but maybe I can find my way to tamp you down and feel okay with the problematic parts of you I still feel inside.* I took another long breath. *Did you know that I sometimes can't even look in the mirror because my face reminds me of you? Other times, I find myself staring at a wall or ceiling, wondering how our lives would have been different if it hadn't been for your contemptible abusiveness, though your likable charisma cushioned it.*

Elaine raised her head. She turned my way, her voice a touch harsh. "Harvy, he certainly was a hard man to love."

I shook off my thoughts and turned to her. I worked to keep my face relaxed. "Yes, I know, Elaine. He's the kind of guy you want to hug for his boyish charm and joking around, then slap him in the face for his senseless hardheartedness to the people who loved him, and then go have a drink with him for his big-heartedness and sincere friendship."

Elaine's eyes met mine. "I find there's a lot I still want to say to that man!"

I looked right back at her and nodded my understanding. Part of me wanted to raise my voice and say, *Lady, take a number and get in line. There are others here ahead of you.*

Yet I stood there, stared at her, and didn't say a word.

* * * *

Johnny ~~Noose~~ Loose Ends

The next time I saw Elaine was a few Januarys later while my family and I vacationed in Fort Lauderdale. Our handsome teen son, our sweet daughter, and Gloria and I had lunch with her. Our meal was full of remembrances about Dad. Afterward, Elaine wrote an email.

> Harvy:
> It's always good to see you and your family. Your kids are very grown and mature. You and Gloria have done an excellent job.
>
> Our lunch conversation has me still thinking about your father. I think I described (in earlier emails) about being served divorce papers by your father's attorney and then having to hire an attorney to respond. I still haven't fully coped with Johnny's betrayal, and I am still shaking my head in disbelief—even after all these years. When I've thought I'd made peace with him, I want to scream at him again!
>
> Can't blame your mother for screaming at him too! I know it was hard for you, BUT what he put his women through was cause to erupt!
> E

I wrote back.

Elaine:
I truly understand your pain. I get moments of darkness myself. It's the predominant reason I feel so compelled to dredge up the past and write my memoir—which, in part, I see as our story!
Harvy

Later, she wrote again.

Harvy:
Did you ever hear the one about the RCMP arriving at your mother's door to check her jewellery box?! They were looking for a ring your Dad had bought in Las Vegas. He charged it to his Diner's Club card but never reported the purchase upon returning to Canada.
E

Whoa! I hadn't heard that one. I couldn't let her leave me on the hook, as my father might say. I immediately emailed her back.

Elaine:
I never heard about that ring story. Wonder how the RCMP knew to look. I guess homeland security came to Canada a long time ago. Might you know more about what happened to that ring and when that was? It sounds like a typical Johnny Simkovits move!
Harvy

Later that day, she responded.

Harvy:
Your father delighted in telling stories about how he evaded the authorities. I remember his mentioning that particular one at the Troika to his many 'friends.'

Johnny had gone to Vegas for the Consumer Electronics Show. There he met a 'lovely young lady' whom he 'dated' during the week. Johnny bought her a ring, charging it to his Diner's Club card so he could put it through his company as an entertainment expense. I have no idea what year that was, but he was still with your mother.

Johnny ~~Noose~~ Loose Ends

When Johnny returned to Canada from the show, he never reported the purchase to the customs officials. Months later, the RCMP arrived at your mother's door, and they wanted to search the house. The story goes that Anna called your father at the office. He then told her, 'Don't worry! You don't have the ring they're looking for; you can show them your jewellery box.' So she did.

Your father came home right away—his factory had been only fifteen or twenty minutes away. Johnny told the RCMP that he had purchased the ring for a gal that he met in Vegas—that she was an American and had taken the ring home with her—that he had not imported it into Canada. That ended the investigation......but imagine how your mother must have felt???
E

I thought I had heard it all about my father, but this was another tale about his brazenness, deception, and betrayal. After Elaine had listened to Dad's story, she may have thought, *Is that going to happen to me?*

I agonized for my mother, who had probably become worn out from turning again and again in her grave. And, after what I had suffered through, written about, and divulged, I wondered how anyone could survive a charismatic, audacious, and sometimes heartless man like my father.

* * *

Some years later, I visited an old friend of my father who lived in South Florida, a woman named Terri. Living as a recluse, Terri allowed me to see her after I sent her my first book. I had not seen her since my father's 80th birthday party, 18 years earlier.

During our reminiscing about my father and the people she and he had known, Terri offered, "Your father and I were good friends, but we never had an intimate relationship. He wasn't my type romantically, but he always came to talk whenever he was having trouble with your mother or brother. I cared for him very much. He was a good man, generous to his friends."

I interrupted Terri's recollections. "Yes, I know that good part of him. He could go to the ends of the earth for his friends." I took a breath. "But what about his continual finagling and hiding of money? He also did many foolish things as a husband and father."

She didn't lose a beat. "Everyone knew your father was a crook and an adulterer." She looked straight into my eyes. "But he was so nice about it that everyone still loved him."

I often recall the words of the rabbi who presided over my mother's funeral. Near the end of his speech about her life, he elevated his hand, pointed to my mother's casket, raised his voice, and almost shouted, "Don't let what happened to Anna Tatransky happen to you!"

I prefer to transform those words into, "Don't let what happened to my tumultuous family happen to yours!"

Each of us has our unique family story that we and others can learn from! It's valuable to know and understand your family of origin, as long as it doesn't define you.

And remember: *There's a lassen in everything if you just lassen for it!*

* * * *

Acknowledgements

A heartfelt appreciation to Elaine for her unending stories about my dad and her life with him; my memoir would not have been as compelling and complete without her poignant perspectives and profound recollections.

An unending appreciation to my wife and kids for putting up with me for the fifteen years it took me to complete my sometimes seemingly endless Simkovits odyssey. Be assured that my paper mistress will be out of our house soon.

Another shout-out to my wife for her excellent comments and ideas for my manuscripts. And the same to Susan, for her caring and careful proofreading.

About the Author

For too long, Harvy Simkovits followed in the path of his crafty and conniving patriarch. Harvy's WWII surviving, Soviet communism escaping, Canada immigrating, Montreal business building, government tax skirting, and blatant womanizing father told him, "Harvy, I want you to finish engineering school, business school, and then law school." The family's flamboyant forbearer longed for his second son to become somebody. He then wanted Harvy to come into the family business where he'd brashly say, "*Lassen* to me, son, for I have more experience than you!"

Harvy, a loyal and impressionable youth, heeded his predecessor's wily wisdom for a while. After completing his bachelor's and master's degrees in engineering at MIT and a stint at Harvard Business School, Harvy realized that he was following his father's designs and not creating his own dreams.

Harvy dropped out of Harvard and discovered his passion in the fledgling field of organizational development. After completing another master's degree in that discipline, Harvy enjoyed a twenty-five-year management consulting and executive coaching career. He helped many owner-managed companies and family businesses not to make the same mistakes that his father and family had made in their business of over thirty years.

Then, in 2005, years after his dad's death, Harvy felt he had to make peace with his past. He started to write not only about how his charming, hard-driving, and finagling father built his success in Canada but also about how those qualities had had an insidious impact on their family, the family business, and (of course) Harvy. The second son of Johnny had to reconcile, repudiate, and rectify the moral and ethical dilemmas he faced with his furtive father and the rest of his thorny family so that he could successfully survive his survivor patriarch.

Harvy Simkovits has been writing and publishing stories about his Canadian immigrant family and their family's business since 2005. *Just Lassen to Me!* is Harvy's full-length memoir turned book series. He resides in Lexington, MA, with his wife, two kids, and two cats.

Visit Harvy at his website:
www.HarvySimkovits.com
to read the latest news regarding his memoir series.